Organisational Behaviour

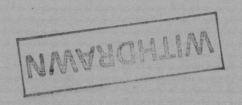

Organisational Behaviour

Individuals, Groups and Organisation

4th edition

Ian Brooks

FT Prentice Hall
FINANCIAL TIMES

An imprint of **Pearson Education**
Harlow, England • London • New York • Boston • San Francisco • Toronto • Sydney • Singapore • Hong Kong
Tokyo • Seoul • Taipei • New Delhi • Cape Town • Madrid • Mexico City • Amsterdam • Munich • Paris • Milan

Pearson Education Limited
Edinburgh Gate
Harlow
Essex CM20 2JE
England

and Associated Companies throughout the world

Visit us on the World Wide Web at:
www.pearsoned.co.uk

First published 1999
Second edition 2003
Third edition 2006
Fourth edition published 2009

ISBN: 978-0-273-71536-8

British Library Cataloguing-in-Publication Data
A catalog record for this book is available from the Library of Congress

Library of Congress Cataloging-in-Publication Data
Brooks, Ian, 1956–
    Organisational behaviour: individuals, groups and organisation / Ian Brooks.—4th ed.
        p. cm.
    Includes bibliographical references and index.
    ISBN 978-0-273-71536-8 (pbk.)
    1. Organizational behavior.   I. Title.
    HD58.7.B7545 2009
    302.3'5—dc22

                                                    2008040495

10 9 8 7 6 5 4 3 2
12 11 10 09

Typeset in 9.5/12.5 Stone Serif by 30
Printed and bound by Graficas Estella, Spain

The publisher's policy is to use paper manufactured from sustainable forests.

For Lucy, Connor, Cara, Hannah and Bernie

Contents

3   Perspectives on individual behaviour   41

Jon Stephens

4   Motivation at work   79

5 Groups and teams   111

Hugh Davenport

6 Management and leadership   157

7   Organisation structure   189

Stephen Swailes

8   Organisational power, politics and conflict   233

9   Organisational culture   259

10   The impact of national culture on organisational behaviour   283

Jon Stephens

Case studies 321

Supporting resources

Visit **www.pearsoned.co.uk/brooks** to find valuable online resources for lecturers, including:

- PowerPoint slides of the book's figures and tables
- Teaching notes for lecturers

For more information please contact your local Pearson Education sales representative or visit **www.pearsoned.co.uk/brooks**.

Contributors

Dr Ian Brooks

is Dean of Northampton Business School at the University of Northampton. His research interests include the study of organisational culture and subculture, change and the NHS.

Hugh Davenport

is a Senior Lecturer in Organisational Behaviour and Occupational Psychology in Northampton Business School.

Jon Stephens

is a Senior Lecturer in International Business in the Northampton Business School, with research interests in international and comparative management.

Dr Stephen Swailes

is a Senior Lecturer at the University of Hull. His research interests include the study of organisational commitment, particularly among professional employees, and the performance of management teams.

Acknowledgements

We would like to thank the reviewers listed below for their valuable feedback.

- Christian Waldstorm, Associate Professor PhD, Aarhus School of Business, Denmark
- Val Finnegan, Leeds Metropolitan University
- Sarah Hurlow, Lecturer in Organisational Behaviour, Cardiff Business School
- Asa Kafling, Associate Professor, Department of Management and Engineering, Linköping University, Sweden
- Dr Martin McCracken, Lecturer in Organisational Behaviour, School of Business Organisation and Management, University of Ulster
- Nigel Marlow, Principal Lecturer Business and Consumer Psychology, London Metropolitan University and Editorial Group Association of Business Psychologists
- Dr Samantha Lynch, Kent Business School, University of Kent.

We are grateful to the following for permission to reproduce copyright material:

Figure 2.2 and Tables 5.3 and 5.4 from Mullins, L.J. (2002) *Management and Organisational Behaviour*, 6th Edition, Financial Times/Prentice Hall; Table 3.2 was published in *The Scientific Analysis of Personality and Motivation*, Cattell, R.B. and Kline, P., Copyright Academic Press (1977); Table 3.3 from Nelson, D.L. and Quick, J.C., *Organizational Behavior*, 1st Edition, © 1995 South-Western, a part of Cengage Learning, Inc. Reproduced by permission. www.cengage.com/permissions; Table 6.4 and Table 6.5 from *Personal and Organisational Transformations: The True Challenge of Continual Quality Improvement*, Fisher, D. and Torbert, W.R. © McGraw-Hill Companies, Inc. 1995; Figure 8.9 from Thomas, K. (1976) Conflict and conflict management in M.D. Dunnette (ed.) *Handbook of Industrial and Organizational Psychology*, Chicago: Rand McNally, 1976; Figure 9.4 from Johnson, G. and Scholes, K. (2002) *Exploring Corporate Strategy: Text and Cases,* 6th Edition, Financial Times/Prentice Hall; Figure 9.6 from ACADEMY OF MANAGEMENT JOURNAL by Isabella, L.A., Copyright 1990 by Academy of Management (NY). Reproduced with permission of Academy of Management (NY) in the format other book via

Copyright Clearance Center; Tables 10.3 and C1.1 from Geert Hofstede, *Culture's Consequences: Comparing Values, Behaviors, Institutions and Organizations Across Nations*, Second Edition. Thousand Oaks, California: SAGE Publications, 2001.

We are grateful to the following for permission to reproduce the following texts:

Mini case 1.1 from http://www.uksport.gov.uk/pages/standards_in_sport_equity/ with permission of UK Sport; Mini case 2.3 reprinted from *Long Range Planning*, 29(4), Brooks, I. and Reast, J., Redesigning the value chain at scania trucks, pp. 514–525, Copyright 1996, with permission from Elsevier.

In some instances we have been unable to trace the owners of copyright material, and we would appreciate any information that would enable us to do so.

1 Introduction

Learning outcomes

On completion of this chapter you should be able to:

- understand the nature and scope of organisational behaviour (OB);
- understand the value of a behavioural approach to management;
- know how the book is structured;
- understand the importance of the four themes of diversity, change, conflict and communications to the study of organisational behaviour.

Key concepts

- individual behaviour
- group behaviour
- organisational behaviour
- organisational analysis
- multidisciplinary study
- theory to practice
- diversity
- change
- conflict
- communications.

Introduction

Organisational behaviour (OB) is the study of human behaviour in organisational contexts, with a focus on individual and group processes and actions. Hence, it involves an exploration of organisational and managerial processes in the dynamic context of the organisation and is primarily concerned with the human implications of such activity.

Studying organisational behaviour

Organisational behaviour (OB) is the study of human behaviour in organisational contexts with a focus on individual and group processes and actions. Hence, it involves an exploration of organisational and managerial processes in the dynamic context of the organisation and is primarily concerned with the human implications of such activity. The subject is rooted in the behavioural sciences, notably sociology and psychology, and underpins in many respects the study of management. It is an applied behavioural science which seeks to draw on a broad and extensive theoretical and practical knowledge base to advance our understanding of the complexities of human behaviour in organisations and to inform management thinking and activity. Both OB and management are social sciences informed partly by research and partly by debate in the traditional subject disciplines of psychology, sociology and, to an extent, anthropology, political science and economics. Psychologists are generally concerned with the study of individual human behaviour and the personality system, whereas a branch of that subject, social psychology, looks at group, including organisational, behaviour. Sociologists focus on social behaviour and are particularly concerned about societal structures and control. Anthropologists explore culture, that is, the symbolic, attitudinal and behavioural factors which unite various social groups. In so far as it relates to OB, political science is the study of power and control between individuals and groups whereas economics attempts to provide a rational explanatory framework for individual and organisational activity. As organisational behaviour has roots in many traditional academic fields, it is considered to be a multidisciplinary subject.

A knowledge of OB should enable you to explain and predict human behaviour in organisations and even control it if appropriate. Additionally, OB is both informed by and contributes to organisational theory and management theory and, as a consequence, it forms an integral part of most Masters and undergraduate programmes in business studies, management and leadership. Moreover, it is an important subject for all who work and manage in organisations.

Many of the theories and arguments presented in this book have value to the work of managers and other employees in organisations. Even for students with little or no formal organisational work experience, the ability to apply OB to other 'organisational' contexts should prove possible and valuable. Your family, your circle of friends, your sports or other clubs and the university or college in which you study are all organisations. Organisational behaviour is relevant to your work, study and play.

As a result of studying this subject it is quite possible that you may alter your 'management philosophy' including, perhaps, long-harboured beliefs, and you may obtain the answers to outstanding questions about issues such as: how people are motivated or led, how groups or teams function, why the structure of an organisation influences the behaviour of people who work in it, and how both the culture and power relationships in organisations affect human behaviour at work.

The study of OB should enable you to diagnose organisational problems with some insight and expertise. Following that diagnosis you may be able to develop solutions to problems, ways of dealing with difficult 'human' issues or, perhaps crucially, ways of avoiding certain problems in the first place. In short, there is something very practical about many of the theories presented in this book: you, the scholar and the 'manager', will, however, need to interpret and apply them to the particular context in which you operate. That, if achieved, would represent a highly worthwhile, constructive and meaningful learning experience and should make you a more effective manager.

Human behaviour in organisations is complex as it is affected by, and in turn influences, an array of factors, including managerial action, changing competitive circumstances and new technologies. People in organisations interact with their environment, with stakeholders and with others in the organisation. There are significant differences in personality between individuals, many people behave differently in groups than when working alone and most are influenced by the norms and values of the organisation and of the society in which they live and work. These influences and interconnections make the study of OB inherently interesting and enlightening, especially for those concerned with human or people issues in organisations.

Four themes: change, diversity, conflict and communications

Four themes inform and influence a number of the topics covered in the book. These themes, organisational change, diversity (e.g. of gender and race), communications and conflict, often form separate chapters in OB texts. However, in an attempt to illustrate the interconnectedness of organisations and the all-embracing significance of these four themes they are integrated into each key chapter. To a large extent behaviour in organisations is influenced by and in turn influences the nature of change, diversity, communications and conflict in the workplace. All four are omnipresent in organisations. They are part of the fabric and reality of organisational life. The degree of success in the management of change, the management of communications and the management of diversity and conflict influence the competitiveness of the organisation and its ability to meet its objectives.

The four themes closely relate to the main topics covered in this book, such as motivation, teamwork, structure, politics and culture. For example, organisational culture is often seen as 'an intangible glue' (Morgan, 1986) which binds people together. As such, it is argued, culture reduces potential conflict in organisations which have a strongly held value and belief system. Organisational change often goes hand in glove with cultural change; an appreciation of the former involves knowledge of the latter, whereas communication, in its broadest sense, is the mechanism whereby culture is learned and changed. Hence, these four themes improve our understanding of and enrich the concept of culture and the other topics covered. This approach should enable you to understand better the complexity of organisational reality.

Diversity in the workplace

Most organisations employ a diverse array of people. Chapter 2 in this book explores individual differences and demonstrates how such differences can influence how organisations function. However, in addition to generic differences in personality, perception, learning, communication styles and so forth there is also diversity of gender, age, race or ethnicity, abilities and disability, religious belief and sexual orientation. Organisations are rich human environments – environments which require of all employees and leaders recognition, tolerance and, hopefully, celebration of individual and group differences. Within each chapter of the book we will attempt to reflect, albeit briefly, on diversity in the context of organisational behaviour. Moreover, we ask the reader to reflect further on this vital aspect of organisations. We briefly explore here some of the issues of relevance to OB.

Traditionally formal organisations (refer to Chapter 7) enjoy close links to male stereotypical behaviours. The male stereotype is a logical, rational, aggressive, strategic, competitive decision maker while formal organisations support and generate such behaviour. It is argued that these behaviours and the values that underpin them promote men and hold back talented women in the workplace – the barriers have often been referred to as the 'glass ceiling'. Women who are perceived to be successful are often considered to be unfeminine or to have exhibited male behaviours.

Feminine stereotypical behaviours are said to derive from women's historical role as family-orientated carers and peacemakers making them more sensitive to others' needs and having good non-verbal and perceptual skills, intuition and interpersonal skills. Some research evidence supports stereotypical differences. Behaviourists believe that differences between sexes and races are learned, from early childhood, and often sustained and developed in the workplace.

Although many forms of discrimination in the workplace have been outlawed for many years, it can pervade national and organisational cultures and subcultures in subtle ways. It can be argued that biased attitudes and behaviours can prove to be obstacles to the advancement of non-traditional managers.

There are conflicting views and practices regarding working with diversity in the workplace. For example, some suggest that people in the workplace should largely ignore differences between the sexes, races and so forth. Others argue, in a sense, quite the opposite: that an organisation that celebrates differences and recognises the value each can bring to the organisation might not only provide for a more pleasant work environment but also promote organisational goals.

Over recent years there has been the emergence of the concept of institutional racism (or discrimination). Whilst controversial and subject to much debate, this concept has influenced government policy and the content of new discrimination laws – particularly the Race Relations (Amendment) Act 2000 and the Equality Act 2006. In particular, the requirements that public bodies (not private organisations or companies) have statutory duties to both eliminate discrimination and promote equality have been introduced.

Whilst the concept of institutional racism or discrimination is not defined in law, there are similarities to the legal concept of 'indirect discrimination'. The Equality and Human Rights Commission suggests that 'this occurs when a provision, criterion or practice which, on the face of it, has nothing to do with [race or gender] and is applied equally to everyone:

- puts or would put people of the same (race or ethnic or national origins/gender) at a particular disadvantage when compared with others
- puts a person of that (race or ethnic or national origin/gender) at that disadvantage
- cannot be shown to be a proportionate means of achieving a legitimate aim.'

As a consequence many 'public' organisations have developed overt statements of intent aimed at avoiding institutional discrimination – refer to Mini-case 1.1 on UK Sport.

Mini-case 1.1: UK Sport standing against institutional racism

'UK Sport will take positive action to:

- eliminate individual and institutional discrimination
- comply with statutory/legislative obligations and, wherever possible, best practice
- meet the needs of our employees and partner organisations
- make equality and equal treatment a core issue in the development, delivery and refinement of our policies, initiatives and services and in the way we manage our employees.'

Traditionally, it is fair to say, people were generally not expected to allow their personal or home lives to impact their working lives. There is now increasing recognition that people do manage complex lives and need to balance the range of demands on their time, energy and emotions. In more recent years the term 'work/life balance' (WLB) has been used to refer to the holistic recognition of employees' broader life commitments. The pressures to achieve some form of balance varies between different people, at different stages of their lives and is often related to gender and cultural background as well as personal circumstances. WLB is a key aspect of diversity and, hence, management in organisations. Increasingly many people are concerned about quality of life (QL) and quality of work life (QWL) issues and seek a balance between the material wealth that demanding and full employment can bring and the benefits of fewer workplace commitments or more enjoyable and fulfilling commitments. Consider how individuals in different circumstances – perhaps yourself – may require or consider WLB and QL or QWL.

Conflict and communication

Communication is the process of sending, receiving and understanding information. It sounds quite simple but communication problems are frequently noted by employees as a key organisational weakness. It is all too often a source of frustration, division and uncertainty for some. It is doubtful, in fact, if any medium or large organisation actually satisfies all of its employees', including managers', needs for communication. People differ immensely; so do their needs for communication and the timing and forms in which it takes place.

Communications are interpreted by the receiver (and the sender) such that even 'simple' messages are often understood in different ways by different people. Communication becomes not merely transference of information by an exchange of shared meaning. The former is often difficult in large complex organizations, while the latter is particularly challenging. Even in one-to-one communications between people we know we are often left saying 'what did she mean by that?' or 'slow down, I can't take all that in at once'. In an organisation where communicators compete to get their message across, achieving shared meaning is often an unobtainable ideal. Communications is as much about active listening and understanding as it is about sending information. Even our body language communicates – often not the sort of message we intend the world to receive.

The process of communications in an organisation is closely related to employee motivation, to team and group work, management and leadership and the structure of organisations and to the political processes of organisation. Hence, it is a fundamental aspect of organisational behaviour and managers and leaders at all levels in organisations need to understand communication processes in order to achieve sustained success.

Just as the intricacies of communication are often a mystery, particularly to those with little organisational life experience, so too is organisational conflict. Yet conflict is a natural part of organisational life both in a macro sense with potential for fundamental difference between, for example, 'workers' and 'management' and in the minutiae of individual, group and department dealings which take place daily in all organisations. Chapter 8 refers to radicalism and pluralism, two perspectives which can be taken when viewing organisations. In both approaches the acceptance of difference between individuals and groups within organisations is accepted as commonplace and inevitable. Differences in personal objectives, resource levels, gender, ethnic background or culture and motivation levels can all create conflict. In reality a unity of interest within organisations simply does not exist; people want different things from their workplace.

Organisational change

Few if any organisations can claim to operate in a stable environment. Change is often rapid, complex in its implications and even unpredictable. Change can and does take many forms. It can directly impact the nature and level of competition, for example, while transformational technology can make old products, services or organisational processes redundant. Everyone in the workplace faces change, sometimes requiring quiet dramatic personal, group or organisational responses.

Change impacts all aspects of the study and understanding of organisational behaviour. One cannot fully understand management or leadership without an appreciation of the changing external and internal context in which people operate. Similarly, power, politics and conflict in organisations both influence and are influenced by changes in organisations and their objectives and ways of working. Being aware of change and its unpredictability is an essential requirement for all who wish to understand behaviour in organisations.

Overview of the book

In order to make the study of OB manageable, we have subdivided the broad subject into nine further chapters. This chapter is followed by:

- **Chapter 2** outlines the development of thinking about organisations and management. It recognises that the way we work, think and behave in organisations is, in part, a product of organisational norms and accepted ways of organising. Knowledge of organisation and management theory gives you a particular insight into the development of modern organisations. We explore contemporary views and research in this regard and take a look at organisations through many different 'lenses' and from various perspectives. This enables you to appreciate the complexity of organisations and of people's behaviour.

- Consideration of the individual – **Chapter 3** focuses upon each person's unique set of attitudes, perceptions and values which influence their personality and behaviour. This personality set affects the way people work, how they communicate with others and their propensity to cooperate in teams and be motivated and managed. Hence, the chapter looks at personality and perception, values and attitudes, learning and decision making.

- The examination of human motivation – **Chapter 4** remains largely, but not exclusively, at the level of the individual. This is a critically important aspect of OB and of management theory and practice. The chapter explores some of the extensive and wide-ranging theoretical work and empirical research findings which inform our understanding of how people are motivated, and indeed demotivated, in the workplace.

- Groups and teams – **Chapter 5** begins by focusing on the various personality types that are thought to make up a successful team. We explore the process of group formation and the nature, causes and consequences of inter- and intra-group conflict and communications, in addition to the characteristics of successful group work.

- Exploring the nature of management and of leadership – **Chapter 6** discusses some of the principal schools of thought in this regard and examines contemporary thinking, particularly about leadership. The chapter also seeks to determine the qualities of successful leadership and explores the intrinsically behavioural nature of both leadership and followership.

- Examining how organisations are structured and controlled – **Chapter 7** discusses contemporary and possible future developments towards flexibility, and flexible organisations, drawing on a burgeoning research base.

- Exploring the constant struggle for control in organisations – **Chapter 8** investigates power, politics and conflict. We look at powerlessness and empowerment.

- Focusing on the concept of organisational culture – **Chapter 9** recognises how important the study and awareness of organisational culture has become in the past two decades. It is widely believed that the culture of a company may have a major bearing on its attempts to change, on both the process and the outcome of managerial decision making, on its competitiveness and upon its performance.

- Examining culture in a broader global context – **Chapter 10** fascinatingly explores the nature and influence of national culture and cultural differences on managerial and workplace activity.

In the interests of focus and brevity this text does not cover all the topics that are often considered within the 'territory' or remit of organisational behaviour, or at least, does not provide detailed coverage of them. These include aspects of human resource management (HRM), organisational development and stress, for example. Certainly, OB underpins and informs these functional areas and knowledge of OB is a useful, if not essential, prerequisite for any HR manager and all managers who, as part of their line responsibilities, work with people. It is, however, not essential for an OB book to discuss the various HR considerations which are adequately covered elsewhere. These topics are important yet would, if covered in appropriate detail, necessitate a far weightier tome than this. The contents of this book represent the areas of focal importance in the subject and its design is, largely, derived from research conducted among academic tutors of organisational behaviour in over thirty universities and higher education organisations.

Case studies and examples

Each chapter in the book contains a small number of mini-cases which serve to illustrate a particular aspect of the material covered. They aim to provide an insight into a 'real-life' scenario and are worthy of further analysis and debate. Some of the scenarios can be critically analysed or explored from a number of perspectives. Some encourage a management problem-solving approach whereas others invite fresh insights in order to better understand organisational behaviour.

A number of medium-sized case studies grouped at the end of the book illustrate the subject of OB. They aim to develop your understanding of OB further by encouraging you to apply many of the theoretical ideas covered in the book and explore explanations for observed behaviour. It is hoped that you will attempt to demonstrate your capacity for critical thinking when tackling the cases and make efforts to get beneath the surface in your analysis. It is also hoped that the cases will assist you to appreciate that organisational life is complex and rich and will help you to develop the capacity to engage in rigorous analysis of behavioural scenarios in organisations.

Illustration in film

Throughout the book a number of mini-cases focus on the learning which can be achieved by viewing and discussing an excerpt from a well-known film (usually a 'classic' if not contemporary) or television programme in the context of the theory being discussed. Some films and TV programmes contain a wealth of learning experiences of relevance to human behaviour, individually or collectively, in organisations. Ideally, in each case you or your tutor would access the film or programme in question and incorporate it into the learning experience. The lessons are often more memorable than the words available to us!

Figure 1.1 illustrates the structure of this book. It indicates the main topic of each chapter, plus the four themes that are integrated throughout and the three levels of analysis: individual, group and organisation. The whole is enclosed in a circle, illustrating the global context in which organisations operate, reminding you of the significance of context in the study and appreciation of OB. The relentless trend towards globalisation, driven by technology in the fields of communication and information dissemination, together with the rapid pace of sociopolitical changes, are creating the highly dynamic global environment within which organisations now have to operate. Change in organisations can be said to be omnipresent and discontinuous, that is, it is not always predictable in its direction, its nature or its pace. Ironically, and often not particularly usefully, most OB theories are not themselves dynamic.

The changes taking place in most organisations often have immediate and far-reaching implications for people and for their behaviour. An awareness of context and change is stressed in this book, particularly in Chapter 10, but also as an ongoing theme. You will also need to relate the materials covered in this book to your own experiences and to your world, recognising, of course, that the world is itself ever changing. We are all left with a significant challenge, but one which may be better informed by gaining a useful insight into the subject of organisational behaviour.

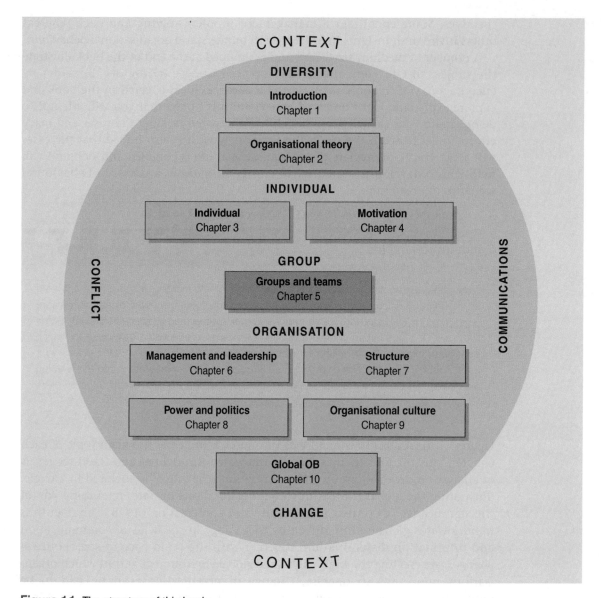

Figure 1.1 The structure of this book

Reference

Morgan, G. (1986) *Images of Organization*. Newbury Park, CA: Sage.

Further reading

Champoux, J. E. (2001) *Using Film to Visualize Principles and Practices*. Winfield, KS: Southwestern College Publishing.

Fineman, S. (ed.) (2000) *Emotion in Organizations*, 2nd edn. London: Sage Publications.

Kakabadse, A., Bank, J. and Vinnicombe, S. (2004) *Working in Organisations*, 2nd edn, Aldershot: Gower.

Mullins, L. J. (2007) *Management and Organisational Behaviour*, 8th edn. Harlow: Financial Times Prentice Hall.

Internet sites

Any good search engine will reveal many sites, some of value, on all aspects of organisational behaviour. Wikipedia provides useful definitions and extension notes on literally hundreds of terms and concepts relevant to organisational behaviour.

2

Organisational theory

Learning outcomes

On completion of this chapter you should be able to:

- understand the main developments in organisational theory;
- understand how organisational theory underpins both the principles and practices of organising and of management;
- value organisational theory as a tool for understanding behaviour in organisations, for diagnosing likely causes of organisational problems and for working towards potential solutions to those problems;
- recognise the close relationship between developments in organisational theory and organisational behaviour;
- acknowledge some of the contemporary themes in organisational analysis and acknowledge the dynamic nature of the subject.

Key concepts

- classical theory
- bureaucracy
- scientific management
- Taylorism
- human relations
- contingency theory
- sociotechnical systems
- organisational behaviour
- environmental behaviour
- enactment
- frames, perspective and paradigms
- organisations as machines, as cultures and as political entities
- learning organisation.

In order to appreciate why organisations, and people in them, behave as they do it is important to explore the influences on them and the theoretical and empirical work conducted, largely in the last one hundred years, in this regard. To enhance our understanding of modern organisations it is essential to appreciate what has gone before, for this has a profound and lasting influence on today's organisations.

Introduction

This chapter opens by briefly exploring a number of macro or broad theoretical approaches to the study of organisations before examining classical organisational theory (*see* Chapter 6 for greater coverage of leadership and management theory). You will appreciate that much of the theoretical work conducted in the first half of the twentieth century in this field has a significant bearing on current thought and practice in organisations. The text continues by exploring the main arguments of the human relations school: work conducted, largely since the 1930s, which enhances our understanding of organisations not as mechanical structures and relationships but as human communities. This crucial underpinning will inform the exploration of systems theory and contingency theory, both of which provide

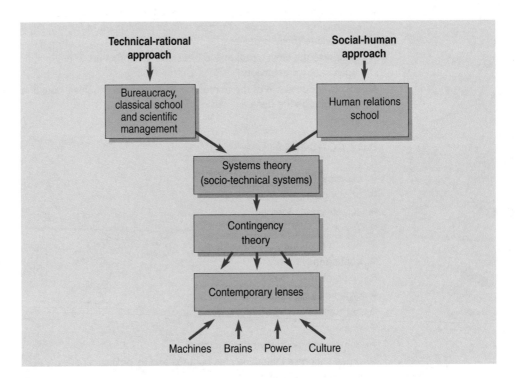

Figure 2.1 Organisation theory

useful explanatory frameworks and add rigour to our understanding of OB. The chapter then briefly explores the behaviour of organisations in their environmental context, before, finally, discussing some contemporary views of organisations and behaviour by taking a look at organisations as if through a series of lenses or from a variety of perspectives. This will give added insight and enable you to recognise that, to put it simply, 'what you see depends on how you look'. Figure 2.1 illustrates the content of this chapter and, albeit rather simplistically, links the various contributions. The theme of change is fully integrated within the chapter. We will then, again briefly, examine some contemporary themes of organisational analysis which, although not covered in detail in this book, may prove to be tomorrow's mainstream OB.

A knowledge of organisational and managerial theory will improve your ability to diagnose and resolve organisational problems. It will underpin and inform your understanding of this book, of management and leadership, organisational structure, change, politics and power and of organisational culture.

 ## Macro-organisational theories

Let us explore some broad perspectives on organisation. Each is developed by a series of academics and researchers as a way of studying and understanding organisation. Perspectives include:

- The population-ecology model suggests that environmental factors select organisational characteristics which best fit the environment in which they operate. Organisational types, structures and so forth that survive are those that enjoy the closest fit with the demands of their environment. Organisations fill niches in their environment. The research of the school is not concerned with individual organisations but rather 'populations' of organisations.

- The resource-dependence model suggests that organisations make decisions mediated through their political context. Rather than being passive recipients of environmental forces, organisations, particularly their management, will mould their environment and make strategic decisions.

- The rational-contingency model suggests that through a combination of rationality and contingency (recognition that there is not one best way), organisations will deal with their environment. The model underplays the political or non-rational decision-making process yet stresses the importance of contingent factors.

- The transaction-cost model derives from the field of economics and attempts to explain the existence of organisations in the private sector. It suggests that individuals act in their own best interest and by collecting into hierarchies to conduct business they incur transaction cost but reduce uncertainty and untrustworthiness by appropriate organisational monitoring and control.

- The institutional model suggests that orgnisations exist alongside others in the same field and take on many of the same characteristics as each other – hence one university is very similar to another. These similarities are encouraged by being subjected to similar environmental forces and networks, encouraging mimicry.

Technical–rational approach

Bureaucracy

Max Weber (1864–1920), a German philosopher and sociologist, introduced the term 'bureaucracy' to organisation studies to capture the ideas that:

- people in organisations have their own well-defined tasks and responsibilities;
- organisations contain hierarchical reporting structures which means that most employees report to another person and may have management responsibilities for others;
- organisations develop their own rules and procedures for completing tasks;
- employees occupy positions in the organisational hierarchy on the basis of merit as judged by others in the organisation;
- employees act in an impartial and unemotional manner, being motivated by a sense of duty towards achieving organisational goals.

It is important to realise that the term 'bureaucracy' has taken on a negative meaning in recent years, with organisations or processes seen as bureaucratic being regarded as self-serving, slow and uncaring. This negative meaning was not part of Weber's ideas and should not be confused with his thinking. Weber held that organisations were bureaucracies to different extents and that increasing bureaucracy would lead to increasingly efficient operations.

With the growth of large organisations in the early twentieth century, bureaucratic forms of organisation increased. There was an increase in the specialisation of jobs and sophisticated rules and procedures for working were created. As we will see, there are some disadvantages associated with bureaucracy: for example, employees can be disaffected if they perceive rules and procedures to be unhelpful or unreasonable, suppressing individual initiative and creativity. Primarily, when business environments were thought to be more stable and predictable it was, arguably, far more straightforward for top management to make good business decisions about products and markets. Now that most organisations exist in intensely competitive environments and many rely on complex technology, they are highly dependent on supportive attitudes and behaviours from the workforce in order to be successful. Far more than was the case previously, managers have to harness the particular knowledge that employees have about customers, products and markets.

Nevertheless, Weber's writing on bureaucracy remains an influential element of organisation theory but the idea that increasing bureaucracy leads to increasing effectiveness is less fashionable. Indeed, current thinkers often argue that bureaucracy should be reduced to give organisations the room to think and manoeuvre in order to sustain high performance.

Illustration in film

Brazil

In the film *Brazil*, directed by *Monty Python* star Terry Gilliam, a science-fiction future is portrayed. This world is a global bureaucracy and the story comically follows an individual's attempt to rectify an administrative error. As a result of his actions he becomes an enemy of the state. It's an entertaining film which illustrates many of the less attractive characteristics of bureaucracy.

The classical school

Contributions to organisational theory in the early twentieth century were dominated by efforts to identify principles which, advocates suggested, would, if followed, ensure success. The assumption was that these simple laws or principles represented the single best way to manage and organise. Inspiration came from the armed forces which had organised large numbers of personnel, often in dynamic and difficult situations. Even today considerable military language infiltrates common organisational discourse; for example, groups of employees are often referred to as 'the troops' and bureaucratic organisations have 'lines of command'. Organisational members who might question decisions are often advised not to 'put their heads above the parapet', and the conventional distinction between line and staff remains in many traditional organisations. In addition to military discourse, mechanistic analogies dominate. Organisations are often viewed as machines, hence the belief that a 'well-oiled machine' is analogous to a sound, efficient operation.

Much of the early work on organisational theory comprised a distillation of managerial experience and most modern companies incorporate some of these ideas. Classical organisational and management theorists suggested that the principles of management and of organisation were a non-contextual, technical, issue. That is, those principles could be applied to all organisations irrespective of size, environment, nature of their outputs or of the technology utilised. Writers such as Henri Fayol and Lyndall Urwick, Frederick Taylor, James Mooney and Mary Follett suggested a 'one best way' to organise and to manage which is referred to as 'structural universalism'. Their prime concern was to suggest efficient mechanisms of control, of how to allocate tasks and to reward people and how to structure organisations. Emphasis was placed on the existence and the need for bureaucratic structures and processes. These included transparent and narrow lines of command or spans of control which embodied clear hierarchical relationships, detailed job descriptions and clear procedures.

Although the rather simple prescriptions of classical theorists still inform much activity today, a number of largely environmental factors have been identified which encourage the questioning of these injunctions, including:

- recognition that context, that is, the size of the organisation, its products or services, the level of technology employed, its cultural environment and other factors, can and do influence both the most efficient and most effective way of organising and managing;
- recognition that the workforce has, arguably, become a more critical factor in determining organisational success; the need to attract, retain and motivate a skilled workforce is paramount in most organisations;
- the dynamism of the business environment and the complexity of the marketplace and the global economy require organisations to be flexible and innovative;
- it is widely believed that bureaucratic organisations, built on the principles of the classical school, are ill equipped to embrace change and are more suited to repetitive activities and known territory;
- changes in social expectations and the political and legal environment have ensured that many of the excesses of the late nineteenth- and early twentieth-century organisations have become unacceptable, unethical and/or illegal;
- recognition that, partly due to dynamism in the business environment, organisations have increasingly sought people with leadership qualities as opposed to mere mechanical management or administrative skills.

Scientific management

The emphasis on rationality, and lack of consideration for human aspects of organisation, led to the application of scientific principles to work management. It can be argued that scientific management comprises a subset of the classical school: the latter is mainly concerned with the wider organisation and its structure, whereas the former focuses on job design. Scientific principles, it was suggested, should be applied to work organisation in order to seek the 'one best way' of conducting any job. The consequence would be significant efficiency gains, an increase in productivity and, hence, in both wage rates and profitability and, arguably, a more de-humanised workplace. The school's most influential exponent was Frederick Taylor (1856–1915), and other valuable contributions were made by Frank Gilbreth (1868–1924) and Henry Gantt (1861–1919).

Frederick Taylor

Taylor argued that efficiency, standardisation and discipline would result from a process of scientific management of work tasks. To be more precise, he suggested that:

- a clear distinction should be made between planning a job, a management role, and conducting the tasks, a worker's role;
- a scientific selection process should identify the correct person to perform the task;
- jobs should be standardised and simplified;
- each worker should conduct a minimum of movements, preferably involving just one set of actions;
- there was 'one best way' of organising any set of tasks to be performed and it was management's responsibility to conduct exhaustive measurements in order to achieve this desired state.

Taylor argued that this would raise productivity (his consultancy work invariably bore out this contention) and so give working people the higher wages they sought. He suggested that increases in productivity should be accompanied by the introduction of piecework, *an incentive payment system which relates bonuses to level of output*, and hence worker satisfaction and motivation would be ensured. Unfortunately, Taylor underestimated the strength of worker alienation and rejection of his philosophy, as the example presented in Mini-case 2.1 illustrates.

It is important to locate developments in scientific management in their historical context. In the early twentieth century, management was a very imprecise activity. Little systematic research had been conducted and practices varied considerably. Meanwhile, workers tended to believe that an increase in productivity on their part would merely result in job losses. Understandably, they took advantage of poor management controls to slow production. This was made possible as workers themselves often designed or organised their own efforts and had little interest in seeking efficiency.

Mini-case 2.1: experiments with scientific management

Taylor's work in a steel plant

Taylor's work at the Bethlehem Steel works in the USA, involving the efforts of a pig iron handler called Schmidt (an alias), is discussed in most OB and organisational theory texts. Taylor sought to alter fundamentally the way in which a simple task, the movement of iron, was conducted. As a result of his detailed time-and-motion observations and measurements, productivity in the process was raised four times, that is, by 400 per cent. In other words, only one-quarter of the workers would be required to move the same quantity of iron; alternatively, the company could move four times the quantity of iron using the same number of workers (although not necessarily the same individuals).

As a result of Taylor's work at the steel works, wages were increased by 60 per cent. The cost of pig iron supplied to all manner of engineering companies declined (Taylor, 1911). Nevertheless, these 'economic' benefits were not often warmly greeted and resulted in almost universal hostility, from workers, management and the US government (Taylor appeared before a House of Representatives committee following investigations into a major strike in 1912).

Taylor's principles were first applied in Britain in 1905 and were criticised by the Iron and Steel Federation. Similarly, in Germany in 1912 they were greeted with considerable hostility, and in France (Renault) they resulted in strike action and violent protest. However, in the USSR, Lenin, shortly after the Bolshevik revolution, established the League for the Scientific Organisation of Work in 1918.

The reader might be forgiven for gaining the impression that such practices are rare, socially unacceptable and no longer considered viable in economic terms. In some industries this is the case. The contemporary need for multiskilling, for workers to be encouraged to show initiative and for them to take responsibility makes the strict application of scientific principles difficult. However, many organisations thrive on scientific management principles and organise accordingly. Perhaps the best examples lie in catering (more specifically in fast food consumer outlets in companies such as McDonald's). In McDonald's outlets, staff have clear and narrowly defined jobs which require limited training, are carefully designed to minimise unproductive movement and scope for human error and are not designed to motivate the employees. There is little or no staff discretion allowed: for example, cooking times are prescribed. The benefits to customers appear to be a standard product, the same every time, delivered rapidly and at a reasonable price and with consistency of service.

Taylor's thinking preceded the widespread adoption of mass production techniques, possibly best demonstrated by the early (1920s) motor manufacturers, notably by Henry Ford in the USA.

Illustration in film

Modern Times

As the old black-and-white film *Modern Times*, starring Charlie Chaplin, satirically portrays, workers performed simple and highly repetitive mechanical tasks. They were no more than 'cogs in the wheel' of a 'well-oiled machine'. Chaplin is seen tightening bolts on items placed on a fast-moving conveyor belt. He's bored stiff by the simple task and easily distracted. He brings great humour to the scene but nevertheless the more depressing message is clear.

It is also important to note that many modern organisations adopt similar principles in order to maintain or increase productivity. This is particularly the case when similar or identical outputs are required on a near-continuous process. Most readers will be familiar with fast food outlets where work processes embody many of the characteristics identified by Taylor. For example, clear instructions are given concerning the exact duration that fries should be immersed in the hot fat or the time required to cook a burger. Very little, if any, discretion is given to employees (refer to Mini-case 2.2).

Whereas Taylor's work was revolutionary in its time, it is now largely taken for granted. Increasingly, aspects of it have been rejected in favour of more 'human' or social considerations and the whole approach has proven less valuable in many contemporary contexts. Nevertheless, the principles of division between managerial and worker roles, of standardisation and specialisation, of division of labour and efficiency, continue to remain as central precepts in many organisations.

Gilbreth and Gantt

It was not Taylor but Frank Gilbreth who first advocated the use of time and motion methodologies. Like Taylor, he worked at reducing the extent and frequency of 'unnecessary' motions involved in completing a task. He conducted his early work in the building industry. By reducing unnecessary motion, he argued, it would be possible to reduce worker fatigue. It was fatigue, he suggested, that hampered efforts to increase productivity; hence he suggested reductions in the working day and regular brief rest periods at work. By also seeking to influence the work environment by altering lighting conditions, considering permitting music to be played, providing canteen facilities and even chairs for periods of rest, Gilbreth was the first researcher seriously to consider that workers have complex needs.

It was Henry Gantt who introduced detailed instruction cards for workers to lead them through, step by step, complex but repetitive tasks. 'Desk instructions' are still to be found in many, particularly clerical, tasks today. He also developed

Mini-case 2.2

The fast-food outlet: a personal reflection on work

When I came to Northampton I realised that I needed to work to pay my way through university. I was so lucky, or so I thought, when a second-year student told me that one of the fast-food restaurants in town needed staff, now! I went for an interview; they liked me and I started just two days later. I worked all day Saturday and Sunday – long shifts but the money was OK. Because I'd done some bar and shop assistant work previously they put me on the counter. I was so nervous at first – it seemed so complex – but no more than 3 or 4 hours into the first shift and I'd learned the till and the main orders with some help from Jerry the supervisor. It was very tiring, standing up for so long, with just a couple of breaks. There were some unhelpful customers. It was always busy. I didn't quite look forward to going in on Sunday as I had on my first day, but after a few minutes the crowds came in and it all fell into place.

In fact it started to get a bit boring. You couldn't really talk with any customers even if you wanted to. I got to the point within a couple of weeks that I really didn't have to think about what to do. What I thought at first was complicated was after just a couple of days all very simple and repetitive. I started to count the minutes and the pay; I worked it out that I was getting about 8p a minute so when I did a big order which took 5 minutes I calculated in my head that I earned 40p. Three of those and I could get a Coke in the pub, 8 and I could put something in it worth drinking!

Then I noticed something changing in me which I didn't like. I got grumpy with some customers. Some would wait ten minutes in a queue and get to the counter before working out what they wanted. 'Does that come with fries', one old guy said when looking at the picture of the meal he'd ordered with a bloody big pile of chips on it! I just pointed at it and mumbled "yes". And, whereas I used to love burgers, I'm not so keen now. It's not exactly thrilling visiting the place now. I need the money but I also need to do something where I need to think (and where I don't leave stinking of greasy burgers).

How people do this sort of work all their lives I'll never understand. It's just too boring and mindless – too easy, if that makes sense. If you're a thinking person it drives you crazy.

new payment systems, combining basic and bonus schemes. Furthermore he recognised the 'human' element in work design considerations. For example, if an employee failed to meet the necessary standard (usually by being unable to work at sufficient speed) the foreman was required personally to demonstrate that the work could realistically be done at the pace required.

A critique

There is little doubt that the work of Frederick Taylor and others influenced work organisation practices in many organisations, first in the USA and later elsewhere. It could be argued that their efforts stimulated changes which led to significant increases in productivity and facilitated mass production techniques and wage rises which enabled mass consumption. This, in turn, stimulated rapid economic growth in North America and Europe. It would be somewhat naive to argue that such a transformation of the global economy was the result of Taylor's work, but changes he stimulated undoubtedly had some influence on these dramatic events. That said, it is important to evaluate his scientific principles critically and note the drawbacks which have arisen.

Taylor suggested that his fundamental principles could, and should, be applied to any organisation: a claim that they were of universal applicability. This remains a hotly disputed contention. A whole host of intervening factors can and do influence 'the one best way' of managing and organising work. These are further explored later in this chapter. Practical and effective problems encountered with Taylorism include:

- widespread, often violent, opposition from workers;
- significant resistance in the early twentieth century from management, who saw his work as critical of their efforts, and from the US government which questioned the implications of his approach and its consequences for worker morale and alienation;
- decline in worker morale, not least because of the highly boring and repetitive nature of their work;
- decline in skill requirements for workers, reducing flexibility through lack of multiskilling and enabling management to offer lower wages.

These problems arose due to:

- a failure to recognise the emotional and social needs of workers; they were viewed, by Taylor in particular, as individual units of production, in much the same way as a machine;
- the assumption that pay was a sufficiently powerful source of motivation to elicit cooperation: although Taylor, rather like classical economists, assumed that workers were rational economic thinkers, who would respond to financial incentives, there are many other variables affecting motivation (*see* Chapter 4);
- the approach clearly represented an overt exercise of management control over working people: it removed any decision making right from workers.

Subsequent research (*see* the discussion on human relations below) demonstrated that the social needs of workers are significant and include the need to form relationships, to experience meaningfulness or achievement at work, to have some job satisfaction and task variation, and enjoy a sense of responsibility. These aspects were largely ignored by scientific management theorists. Additionally, Taylor, in particular, underplayed the significance of the work group and the breadth of capabilities workers possess. His techniques aimed to reduce difference or individualism – characteristics which, in many situations, are of value.

 Socio-human approach

Human relations school

It is possible, although probably not entirely fair, to consider the work and prescriptions of the classical school as characterising the 'forces of dark' and the human relations school as the 'forces of light'. This polarised view emphasises the radical differences between the two schools. It suggests that human relations theorists rejected the view of organisations as mechanistic, rational and impersonal entities which embody strict lines of command and hierarchical positions, specialisation of labour and rules and procedures to cover all activity, in favour of an emphasis on people, involving a consideration of broader issues of motivation, autonomy, trust and openness in managerial and organisational matters.

Chester Barnard (1938) proposed the first new theory of organisations, arguing that they were cooperative social systems, as opposed to machine-like technical structures. Hence, he noted the existence of the informal organisation, of natural, as opposed to managerially instigated, groups in organisations, of complex information flows, of authority from below; for example, the power of individual teams to either under- or over-achieve against targets. His work immediately preceded the publication of the now-famous Hawthorne studies (Roethlisberger and Dickson, 1939).

Research was conducted at the Western Electric Company in the USA between 1924 and 1932. Its intent, as with most organisational and management research, was to explore influences on levels of productivity with a view to improving, in true classical style, worker output. However, the research achieved a number of significant and unintended outcomes. The investigators altered certain 'physical' conditions among a control group of workers. Changes to the level of lighting were expected to lead to increases or declines in productivity. However, they found that on almost all occasions when lighting levels were changed productivity increased (even when the light was believed to be insufficient to conduct the task accurately and speedily). Further experiments involved planned changes to hours of work and rest and to other interventions, such as refreshments and consultation with supervisors. Again, invariably, productivity increased as a result of *any* form of intervention.

The research suggested that:

- it was the attention that the control group of workers received which contributed to productivity improvements;
- more complex human needs were involved than had been considered previously by classical theorists;
- workers in groups were able to influence the level of their output and exerted social pressures, via informal group mechanisms, to control that output;
- workers did not necessarily seek to maximise production in order to receive enhanced bonuses – social pressures on individuals were often stronger than managerial concerns for enhanced work rates.

Even today 'the Hawthorne effect' is a term used by many to describe the changes in behaviour that occur when individuals, groups or whole organisations are in some way scrutinised. Often, no direct management intervention is required to create a change in behaviour or emphasis, merely the belief that the new direction is what is required can, sometimes, prove sufficient to stimulate change. But don't rely on it!

These experiments, although methodologically imperfect, generated new insights into motivation, group work, leadership/management and the informal organisation which have, subsequently, inspired considerable research and the blossoming of a significant branch of social study. It should be noted, however, that the human relations approach does not represent a 'getting soft' orientation. The school sought to discover ways of improving output or productivity and, ultimately, profitability. However, the approach moves away from the overt managerial perspective, adopted by the classical school, to consideration of the vital importance of human/social activity as a determinant of productivity and organisational well-being. It became increasingly recognised that people have a complex set of needs and that they seek to satisfy many of these needs in the workplace.

The work of this school has been continued by many researchers, including some referred to in Chapter 4, for example Herzberg, who stressed the importance of intrinsic needs in the motivation equation, and McClelland, who argued that style of management reflects an individual's attitude to their subordinates. McGregor (1960), whose Theory X/Theory Y is now renowned in this regard, is discussed in Chapter 6.

Systems theory

The systems approach to the study of organisations combines the often contrasting positions and considerations of the classical and human relations schools and embraces both the technical and social aspects of organisation. It also recognises the presence of contingent environmental factors which, even though they may lie outside the organisational boundaries, nevertheless influence organisational activity. Attention is focused on the whole organisation, the relationships between its technical, mechanical or structural parameters and its behavioural, social or human elements and its relationship with the business environment.

An organisation is considered to be an open system: *'open' suggesting that it interacts with other, broader, systems outside the organisation* (*see* Figure 2.2). These external systems are part of the organisational environment. When viewed as a system, the organisation is an integrated and complex web of relationships between structures, technology, employees and all manner of technical and social processes.

Research conducted at the Tavistock Institute of Human Relations in the UK suggested that the interaction between coal-miners and the technology they used was a critical factor in determining productivity. 'Improvements' in technology did not always lead to productivity gains as they altered the delicate psychological and sociological conditions. Old ways of working were changed by technological advance, resulting in damage to the social fabric of the work team and consequent, lower than expected, productivity. The relationship between the technical and social aspects of organisations was highlighted by this research. Table 2.1 illustrates some of the two sets of components.

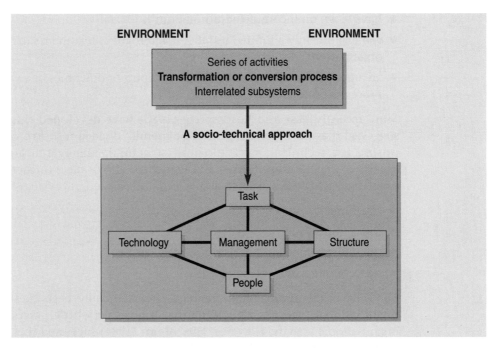

Figure 2.2 An open organisational system
Source: Mullins (2002), p. 115.

Table 2.1 Illustration of technical and social subsystems

Technical subsystems	Social subsystems
Physical location	Social needs
Stages in operational process	Psychological needs
Use of materials	Human relationships
Technical equipment	Formal/informal communications
Maintenance	Skills and learning
Logistics/material flows	Meaningfulness of work

The challenge or design problem presented by the range of social and technological subsystems is to create the most appropriate 'fit' between them and continually to modify that to accommodate organisational change. This area of research is often referred to as the sociotechnical approach. It focuses on the interrelationships between technical or structural aspects of organisation, including the use of technology itself, and the human side or interface with that technology. The modern study of ergonomics embraces aspects of this approach. In reality, of course, suboptimisation (i.e., less than 'best', or what March and Simon (1958) refer to as 'satisficing'), is bound to occur as people:

- have to act on incomplete information;
- can explore only a limited number of alternatives relating to any managerial or organisational decision; and
- are unable to attach accurate values to inputs or outcomes of a variety of processes or decisions.

More recently Kast and Rosenzweig (1985) have developed this approach and suggested that the organisation can be usefully divided into five subsystems comprising the technical, psychological, structural, managerial and goals/values aspects of organisation. Hersey and Blanchard (1993) have further developed this work, suggesting the existence of just four, interrelated, subsystems:

- the human or social;
- the administrative and structure;
- the informational and decision-making; and
- the economic and technological.

The value of this approach has, perhaps understandably, been questioned by many organisational theorists who argue that it gives very little practical insight into organisational activity. However, Hirschhorn (1984) suggested that, because of the changing nature of manufacturing, involving semi-autonomous groups and greater delegation of decision making and problem solving, work based on sociotechnical principles warrants careful consideration. Of particular significance is the finding of the Tavistock studies which suggested that work in groups is more meaningful for its participants and that technology need not, if applied appropriately, unduly influence this form of work organisation. It is not therefore surprising that many recent changes in organisational structures place emphasis on the team or group as one of the best ways of managing difficult problem-solving tasks and coping with the needs for organisational flexibility and change.

 ## Contingency theory

The work of theorists from the classical school in particular, and to an extent the human relations school, offered all-embracing, 'one best way' prescriptions on how best to organise and to manage. These panaceas were proposed to be universally applicable.

Research conducted from the early 1960s questioned many of these organisational prescriptions. For example, Woodward (1965) found that the level and type of technology, being central to the organisation's activity, influenced the structure of the unit. Similarly, others provided empirical evidence to suggest that organisational size, the nature of its output and, more significantly, the characteristics of the business environment in which it operated (e.g. the nature of competition), had a significant, measurable effect on the organisational structure, work organisation or job design, and upon management. The plethora of research in the 1960s, and since, on many aspects of organisational activity largely rejected the 'one best

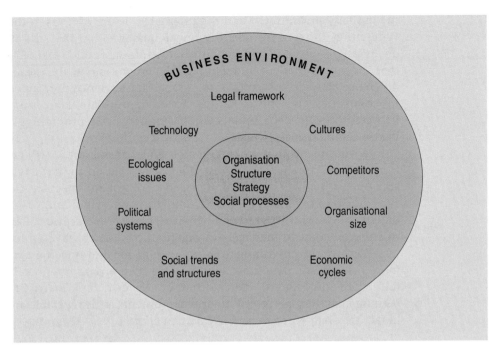

Figure 2.3 Contingency factors: the organisational context

way' philosophy, arguing instead that organisations in many ways reflect the situation in which they find themselves and the strategy they pursue, and that there is a great variety of ways of organising and managing with each potentially leading to organisational success (or indeed failure). In other words, organisational structure, job design, management practices and most other aspects of organisations are dependent or contingent on a variety of internal and external tangible and non-tangible variables (*see* Figure 2.3). Implicit is the understanding that organisations are social communities and hence, organisational behaviour can be considered as both a response to and a determinant of many of the complex variables which make up organisations and their environments. As the word 'behaviour' implies, the human element in organisational activity is emphasised and recognised by contingency theorists as a vital influencing factor on organisations and one that was largely ignored by earlier classical management theorists.

We will now briefly explore three key factors, alluded to above, which have been found to influence organisational structure and activities.

Contingent factor: the business environment

A study of electronics companies in the United Kingdom by Burns and Stalker (1961) attempted to establish why some companies were able to cope with changes in their environment, specifically dynamism in their product markets, whereas others were inept in this regard. They argued that successful innovators had developed an 'organic' structure whereas those with 'mechanistic' structures were less able to adapt. Lawrence and Lorsch (1967) found a similar relationship between the business environment and the internal structure of firms in the United States. Where they differed from earlier researchers was that they did not believe that organisations or their environments were uniform or unchanging. They postulated that the more turbulent and complex the environment, the greater the degree of difference between sub-parts of the organisation. Hence they argued that successful companies were those that developed appropriate degrees of differentiation between specialist departments while simultaneously promoting integration calling on common goals.

In environments that are certain and stable, organisations will tend to develop a form and structure which is most efficient in relation to that environment, probably one with a high degree of managerial control and mechanistic structures and systems. If an organisation's environment is uncertain and complex, managers design structures with greater flexibility. However, perception may play a part in this process, that is, managers in organisations which have an organic structure may perceive the environment as being dynamic and uncertain whereas those in more mechanistic structures may perceive their environment as being more certain; the reality may be quite different. Nevertheless, many firms have failed because managers 'perceived' their environments as being stable and certain when in fact they harboured destructive dynamic forces.

Contingent factor: technology

Woodward's contention was that companies which design their organisational structure to fit the type of production technology they employ are likely to be successful (Woodward, 1965). She found clear variations in organisational structure between companies and argued that much of the variation was linked to differences in manufacturing techniques. For example, structures differed between organisations engaged in specialised or small batch production and those adopting mass production techniques and technologies. She noted, particularly, that certain factors varied considerably according to the production techniques adopted (*see* Chapter 7 for further details). These included:

- typical spans of control;
- levels in the hierarchy;
- the ratio of managers to other personnel and of the total salary bill to total costs.

In other words, and in contrast to the generalisations made by classical management exponents, considerable variability in structure and management activity occurred between organisations, although this appeared to have little significant or discernible influence on commercial success.

Perhaps not surprisingly, Perrow (1970) found that in organisations where routine technology predominates (i.e., there is considerable repetition of tasks and problem solving and flexibility is less in demand) there tends to be little requirement for decision making at the lower levels of the organisation. Middle managers are powerful and the organisations are characterised by careful planning and little cooperation between groups or departments. Bureaucratic principles dominate and the structure is mechanistic. Conversely, in non-routine environments, there is a high level of discretion at lower levels, greater feedback and dialogue between groups and levels in the hierarchy and significant interdependence between groups. This model approximates to the organic structure outlined above.

Contingent factor: organisational size

The Aston studies (empirical research conducted in the University of Aston largely in the 1960s and 1970s by, among others, D. S. Pugh, J. Child, D. J. Hickson, C. R. Hinings and C. Turner) suggested that organisational size has important implications for organisational design. Despite the fact that organisational size is often problematic to determine and that its influence is difficult to distinguish from the effects of other variables, the Aston studies and the work of Porter *et al.* (1975) and Child (1988) found that:

- size of organisational unit was negatively correlated with job satisfaction, staff turnover and absenteeism from work;
- larger organisations are more likely to be standardised by rules and procedures;
- internal communications and coordination are more difficult in larger organisations and are addressed via structural and procedural mechanisms, that is, line managers have a responsibility to communicate with employees and follow accepted procedures when doing so;
- the relationship between organisational size and productivity was unclear and variable;
- increased organisational size is associated with increased bureaucracy.

Contingency: criticisms and conclusions

There has been some criticism of the contingency approach. First, although extensive research has been conducted which is clearly of theoretical and academic value, the outcome of the work is more difficult to apply to the workplace. By its very nature, it is not significantly prescriptive: the answer to the question 'How should we organise?' is 'It depends'! It depends on a whole host of only partly understood internal and external variables. It is no wonder that the simple, although highly questionable, panaceas offered by the classical theorists had, and to an extent still have, considerable appeal among some managers. Many of the best-selling management books of recent decades tend to offer 'one best way', simplistic prescriptions.

Second, contingency theory can only ever give a partial picture. There are so many variables and combinations of factors which influence organisational activity and company success, and the environment is complex and dynamic, that complete knowledge is unobtainable. Third, the contingency theorists underplay the significance of intensely 'human' aspects of organisation, such as power, the role of multiple stakeholders and organisational culture. Finally, it should be remembered that organisations and their environments are in constant flux. Change is often rapid and discontinuous. The factors influencing the 'correct fit' between structure and environment, for example, at one time, may become less relevant at another time.

With the rejection of 'the best way' of organising, the crucial task of management, and hence the concern of academics and researchers, is to find an appropriate, satisficing 'fit' between the human, task and business environments. Emphasis has subsequently been placed on establishing which variable or variables most influence organisational structure and other organisational variables. The deterministic position suggests that certain key variables will have a significant and measurable influence on organisational structure, job design, the degree of specialisation or standardisation and so forth. However, an alternative position suggests that these organisational variables are themselves strongly and decisively influenced by strategic choice: they are the product of the political power of key stakeholder groups, such as senior management. Others argue that a collective social concept, organisational culture, explains much of the variability found in organisations. Chapter 8 explores this position and the interplay of power and politics within organisations. Clearly, the complex interplay between tangible and non-tangible aspects of organisation and environment provide rich veins for academic and managerial exploration in search of *the*, or *a*, 'truth' or, perhaps more realistically, greater insight into organisations and their behaviour.

Contemporary lenses and postmodernism

Many scholars of organisation suggest that we are in a postmodern era. They view organizations through postmodern lenses. These lenses reject previously considered rational systems approaches to viewing organisations. In recent decades, organisational theory has moved on from an idea of the organisation as a rational decision-making entity and has placed greater emphasis on how humans construct or invent their world, often via their language or discourse. When it is accepted that there will be many world-views or socially constructed realities then it is also apparent that organizations have to recognize and accept that there will be disorder, complexity and paradox in all that they do. The following section further explores the non-rational view of organisations or, rather, views organisations from different perspectives.

Frames or perspectives

Possibly one of the most significant developments in organisational theory in recent years is the recognition that organisations can be many things at the same time, depending on the perspective from which we view them. This approach builds on the extensive work conducted in the field of organisational culture (Chapter 9), organisational politics (Chapter 8), organisational learning and other theoretical developments in OB.

Morgan (1996) suggests a series of metaphors which shape our understanding of organisations. These reflect 'a way of thinking and a way of seeing that pervade how we understand our world generally' (Morgan, 1996: 4). Metaphors, or perspectives with which we view or 'see' organisations, are crucial for understanding, managing and designing organisations. For example, when managers think of organisations as machines, 'they tend to manage and design them as machines' (Morgan, 1986: 13). As a consequence, thinking in metaphorical terms can influence the organisational structure, systems and ways of organising. For example, the mechanical way of thinking, common to many Western organisations, is so engrained in everyday perception that it proves difficult to organise in any other way. In a sense, we are conditioned into believing that 'our' reality is the only reality.

An alternative perspective or frame with which to analyse an organisation is as an 'organism'. Considerable literature is devoted to the study of organisations being categorised into types or 'species', which have 'evolved' via interaction with their environment. This perspective enables us to analyse how organisations are 'born', how they 'develop', 'decline' and 'die', and has led to the development of many 'life-cycle' models. Another popular perspective, the 'structural' frame, is particularly commonplace in Western organisations. So pervasive is this that, as we shall see, it even influences the study of organisational culture. When the structural perspective is adopted, organisational problems are thought to be attributable to deficiencies in structure and, consequently, change initiatives often focus on structural issues, the popular belief being that, if you get the structure right, all else will fall into place. The 'political' perspective is also a commonly used diagnostic and analytical tool.

Illustration in film

The Truman Show

In the 1998 film *The Truman Show*, a television producer and director created a 'real' world for an individual (Truman Burbank, played by Jim Carrey) and determined that man's reality. Truman's life was filmed, without him being aware, and was shown on television across the world as 'real-life' soap. His life was, for most of us, a very unreal existence but for Truman, who knew nothing else, it was the only world – it was normal. He saw only that world – people were always very friendly and warm to him, there were no pressures at work, no crime and he was surrounded by beauty and tranquillity. The film became exciting and meaningful as he increasingly began to question that reality. A message from this film is that it is all too easy to settle for our known world, to live with its simple and unquestioned reality, but this restricts our learning, understanding and wisdom, perhaps even our freedom.

It is argued by proponents of this school of thought that patterns of power and control fundamentally influence organisational activity and ways of organising. There are very many perspectives or paradigms which can be adopted when managing, analysing or researching organisational form and activity. If used as a problem-recognition and problem-solving tool each perspective might identify different problems and generate alternative solutions. Figure 2.4 indicates just some of the alternative perspectives or ways of seeing organisations.

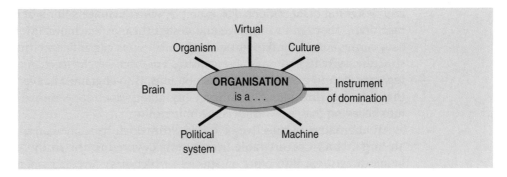

Figure 2.4 Ways of seeing organisations

The cultural perspective

The cultural or symbolic metaphor is one very powerful way of viewing organisations. The organisation can be viewed as a culture, in which case even the more
mechanical characteristics, such as the structure, rules, policies and systems, can be
considered to be products of the culture, or cultural artefacts, which help shape the
ongoing reality for people in the organisation. Adopting this perspective ensures
that every aspect of the organisation is rich in symbolic meaning so that the familiar appears in a new light. Meetings, other routines and ceremonies, such as
selection and promotion boards, become rituals which serve an important cultural
purpose. Morgan (1986, 1996) identifies the strengths of the cultural metaphor. It
directs attention to the symbolic significance of even the most rational aspects of
organisational activity and focuses attention on the human side of organisation.
Additionally, culture focuses on shared systems of meaning and hence provides a
new focus for the creation of 'organised' action. Hence, if it is possible to influence
the symbolic elements of organisations, such as language, norms, rituals and other
practices which communicate key values and beliefs, managing, or at least influencing, culture may become possible. Culture also influences the way organisational
members interpret the nature of their business environment, as knowledge of the
relationship between the organisation and its environment is an extension of the
organisational culture; the environment is viewed through 'cultural lenses'. For
example, firms in an industry often develop a language for making sense of their
market: they might argue that it is a 'dog eat dog' culture, or suggest that 'he who
dares wins'. This language tells us something about the culture of the organisation,
not merely about the competitive environment in which it operates.

Weick (1979) and Morgan (1986) argue that organisations 'enact' the realities
with which they have to deal. For example, a competitive ethos within firms is
likely to produce a competitive business environment. That is, if all or many firms
in a business sector believe that they operate in a highly competitive arena, their
subsequent action might ensure that competition is rife; they might engage in
competitive pricing, special offers, improvements to delivery times and so forth.
This has important implications for the analysis of organisational strategy, as strategy itself derives from organisational culture and is influenced by its enacted
business environment. Finally, the cultural perspective sheds invaluable light on

the process and success, or otherwise, of organisational change. It can be argued that effective organisational change must imply cultural change. This issue is developed further in Chapter 9.

Metaphors have been used to characterise how the culture of an organisation serves as an integrating force. These often portray a graphic, subjective and meaningful interpretation of the concept of organisation. For example, culture can be viewed as an intangible 'social glue' or 'normative glue' that binds and holds everything together (Morgan, 1989). Culture and organisation can be viewed as an 'iceberg', a metaphor which suggests that what you see on the surface masks a much deeper, mystical and powerful reality. The warning to change agents, that is, *those whose prime role is to manage and encourage change in an organisation*, implied by this metaphor, is clear: it may be possible to change surface appearances but to have lasting impact the deeper reality needs to be addressed.

Organisation as a brain: the learning organisation

From the perspective or paradigm of the learning organisation we can analyse organisations as systems of complex information, communication, decision making and learning. Considerable work in Management Information Systems (MIS), Operations Research (OR) and Management Decision Systems (MDS) has attempted to develop decision-making tools and data management principles and practices, in some ways reminiscent of the human brain. The resultant complex systems of data management, in the fields of logistics, production, finance and marketing and the implementation of teams that can 'think' for the rest of the organisation and control activities, is reminiscent of a centralised brain that regulates activity (Morgan, 1996).

An area of particular interest to modern organisational behaviour is the learning capability of an organisation (as opposed to the learning capability and capacity of a series of individuals within an organisation). A contemporary question inviting considerable debate and interest is whether organisations can learn. If they can, it is argued, they are better able to embrace organisational change because they can learn to manage and cope with circumstances which have not previously been experienced.

Argyris and Schön (1974, 1978) suggest that most organisations (and individuals) engage in, and are proficient at, single-loop learning. That is, *learning within accepted limits where an organisation is able to scan its environment, set objectives and monitor its performance to keep it on course, usually resulting in 'same-again', single-frame solutions.* In bureaucracies, for example, the fundamental organising principles, based on precedent, rules, procedures and regulations, often obstruct the learning of different ways of working, organising or managing. The same, or similar, solutions are generated as a response to perceived organisational problems, with the result that the organisation is locked into single-loop learning and defensive routines. Double-loop learning can only occur when *organisations and individuals reflect on practice, challenge accepted practices and norms, recognise that solutions do not lie in previous experiences and allow alternatives to emerge.* For these actions to occur requires an organisation to be able to break free from the paradigm into which it is locked.

Organisational analysis: contemporary themes

Many academics, largely from the fields of business, management, sociology, psychology and philosophy undertake research about human activity in organisations. They are concerned with finding explanations for all manner of human behaviours and activities. For example, a more recent theme of some of this work explores how people exhibit, use and abuse emotions in organisations. Other academics have focused on time and the different interpretations made of it in an organisational setting. Knowledge management and inter-organisational networks are two of the more popular contemporary concerns.

Academics have for some time now explored values, beliefs, stories, myths and other symbols in organisations. Knowledge of these helps us to appreciate the complexity of human interaction in an organisational setting and to reject the simplistic and rational philosophies that dominated Western organisational theory for so long. We will briefly explore just two 'contemporary' themes: emotions and time.

Emotion in organisations

Pleasure, sadness, anger, jealousy, lust, guilt and love are experienced and displayed in organisational as well as in everyday life. Deeply rooted in Western culture is the belief that organisational order and efficiency are a matter of rational, non-emotional activity. In other words, it is often considered that messy feelings interfere with orderly, efficient decision making and activity. For many decades now researchers have questioned these beliefs and more recently have discussed the role played by emotion in organisations.

Hence, research has examined the way that people bring the influences of their childhood into their interpersonal encounters at work (refer to Hirschhorn, 1988; Schwartz, 1987). Fineman (1993) has investigated the psychology of emotions in organisations. Mumby and Putnam (1992) suggested 'bounded emotionality' and, together with Simon (1989), have recognised that decision making is likely to be influenced by both 'rational' considerations and emotions. Abramis (1988) considers joy, excitement, humour and play in the workplace. It has also been shown that an understanding of our own and others' emotions in the workplace can influence how we communicate and motivate people.

Emotions at work can be exploited to further organisational objectives. In marketing and advertising emotional appeals often play a part. In all manner of care work, such as nursing, emotions, whether surpressed or not, are important. In Chapters 8 and 9 we explore organisational culture and politics, recognising that there is an emotional dimension to these two concepts.

Time and organisations

Time has always been important in organisations but has been stressed more recently as it is seen as vital in influencing organisational competitiveness. Let us briefly look at just three aspects of time-based language and thinking:

- Time can regulate and fundamentally control our daily lives: when we start and finish work and how we are evaluated in the workplace. Productivity, for example, is a measure of how much we achieve in a given time. Time (temporal) flexibility is often stressed as a source of competitive advantage and is a source of ongoing tension between employers and employees in organisations (e.g. length of working day, shiftwork arrangement, notice periods).

- Organisations also think of time in terms of short-term and long-term positions. A company might use some existing knowledge to gain short-term competitive advantage while another firm may seek to develop new knowledge in order to gain long-term competitive advantage – these two hypothetical companies will differ in very many ways. Similarly, organisational cultures may differ in their consideration of time. Some organisations may have a short-term focus while others have a long-term emphasis. They may not be aware of this culturally engrained orientation. As Mini-case 2.3 indicates, this may cause problems not least at the interface between organisations with different time frames.

Mini-case 2.3

Friction between the manufacturer and its dealerships: a time-based observation

Research in Scania, the successful Swedish truck manufacturing, marketing and servicing organisation, indicated that labels 'long term' and 'short term' have quite different meanings in different parts of the wider multinational organisation. At the Swedish manufacturing headquarters concern is often about product and process life cycles, eco-friendly truck design and emerging European legislation. Product life cycles in this industry are often 10–15 years so the label 'long term' often means in excess of 10 years, whereas 'short term' can refer to the current production and planning cycle which is at least one year.

At the other extreme, dealerships manage day-to-day activities with customers including the sales of new and second-hand trucks and servicing and repairs. In these organisations, the words 'short term' often means 'today'. A typical short term concern would be whether they can access a key part in order to immediately repair a truck which is off road due to breakdown and consequently costing their client dearly in lost business. Long term in such dealerships is not a term often considered but is thought to be a period of time up to about 3 years. Words like 'urgent' take on a range of meaning in different parts of the wider organisation!

Source: Brooks, I. and Reast, J. (1996) 'Redesigning the value chain at Scania Trucks, *Long Range Planning*, 29(4).

- Some researchers and managers think of company and product life-cycles. Hence, companies are thought to go through a series of stages, rather like people themselves, before they eventually decline while products also eventually reach maturity and eventually 'die'.

What is more, change management, an important theme in organisations and in this book, implies difference (change) over time. In change management we consider terms like revolution, evolution, incrementalism or quantum changes, all of which require us to understand the passing of time. Management thinking suggests concepts of the past and future are important; that is, we look at where we have come from and plan where we hope to go. Organisational reality, however, often stresses the present, the crises and responsibilities that we face and which preoccupy us in the present.

Managerial implications

Organisational theory has a fundamental impact on organisational activity. It can inform our understanding of how organisations are structured and managed, grow, change and decline, and even help us to understand what organisations actually are. The managerial implications that arise from gaining some knowledge and understanding of this theoretical base are significant and include the following.

1 Managers need to recognise that their 'taken for granted' assumptions about how to organise and manage are profoundly influenced by classical theory, traditional practice and all manner of life experiences.

2 The principles outlined by Taylor and others have transformed organisational and socioeconomic conditions in the twentieth century. These principles are still applied, and will continue to be applied in many organisations. Managers might examine the benefits and drawbacks of managing scientifically and consider, in the light of the human relations approach, the human implications of the way we organise and manage.

3 Managers might benefit from an understanding that organisations are complex sociotechnical systems and that there exists a complex interrelationship between all human and technical aspects of organisation. This knowledge, together with the development of skills to manage such interrelationships, might enable managers to cope with and manage successful organisational change. It should enable managers to better assess the likely impact of their activities on colleagues.

4 Organisational behaviour is not confined to traditional organisational boundaries. Managers need to be aware that the environment in which they, as individuals, and their organisation, operate is likely to be subjectively defined and, in part at least, enacted. The testing of assumptions about the internal and external environment may yield positive results.

5 Recognition that 'what we look for we tend to find' or 'when we wear certain lenses we will only "see" specific things' might enable managers to experiment with alternative 'lenses' or ways of seeing in order to improve their insight into organisational activity. In turn, that improved insight can inform action and enable managers to cope with and manage conflict, communications and change more effectively.

Summary of main points

This chapter has examined many of the prime developments in organisational theory in the twentieth century. The main points are:

- classical theorists aimed to design organisations and develop management principles which were universally applicable and based on rational, ordered technical arrangements;

- scientific management, a subset of the classical school, focused on job design and work organisation: the human or social element of the work was largely overlooked;

- the classical and scientific traditions remain influential, particularly in Western organisations, although many fundamental criticisms can be levelled at these principles;

- situational or contingent factors were shown to influence organisational and management activity, with the result that the search for a 'one best way' approach was considered hackneyed and inappropriate;

- organisational size, levels and types of technology, the business environment and all manner of internal social aspects act as contingent factors and, consequently, affect organisational activity;

- organisations can be viewed as open systems which embrace complex interrelationships between technical and social subsystems;

- organisations can be viewed through different 'lenses', for example as cultures, brains or machines. Whichever perspective or paradigm is employed will fundamentally influence our reading of organisational practice.

 ## Conclusions

Probably the most significant lesson to be learned from the study of organisational theory is the recognition that our understanding of organisations today, as individuals or collectively, is strongly influenced by historical context, by past and current organisational practice, by the writings of a relatively small number of key researchers in the field and by our own life experiences. As suggested above by Morgan (1996), when, as is often the case, we are locked into a particular way of seeing and thinking (a paradigm) it is difficult to imagine or devise feasible alternatives to what we take for granted. The early classical theorists did not so much ignore or rule out the possibility that social factors might influence productivity and ways of organising: as early researchers they were largely unaware of the significance of these factors. The frames of reference into which they were 'locked' prevented them from 'seeing'. Similarly, if we consider the social needs of people in the workplace, in isolation from technical, structural, managerial or environmental matters, then we may become locked in an equally unsatisfying paradigm. The final section of this chapter raises our awareness of the value of 'paradigm hopping', a skill which can be well worth exploring, while reminding us that there are very many ways of seeing organisations and that each will give us a quite different view of how and why people behave as they are believed to do.

Questions

1 What are the important differences between the Classical School of Management (including Taylorism) and the Human Relations School? Why are these important for how we work and manage in organisations?

2 How would you organise the preparation of food and service within a fast food outlet? In what ways do these practices reflect Frederick Taylor's approach?

3 How is a manager's work influenced by how he or she 'sees' the organisation? For example, if they view it as needing to be a 'well-oiled machine' how would they manage? If they saw their organisation as a complex culture how would they manage?

References

Abramis, D. J. (1988) 'The upside of emotions in work: joy, excitement, humor, play and fun'. Paper presented at the annual meeting of the Academy of Management in Anaheim, California.

Argyris, C. and Schön, D. A. (1974) *Theory in Practice*. San Francisco: Jossey-Bass.

Argyris, C. and Schön, D. A. (1978) *Organizational Learning: Theory of Action Perspective*. Reading, MA: Addison-Wesley.

Barnard, C. (1938) *The Functions of the Executive*. Cambridge, MA: Harvard University Press.

Burns, T. and Stalker, G. M. (1961) *The Management of Innovation*. London: Tavistock.

Child, J. (1988) *Organization: A Guide to Problems and Practice*, 2nd edn. London: Paul Chapman.

Fineman, S. (ed.) (1993) *Emotion in Organisations*. London: Sage.

Hersey, P. and Blanchard, K. (1993) *Management of Organizational Behavior*. Englewood Cliffs, NJ: Prentice-Hall.

Hirschhorn, L. (1984) *Beyond Mechanization*. Cambridge, MA: MIT Press.

Hirschhorn, L. (1988) *The Workplace Within: Psychodyamics of Organizational Life*, Cambridge, MA: MIT Press.

Kast, F. E. and Rosenzweig, J. E. (1985) *Organization and Management*. New York: McGraw-Hill.

Lawrence, P. R. and Lorsch, J. W. (1967) *Organization and Environment*. Cambridge, MA: Harvard Graduate School of Business Administration.

McGregor, D. (1960) *The Human Side of Enterprise*. New York: McGraw-Hill.

March, J. G. and Simon, H. A. (1958) *Organizations*. New York: John Wiley.

Morgan, G. (1986) *Images of Organization*. Newbury Park, CA: Sage.

Morgan, G. (1989) *Creative Organization Theory*. Newbury Park, CA: Sage.

Morgan, G. (1996) *Images of Organization*, 2nd edn. Newbury Park, CA: Sage.

Mullins, L. J. (2002) *Management and Organisational Behaviour*, 6th edn. Harlow: Financial Times Prentice Hall.

Mumby, D. K. and Putnam, L. L. (1992) 'The politics of emotion: a feminist reading of bounded rationality', *Academy of Management Review*, 17(3): 465–86.

Perrow, C. (1970) *Organisational Analysis. A Sociological View*. London: Tavistock Publications.

Porter, L. W., Lawler, E. E. and Hackman, J. R. (1975) *Behavior in Organizations*. Maidenhead: McGraw-Hill.

Roethlisberger, F. J. and Dickson, W. (1939) *Management and the Worker*. Cambridge, MA: Harvard University Press.

Schwartz, H. S. (1987) 'Anti-social actions of committed organizational participants: An existential psychoanalytic perspective', *Organization Studies*, 8(4), pp. 327–40.

Simon, H. (1989) 'Making management decisions: The role of intuition and emotion', in Agor, W. H. (ed.) *Intuition in Organizations*, Newbury Park, CA: Sage, pp. 23–39.

Taylor, F. W. (1911) *The Principles of Scientific Management*. New York: Harper & Brothers.

Weick, K. (1979) *The Social Psychology of Organizing*. Reading, MA: Addison-Wesley.

Woodward, J. (1965) *Industrial Organization: Theory and Practice*. Oxford: Oxford University Press.

Further reading

There are a host of good texts in the field of organisational and management theory and organisational design. For synthesised versions you might consider:

Daft, R. L. (1992) *Organizational Theory and Design*. St Paul, MN: West Publishing.

Alternatively, if you require a more focused approach, most good OB textbooks cover much of the material presented in this chapter. Examples include:

Huczynski, A. and Buchanan, D. (2007) *Organizational Behaviour: An Introductory Text*, 6th edn. Harlow: Financial Times Prentice Hall.

Mullins, L. J. (2007) *Management and Organisational Behaviour*, 8th edn. Harlow: Financial Times: Prentice Hall. This high-quality OB text covers much of the ground reviewed by this chapter in further detail (with the exception of the contemporary lenses material).

Morgan, G. (1996) *Images of Organization*, 2nd edn. Newbury Park, CA: Sage. This international bestseller investigates with insight and skill, as the name suggests, a variety of 'images' or perspectives of organisations.

Internet sites

Google and other search engines will help you locate sites on most of the concepts and theories contained in this chapter – try Taylorism, for example. Wikipedia gives excellent definitions and some extension notes on each term also. Some university lecturers post their slides or notes on open access within university web sites; these can be useful for reference.

3

Perspectives on individual behaviour

Jon Stephens

Learning outcomes

On completion of this chapter you should be able to:

- understand how different aspects of organisational behaviour can impact on the organisation as a whole;
- appreciate different theories about personality formation and evaluate the extent to which personality testing is an effective method of recruitment;
- have a clearer idea of the process of perception and how perceptions might change at individual level;
- understand how values and attitudes are formed, and the implications for organisational change and conflict;
- evaluate different perspectives of the learning process at both the individual and the organisational level;
- identify the importance of effective decision making and the significance of cognitive style;
- appreciate the increased roles of emotional labour and emotional intelligence in organisations;
- understand all of the above within the context of change, conflict and communication.

Key concepts

- individual personality and behaviour
- personality in the organisation
- personality testing
- perceptual processes
- attribution theory
- attitudes and values

- individual learning
- learning styles
- individual decision making
- psychological contracts
- emotional intelligence
- emotional labour.

An organisation comprises the individuals who make up its membership, and it is the behaviour and interaction of these individuals which influence all other areas of organisational behaviour, whether group behaviour, leadership or the corporate culture of the organisation itself. Thus an understanding of individual behaviour is an essential tool to help us understand the way people behave and how they interact with each other and perhaps, even, to understand our own behaviour in an organisational context.

 ## Introduction

An organisation, by its very nature, is composed of individuals who are 'organised' in some way or form in order to achieve certain objectives. Thus, individuals are the basic building material around which an organisation functions, and an understanding of individual behaviour is an essential prerequisite to the exploration of how individuals work in groups and how the organisation itself behaves. Organisations sometimes forget this point in the struggle for corporate survival. However, it could be argued that the radical changes being forced on organisations as a result of increasingly turbulent environments are forcing them to reassess the role of individuals in terms of their capacity for individual and collective development and the potential which this has for revitalising the organisation. It is interesting that one of the most significant developments in recent years has been the concept of the learning organisation (Senge, 1990; Burgoyne, 1995), which seeks to develop people so that the organisation can constantly learn from good practice and continually adapt itself in a fast-moving environment.

Emphasis is being placed increasingly upon individuals in terms of assessing the significance of the personality of the key players in the organisation, how learning occurs in an organisation, how decisions are made, how values and attitudes are determined and how they can be changed, and how perception influences all of these. This chapter examines some of these issues in the light of relevant theories and recent trends. The context of change and conflict in the organisation and the importance of communication as the effective cement which holds the organisation together are also considered.

 ## Individual behaviour and personality

The starting point for an examination of individual behaviour in the organisation is personality. Personality theory overlaps strongly with other disciplines, most notably psychology, and there are a large number of personality theories (Ewen, 1988), each taking a different perspective. There is a similarly wide range of definitions of personality which can make the concept more complex. For our purposes we will define personality as: *specific characteristics of individuals which*

may be open or hidden and which may determine either commonality or differences in behaviour in an organisation.

The definition given above suggests that personality affects other people in an organisation through interaction but also that it affects how individuals see themselves and thus the extent to which individuals are a positive or a negative force in the organisation. For example, personality differences can lead to hostility between individuals, which could hinder the development of effective teams, although the right mix of different personalities can lead to the formation of efficient teams (Belbin, 1996). Attitudes and motivation are influenced by personality in terms of how individuals respond to motivational stimuli or, more negatively, how a negative concept of self can lead to attitudes which might hamper attempts to motivate individuals at an organisational level. Leadership styles are also affected, and the ability to create commonality of purpose may be significant in relation to the process of developing a strong organisational culture.

Furthermore, it could be argued that personality may have a major bearing on the way people behave in an organisation. An issue often debated is the *extent* of this interaction, as it is argued that behaviour is determined by a number of innate factors, based around personal attributes, and also by a number of environmental factors outside the control of the individual. Some of these factors can be seen in Table 3.1.

The concept of factors affecting behaviour was developed by Lewin (1951) with the model

$$B = f(P, E)$$

where B is behaviour, P is person (innate) and E is environment. Lewin's theory suggests several ideas which have been developed by interactional psychology and which argue that people are influenced by both innate and environmental factors and that behaviour results from the continuous interaction between these factors. Furthermore, it suggests that environmental factors can be changed by situations in the organisation but also that they have the capacity to change the organisation. The person aspect indicates that people are influenced by many innate factors. The theory proposes that individual behaviour should be examined both from the organisational perspective (objective) and from the individual's perspective (subjective). In this chapter we focus primarily on innate individual characteristics, although we also look at organisational factors that influence, or are influenced by, different aspects of behaviour.

Table 3.1 Variables affecting individual behaviour

Innate factors	Environmental factors
Personality	Organisation/work factors
Perception	Family
Values	Peer-group pressures
Abilities	Personal life experiences

Illustration in film

Television example: the Big Brother *phenomenon*

The television show *Big Brother* originated in the Netherlands, has since been syndicated in most European countries, and is currently well into its fifth or even sixth edition. It has spawned a whole host of 'reality TV' shows where contestants have to share a house whilst undertaking other tasks (e.g. *The Apprentice* series on BBC starting in 2005). The concept of *Big Brother* is a simple one. Ten to twelve contestants share a house over several weeks and their behaviour is observed through a battery of hidden cameras. The contestants are given tasks to fulfil and tension is created at the end of each week as the contestants have to vote for the two people they would most like to leave the house, with the final decision being made by the television vote, via phone-in or the Internet. Eventually there will only be two people left, and the winner is the one who wins the TV vote at this stage, for which they receive a financial prize. The shows have been massively successful across Europe with many people becoming addicted to the series, sometimes using the 24-hour video link with the show or through the Internet (in the UK counselling was offered for the worst cases).

So why was it so successful and why is it our chosen illustration for Chapter 3? The answer lies in the fascination of watching individual interaction and in relating the behaviour observed in the house to our own. The series has a number of areas of interest for the student studying organisational behaviour. There is the emergence of leaders within the group, whether the group develops successfully and whether there are 'outsiders' who don't accept the group norms. From the perspective of this chapter there is the observation of individual behaviour and how the individuals interact with each other – an issue which is at the heart of any organisation. The examples used in this chapter relate to the second series of *Big Brother* (see Ritchie, 2001).

Personality theories

If we accept that personality is the driving factor influencing a range of innate characteristics of the individual, then we have to look at how personality is formed and to explore some of the typologies which relate to personality. However, just as with behaviour, there is a debate concerning the extent to which personality is innate or is determined by environmental factors such as those identified in Table 3.1. These two perspectives have been called a nomothetic perspective and an idiographic perspective (*see* Hicks, 1996). The **nomothetic** approach strongly supports the view that personalities are fixed and determined by heredity and cannot be significantly influenced by environmental factors. This approach would suggest that there are a number of clear personality types that can be identified and which it is possible to measure, and thus that it might be possible to predict behaviour in the organisation.

The **idiographic** approach takes the opposite perspective and, while recognising that individuals do have unique innate characteristics, it also suggests that personality can be moulded and that both personality and behaviour are influenced by specific environmental experiences. On this basis supporters of this approach are less willing to accept the belief that personality can easily be identified by testing.

It is clear that the debate about whether personality is influenced by nomothetic or idiographic factors has implications for education and crime issues, but in this chapter we look at personality theories from an organisational perspective.

Trait theories

Trait theories clearly fit the nomothetic approach in the sense that it is suggested that *people have certain inherent traits which determine their personality* and thus their behaviour (*see* Chapter 4 for a discussion of trait theories of motivation). These theories have been popular since the days of Hippocrates, who identified four main types of personality – phlegmatic, sanguine, melancholic and choleric – which were often incorporated into medical examinations in ancient times with often-bizarre medical remedies being used to treat or temper these 'conditions'. The concept was developed further by Allport (1961) and Eysenck (1973), among others.

Eysenck (1973) identified a range of personality characteristics along scales from extrovert to introvert and neurotic to stable. Thus, phlegmatic could be seen as stable introvert, sanguine as stable neurotic, melancholic as neurotic introvert and choleric as neurotic extrovert. From this Eysenck suggested that if the relevant traits of an individual can be identified then that person's behaviour can be predicted. Although Eysenck's theory can be criticised for its relatively simple approach to a complex issue, it has attracted considerable attention from managers who saw the appeal of trait identification as a means of selection in the organisation. This led to the suggestion that it might be possible to use some of these theories to develop means of testing personality within the organisation, especially in the context of recruitment and selection, where the organisation may have specific traits that it is looking for in employees and which can in turn be identified by the use of a personality test. This idea was further developed by Cattell and Kline (1977), who devised a much more sophisticated range of traits which could be used as the framework for personality testing. These are shown in Table 3.2.

Trait theorists have argued (*see* Weiss, 1996) the existence of five main personality traits which are the most significant for determining behaviour. These key traits are:

- *agreeableness* – an individual can be seen as very agreeable or very uncooperative;
- *openness to experience* – the range is from very open-minded to closed and narrow-minded;
- *extrovert or introvert* – the range is from very sociable and outgoing to more reserved and cautious;
- *conscientiousness* – the range is from responsible to irresponsible;
- *emotionally stable* – the range is from an ability to control emotions to a more unstable emotional pattern.

Table 3.2 Cattell and Kline's 16 personality factors

Factor	Low score description*	High score description*
A	Reserved	Outgoing
B	Less intelligent	More intelligent
C	Affected by feelings	Emotionally stable
E	Humble	Assertive
F	Sober	Happy-go-lucky
G	Expedient	Conscientious
H	Sly	Venturesome
I	Tough-minded	Tender-minded
L	Trusting	Suspicious
M	Practical	Imaginative
N	Forthright	Shrewd
O	Self-assured	Apprehensive
Q1	Conservative	Experimenting
Q2	Group-dependent	Self-sufficient
Q3	Undisciplined	Controlled
Q4	Relaxed	Tense

* On scale of 1 to 10.
Source: Cattell and Kline (1977), Table 4.1, pp. 44–5.

Such theories continue to be the subject of criticism, however, on the grounds that so close a focus on innate personality traits can mean that the influence of other factors is diminished or sidelined. There has also been criticism that some of the factors mentioned by Cattell are too close to one another, and it could therefore be argued that it is too simplistic an approach to yield meaningful insights into a very complex issue.

Humanistic approach

The humanistic approach, developed by Rogers (1970), also focuses on the individual and is nomothetic in parts. A central part of the Rogers view is that individuals experience a need for personal growth and fulfilment ('self-actualisation'). This approach is very much focused on the development of the individual but also explores the concept of 'self' and the self-concept, that is, how people perceive themselves. The potential fulfilment for the individual will depend upon the self-concept as much as, if not more than, on any objective measures of fulfilment or development.

Psychodynamic theory

Psychodynamic theory relates to the work of Freud and certainly possesses an idiographic (environmental) perspective in that Freud saw personality as being developed by a number of environmental factors, most notably parental relationships and the effects of various types of trauma. One significant aspect of Freud's work in the present context is the theory that behaviour can be driven by unconscious or hidden personality factors and that these influences can sometimes be used to explain various types of irrational behaviour. For Freud, behaviour and personality were determined by a constant battle between the id (which is the basic drive in the personality which can often act irrationally and on impulse), the superego (which imposes a whole range of environmental influences such as parental and societal factors on to the mind or conscience) and the ego (which seeks to balance the often-conflicting directions of the id and superego).

It is suggested that it is this compromise by the ego which leads to certain behavioural characteristics. Some of these may be significant for the organisation, such as 'denial' – where the individual refuses to recognise a change which can be harmful and so ignores it. 'Compensation' is another behavioural characteristic – where an individual compensates for weaknesses in one area by doing too much in another, for example, avoiding making important strategic decisions by making numerous small operational ones which still avoid the main problem. It also adds to understanding of individual defence mechanisms and thus the behaviour of managers who might feel threatened in a change situation, i.e. over-reaction.

Although Freud's work has led to the development of psychoanalysis, it has been criticised in an organisational context as many of the suggestions have not been proven. Nevertheless, the concept of the subconscious and some of the behavioural patterns identified by Freud are useful for understanding personality. Some of these issues are used with the Johari Window technique, which is discussed later in the chapter.

Jung's personality theory

The personality theory developed by Carl Jung is linked to some aspects of psychodynamic theory but also has more practicable implications in that it has led to the design of different types of personality testing. Idiographic in nature, Jung's theory looked at four dimensions of personality. He started from personality types also identified by Eysenck, namely 'extrovert' or 'introvert', and then went on to pick out two types of perception, which he called 'sensing' and 'intuiting' and which referred to the way in which people get their information. The third dimension of this theory concerned judgement, which he differentiated into two types, which he called 'thinking' and 'feeling', terms which also refer to decision-making styles. The fourth dimension is that of judging or perceiving, which reflects how we relate to the environment. The significance of Jung's analysis, apart from its place in the development of psychology as a discipline, was that his concepts were used by Myers (1987) to develop the Myers–Briggs Type Indicator (MBTI), which can be seen in Table 3.3 and again is a basis for personality testing.

Questionnaires, informed by the criteria illustrated in Table 3.3, are used to evaluate personality and develop profiles based on combinations of characteristics identified in the table. These are used extensively in organisations as a tool in staff selection, development, promotion and even redundancy, although the validity of personality testing has been questioned.

Personality in the organisation

There are a number of organisational situations in which personality has an impact but, equally, there are certain personality characteristics which might be more important for understanding people who work in organisations and which can be used to explain the behaviour of individuals in organisations.

One area of significance is that of locus of control, which is *the amount of control that individuals feel they have over a situation*. If an individual feels that he or she has a high degree of control over what happens to him or her then that person is said to have an internal locus of control, whereas an individual who feels that he or she is primarily influenced by other people, or the organisation, is said to have an external locus of control. Those with an internal locus of control tend to be more motivated and committed as they believe that they can influence outcomes in terms of their career progression, whereas those with an external locus of control are less likely to take this view. The motivational aspect can be linked to expectancy theory (refer to Chapter 4), which states that where individuals feel that they can influence the environment in which they operate, they will generally exert more effort to achieve, and may work more independently; the individual with an external locus of control is more likely to need a more structured environment such as is found in bureaucratic organisations. In the *Big Brother* scenario, one of the contestants with a strong internal locus of control sought to exercise this control by the use of winking by deliberately including some people in secret winks whilst excluding others, and to reinforce the perception that he was in control of the situation (*see* Ritchie, 2001, p. 113).

A key factor in this regard is how individuals perceive themselves within the organisation. This is particularly pertinent in the areas of self-esteem and self-efficacy. The concepts of self-esteem and self-fulfilment relate back to Rogers's humanistic theory. Self-esteem is seen as *an individual's evaluation of self-worth*: basically, this relates to how good the individual feels about him- or herself in the organisation. Obviously, if a person has high self-esteem this person will be more confident, although there is always a danger of overconfidence in that the individual's perception of his or her self-worth may not be matched by the organisation's perception. However, positive self-esteem can lead to an individual adopting a positive attitude in the organisation, and this will affect that person's motivation, attendance record and ability to handle stress. The more serious issue for the organisation is that of low self-esteem, which may lead to a more negative outlook towards issues relating to the organisation and an individual's worth to the organisation.

This concept of organisation-based self-esteem (OBSE) is being increasingly recognised by managers as a mechanism whereby self-esteem can be built up in organisations. It has implications in terms of the extent to which managers should seek to encourage or control it. Self-efficacy is linked to self-esteem in that it relates to *an individual's perception of his or her ability to complete a task*. Given the complexity of many tasks in the modern organisation it is important to help individuals develop their self-efficacy and to encourage them to believe that they can complete tasks effectively, perhaps through training in time management and other techniques. If an individual has low self-efficacy then it may affect that person's behaviour and ability to complete tasks. In a task-based culture, failure in this respect could be detrimental to the individual concerned and the organisation's development. It should also be noted that the concept of 'self' may vary between one national culture and another. Factors that may cause high self-esteem and self-efficacy in one culture may not transfer so readily to another (refer to Chapter 10).

Table 3.3 Myers–Briggs type indicators

Personality type	
Extrovert	**Introvert**
Outgoing	Quiet
Publicly expressive	Reserved
Interacting	Concentrating
Speaks, then thinks	Thinks, then speaks
Gregarious	Reflective
Perception	
Sensing	Intuitive
Practical	General
Specific	Abstract
Feet on the ground	Head in the clouds
Details	Possibilities
Concrete	Theoretical
Judgement	
Thinking	Feeling
Analytical	Subjective
Clarity	Harmony
Head	Heart
Justice	Mercy
Rules	Circumstances
Relating to environment	
Judging	Perceiving
Structured	Flexible
Time-orientated	Open-ended
Decisive	Exploring
Organised	Spontaneous

Source: Adapted from Nelson, D.L. and Quick, J.C. (1996) *Organizational Behavior: The Essentials*. © 1995 South-Western, a part of Cengage Learning, Inc. Reproduced by permission. www.cengage.com/permissions.

A further area which could be of significance is how individuals in an organisation handle stress. A number of approaches have been developed to evaluate stress and an individual's ability to handle stress. One such approach attempts to categorise people into personality types, type A or type B, in relation to how they deal with stress. The type A personality profile is of an individual who is always moving, who talks rapidly, is impatient, feels continuously under time pressure, is competitive, is obsessed by numbers and is often aggressive. The type B personality is more patient, less concerned about time, and tends to be more relaxed in his or her approach to work. As one may surmise, the type A personality is more likely to suffer from stress, although possibly is more successful in career terms. In addition, type As are also more prone to heart diseases and other stress-related illnesses.

One of the organisational areas where personality issues are most significant is personality testing. Such testing can inform decisions in relation to selection and advancement and can even be used to facilitate downsizing. We have already seen two examples of personality tests – Cattell's Trait Analysis and the Myers–Briggs Type Indicators based on Jung's analysis. Although other forms of testing are used in organisations, such as graphology, which is favoured in France, personality tests are still used widely. In the UK, for example, some 51 per cent of companies use tests to recruit executives and 40 per cent use them for non-executive appointments (Willis, 1997).

There has been some criticism of personality testing. Viswesvaran *et al.* (2007) surveyed the literature on the topic and the two main issues appeared to be, first, the magnitude of the validity coefficients, i.e. how valid were the data from personality testing, and, secondly, the question of respondents faking their responses to personality tests, in terms of trying to provide the answers they think will reflect them in a good light rather than responding honestly. Klehe and Anderson (2007) have argued that the validity of the personality tests will also be influenced by social and cultural factors, and they focus particularly on the variables of power distance and collectivism (*see* Chapter 10). In terms of the faking, there is again mixed evidence, but it seems that personality tests will still give useful information, especially if they are linked with observer ratings (Connolly *et al*, 2007). Other issues are raised in Mini-case 3.1.

Emotional intelligence: a personality trait for the twenty-first century

There has been considerable interest in recent years in the concept of emotional intelligence (EI) and whether it is a significant personality trait that organizations should be seeking to identify in current or prospective employees. Mayer *et al.* (2008) see it as an inherent ability to carry out accurate reasoning about emotions, together with the ability to use emotions and emotional knowledge to enhance thoughts and actions. Although the term 'emotional intelligence' was first used by Salovey and Mayer (1990) it was the work of Goleman (1996) which began to develop the concept in practical terms as a predictor of successful leaders – in fact he saw this as more important than technical knowledge. It is based around understanding your own emotions through self-awareness and self-management and also understanding the emotions of others through empathy and relationship skills (Morrison, 2007). Goleman (1998) has developed an Emotional Competence Inventory which seeks to test an individual's emotional intelligence through evaluating areas such as:

- self-awareness
- emotional resilience
- motivation/drivers
- empathy/sensitivity
- influence/rapport
- intuition
- conscientiousness.

There is some debate as to whether EI is a personality trait or whether it is an ability that can be learnt, although the evidence suggests that it is a trait linked to other personal attributes which may well be linked to social upbringing. This area also links into the theme of cultural intelligence (CI) where emotional responses may be conditioned by national cultural characteristics.

With the increased complexity of business in the twenty-first century and the increased shift towards personal interaction and group working, it could be argued that emotional intelligence will get greater prominence when we look at the personality traits needed to work in the modern organization. Morrison (2007) has looked at the significance of EI in the context of social work, a sector which has undergone substantial and rapid changes and he suggests that the ability to handle one's own emotions and to recognise and manage other people's emotions will be increasingly needed in this sector.

Perception and the perceptual process

Perception is an essential factor in determining individual behaviour both inside and outside an organisation. We all look at events that happen to us, or situations that occur, in different ways. Imagine your favourite team losing a match. As a supporter I might perceive that this has been caused by the team having poor players; a fellow supporter may see the outcome as a result of poor management; and yet another supporter may see it as a significant improvement on previous defeats! We are all looking at the same situation (the actual match) but from a different perspective and thus our reactions to the situation may differ considerably. Within an organisation a continual stream of things may take place and yet these can be perceived very differently by individuals. Imagine an organisation announcing an impending reorganisation. This may be perceived by some in the organisation as an opportunity for advancement through new job opportunities, whereas others might see it as a threat to their existing job: thus some may welcome the change and others may seek to resist it.

Mini-case 3.1: Criticisms of personality testing

Testing times for personality tests

Personality testing is something which many of us will undergo during our careers, with an interview being preceded by a bank of questionnaires which are meant to give our current, or prospective, employer an idea of our personality, personal characteristics and potential. However, recent developments are suggesting that personality testing may not be as effective as it was intended to be.

One problem has been that some candidates manage to 'second-guess' the tests and give answers that they believe would please the employer rather than give their true response. This is particularly true with some well-known types of tests about which candidates can find out before the interview. As a result the Halifax Bank, worried about the manipulation of tests, has turned away from traditional psychometric tests towards more work-related aptitude tests.

A second area of concern has been the fear of legal action by individuals who feel that the tests have discriminated against them, especially on a racial basis. A series of race-bias cases has led to a sharp decline in the use of personality testing in the USA. In the UK, Asian guards at Paddington station feared that their career prospects would be diminished after they achieved poor test scores. It was shown by the Council for Racial Equality that cultural differences would affect the candidates' responses to tests. This case was settled without going to court and the procedures were amended.

The issue of Western cultural bias in personality testing has also surfaced, especially when multinational organisations have used personality testing on a global basis (Cronbach, 1995). Some of the problems that have been encountered are familiarity with the types of questions encountered, language awareness, the speed at which responses are expected, and different social and cultural norms. Thus a UK-derived questionnaire may lead to distorted results if applied in English to a group of Indonesian managers.

So what is perception? In simple terms it is *how we view and interpret the events and situations in the world about us*. It can be looked upon as a cognitive process and a social information process whereby we go through the process of:

- picking up some external stimuli, such as some event or perhaps some personal interaction;
- screening, when we only acknowledge the stimuli we choose to acknowledge;
- some interpretation and categorisation of these stimuli, possibly based on previous experience or on our upbringing.

Thus, in the previously mentioned example, perhaps the external stimulus is hearing that my team has lost yet again. I may screen this information in a negative manner, assuming that something is wrong with the team rather than that it has just had a bad day. Finally, I may interpret this information on the basis of previous experience of supporting the team, and decide that it is a further example of bad management.

Within organisations, perception has a major impact on such matters as selection interviews, but it can apply to a range of situations, one of which we use to illustrate the basic model of social perception – *see* Figure 3.1.

Imagine a situation where a new leader has arrived in an organisation and he or she is perhaps seeking to bring about a cultural change by addressing some

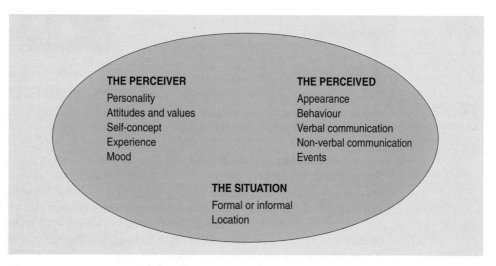

Figure 3.1 The perceptual process

middle managers on the need to adopt new objectives or to create a new vision for the company. In other words, this is a change situation. Much of the success of the change process will depend on the nature of the perceivers (the middle managers), who may initially be suspicious of the new leader because of their experience of other leaders, or because they have low self-esteem or because they may associate change with job losses. Much will therefore depend on the abilities of the perceived (the new leader) to overcome their fear and suspicion and thus change their perception of him or her. The new leader will need good presentational skills – using positive verbal and non-verbal communication – backed by a reassuring appearance and the ability to convince them of the value of the change. The situation may also be significant, that is, whether the presentation is made in an office at work during their lunch break or on an away day, where the middle managers can focus on the change issues under consideration and mix both formally and informally. Ultimately, this interaction and the perception of the new leader by the middle managers may have a crucial bearing on whether the change process is successful.

However, one must be aware of a number of factors that can distort this whole process. One of the most common of these is perceptual stereotyping, *where generalisations are made about certain groups of people*. What will happen if the new leader is a young woman and the middle managers all older men? There is, of course, the danger that the middle managers hold stereotypes of younger women which will interfere with her ability to get her message over to them. There are many areas where the ethos of male managers dominates despite the lack of any apparent rational reason for this (Hansard Society Commission Report, 1990), and where women have trouble reaching the top of the organisation. This tendency can be very pronounced in male-dominated national cultures such as that of Japan, where Hofstede (1984) has indicated that the high masculinity index found in that country makes it very difficult for women managers to progress in organisations (*see* Chapter 10).

Illustration in film

Tootsie and *Working Girl*

The issue of selective perception has been used in many films. One of the best of these was *Working Girl* (1989) starring Melanie Griffths and Harrison Ford. Griffiths plays a secretary who poses as her unpleasant female boss and thus creates confusion in how she is perceived by other members of the organisation, especially as she is very good at managing.

Another film which follows this theme is *Tootsie* (1982), starring Dustin Hoffman and Jessica Lange, in which the perceptual confusion is gender-based, wherein a young male actor, unable to get a part, dresses up as a woman to get a part in a leading hospital soap and finds people's perceptions of him in his female role are different than those of him as a male. Interestingly, Hoffman's personality seemed to change when he was dressed as 'Tootsie' and the film crew realised that if they had bad news for Hoffman, they would keep it from him until he was in his female persona because he 'was much nicer as a woman' !

Selective perception is a further development of stereotyping, in that *the perceivers may already be conditioned as to how they perceive the perceived*. In the example quoted above, the new leader may have brought from a previous organisation to the new organisation a reputation as a 'job cutter'. Thus, given the initial suspicion of the group, it may prove almost impossible to change their attitudes if they only perceive the new leader as someone who has come there to cut jobs (probably their jobs) in the organisation. It is probable that other 'messages' that do not conform with the expected stereotype are screened out or ignored. The result of a meeting between the middle managers and the new leader can be fairly easily predicted.

On the other hand the 'halo effect' may apply, where *the perceivers pick upon a particular attribute of the perceived and it is this which determines their overall perception*. It may be that the perceived communicates well, or has a good sense of humour, or is seen as 'one of the gang' in a social setting, and this may influence perceptions irrespective of the new leader's ability. Sometimes a new leader arrives with a high reputation which leads to an initial positive perception and, consequently, the newcomer may enjoy a 'honeymoon' period.

Another possible distortion can arise from self-fulfilling prophecies – *the expectation that others will act in certain ways no matter what they actually do or say*. Returning to our example, the new leader may be trying to explain a much wider strategic change in the company but the middle managers may only pick up on any comment or issue which could be seen to affect jobs. Thus, whereas the overall theme of the talk by the new leader may be strategic and positive, it will be perceived by the middle managers as operational (that is, dealing with the possibility of job losses) and negative, that is, it is fulfilling their prophecy.

Mezias and Starbuck (Hodgkinson, 2003) have studied key factors affecting managers' perceptions and found they were conditioned by the degree of their experience, their level of training and interpersonal skills, the nature of the organisational culture and the individual's position in the hierarchy, although they did note that managers may bias information in order to improve their own position.

An interesting extension of the importance of perception at organizational level is the growth of **employment branding** where organizations are seeking to develop and improve the perceptions of stakeholders about working for their organization so that they can both retain and attract good candidates. Many are doing it through developing employer value propositions to seek to show the advantages of working for their organization and this is particularly prevalent at international level where there may be strong competition for available talent (*see* Brewster *et al.*, 2007).

Attribution theory

The concept of attribution is related to perception in that it seeks to evaluate the way we perceive our own behaviour and the behaviour of others: that is, we seek causes or attributes of our own behaviour and of that of people with whom we come into contact inside the organisation. The original work on attribution (Heider, 1958) was developed by Kelley (1973) with his attributional theory.

Attributions, that is, *the perceived causes for our behaviour or the behaviour of others*, can be seen to be internal, that is, being derived from our own personal attributes. Thus, we have some control over them: in other words, we enjoy a high locus of control. External attribution, on the other hand, suggests that external forces, such as factors in the organisation, are the cause of our attributes. Obviously we all have different patterns of attribution. Achievement-orientated individuals may well see their attributions as being based primarily on internal factors and their own ability to achieve success. Kelley developed this concept by looking at whether we attribute other people's behaviour as being a product of either internal or external causes. He based this analysis on three key factors:

- *Consensus*: do other people in the same situation behave in the same way?
- *Distinctiveness*: was the observed behaviour distinctive or does the person behave in the same way in other situations?
- *Consistency*: has the person always behaved in this way over a period of time?

The answers to the above questions depend on the judgement of the perceiver. Imagine that you (as a senior manager) receive a complaint about the behaviour of one of your middle managers towards a client. If on investigation you find that no other client has complained about any other manager, this would imply low consensus, whereas if there were a number of complaints about a number of managers it would imply high consensus. If there had been complaints about the same manager in a different context it would imply low distinctiveness, but if there had not been any previous complaints about this manager in different areas of the organisation it would suggest that the manager's action was very distinctive and thus had high distinctiveness. Finally, if there had been complaints about this manager over a period of time it would suggest high consistency, whereas if there were no history of complaints about the manager it would suggest low consistency.

If, following this analysis, you ascertain that the attributional characteristics of the manager are low consensus, low distinctiveness and high consistency, this would imply that the behaviour of the manager arose from internal characteristics rather than being the result of external forces. This is a case of **internal attribution** and you may consider that there was something about the behaviour of this manager that needed further investigation. If, however, a pattern of high consensus, high distinctiveness and low consistency emerged, it might suggest that the action of the manager was primarily determined by external factors, that is, it was a case of **external attribution**. As a result you may consider that this was a unique event which may reflect more on the nature of the complainant than on the specific behaviour of the manager concerned.

It was previously stated that attribution is to a large extent based on perception and there is still therefore the danger of bias or distortion of perception, as mentioned earlier. One type of distorted perception is known as 'fundamental attribution error'; in this we tend to look at other people's behaviour from an internal attribution bias. We assume that aspects of their attribution are determined by their own personality, intelligence, moods and so on rather than accept that external factors may have had some impact on their behaviour. For example, we may observe a colleague who is forgetting things or snapping at other people and attribute this to their personality, whereas in reality it may be a stress reaction caused by external factors over which the individual has no control. The second distortion can come from a self-serving bias by which *any successes we have we attribute to our internal factors* (intelligence, skill and so forth), and any problems or lack of success that we encounter we attribute to external factors (usually linked to some aspect of the organisation). For example, you may receive a poor mark for an essay, and argue that this is because the question was phrased badly or too little time was given for its completion. Finally, we have to be aware of cultural differences. In some cultures, behaviour and outcomes are viewed as a product of fate rather than as something that can be determined by our own actions. In such cultures behaviour would be seen as having an external rather than an internal attribution. Mini-case 3.2 illustrates this.

Attitudes and values

Attitudes

Attitudes, especially personal attitudes, have a key bearing on how an individual functions within the organisation, particularly as these attitudes may be reflected in positive or negative behaviour. Sometimes attitudes may be influenced by the organisation itself, and one of the challenges facing the modern manager may be how to effect an attitude change in the organisation within the broad context of cultural or strategic change.

Mini-case 3.2: Perceptual bias

The perception of older workers

Although perceptual bias and distortion are frequently linked to racial and sexual discrimination in the organisation, an area which is of increasing importance is how older people are perceived within the organisation. This issue has acquired greater significance as the number of older people in the population has seen a substantial increase and, furthermore, these people are increasingly fitter and more active than at any time in the past. At the same time, organisations undergoing restructuring and shifting towards more flexible types of operations have tended to 'downsize' by removing many in this age range from the workforce. According to Casey (1990), Lyon and Pollard (1997) and the *Personnel Today* survey (2004), common stereotypes of older people are that they are slow, are physically unfit, cannot cope with new technology, can be cynical, adapt less well to change and learn less quickly. The positive perceptions are that they are more loyal to their employer, are more reliable, are more customer-conscious, that they work harder and that they add value through experience. Although older workers who are 'known' in an organisation are often considered effective, the problem arises when they leave the organisation for whatever reason and are seeking new employment: invariably their perceived characteristics as older workers can militate against them in competition with younger workers.

The *Personnel Today* survey of 2004 looked at perceptions of older workers based on a sample of 500 human resource managers and 1000 members of the general public. Of the HRM professionals 91 per cent felt that companies discriminated against employing older people compared to 61 per cent of the general public, although the majority of the HRM professionals stated they were positive about employing workers over 50 from their own experiences with these workers. Most interestingly 69 per cent of the HRM professionals thought that their own companies were not preparing adequately for the recruitment implications of an ageing population.

The extent to which perception fits with reality can be debated. There are cases of older workers struggling with new information technology, for example, but in many other respects the perception can be seen to be a false one, yet one which disadvantages a large number of people. A different perspective can be seen in the study by Hogarth and Barth (1991), who studied the experiment by the B&Q store group which recruited 55 people in its Macclesfield store exclusively from those aged over 50.

The outcome was that the store outperformed other local outlets competing in the same sector, in terms of profitability, low staff turnover, good product knowledge and high productivity; even absenteeism through illness was lower than that in some of the store's rivals. These results probably changed the perception of B & Q, which now sees older people as a valuable alternative source of employees. The firm has since designated more stores as employers of the over 50s. It should be stated, however, that many of these workers aged over 50 had previously been employed in higher-status jobs and been made redundant. Their skills were, therefore, higher than those of workers who normally applied for jobs at that level.

Many other companies have followed B & Q's approach including ASDA and Domino's Pizza (for further examples, see **www.agepositive.gov.uk**), and ASDA has flexible working options such as 'Benidorm leave', which is three months' unpaid leave between January and March, and grandparent leave, which gives a week of unpaid leave after the birth of a grandchild.

One could also widen this discussion to the level of national culture. Age is much respected in some cultures, such as in Asia, where the perceptions of older people differ accordingly.

An individual's attitude may result from a number of factors acting together. An attitude may have an emotional element, reflecting feelings or moods about an individual or an event, a cognitive component, based more on beliefs, opinions and knowledge held by an individual and, finally, a behavioural aspect, based on an individual's behavioural pattern. For example, if an employee is asked to undertake some weekend work when he or she is conditioned to the Monday to Friday pattern, the response may vary. The attitudinal response may depend upon the employee's emotional response to working a weekend, the effect on his or her behavioural pattern (e.g. whether it disrupts a regular commitment on the Saturday morning) and what this person thinks about the policy of weekend work (e.g. whether it is seen as an opportunity to earn more overtime or an undesirable and inevitable trend in the particular industry). If the individual is unhappy about changing from the current employment pattern and feels it would disrupt the normal weekend behavioural pattern and, further, disagrees with the concept of weekend working, there is a strong likelihood of a negative attitude. On the other hand, if the individual would quite like a change, does not feel it would greatly disrupt the weekend behavioural pattern and agrees with the logic of weekend working (and, possibly, higher pay rates), the attitudinal response is likely to be more positive.

Attitude formation is partly a reflection of personality formation. Attitudes are formed from the interaction of a mixture of external events with the individual's own personality. Sometimes direct experience is a powerful moulder of attitudes. If you had an unhappy time studying physics and did not get on with your teacher, this may prejudice your attitude towards the subject for the foreseeable future. Attitudes based on direct experiences can be very strong and very hard to break. For example, if members of the workforce feel that they have been seriously let down by their managers over a particular issue, this direct experience can lead to the formation of attitudes which current, or any future, managers may find it very difficult to change. The other source of attitude formation lies with social learning, which reflects attitudes picked up from our peer groups, from our families or from other social influences in our life. The peer group factor can be especially strong and can be seen in group behaviour. Once a group-behavioural norm is set, it becomes very hard for members of the group to go against the group attitude (*see* Chapter 5 for a discussion of cognitive dissonance and the phenomenon of group-think). Very often any dissenting action may lead to isolation from the group so that dissenters prefer to adapt their attitudes to those of the group.

Also of significance in this context is the concept of modelling, where an individual 'models' him- or herself on another and seeks to follow and reproduce that person's behaviour. Role models often, but not always, have a benign influence inside and outside the organisation.

One of the central issues about attitude is the extent to which knowledge about an individual's attitudinal set can be used as a predictor of that person's behaviour inside the organisation. There has been considerable debate around this issue, but no clear conclusion has emerged. One can, however, postulate certain tendencies. For example, if an individual has a very strong attitude on a particular issue (possibly based on strongly held beliefs) it might affect that person's behaviour more directly: that is, strongly held religious or political beliefs might trigger an immediate behavioural response in certain situations. If an issue is very threatening (for example, if there is a proposed job reorganisation directly affecting an individual's job), attitudes will be very focused, so triggering a strong behavioural response. Obviously personality factors influence attitudinal responses, but it must also be remembered that there are a number of strong social constraints in any organisation which might dampen an attitudinal response. For example, an individual may disagree strongly with a viewpoint taken by a line manager but is unlikely to respond too aggressively because (a) aggressive attacks on colleagues may go against the prevalent social norm or culture and (b) antagonising the line manager may weaken the individual's position in the organisation. Thus, a restrained attitudinal response is called for.

One factor that influences attitudes in the organisation is cognitive dissonance. This results from *a conflict between the behavioural and cognitive aspects of attitude*. An example of this might be a middle manager who is promoted and is put in charge of a group of middle managers who were previously his or her colleagues. The immediate reaction may be a behavioural one, in that he or she strives to keep on good terms with previous friends and behaves in a casual, relaxed manner as they may have done previously. However, the demands of the new job, which will be cognitive in nature, may put the senior manager in the position of disciplining one of these old friends or even of making one of them redundant. Thus the behavioural aspect comes into conflict with the cognitive needs of the new job and the result is cognitive dissonance. This may cause confusion, which may have to be resolved by:

● the changing of his or her attitude to the old friends and distancing him- or herself from them; or

● getting someone else to make the decision, to avoid being put in this quandary; or

● quitting the job if the tensions are too great.

A topical application of this might be that of a football player who is promoted to manage the team at short notice and who may have to make immediate decisions about changing the team formation or team personnel.

Managers in organisations are obviously concerned about attitudes to work in their organisations as they may have a significant bearing on achieving high productivity and developing innovation in the organisation. For example, it may be difficult to achieve these when there is latent hostility between the management and the workforce or between the managers themselves (the 'them and us' phenomenon). This can be contrasted with the experience of Japanese companies, where there is a strong commitment to work, so much so that the danger of overwork has been a problem (Japan is one of the few countries that has a word – *karoshi* – which means *death through overwork*). Many surveys are carried out to measure individuals' attitudes to work and especially their level of job satisfaction. It is argued that, if problems in attitudes to work can be identified, they can be corrected by organisational changes. However, although one would anticipate that a high level of job satisfaction would lead to high performance, the evidence is that there is little correlation, as the issue of job performance is a very complex one.

Change at individual level: changing attitudes

We have seen that it is hard to measure attitudes clearly and that it is difficult to establish simple links between attitude and behaviour and job performance. This is an area of great concern to managers. The issue of changing attitudes may be highly significant for a manager who is seeking some form of change in the organisation. Many of the previously state-owned industries, British Rail and British Gas for example, had to make significant changes in their operations when they changed from being state-run industries with no competition, to being part of a much more competitive privatised sector. Suddenly they had to become 'leaner', had to respond more quickly to the marketplace and, thus, had to change attitudes in the organisation, for example by becoming more customer-focused. How, as a senior manager, can you effect a change in attitude in the organisation? Much will depend upon issues already covered, such as personality and perception, although the issue of communication is vital here too, as can be seen in Figure 3.2.

As already indicated, much depends on the nature of the person carrying out the change or 'the source'. The issue of perception is crucial in this context. The better the communication skills and 'charisma' of the source, the stronger will be the source's chances of changing attitudes and perceptions. It is no surprise that politicians are coached in performing in front of cameras, as their performance may have a major influence on people's perception of them and, thus, on their ability to lead change. It seems a modern trend for political leaders to have to be telegenic in order to change attitudes, although such a need is perhaps less evident in the business world. The nature of the target audience affects the process of changing attitudes. If we return to the change scenario previously considered, we can appreciate that the senior manager may have to address and convince people at different levels in the organisation for the change to succeed and thus will have to think very carefully about whether the same approach should be used with different groups of people. All groups may need reassuring, though what may be a reassuring message for one group might be perceived as a threat by another and thus might engender a different attitudinal response: one group might welcome the change, another resist it.

A further factor is how the message is presented: whether it is in simple or complex language, whether both negative and positive aspects of the change are discussed or only the positive aspects. Paradoxically, the identification of negative factors may lead to a more realistic response from the target audience than if only the good points are emphasised.

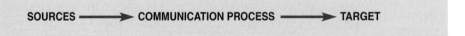

SOURCES ⟶ COMMUNICATION PROCESS ⟶ TARGET

Figure 3.2 Aspects of changing attitudes in organisations

Values

Another factor that influences individual behaviour is values. Many people would suggest that attitudes and values are fairly closely related, yet it may be strongly argued that values are deeper than attitudes and more embedded in our character. It is also suggested that values are longer lasting and that they give us a sense of what is right and wrong and what is good and bad. Values are developed over time and may be strongly linked to societal factors like family or peer group or strongly held beliefs emanating from membership of organisations or deriving from particular creeds. Organisations have become increasingly interested in both the individual and the collectively held values which permeate the organisation. Of particular significance is the issue of ethics in the organisation. The organisation may seek to portray a strong ethical stance in its operations, reflecting commonly held ethical values inside the organisation. The Co-operative Bank is a good example of this, particularly in relation to its ethical investments. The other reason why an organisation may be interested in values is that if it can develop a set of commonly held values among its workforce then it is, in effect, creating a specific corporate culture which might differentiate it from its competitors, thus giving it competitive advantage.

The question, then, is how to identify values. Rockeach and Ball-Rockeach (1989) divided values into terminal values and instrumental values. Terminal values can be seen as desired outcomes, for example peace, harmony, security, happiness, partnership, love and so forth, and instrumental values can be seen as means of behaviour to achieve these terminal values. The most significant values found in the survey carried out by Rockeach and Ball-Rockeach were honesty, ambition, responsibility, a forgiving nature and open-mindedness. It should be noted, however, that this was essentially an American study of an area in which there might be distinctive national differences as to what constitutes values. From Rockeach and Ball-Rockeach's American values survey, you can see why the issue of ethics is quite strong in many American companies. A different set of national values, however, could put a totally different complexion on issues like, for example, the receiving of gifts. What might be seen as corrupt behaviour in one country would be seen as essential politeness in another. This is why the ethical stance of multinational companies may have to be more complex than those of organisations which operate only in their home country. Indeed, values are one of the main drivers of national cultural differences, as is explored further in Chapter 10.

When terminal values are transferred to an organisation, they may comprise the achievement of excellence or high quality, becoming innovative or, perhaps, becoming an ethical organisation. When an organisation tries to inculcate terminal values such as these among its workforce, it may seek to promote or develop instrumental values that will lead to these objectives. These could be attempts to develop attitudes to work or ways of communicating in the organisation. Ideally the instrumental values can be developed to create some terminal value or values which will help determine the new culture of the organisation. They may even be enshrined in the organisation's mission statement. For example, Mercury Communications, in its 'Mercury 97 imagine' programme, proclaimed its values as follows:

- we always put the customer first;
- we are innovative and creative;
- we are true to our word;
- we communicate openly, honestly and with responsibility;
- we all make a difference;
- we value teamwork;
- we produce results.

However, with values as with attitudes, there is a danger of value conflicts occurring between individuals and groups within the organisation. Therefore it can be difficult to reconcile these values with organisational values.

 ## Individual learning in the organisation

The issue of learning has become an increasingly important one, both for the individual in his or her own right and also in terms of the role of individual learning in the organisation. One reason for this is that restructuring into 'flatter' organisations (i.e., having fewer levels between senior managers and the lowest level of worker – *see* Chapter 7) is leading to more 'empowerment', with decisions having to be made lower down the organisation. Increased use of teamwork is requiring individuals to learn within a group context. Furthermore, as we move into the twenty-first century, the increased complexity of the nature of work has meant that there is an added need for people to be able to adapt and to develop in the organisation. There is a large group of workers seen as 'knowledge workers' whose importance in the organisation lies as much in their skills and ability to learn as in their adaptability to new technology. It is probable that this category of worker will increase in the future at the expense of traditional, manual trades. Thus the issue of individual learning and of how individuals can learn within the organisation has gained prominence. We can even talk of the 'learning organisation' – one which seeks to learn through its experiences in order to adapt to rapidly changing environments.

Studies of individual learning often have their roots in the field of psychology. One of the most significant schools is that of the behaviourists, which includes the work of people such as Pavlov and Skinner. Pavlov (1927) is famous for his work with dogs and, in particular, for the experiment in which a plate of food was put in front of the dog, making it salivate. If a bell was rung when the plate of food arrived, there would eventually come a time when the dog would salivate on hearing the bell, regardless of whether food was there. This indicated that the dog had 'learned', or had been conditioned, to react to the sound of the bell. Its behaviour had been modified. This is called the stimulus–response model as it implies *a behavioural response to some sort of stimulus*. This approach was further explored by Skinner (1974), who developed the concept of operant conditioning, which suggested that the vast majority of learning is due to what happens *after* we carry out a certain action. That is, learning is driven by the behavioural consequences. A dramatic example might be if you are travelling on the Underground and a warning is issued for people to be vigilant for pickpockets. Would this change your behaviour when you are in a crowded carriage with people pressing close to you? Your behavioural response may have been affected by this stimulus (the announcement). Linked to operant conditioning is the concept of reinforcement theory, which suggests that behaviour can be changed, or we can 'learn', by encountering specific responses to our actions. Reinforcement can be of two types. Positive reinforcement can suggest that your behaviour has been condoned and even appreciated by other people in the organisation: therefore you are more likely to repeat this behaviour. For example, if I have put in extra time to finish a report and my boss seeks me out to thank me and compliment me on the report then I am going to be much more motivated to carry out this action again. Negative reinforcement is the opposite: for example, if one is singled out for criticism for some prior action, one will probably not repeat that action.

There has been criticism of reinforcement theory as a means of behaviour modification as it is argued that self-reinforcement is the vital factor, that is, the individual's decision to change his or her behaviour through self-motivation, rather than through the negative or positive responses of other people. There is also the risk that a person could appear to change his or her behaviour in order to achieve some short-term reward but may revert to type later on. The behaviourist school has also been criticised for oversimplifying human behaviour and for the fact that too much of the theory is based purely on laboratory tests.

The cognitive school derives from the work of Tolman (1932) and sees learning as more complex than just a response to a stimulus. It sees learning as a cognitive process which is based on *expectations and on the connection in the mind between two or more stimuli: that is, it is a thinking process rather than a purely reaction-based response*. Learning depends, according to this theory, more on values and beliefs and on whether expectations based on values and beliefs are confirmed as behaviour takes place. Hence this school suggests that if an individual believes that his or her friendly behaviour towards other people will tend to be followed by a friendly response and this then happens, this person is likely to repeat this behaviour. Similarly, if a person discovers over time that there are certain times when humour can help a situation and other times when it cannot, then that person starts to develop a 'cognitive map' which will help guide him or her in future situations.

Learning styles

What might be of more significance to the organisation than the cognitive process or the behavioural responses is an awareness of learning styles and the ways in which people learn. One of the most significant styles of learning is illustrated by Kolb's learning cycle. Kolb (1976) sees learning as a continuous process which is based on experiences we encounter and depends on how we interpret and respond to these. Figure 3.3 illustrates this.

In a sense, Kolb's model can be seen as experiential learning, constructed on the belief that *we learn by our experiences*. Let us assume that my goal is to communicate with another part of the organisation. I might decide to develop an internal

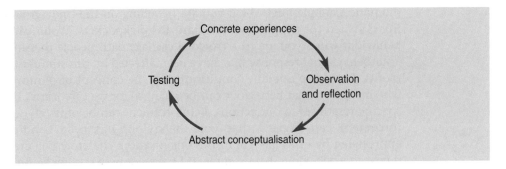

Figure 3.3 Kolb's learning cycle

web page which means that I can spread information more easily around the organisation. Thus my concrete experience is attempting to set up the web page electronically. I may then observe that I appear to be receiving more feedback from colleagues in the organisation than I did previously. Following this observation, and having reflected on it, I may then start to draw the conclusion that internal web pages are a much more efficient method of sending information around the organisation than methods I had used previously (the abstract conceptualisation phase). Having made this conclusion I may then seek to test it out a little more, for example, by developing content on the web pages and making it more interactive and visually attractive. If this confirms my conclusion that internal web pages are more efficient then I will probably change my behaviour and use them much more. In essence I have learned through experience, reflection and action. In fact the process might not stop there: Kolb's model suggests the idea of continuous learning through experiences. In the example just discussed, the success of my use of internal web pages may encourage me to experiment with other forms of electronic information interchange, such as electronic yellow pages.

It is clearly attractive to the organisation to have an element of continuous learning taking place as this will improve the skills and flexibility of the workforce. Given the trend towards an increased dependence on knowledge workers and more complex business environments, this could give the organisation some form of competitive advantage over its rivals. An example of this is EDAP (Employee Development and Assistance Programme), implemented by Ford UK, which originated in 1987 and which sets up a whole range of courses within and outside the organisation (e.g. learning how to use e-mail) with the objective of developing their employees as individuals. Employees are given up to £200 a year for learning or health and fitness activities as long as they are not directly related to work. The firm sees this programme as being clearly linked with the well-being of the company. Kolb's cycle is, therefore, a useful model that can be used in an organisation, but the challenge is to ensure that, in order to achieve learning within the organisation, individuals must have clear goals – otherwise they might not seek new experiences. We should also remember that concepts such as reflection, and the development of abstract concepts, may well create different results in different cultures and thus may potentially affect learning within the organisation.

Kolb's model also led to the development of studies on cognitive styles – that is, *the way we organise and process information*, which may or may not be linked to cognitive ability (Sadler-Smith, 1998). This was explored by Honey and Mumford (1982), who based their model on Kolb's cycle and related it to management in the UK. They identified four cognitive styles linked to the phases of Kolb's cycle: the activist (linked to concrete experimentation), the reflector (reflective observation), the theorist (abstract conceptualisation) and, finally, the pragmatist (active experimentation/testing). Their work led to the development of a learning styles questionnaire which could be used in organisations for selection and evaluation. This model, in turn, was tested by Allison and Hayes (1988), who felt there were two broad cognitive styles which they identified as the 'analytic' style, which is reflective and theoretical, and the 'action' style, which is more activist and impulsive in nature. In later work Allison and Hayes (1996) suggest that these two approaches might reflect different parts of the brain (intuition and immediate action from the right side of the brain and analysis and reflection from the left side of the brain). In turn they have developed a cognitive style index which seeks to measure this in individuals.

If one accepts that clearly different cognitive styles are used by different people and that these can be measured, this differentiation can be useful in terms of analysing and developing learning in the organisation. This applies both for the individual, in terms of developing a more effective way of dealing with information, and also for the organisation, in placing people with a cognitive style in the right role, congruent with the needs of the organisation and the environment. The concept of single- and double-loop learning (Argyris and Schön, 1978) can also be applied to both the individual and the organisation, especially in terms of how the organisation can learn from changes in its environment and move towards becoming a Learning Organisation. (These concepts are discussed in Chapter 9.)

 ## Decision making

The final area of individual behaviour covered in this chapter is that of how individuals formulate decisions. One of the biggest challenges facing organisations is to ensure that people achieve effective decisions, in terms both of speed of the decision making and of the quality of the decisions made. Decision making is obviously important for managers, but, as decision making is increasingly being devolved as we move to 'flatter' organisations, people throughout the organisation are required to be able to make effective decisions. Nutt (1997) suggests that the quality of management decision making is often poor, primarily because managers rush into decisions or become fixated on aspects of a particular solution, even if it has been shown not to work. Poor decision making is often the result of short-term target setting, which is a particular feature of the decision processes of chief executives who are on fixed-term contracts.

Therefore, we need to look at the process of decision making by individuals and ascertain whether this process can be distorted by factors which might diminish the effectiveness of the decisions made. Our starting point is what is known as the *rational model* of decision making, which views the making of a decision as a rational, linear process which will produce rational outcomes. This model is used to explain microeconomic behaviour, such as how an increase in price is likely to lead to an individual deciding to reduce his or her demand for a product or service, all other factors remaining equal. It implies that when faced with a decision, people first identify some problem which will need a decision to be taken; second, they gather information and materials which will help them to solve the problem; third, they generate some potential solutions to the problem; and fourth, they make a rational choice and select the best solution, which is then implemented. It suggests that a person will always make a rational decision based on the ability to evaluate all the alternatives and effectively calculate the potential success of each alternative. It also suggests a situation where the environment within which the decision is being made is stable and slow moving: that is, the decision maker has plenty of time to gather information, reflect on all the alternatives and reach the rational solution. Most people who have worked in environments where decisions are made under considerable pressure, and are needed quickly, would probably soon begin to question the effectiveness of the rational model as a practical tool.

The potential weakness of this model was first identified by Herbert Simon (1960). He introduced the concept of bounded rationality, which accepted that, in practice, decision makers in organisations are under pressure and thus are likely to reach a decision 'that will do' or, to use Simon's phraseology, will 'satisfice'. This often means that they choose the first solution they come across that will satisfice or achieve some sort of satisfactory solution. Finding a solution quickly makes life more comfortable for the manager, so he or she may be keen to make quick decisions on issues. Managers therefore often develop 'short cuts' (sometimes called 'heuristics') to solve problems and reach quick decisions. This suggestion was supported in the study by Nutt (1997), which showed that in practice this was how many managers do reach their decisions. One factor that is relevant in this context is that people tend to be risk-averse and so seek an immediate, expedient solution, rather than explore all the options – an exercise in which more risky solutions might present themselves for evaluation. Such an approach might in turn reflect the corporate structure and culture of the organisation (*see* Chapters 7 and 9).

Another question we have to examine is how some organisations seem to have an erratic and somewhat unpredictable approach to decision making. This may be significant in organisations operating in very volatile business environments where even a satisficing approach may be difficult to implement. This is where the 'garbage can model' (Cohen *et al.*, 1972) may be useful. It suggests a scenario where decisions have a random element to them. Within an organisation there are a number of individuals, a number of problems floating about, potential solutions to these problems that can be found, and finally (and critically) a number of opportunities for choices to be made by the individuals. For an effective decision to be reached, the problems and solutions must come together. Bringing them together may be seen as a challenge for managers. They have to develop the ability to identify relevant problems and to seek radical solutions by bringing the right people together at the right time in order for them to reach the sometimes radical decisions that will be needed in often-turbulent environments.

The rationality and objectivity of decision making may also be compromised by the existence of cognitive biases. As already discussed, an individual's cognitive structure develops over time and is influenced by beliefs, attitudes, values and the person's own personality. The individual's cognitive mindset inevitably has some bearing on the quality of decisions made. The issue of cognitive dissonance has already been discussed in the context of attitudes, where it was explained that this refers to the situation where a clash exists between a person's beliefs and actions. For example, the evaluation of various options for solving a problem may produce a logical solution, but this may still go against the decision maker's beliefs or attitudes and thus the rational solution to the problem may be resisted.

Other cognitive biases which could influence decision making include the illusion of control, which means that *an individual believes he or she can handle a complex problem but does not have the capability to do so*. For example, the person may feel confident of being in control of everything and have the need to maintain this illusion no matter how difficult the problem becomes. This can lead to poor decision making for both the individual and the organisation, particularly in a complex and fast-moving business environment. This bias could be linked to that of escalation of commitment. An example of the latter could involve a manager who is in difficulty through the illusion of control. Perhaps she or he has made a deal on forward foreign exchange for the company which is in fact more complex than had been imagined and as a result the company is potentially exposed to some losses. The rational decision to make would be to abandon the deal and take the loss before setting up a better deal. However, it appears that managers who have made mistakes such as these tend to continue in their course of action and often increase, or escalate, their commitment. That is, they increase their foreign exchange exposure, hoping for some turnaround which will offset their initial losses, often running the risk of even further disasters for the company. The classic case of this would have to be that of Nick Leeson, who was working in the global derivatives trading market for Barings Bank Plc and who, by February 1995, had managed to lose $1.3 billion for the company with the result that Barings collapsed and was finally sold for £1 to the Dutch group ING (Hill, 1997). There is clear evidence that Leeson, despite realising that he had made horrendous losses, kept on speculating in an attempt to recoup his losses, incurring still further deficit and ultimately bankrupting his employers. Perhaps he did not want to admit that he had made mistakes as a result of an illusion of control or ego-defensiveness, by which he interpreted what was happening in a positive way – that he could 'correct' his mistakes – so hiding from himself the gravity of the situation. No matter what the cause, the poor quality of decision making in this case was a disaster for the organisation, and for Leeson himself.

Communication, change and conflict

We have seen in this chapter a number of factors that can influence individual behaviour in the organisation, including individual personality, perception, values, learning and decision making. It is clear that these in turn are affected by communication, change and conflict. Examples of areas where this applies are discussed below. First, we examine how communication can change perception by means of the concept of the Johari Window, and second, we look at how change affects the psychological contract and the potential for conflict that this creates inside the organisation.

The Johari Window: using communication to change perception

One of the most significant ways in which communication can influence individual behaviour is through its ability to change individual perceptions and perceptual bias. We have already seen that people in an organisation have a range of personalities and that they are likely to have differing perceptions of other people within the organisation. Very often their perceptions are conditioned by the structure of the organisation wherein people are pigeonholed in a specific part of the organisation and thus have little contact with people outside their particular area (*see* the discussion of traditional functionalist structures in Chapter 7). Indeed, they may well have negative perceptual stereotypes about people in different parts of, and at different levels in, the organisation. With the move towards flatter, more flexible types of organisation there has been a move towards greater teamwork involving people across the organisation. This brings individuals increasingly into contact with people for whom they may have existing negative perceptual stereotypes. If this occurs within a teambuilding context (*see* Chapter 5), the development of new task teams in the organisation, based on drawing together people from different parts of the organisation, may be hindered.

Thus the challenge facing organisations is to change the perceptions that people in one part of the organisation may have about people from another part, in order that they can work more effectively together. The key to success in this process is effective communication, because it is through this that perceptual stereotypes or biases can be changed. It is not uncommon, therefore, for organisations to undertake training weekends or days, when they bring together people from different parts of the organisation, in order to tackle these problems and to seek to improve communications throughout the whole organisation. One of the techniques which could be used here is the Johari Window (Luft, 1970).

As Figure 3.4 shows, there are four areas of awareness about an individual. The top left-hand box represents the 'public' open area, *that which is known about the individual by others and which the individual knows about him- or herself*: for example, 'Mr Scholes is quite young and works in the marketing department'. This area may, initially, be limited in scope, constitutes only a minute part of the square, and is probably conditioned by perceptual stereotyping and bias (someone working in the production department may, for example, have a negative perception of people

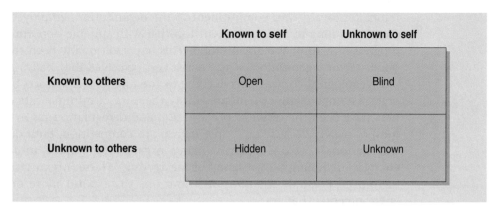

Figure 3.4 The Johari Window

who work in the marketing section). The 'blind' section refers to *aspects of an indi-vidual's behaviour which may be known to other people but of which the individual is unaware*: for example, an annoying personal habit or trait. The 'hidden' section refers to *facets of an individual that are known to the individual but which are unknown to other people.* The 'unknown' area *may lie in the subconscious* and it may be danger-ous to allow untrained people to explore this area.

When new groups of individuals are working together, the aim is for individuals to communicate more information about themselves to other members of the group (widening the 'hidden' area) and for the group to identify aspects of an individual's behaviour about which that person is unaware (widening the 'blind' area), preferably without straying into the 'unknown' area. In practice, most of the progress is usually made on widening the 'hidden' area and, as this happens, perceptual stereotyping and biases are broken down. If this can be achieved, more positive perceptions can be developed between people from the different parts of the organisation, improving communications and the flexibility of the organisation.

This concept could also be applied in other situations, such as integrating the management of two companies which have merged or in the context of joint ventures and strategic alliances. As will be seen in Chapter 10, perceptual prob-lems may also occur at an international level, and the process of breaking down national perceptual stereotypes may well determine the success of international alliances or projects.

Psychological contracts: will organisational change lead to more conflict?

According to Roehling (1997) the phrase 'psychological contract' was first used by Argyris in 1960 and Levinson *et al.* in 1962 but the concept was considerably developed with the work of Rousseau (1989) who looked at obligations between employers and employees based on *perceived* promises between them. These prom-ises are 'psychological' in the sense that they are not written contracts but represent expectations and beliefs, particularly of employees. For example, in return for loyalty and commitment to the organisation, employees are given the security of long-term employment together with suitable opportunities for career progression within the organisation. This has traditionally been the case in many public-sector organisations where employees perceived they had 'a job for life'.

Psychological contracts have come to the fore in recent years because of rapid organisational change where previously there was a minimal rate of change. This may have been the result of privatisation and deregulation (as in the public utilities) or merely because of a rapid increase in competition, both domestically and internationally. Consequently many organisations have undergone radical changes, including 'downsizing' or 'delayering'. Flatter organisational structures have been created, enabling organisations to respond more quickly to rapid environmental changes.

These changes have led to a re-evaluation of the psychological contract, especially from the perspective of employees who see change as being imposed in a top-down way, without much consultation. Employees are increasingly seeing a shift from 'relational contracts' based on a long-term relationship between the organisation and the employee towards 'transactional contracts', which are often of shorter duration and which may carry extra burdens for the employee, together with greater uncertainty and potentially greater levels of stress. One way in which this shift may be encouraged is through increased use of performance management (Styles *et al.*, 1998), whereby key aspects of the psychological contract, such as career development, bonuses and, by implication, employment retention, may be dependent on the success of the employee in the performance appraisal. Styles also suggests that performance management is being used to shift attitudes within organisations away from relational-style contracts towards transactional-style contracts.

The questions we must consider at this point are whether this change in the psychological contract will alter the individual's relationship with the organisation, and whether it could lead to conflict in the organisation. Hendry and Jenkins (1998) have suggested that changes in the psychological contract, especially if linked to longer hours, less security and greater stress, will almost certainly lead to changes in attitudes among employees. If employees perceive that the organisation has changed the old psychological (relational-style) contract, these authors suggest it will lead to an increased sense of powerlessness, a loss of trust in the organisation and consequently less loyalty towards the organisation. Whether there will be greater conflict in the organisation may depend upon individual behavioural characteristics and how individuals respond to the perceived change in the psychological contract. Sparrow (1997) suggests that some individuals will be more flexible and see the changing nature of work towards transactional contracts in a positive light and possibly as a means of advancement. However, it is equally certain that many individuals, who may by nature be resistant to change, will view the change in a negative manner. Some may choose to respond by 'getting out' by means of early retirement, whereas others may seek to respond by 'getting even' with an organisation they feel has let them down; and it is in this area that the potential for conflict in the organisation will arise.

Guest and Conway (2002) have identified that if there is a positive psychological contract, supported by high levels of communication between employers and employees, then it can have positive effects on business performance as a result of increased employee commitment and satisfaction, but they also identify the negative effects mentioned above when the psychological contract breaks down. With the shift towards knowledge workers in the twenty-first century, many employees will have an increased amount of discretion about how they do their job, and if they feel they are being fairly treated (i.e. there is a strong psychological contract) then they will use this time discretion positively, which can lead to high performance working (Purcell *et al.*, 2003).

Emotional labour

Another area where change has the potential to cause individual conflict is in the growing field of emotional labour. This concept was first described by Hochschild (1983) as the induction or suppression of feeling in order to sustain an outward appearance that produces in others a sense of being cared for in a convivial safe place. It was traditionally linked with women's work and the role of the mother (especially the working mother) in the family, and has been developed by Smith and Gray (2000) when looking at this in the context of the nursing profession, which is undergoing rapid change. As James (1989) suggests, the regulation of emotion may be important when dealing with other people's feelings, but this may place a strain on the individual.

This may become enhanced when the regulation of emotion is demanded as part of the job conditions and in which organisations might implicitly or explicitly specify what emotions are to be expressed and how emotions should be expressed, even if this requires acting by the employee. The individual conflict may arise if what the employee is expected to express is at variance with what the employee feels, as this can lead to emotional dissonance and hence emotional exhaustion. This potential conflict has been examined by Totterdell and Holman (2003) when looking at emotional labour in call centres. Here employees are expected to display positive emotions all the time, irrespective of their individual feelings. They found that the employees who were naturally positive (i.e. had a low level of emotional dissonance) felt less drained and exhausted than those who were less positive and often had to fake emotions on the phone and who hence felt a higher level of emotional exhaustion. This may have wider implications for staff retention and recruitment in the industry.

Managerial implications

A series of implications for managers arises from a knowledge of organisational behaviour at the level of the individual. These include:

1 A manager needs to realise that the organisation is built up of individuals who will have a range of different personalities and behavioural patterns. The results of actions taken by managers may, therefore, differ according to the individuals concerned.

2 Personality testing can be used to identify behavioural characteristics in individuals, but care should be taken in using such tests and in interpreting their results.

3 Managers should be aware of how perception may influence an individual's behavioural pattern in relation to other people in the organisation. The perceptual process can be distorted by perceptual bias and stereotyping, but effective use of communication, including use of the Johari Window technique, can significantly change these perceptual distortions.

4 It is useful for managers to have an awareness of how values and attitudes develop in the individual and how these may relate to the organisation. Managers may need to change attitudes in an organisation if faced with a change situation or if they are seeking to change the corporate culture.

5 It is advantageous for the manager to have some awareness of how learning occurs both at individual level and overall in the organisation. With an increasing number of organisations being dependent on 'knowledge workers', managers will benefit from having knowledge of cognitive styles.

6 Effective decision making is crucial to the well-being of the organisation, especially when an increasing number of decisions are being taken further down the organisation. An understanding of the process of decision making and of how it gets distorted is of value.

 ## Summary of main points

This chapter should have provided an understanding of:

- the complex nature of the factors that influence personal behaviour;
- how personality may be explained through trait, humanistic and psychodynamic theories;
- the way in which the perceptual process takes place and how this is affected by perceptual stereotyping, selective perception, the halo effect and self-fulfilling prophecies;
- the significance of attribution theory in developing our understanding of how we perceive our own behaviour and the behaviour of others;
- how values and attitudes are formed by individuals and how this may lead to cognitive dissonance;
- the process of individual learning, the differences between the behaviourist and cognitive schools of thought on this topic, and how learning may be influenced by cognitive styles;
- the process of decision making, how this can be explained in terms of the rational model, the bounded rational model and the garbage can model, and how it can be influenced by cognitive biases;
- the ways in which communication, change and conflict can influence, or be influenced by, aspects of individual behaviour, especially in terms of the Johari Window, psychological contracts and emotional labour.

Conclusion

This chapter has sought to give an overview of some of the main theories which can help us to understand aspects of individual behaviour in an organisation. An organisation represents the coming together of individuals to achieve some common purpose and yet we need to acknowledge the diversity of individual behaviour that is likely to occur when individuals 'organise' themselves together. Thus the danger of assuming that organisations are going to be governed by rational and logical actions and behaviour should not be underestimated. These issues are becoming more important as we move fully into the era of 'post-Fordism', with the shift towards organisations becoming increasingly flexible in business environments that are becoming ever more complex. These flatter and more flexible organisations are putting greater pressures on the people who work in them. The development of behaviour, values, beliefs, learning and decision making is being carried on against a backdrop that is constantly changing. One of the dangers posed to individuals by rapid change is the potential for increased conflict, as we saw in our discussion of the implications of psychological contracts, together with increased stress and insecurity. These will place an ever-heavier emphasis on the role of communications in the organisation because it is through effective communication that perceptions, attitudes and beliefs about change can be altered and individuals can learn about the potential benefits of change. Without effective communication, existing values, perceptions and beliefs can harden and ultimately individuals may seek to resist change, again engendering more conflict within the organisation.

Questions

1 Identify three leading characters who have been in the news during the last two weeks and identify their behavioural characteristics and personality traits, drawing on material from the chapter. What are their main differences and why?

2 'Personality tests have no value in terms of contributing to the recruitment process.' Discuss.

3 Given that perceptual impressions are usually made in the first two minutes of meeting someone, evaluate the extent to which these perceptions might be altered. What are the implications of this process for the organisation?

4 Try and identify three key decisions that you made this week and relate these to theories on decision making discussed in the text. To what extent do you feel you are a rational decision maker and are there ways you could improve the quality of your decisions?

5 Look at some learning situations that you have been in this week from both a stimulus–response perspective and a cognitive learning perspective. Which of these has been more effective and why?

6 What issues do you imagine employees look for in the psychological contract? Can job security still be one of these in the twenty-first century? How can employers build a sense of trust when job security is no longer guaranteed?

References

Allison, C. and Hayes, J. (1988) 'The learning styles questionnaire: An alternative to Kolb's inventory?', *Journal of Management Studies*, 25, pp. 269–81.

Allison, C. and Hayes, J. (1996) 'The cognitive style index: A measure of intuition-analysis for organizational research', *Journal of Management Studies*, 33(1), pp. 119–35.

Allport, G. (1961) *Pattern and Growth in Personality.* New York: Holt, Rinehart.

Argyris, C. (1960) *Understanding Organizational Behavior.* Homewood, IL: Dorsey Press.

Argyris, C. and Schön, D. A. (1978) *Organizational Learning: A Theory of Action Perspective.* Reading, MA: Addison-Wesley.

Belbin, M. (1996) *Management Teams: Why they Succeed or Fail.* Oxford: Butterworth-Heinemann.

Brewster, C., Sparrow, P. and Vernon, G. (2007) *International Human Resource Management*, 2nd edn. London: Chartered Institute of Personnel and Development.

Burgoyne, J. (1995) 'Feeding minds to grow the business', *People Management*, 21 September.

Casey, B. (1990) *Firm Policy, State Policy and the Recruitment and Retention of Older Workers.* London: Policy Studies Institute.

Cattell, R. and Kline, P. (1977) *The Scientific Analysis of Personality and Motivation.* London: Academic Press.

Cohen, M., March, J. and Olsen, J. (1972) 'A garbage can model of organisational choice', *Administrative Science Quarterly*, 17, pp. 1–25.

Connolly, J., Kavanagh, E. and Viswesvaran, C. (2007) 'The convergent validity between self and observer ratings of personality: A meta-analytic review', *International Journal of Selection and Assessment*, 15, pp. 110–17.

Cronbach, L. (1995) *Essentials of Psychological Testing*, 5th edn. London: HarperCollins.

Ewen, R. (1988) *An Introduction to Theories of Personality*, 3rd edn. Hove, East Sussex: Lawrence Erlbaum Associates.

Eysenck, H. (1973) *Eysenck on Extroversion.* London: Crosby, Lockwood & Staples.

Goleman, D. (1996) *Emotional Intelligence: Why It can Matter More than IQ.* London: Bloomsbury.

Goleman, D. (1998) *Working with Emotional Intelligence.* London: Bloomsbury.

Guest, D. E. and Conway, N. (2002) *Pressure at Work and the Psychological Contract.* London: Chartered Institute of Personnel and Development.

Hansard Society Commission Report (1990) *Women at the Top.* London: The Hansard Society.

Heider, F. (1958) *The Psychology of Interpersonal Relations.* New York: Wiley.

Hendry, C. and Jenkins, R. (1998) 'Psychological contracts and new deals', *Human Resource Management Journal*, 7(1), pp. 38–43.

Hicks, L. (1996) 'Individual differences', in Mullins, L. (ed.) *Management and Organisational Behaviour*, 4th edn. London: Financial Times Pitman Publishing.

Hill, C. (1997) *International Business*, 2nd edn. New York: Irwin. *See* especially pp. 342–8.

Hochschild, A. (1983) *The Managed Heart: Commercialization of Human Feeling.* Berkeley: University of California Press.

Hodgkinson, G. P. (ed.) (2003) 'Managers and their inaccurate perceptions: Good, bad or inconsequential?', John M. Mezias and William H. Starbuck debate with Kevin Daniels, T. K. Das, A. John Maule, Gerard P. Hodgkinson and Sidney G. Winter. *British Journal of Management*, 14(1), Special Topic Forum, pp. 1–47.

Hofstede, G. (1984) *Culture's Consequences: International Differences in Work-related Values* (abridged edn). Beverly Hills, CA: Sage.

Hogarth, T. and Barth, M. (1991) 'Costs and benefits of hiring older workers: a case study of B&Q', *International Journal of Manpower*, 12(8), pp. 5–17.

Honey, P. and Mumford, A. (1982) *The Manual of Learning Styles*. Maidenhead: Peter Honey.

James, N. (1989) 'Emotional labour: Skill and work in the social regulation of feelings', *Sociological Review*, 37(1), pp. 15–42.

Kelley, H. (1973) 'The process of causal attribution', *American Psychologist*, February, pp. 102–27.

Klehe, U. and Anderson, N. (2007) 'The moderating influence of personality and culture on social loafing in typical versus maximal performance situations', *International Journal of Selection and Assessment*, 15, pp. 220–31.

Kolb, D. (1976) *The Learning Styles Inventory*. Boston: McBer & Co.

Levinson, H., Price, C. R., Munden, K. J., Mandl, H. J. and Solley, C. M. (1962) *Men, Management and Mental Health*. Boston, MA: Harvard University Press.

Lewin, K. (1951) 'Formalization and progress in psychology', in D. Cartwright, (ed.) *Field Research in Social Science*. New York: Harper.

Luft, J. (1970) *Group Processes: An Introduction to Group Dynamics*. New York: National Press.

Lyon, P. and Pollard, D. (1997) 'Perception of the older employee – is anything changing?', *Personnel Review*, 6(4), pp. 245–57.

Mayer, J. D., Roberts, R. D. and Barsade, S. G. (2008) 'Human abilities: Emotional intelligence', *Annual Review of Psychology*, 59, pp. 507–36.

Morrison, A (2007) 'Emotional intelligence, emotion and social work: Context, characteristics, complications and contribution', *British Journal of Social Work*, 37, pp. 245–63.

Myers, M. (1987) *Introduction to Type*. Oxford: Oxford Psychologists Press.

Nutt, P. (1997) 'Better decision-making: A field study', *Business Strategy Review*, 8(4), pp. 45–52.

Pavlov, I. (1927) *Conditioned Reflexes*. Oxford: Oxford University Press.

Personnel Today (2004) 'Perceptions of older workers', 26 October.

Purcell, J., Kinnie, N. and Hutchinson S. (2003) *Understanding the People and Performance Link: Unblocking the Black Box*. London: Chartered Insitutute of Personnel and Development.

Ritchie, J. (2001) *Big Brother 2: The Official Unseen Story*. London: Channel 4 Publications.

Rockeach, M. and Ball-Rockeach, S. S. (1989) 'Stability and change in American value priorities 1968–81', *American Psychologist*, 44, pp. 775–84.

Roehling, M. (1997) 'The origins and early development of the psychological contract construct', *Journal of Management History*, 3(2).

Rogers, C. (1970) *On Becoming a Person: A Therapist's View of Psychotherapy*. Boston: Houghton Mifflin.

Rousseau, D. (1989) 'Psychological and implied contracts in organisation', *Employee Responsibilities and Rights Journal,* 2, pp. 121–39.

Sadler-Smith, E. (1998) 'Cognitive style: Some human resource implications for managers', *International Journal of Human Resource Management,* 9(1), pp. 185–200.

Salovey, P. and Mayer, J. (1990) 'Emotional intelligence', *Imagination, Cognition and Personality,* 9(3), pp. 185–211.

Senge, P. (1990) *The Fifth Discipline: The Art and Practice of the Learning Organization.* New York: Doubleday.

Simon, H. A. (1960) *The New Science of Management Decision.* New York: Harper & Row.

Skinner, B. F. (1974) *About Behaviouralism.* London: Jonathan Cape.

Smith, P. and Gray, B. (2000) *The Emotional Labour of Nursing: How Student and Qualified Nurses Learn to Care.* London: South Bank University.

Sparrow, P. (1997) 'Transitions in the psychological contract: Some evidence from the banking sector', *Human Resource Management Journal,* 6(4), pp. 75–92.

Styles, P., Gratton, L., Truss, C., Hope-Hailey, V. and McGovern, P. (1998) 'Performance management and the psychological contract', *Human Resource Management Journal,* 7(1), pp. 57–65.

Tolman, E. (1932) *Purposive Behavior in Animals and Men.* Berkeley, CA: University of California Press.

Totterdell, P. and Holman, D. (2003) 'Emotional regulation in call centres: Testing a model of emotional labour', *Journal of Occupational Health Psychology,* 8, pp. 55–73.

Viswesvaran, C., Deller, J. and Ones, D. (2007) 'Personality measures in personnel selection: some new contributions', *International Journal of Selection and Assessment,* 15(3), pp. 354–8.

Weiss, J. (1996) *Organizational Behavior and Change.* St Paul, MN: West.

Willis, P. (1997) 'Testing times', *Personnel Today,* 30 October, pp. 26–7.

Further reading

Most textbooks on OB have good sections on individual behaviour, but those particularly recommended are:

Mullins, L. (1999) *Management and Organisational Behaviour,* 5th edn. London: Financial Times Pitman Publishing, Chapters 9 and 11.

Nelson, D. and Quick, J. (1996) *Organizational Behavior: The Essentials.* St Paul, MN: West.

Robbins, S. (1989) *Organizational Behavior,* 4th edn. Englewood Cliffs, NJ: Prentice Hall International.

Weiss, J. (1996) *Organizational Behavior and Change.* St Paul, MN: West.

Internet sites

www.psychtesting.org.uk The testing centre of the British Psychological Society
www.aptinternational.org The Association for Psychological Type
www.agepositive.gov.uk Examples of positive discrimination towards older workers
www.traininginstitute.co.uk/itoljournal.htm The British Journal of Occupational Learning

4 Motivation at work

Learning outcomes

On completion of this chapter you should be able to:
- define motivation;
- know the main schools of thought and prime contributors to the theory of workplace motivation;
- know and understand the nature of expectancy theory and assess its value as a frame for analysing motivation theories and for understanding individual motivation;
- appreciate the relationship between motivation and interpersonal conflict;
- assess the effects of organisational change on the psychological contract and on motivation;
- understand how communication and mis-communication can impact upon motivation;
- understand the relationship between motivation and job design;
- appreciate management's role in enhancing workplace motivation.

Key concepts

- motivation and satisfaction
- cognitive and behavioural theories
- contents and process theories
- expectancy model
- goal theory
- needs and self-actualisation
- extrinsic and intrinsic rewards
- equity
- psychological contract
- type-environment
- job design.

Possibly one of the most contentious, important and frequently debated issues in organisational behaviour and workplace practice is 'how do we motivate our staff?' Whether we are a manager or someone being managed, motivation is a prime concern and of considerable social and economic significance. Intuitively, we recognise that poorly motivated staff tend to underperform whereas in all activities well-motivated individuals and teams are an important ingredient of success. Motivated individuals tend to work with enhanced effort and confidence and enjoy high productivity. Additionally, motivated employees are more satisfied with their work and their environment.

 Introduction

Although motivation is a critical factor in individual, group and organisational success there is some debate concerning its definition. In broad terms, *motivation can be considered to comprise an individual's effort and persistence and the direction of that effort.* In simpler terms, *motivation is the will to perform.* It is, perhaps, of more value to identify the characteristics frequently associated with well-motivated individuals. Such people are commonly thought to consistently achieve at work and to exhibit energy and enthusiasm in the process. They often work with people to overcome organisational problems, or obstacles to progress, and frequently demand and accept additional responsibility. They may also be more willing to accept organisational change. In contrast, employees who are demotivated may appear apathetic and may tend to consider problems and issues as insurmountable obstacles to progress. They might have poor attendance and time-keeping records and might appear uncooperative and resistant to change. Clearly, organisations that can motivate their employees are more likely to achieve their organisational objectives.

This chapter focuses primarily on motivation of the individual in the workplace. It explores the influence of organisational change, communication and conflict on personal motivation and is supported by a number of the case studies presented later in the book, notably Case Study 2, 'Organisational change: multiskilling in the healthcare sector' (*see* p. 330). The chapter explores expectancy theory, as a useful analytical frame, and as the vehicle by which to examine, in some detail, the likely nature and sources of motivation. Additionally, concepts such as intrinsic and extrinsic rewards, personal needs and environmental stimulation are discussed. We argue that the different approaches tend, often, to complement one another and add richness to our understanding of this complex topic. The chapter also explores how job design and role characteristics can be developed to better ensure a motivated workforce.

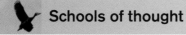 **Schools of thought**

Content and process theories, behavioural and cognitive traditions

Motivation theory has been developed, mainly in the USA, following empirical research activities. It has progressed considerably from the traditional or classical approaches which assumed that people in the workplace acted rationally in an attempt to maximise the economic return to their labour. This rational economic concept assumed that work was inherently unpleasant and that wages compensated workers for their efforts. Indeed the money they earned was considered to be of greater importance to individuals than the nature of the job they performed. People could, it was believed, be expected to tolerate any kind of work if they were paid enough. We saw in Chapter 2 how Frederick Taylor and others in the Scientific School of Management developed this concept.

Broadly, most models and approaches to motivation can be categorised as either content or process theories. Content theories attempt to identify and explain the factors which energise or motivate people whereas process theories focus on how a variety of personal factors interact and influence human behaviour. Quite often the two sets of theories are compatible, in fact, when combined they provide considerable insight into motivation in the workplace.

Additionally, motivation theories derive from either a behaviouralist tradition, where human behaviour is considered to be reflexive and instinctive, a response to certain environmental positive or negative stimuli, or a cognitive tradition. In the latter case it is assumed that people are conscious of their goals and their behaviour and they act rationally and with purpose. Behaviour modification theory and reinforcement theory are located firmly in the behaviouralist tradition. They ignore the inner state of the individual, this being the territory of the cognitive school, and focus instead on the consequences of people's actions. Figure 4.1 graphically illustrates the simple differences between these traditions.

Behaviour modification theory is often associated with both motivation and learning. Broadly, it suggests that behaviour is a function of its consequences, that is, the outcome of a particular behaviour will influence the nature of future behaviour. Both positive and negative reinforcement can increase the strength of a behaviour as people often respond positively to encouraging feedback and/or consider changing their behaviour if it leads to negative feedback. A study among students found that individuals reported higher perceptions of competence and greater task enjoyment relative to others when given feedback on their performance relative to others'.

Negative feedback should not, however, be confused with punishment, the former generally being constructive. Punishment, especially if used indiscriminately, may have unintended consequences. However, it can reduce a particular

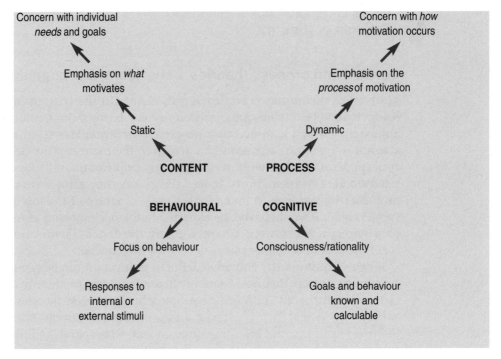

Figure 4.1 Distinction between process/content and cognitive/behavioural traditions

behaviour if it is quick, fair, private, informative, focused and not followed by rewards. Additionally, by their failure to reinforce particular desirable behaviours, managers may encourage that behaviour to be exhibited less. Critiques of behavioural modification or shaping in the workplace suggest that it dehumanises employees. Table 4.1 illustrates a simple classification of motivation theories.

Table 4.1 A simple classification of motivation theories

Content theories	Process theories
● Two-factor theory (Herzberg)	● Expectancy theory (Vroom; Porter & Lawler)
● Needs hierarchy (Maslow; Alderfer)	● Equity theory (Adams)
● Achievement needs theory (McClelland)	● Goal theory (Locke)
	● Attribution theory (Heider; Kelley)

Expectancy theory: a framework for the analysis of workplace motivation

This section outlines the nature of expectancy theory and explores other process and content theories which add insight to the nature of workplace motivation.

Expectancy theory has developed since the 1930s as an alternative to the behaviouralist approaches to motivation. It argues that humans act according to their conscious expectations that a particular behaviour will lead to specific desirable goals. The theory, with all its consequent refinements, provides a popular explanatory framework for a range of employee behaviours, including levels of motivation, performance, employee turnover and absenteeism, in addition to leadership effectiveness and career choice.

Vroom (1964), by an American psychologist, developed expectancy theory from the original work of Tolman and Honzik (1930), producing a systematic explanatory theory of workplace motivation. It argued that *the motivation to behave in a particular way is determined by an individual's expectation that behaviour will lead to a particular outcome, multiplied by the preference or valence that person has for that outcome*. For example, if by working diligently and for long hours an employee expects to receive promotion at some future date and if that worker values promotion highly (the worker is said to have valence) then, rationally, we might expect that employee to show that behaviour. Vroom argues that human behaviour is directed by *subjective probability*, that is, the individual's expectation that his or her behaviour will lead to a particular outcome. The simple expectancy equation is:

Motivation (M) = Expectation (E) $\times$ Valence (V)

It is assumed that the level of motivation an individual displays results from his or her conscious decision-making process: a rational estimate of the likely result of their behaviour. The theory also considers the value that each individual places on the estimated outcome. The basic theory recognises that individuals differ: that we are all unlikely to value the same outcomes equally. The theory also attempts to measure, via a simple calculation, the strength of motivation by multiplying the individual's estimated probability ($E \times V$, above) of an expected outcome by the value or valence that individual places on that outcome. A simple personal example will illustrate this (*see* Mini-case 4.1).

Mini-case 4.1

Expectancy theory: an illustration

A university lecturer considered that she was about 80 per cent (probability, +0.8) sure that she would achieve promotion within five years if she (a) published research, (b) developed new courses, (c) managed budgets effectively and (d) indicated a willingness to change and take the organisation forward. That was her subjective probability or expectation (E).

At the time she valued the prospect of promotion rather highly and believed that it would enable her to manage the changes that she perceived as important,

to more fully utilise her skills and abilities, to develop herself and achieve new outcomes and to earn a little more money. On a scale between −1.0 and +1.0 she would place her valence as +0.9 (*V*).

Hence, at the time she believed it quite probable that by behaving in a particular way, which involved a great deal of hard and thoughtful work, she would quite likely (say four times out of five) achieve an outcome (promotion) that was desired rather highly. Her motivation was:

$M = E \times V$ or Motivation $= 0.8 \times 0.9 = 0.72$

The maximum score possible is +1.0, whereas the minimum is −1.0. If the score is positive it is likely that the individual would behave in the manner which she or he hopes would lead to the desired outcome.

In this case, a score of +0.72 is rather high and positive, suggesting that she would be strongly motivated to work as indicated above (see points (a), (b), (c) and (d)). That she did and she has received the desired promotion. Expectancy theory would suggest that she took a subjective but rational decision; others might argue it was a calculated gamble.

It is worthy of note, however, that despite extensive knowledge of expectancy theory, she did not actually make such a calculation as expressed above. It did not prove a useful tool or source of guidance, and in fact it was never intended as such. Expectancy theory is based on the observation of human behaviour and attempts to depict the cognitive process which individuals are likely to go through. Our lecturer can now reflect on the theory and suggest that in this case it holds some validity.

Locke (1968) proposed a simple and intuitively appealing cognitive theory of motivation that has certain similarities to the expectancy approach. *Goal theory proposes that both motivation and performance will be high if individuals are set specific goals which are challenging, but accepted, and where feedback is given on performance.* Numerous studies appear to support his notion and goal setting is now a popular technique in organisations. Locke *et al.* (1981) identified four ways in which goals influence behaviour. They:

- direct attention;
- mobilise effort;
- encourage persistence;
- facilitate strategy development.

It is argued that self-evaluation and self-monitoring against targets are vital. This has also shown to be important to successful individual learning and a study revealed that individuals who received training in self-regulatory processes demonstrated less absenteeism. Studies have also shown that difficulty in achieving a high-order goal tended to lead to a shift towards a lower-order goal, hence the notion of a hierarchy of goals is seen as valuable, enabling self-regulation and the achievement of longer-term goals.

Organisational bureaucracies often make goal setting difficult and, hence, dissipate the potential motivational benefits from processes such as management by objectives (MBO). It can also be argued that in dynamic environments annual objectives or individual goals often fail to embrace the need for change and flexibility. Additionally, with increasing emphasis being placed on the role of teamwork in organisations, individual goals and rewards can be seen as divisive or even counterproductive. Finally, acceptance of goals by the individual is essential; hence participative goal setting is seen as vital to enhance performance.

Porter and Lawler's expectancy model

The basic expectancy model has been further developed, notably by Porter and Lawler (1968) whose model includes further, hopefully realistic, variables and highlights certain potential managerial implications. In particular it sheds light on the nature of the relationship between employee satisfaction and performance. Figure 4.2 illustrates the more complex expectancy model. Porter and Lawler's model adds to existing theory by suggesting that performance is a product not only of effort but also of the individual's abilities and characteristics together with his or her role perceptions. This adds a certain intuitive realism.

Performance leads to two types of reward. *Intrinsic rewards are intangible and include a sense of achievement, or advancement, of recognition and enhanced responsibility, whereas extrinsic rewards are more tangible and include pay and working conditions.* It can be argued that the relationship between intrinsic rewards and performance is both more direct and immediate than that between performance and extrinsic rewards. As a consequence, Lawler (1973) argues that intrinsic rewards are more important influences on motivation than pay or promotion. Similarly, Herzberg (1968) suggests that intrinsic rewards have a more direct and powerful influence on workplace satisfaction than do extrinsic rewards. This has been recognised for some time with Blum (1949: 132–3) writing that 'the major error in industry has been the oversimplification of the concept of motivation'. Herzberg's two-factor theory, outlined below, sheds light on the motivational effects of these two sets of rewards and makes a useful contribution to our understanding of workplace motivation.

Following receipt of rewards the individual assesses, via social comparison, the equity of the rewards received. Adams's equity theory is discussed below (*see* pp. 97–8). If the individual perceives that the rewards received are equitable, that is, *fair or just in comparison with those received by others in similar positions in or*

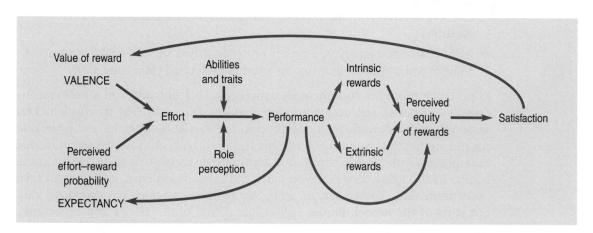

Figure 4.2 Porter and Lawler's expectancy model
Source: Adapted from Porter and Lawler (1968), p. 165.

outside the organisation, then that individual feels satisfied. This perceived level of satisfaction then influences the valence of rewards: if an employee is dissatisfied, the valence or value of those rewards is likely to be low. Hence, if rewards are perceived as adequate and equitable, this gives a fillip to performance and hence satisfaction. A positive or virtuous cycle of motivation may occur.

Tyler and Bies (1990) suggest five factors that contribute to perceptions of fairness in the workplace and, hence, influence perceived equity:

- adequate consideration of an employee's viewpoint;
- suppression of personal bias;
- consistent application of criteria across employees;
- provision of timely feedback after a discussion;
- providing employees with adequate explanations for a decision.

If we refer to the case, discussed above in Mini-case 4.1, of the woman who achieved promotion, and consider the consequences of her not being promoted, it is possible to illustrate how inequity in the workplace may prove an issue. She was 80 per cent certain that promotion, a desired outcome, would be achieved if she showed effort in a number of specific ways. If a colleague had received promotion ahead of her, she might have felt aggrieved if she had perceived that the successful colleague had failed to demonstrate greater talents in the key areas of achievement than she herself had displayed. As a consequence she might have become demotivated due to a feeling of inequity.

Expectancy theory makes a number of important assumptions, which include:

- the realisation that individual behaviour is influenced by various personal and environmental factors;
- an individual makes a series of decisions or choices about his or her behaviour and acts rationally in that process, taking note of such information as is available;
- individuals differ and have a variety of needs, drives and sources of motivation. So what works for one may not for another individual (Mini-case 4.2).

Expectancy theory is complicated, which is both a blessing and a problem. Its complexity better reflects reality yet it makes the testing of its fundamental assumptions by scientific methods difficult. The model assumes, by and large, that people are rational and objective; this is, possibly, a spurious assumption. For example, individuals differ from one another considerably in their perception of equity, in the value they place on particular rewards (valence) and in their own needs from, and expectations of, work. Nevertheless, research has supported various parts of the model. Pinder (1984) found that both valence and expectancy were related to both effort and performance in the workplace, whereas Campbell and Pritchard (1976) confirmed that an individual's motivation is influenced by the value this person places on expected rewards. Additionally, their research indicates that people need to believe that their efforts will lead to enhanced performance and that their performance will result in the desired outcomes in terms of rewards. Additionally, for many routine activities at work, habit or group norms may be a more typical basis for motivated behaviour. This means workers will not always go through the expectancy theory process before displaying motivated behaviour.

Mini-case 4.2

Motivation: what works for one may not for another

Consider two graduates, armed with their upper second class degrees, and starting 'serious' work in the late summer after graduating. Milan got a post in an inner city comprehensive school in Leicester. He has long wanted to help secondary-school-age students to achieve as he did. The salary, although not great, is fine: it's certainly far more than he has ever been used to having. His Head of Department lets it be known that if he settles in well, has good classroom discipline, his students like his classes and their examination results were above the school average, then he would not only pass his probationary period but would have a bright future ahead. He may even make it to second in department after a year or two which would put him in a position to make an even greater contribution to student performance. This is everything Milan wants: a chance to make a difference to children's lives, to help them to achieve by achieving himself. What was more, he got on well with the Head of Department. There was mutual respect and they even met socially. Milan knew what was expected of him, wanted to achieve it and enjoyed the social contact with colleagues. It couldn't get much better than that.

Emma started work for a software company as a sales representative. She entered this business to make money. Some of the good reps, she was told at interview, earned £40,000 a year by the time they were 25 years old, some even more. After two days' product training her manager gave her some ambitious sales targets. It was up to her now. She made a few early sales but also had a number of setbacks. The sales gave her a great buzz, but the setbacks were depressing. After the first month she was called to a meeting with her manager to discuss her targets. She believed she had made 12 sales (and the bonus cut in at 10). Her manager informed her that three of the provisional clients had not paid and the bonus would have to be withheld but that she had started well and clients phoned in to say they thought that she was a welcome addition to the company.

She left the office feeling very low. Was it her fault they had not paid? She wasn't much interested in what the clients thought; she wanted to earn that bonus. On subsequent visits she got a little aggressive with some clients, thinking that they were just the sort to string her along, have the product but later return it or delay payment for as long as possible. Her sales dropped in month two to just 8. She was getting nothing from this job. She wanted to 'work hard and play hard' and earn lots of money; it didn't really matter what she did. She felt that she had been duped by her manager and by the company's clients.

 ## Needs theories

The extent to which certain outcomes will be valued by individuals in the workplace is dependent upon their particular needs. It has been argued that people share a series of hierarchically related needs which will act as a source of motivation. Other 'needs theories' suggest that people's fundamental requirements or needs differ from one person to another and that, as a consequence, their sources of satisfaction and motivation will also vary. Perhaps the most frequently cited needs theory is Maslow's needs hierarchy. Unfortunately, it also warrants criticism: empirical evidence has not supported its main contentions and it is highly ethnocentric. Hence, we will only briefly discuss it here before looking at more recent modifications, and in a little more detail at the work of McClelland.

Needs hierarchy

Maslow, a sociologist writing in 1943, suggested that individuals are motivated to satisfy a set of needs which are hierarchically ranked according to their salience. Hence, man's most basic requirements for food and drink are pursued at all costs until that need has been satisfied. When these basic physiological needs are met he will switch his attention to seeking a higher-order need, that of security. Further fulfilment is then achieved via affiliation with others. Individuals who enjoy sufficient physiological, security and social affiliation may then be motivated to seek the esteem of others and self-respect or self-esteem. Finally, man will attempt to self-actualise, to realise his potential and to achieve something beyond the immediate needs of the body and his social circle (Figure 4.3). Maslow also suggested that freedom of enquiry and expression and the need for knowing and understanding are essential prerequisites for the satisfaction of other needs.

Implicit in this hierarchy is the belief that individuals will strive to seek a higher need when lower needs are fulfilled, that is, the need for self-actualisation, for example, becomes stronger when esteem needs are satisfied but is weak or non-existent until these lower-level needs are satisfied. The model also suggests that once lower-level needs are satisfied they no longer serve as sources of motivation. In order to be motivated, individuals need to be given the opportunity to satisfy the need at the next level in the hierarchy.

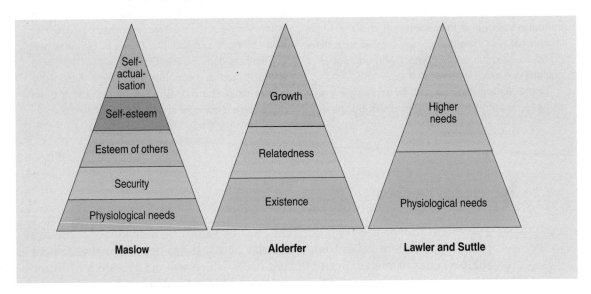

Figure 4.3 Needs hierarchies

Maslow recognised that this was not a fixed hierarchy and that for some, for example, self-esteem might prove a more powerful motivator than affiliation or the love of others. Similarly, for some, particularly creative people, the need for self-actualisation might even displace their motivation to satisfy certain basic physiological requirements. In contrast, some people who might never be motivated to seek to satisfy higher-level needs instead would be satisfied with sound physiological and social fulfilment. He also suggested that a lower-level need would not necessarily require to be fully satisfied before an individual could be motivated to seek to satisfy other needs: these lower-level needs would still carry some, but limited, valence. It is not an absolute requirement that one must be fed and socially fulfilled before one seeks any measure of self-esteem. However, the lower-level needs would take precedence, he argued, if they were not fulfilled. He also argued that the theory was more or less universally applicable, that it was not ethnocentric or influenced by culture (refer to Chapter 10).

Applying this theory to the workplace is fraught with difficulties, although it must be said that Maslow did not intend this theory to be a managerial or organisational tool. Additionally, it has not enjoyed unquestioned empirical support (Hall and Nougaim, 1968; Lawler and Suttle, 1972). A number of problems and deficiencies have been noted. People often achieve higher-level needs via non-work-related activities. Individuals differ and, as a result, some place more value on certain needs than others. Research has indicated that as managers advance within organisations their need for security and safety tends to decrease, whereas social, esteem and self-actualisation needs increase (Lawler and Suttle, 1972). This same research also suggests that individuals rarely satisfy their higher-order needs and they continue to strive for status and autonomy even after experiencing considerable success in these areas. Satisfaction does not necessarily equate to motivation, nor does it always lead to improved work performance. Although a commonly held view is that 'a satisfied worker is a more productive worker', numerous studies have shown that a simple link between job attitudes and job performance often does not exist (Iaffaldano and Muchinsky, 1985). For example, whereas participative decision making has been shown to enhance job satisfaction, studies suggest it has little or no influence on performance (Schweiger and Leana, 1986). There is, however, a link between job satisfaction and each of absenteeism, staff turnover and the incidence of both physical and mental health problems (Schneider, 1985). Furthermore, the model is highly ethnocentric. It applies primarily to average American individuals and might not represent the prime motivational drivers for those of Chinese origin, for example, where social needs, the need for affiliation and belonging, could prove a more fundamental source of motivation than personal physiological needs (refer to Chapter 10).

Lawler and Suttle (1972) suggest, following research in two companies, that the needs hierarchy can be reduced to just two levels: the research indicated that physiological needs existed separately and the second level included all other needs (refer to Figure 4.3).

Alderfer (1972), who adapted Maslow's approach to the workplace, proposed three categories of needs (refer to Figure 4.3):

- existence (basic survival needs);
- relatedness (including social interaction and respect of and recognition from others);
- growth (self-fulfilment, autonomy and success).

Alderfer's model suggests that needs may be activated simultaneously, as opposed to the strict, hierarchical sequence of Maslow. For example, an individual may be motivated by a desire for money (an existence need), by friendship (a relatedness need) and the opportunity to learn new skills (a growth need) at the same time, in parallel. There is something intuitively appealing about this. Think of a 'typical' full time student – they often undertake a university course partly because they recognise that success should lead to enhanced career prospects and a better-paid job in the future (existence need). They also recognise that they will meet many other students and are quite likely have a good time socially (a relatedness need). All this happens while actually learning new skills and developing as an individual (a growth need). University has been for centuries, and looks likely to continue to be, a rather appealing 'product'. Alderfer also suggested that if higher needs are not satisfied an individual will regress in pursuit of lower-level needs. This is referred to as the frustration–regression effect. Although better received than Maslow, this model's broad assertions make it difficult to verify.

Illustration in film

Toy Story

The film *Toy Story* (1995) contains many illustrations of motivation theory in action. For example, when Buzz Lightyear is depressed, Woody manages to pick him up, to motivate him to help save the day. He does this by appealing to Buzz's needs – like the need to be an action hero. It is clear that each of the toys enjoys different needs, some for affiliation with others, some to have power and to lead.

McClelland's achievement needs theory

Perhaps of more significance and potential value to managers and academics attempting to understand motivation in the workplace is the work of McClelland. McClelland's (1961) need achievement theory identifies three basic needs that people develop and acquire from their life experiences. These are the needs for:

- achievement;
- affiliation; and
- power.

Individuals develop a dominant bias or emphasis towards one of the three needs. For example, those with a high achievement need tend to seek situations where they have personal responsibility for solving problems, managing projects and for

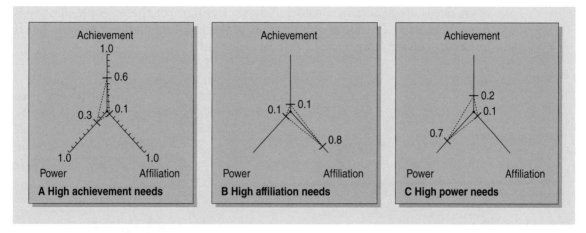

Figure 4.4 Achievement, affiliation and power needs

overall performance, where feedback is often clear and rapid, where tasks are moderately challenging and where innovation is required.

Figure 4.4 illustrates the needs profile of a number of hypothetical individuals. If we assume that each individual's combined achievement, affiliation and power needs total 1.0 we are left with considerable scope for individual variation based on the strength or salience of a particular need. This provides a relative measure which might enable us to enhance our understanding of ourselves and others in the workplace. We can construct three quite different and extreme scenarios. For example, individual A has a high need for achievement (0.6), a moderate need for power (0.3) and a low need for affiliation (0.1), whereas B has a high need for affiliation (0.8) and low power and achievement needs (0.1 and 0.1). Individual C is driven or motivated by the need for power (0.7) and less so by achievement alone (0.2), whereas his or her need for affiliation is low (0.1). Clearly, these are extreme cases. Such individuals will, most likely, forge quite different careers from one another by seeking different ways of meeting their needs. If these three individuals were managed similarly, as is often the case in traditional bureaucracies, then it is unlikely that all would satisfy their needs in the workplace.

In a study in the USA (McClelland and Boyatzis, 1984) it was found that successful managers had high power needs and lower achievement needs. Power appears to be the main determinant of success, particularly when success is measured in terms of status and promotion to senior posts. McClelland distinguished between socialised power and personalised power, the former being useful in assisting managers and leaders in their attempts to achieve organisational and group goals whereas the latter often merely serves the individual in seeking his or her need for domination. The need to achieve is linked to entrepreneurial activity and is viewed as an essential ingredient of organisational and national economic success. Managers tend to have higher achievement needs and lower affiliation needs than non-managers. We are all, perhaps, aware of people who appear, at least, to demonstrate a high need for one of the three drivers identified by McClelland. However, for the achievement of organisational success, those with high achievement needs are generally considered most essential. For these people, money is often considered a measure or indication of success, a method of feedback, but is not a particularly strong motivator in its own right.

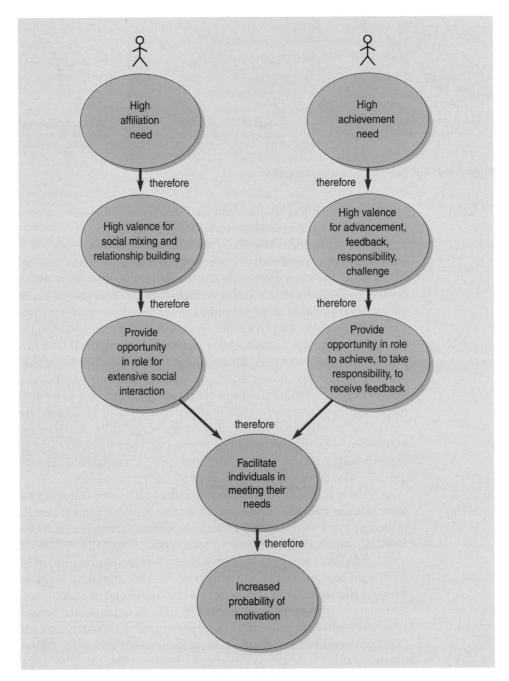

Figure 4.5 Expectancy and needs theory: relationship

McClelland's motives correspond, to an extent, with Maslow's self-actualisation (achievement), esteem needs (affiliation) and love and social needs (power). However, this theory recognises that the relative extent or influence of these needs varies considerably between individuals. McClelland's work emphasises the importance of context, the social environment outside work, for the development of needs or motives, whereas Maslow and others suggest that needs are instinctive.

Of particular interest to managers attempting to instil higher achievement needs in staff is McClelland's (1962) argument that this need can be strengthened by a combination of managerial action and training. He suggests that managers should reinforce successes and give positive feedback (with effects similar to those of Herzberg's 'recognition' motivators), identify role models and successful mentors and encourage employees to emulate these achievers, modify the self-image of staff with lower achievement needs and encourage them to think of themselves in more positive terms.

The implications of this work for expectancy theory are significant (*see* Figure 4.5). For example, an individual with high achievement needs is likely to value highly (valence) an expected outcome involving advancement, positive feedback, enhanced responsibilities and new challenge. Similarly, that individual's potential disappointment at not achieving outcomes of this kind would be severe and would possibly lead to demotivation and, perhaps, to departure from the organisation. Individuals with higher affiliation needs, for example, might be motivated by tasks and jobs which are designed to cater for their need to mix socially and build relationships. It should be clear that the nature of potential outcomes and rewards, as shown in the expectancy model, will influence individuals' motivation levels differently.

Intrinsic and extrinsic rewards

Herzberg's (1968) two-factor theory focused on intrinsic and extrinsic motivational factors and adds considerably to our understanding of what motivates people in the workplace (Table 4.2). In terms of the expectancy model it will affect what individuals perceive as the value or valence of particular outcomes; hence it will influence both their performance and job satisfaction.

Table 4.2 Herzberg's satisfiers and dissatisfiers

Hygiene – context factors Extrinsic rewards	Motivators – content factors Intrinsic rewards
● Company policy and administration	● Sense of achievement
● Supervision/relationship with supervisor	● Recognition
● Working conditions	● The work itself
● Remuneration: pay, salary	● Responsibility
● Relationship with peers and with subordinates	● Advancement
● Status/promotion	● Personal growth
● Job security	

The two-factor theory is appealing, at least intuitively, to many academics, students and managers, although, curiously, when it was first published it represented a somewhat counterintuitive concept as it confronted certain 'accepted' beliefs. It suggests that a series of so-called hygiene factors can create dissatisfaction if individuals perceive them to be inadequate or inequitable, yet individuals will not be significantly motivated if these factors are viewed as adequate or good. Hygiene factors are extrinsic to the actual work itself, and include factors such as salary or remuneration, job security, working conditions and company policies. The suggestion is, for example, that if an employee's wages are not as high as he or she believes to be appropriate, then this might lead to dissatisfaction. However, if the employee's wages are thought to be good, that alone will not particularly motivate, or even fully satisfy, them. These contextual factors cannot sustain motivation, although they may lead to a state of personal satisfaction. This is in contrast to the traditional belief that pay is the prime, or in some cases only, source of motivation. That traditional understanding was reinforced by the work of Frederick Taylor and the Scientific School of Management in the early part of the twentieth century (refer to Chapter 2).

Illustration in film

Blue Collar

In the film *Blue Collar* (1978), Richard Pryor works on a production line in Detroit making cars. It illustrates the nature of such work and the demotivating effect it has on staff. There certainly is little in the way of intrinsic reward here.

Taylorism advocated the application of 'scientific' principles to job design and work management. It was founded on the belief that if jobs were designed to achieve maximum productivity, and if workers were selected with the necessary physical, as opposed to cerebral, capabilities, then wages could be increased: this, Taylor argued, would provide the necessary incentive for workers. Although productivity did increase significantly as a result of carefully, albeit mechanically, planned tasks and careful worker selection, considerable disenchantment and demotivation often resulted, because of the physically highly demanding and repetitive nature of the resultant jobs. Nevertheless, the common assumption, which became engrained in organisational belief systems, was that pay was a major, if not the sole, source of motivation: this view prevailed, and still exists to an extent today, despite the widespread criticism of the work of the Scientific School of Management. Mini-case 4.3 illustrates the experience of a call-centre employee.

Herzberg also identified a series of factors which, he suggested, lead to satisfaction and, he at least implicitly suggested, increased motivation. These intrinsic factors are those directly related to the work itself and include a sense of achievement, recognition from superiors and colleagues, responsibility and opportunity for personal growth and advancement. Hence, the implication is that managers should attempt to enable employees to access intrinsic satisfiers, while simultaneously avoiding the dissatisfaction resulting from the perceived inadequacy of extrinsic rewards. The intrinsic rewards equate to Maslow's higher-level needs, whereas the hygiene or extrinsic factors are similar to his lower-level physiological and security needs. The two factors, satisfiers and dissatisfiers, are illustrated in Table 4.2.

Mini case 4.3

Working in a call centre: an insider's view

The first time I got a job in a call centre I was excited by the prospect of earning £5.50 per hour, which in comparison to my previous employment was a good wage. I was expecting that this would be an interesting job, certainly better than a supermarket or café.

At first the job was great, the first week of training went really fast, learning about the product and how to handle calls was interesting and the trainers were full of enthusiasm. Finally, we were taken to the centre and seated in a group where we would make our first calls. As trainees, we were supervised closely at first, a team leader being available to assist us if we were in difficulty. The first few weeks flew by and I enjoyed them. Then the boredom set in. All the calls were similar and the demoralising effect of dealing with people's problems from morning to night became tedious. So called 'after-call work' was non-existent and pressure to deal with as many calls as possible became apparent, taking one call after another with no break between. The promised £50.00 monthly bonus depended on keeping the call rate as high as possible. It also became obvious that as I became more confident, the supervisors became more reluctant to help out with difficult calls and would decline to accept calls when customers requested a supervisor. My colleagues and I were left alone to handle difficult and abusive clients regularly.

I was a 'temp' and was told by the agency after several weeks that my contract was not being renewed. No indication that there was a problem with my work was given and they had always seemed so pleased with me. The reason given was my timekeeping and I was told that I had 'signed on' the computer late on eleven separate occasions. Due to poor communication between departments, I was not issued with a log-in code of my own and although I made myself available for work on time I had to use other people's codes, often having to go and find a code before starting work.

Keeping motivated in a call centre job is very difficult, at least that is my experience. One agency sent me to a telesales job that was paying £3.00 for each sale, over and above the normal hourly rate of pay. This was a dream come true, or so I thought. I worked for about three weeks, getting 12–15 sales a day, thinking I was going to pay off my student overdraft and have a holiday. Then the crunch came. I was told that I'd have to be employed for eight weeks before I'd get my bonus. This was impossible, as I would be back at university by then. The agency had not told me this fact. I tried to negotiate but left shortly afterwards, but I'm sure my team leader will benefit from my sales.

Telephone work seems to be the sort of job that can only be done for a short while. The expectations of employers seem unrealistically high, bearing in mind that they are employing human beings and not machines. The ability to perform at a high level for any length of time is probably a skill some acquire, but anyone capable of independent thought cannot survive such an atmosphere and any amount of sweets, pizzas and trivial incentives by team leaders can only be a temporary solution.

Source: Nicola Gerrard

The two-factor theory suggests that the prospect of receiving intrinsic rewards (expectancy) will be more likely to motivate individuals than the possibility of, for example, improved working conditions, job security or salary improvements. Salary enhancements and other hygiene factors might be viewed in the short term as advantageous but, Herzberg suggested, they have only a small effect on sustained motivation in the workplace. The opportunity for personal advancement, recognition for one's contribution, enhanced responsibility for the outcome of an individual's or group's effort and the nature of the actual work itself (possibly stimulating, interesting, involving variety) will serve to motivate on an ongoing and sustainable basis.

Kerr (1975) has noted that the reward systems in many organisations serve to 'reward' undesirable behaviours while, simultaneously, ignoring or even punishing more positive ones. The feedback and reinforcement processes appear to be essential to achieve and sustain a motivated workforce, yet many company practices and policies, usually unknowingly, serve to depress employee motivation. As a consequence, when individuals feel that they are not being rewarded for a job well done they become dissatisfied and, potentially, undermotivated.

By and large, prior to Herzberg's work, job satisfaction and performance were thought to result largely, if not exclusively, from extrinsic stimulants, such as pay. He raised the very real spectre that the factors contributing to workplace satisfaction, motivation and performance undoubtedly include intrinsic rewards. Few academics and practitioners now believe that hygiene factors alone will ensure that organisations have motivated, productive, involved and creative employees and most recognise the need to consider the quality of work life as part of the motivation equation and managerial process.

Despite the intuitive appeal of the two-factor theory criticisms can be levelled at its premises and, particularly, at its validity. The original research conducted by Herzberg utilised a relatively small sample size (210) of professional people (accountants and engineers). Therefore, its applicability to other groups has been questioned. Nevertheless, research conducted by Blackburn and Mann (1979) (sample size, 1000) among low- to medium-skilled employees found a wide range of orientations and suggested that individuals are often motivated by factors other than, for example, pay. Many of the respondents in this research were found to have a primary and strong orientation towards many of the intrinsic motivators referred to by Herzberg, such as concern for autonomy and for worth of the work. It also concluded that blue-collar workers differ from one another regarding their prime orientation and likely source of workplace motivation. What it did not find was that pay and other hygiene factors totally dominated their considerations. Numerous other studies, using workers from a variety of sectors, such as nurses, food industry employees, technicians and assembly staff have, broadly, replicated the original findings.

Herzberg used a method of research known as the 'critical incident technique' which requires respondents to consider their work experiences retrospectively. It can be argued that such historical contemplation may distort 'reality' when respondents consider factors which led to either satisfaction or dissatisfaction. Other writers, notably Vroom (1964) and House and Wigdor (1967), have criticised the theory, the latter suggesting that the two-factor approach is an oversimplification of the potential sources of both satisfaction and dissatisfaction.

In summary, the three most common criticisms of the theory are that it has limited application for non-professional or non-manual workers, that it represents an oversimplification of sources of satisfaction and dissatisfaction and that it is methodologically flawed. It should be noted that, despite the often well-considered criticisms, the theory is not invalidated but merely questioned and refined. One could suggest that it is a measure of the appeal of this theory that so much critical attention has been paid to it.

Motivation and equitable treatment

Equity theory, developed by Adams (1963, 1965), gives us a particularly useful, if simple, insight into the relationship between rewards and the likely satisfaction individuals gain from them. It qualifies our understanding of the expectancy model. The level of satisfaction and potential motivation resulting from an individual's receiving a reward cannot be considered in isolation. The rewards and treatment of others also influences an individual's level of satisfaction as people appear to be motivated to receive what they consider a fair or equitable return for their efforts. For example, where expectancy is high, perhaps unrealistically so, if the desired outcome is not achieved then individuals may feel frustrated or even cheated by this experience. This sense of unfairness or inequity may result in dissatisfaction and demotivation.

Adams's model contains three crucial components:

- inputs (the effort an individual makes);
- outputs (intrinsic and extrinsic rewards from the organisation);
- comparison with others.

Clearly, the weighting or value placed on both inputs and outputs is a matter of individual perception and judgement. These two factors equate to 'effort' and 'rewards' in the expectancy model. How this significantly differs from expectancy theory is its recognition that individuals make comparisons between themselves and others when assessing the scale or worthiness of rewards received. Recognition of this critical contextual variable adds important insight.

If an individual perceives that the overall outputs he or she receives from the organisation (e.g. pay, fringe benefits, recognition) in return for their particular inputs (e.g. hours of work, achievements, qualifications) are equal to, or exceed, those received by colleagues in the company or peers elsewhere, then they will view the situation as equitable or even favourable. The opposite effect leads to under-reward inequity where individuals are motivated to reduce such inequality. This may result in their reducing their input. Such real or perceived inequality can also cause conflict between individuals and groups within and across organisations. It may lead to relationship difficulties between, for example, management and employees if the latter group perceive that they are being treated inequitably.

This perception, often held by large numbers of employees simultaneously, is frequently a root cause of union–management strife, worker discontent, or demotivation, and low morale. Equity theory has been shown to hold validity in practice (Goodman and Friedman, 1971). As a consequence the theory underpins the work of managers and, in particular, industrial relations and compensation specialists in HRM. Mini-case 4.4 illustrates potential motivational issues within the context of diversity.

Mini-case 4.4: Motivation and diversity

A company operating in the fast-changing consumer goods market has to continually reorganise in order to compete. In some sectors of the business there is growth, but in others there is a need to 'down size'. The company has a diverse multi-ethnic workforce, a mix of women and men at all levels and is considered to be 'progressive' in its employment practices. The company has a well-established equal opportunities policy.

However, during the last reorganisation it became apparent (and was certainly perceived to be the case) that a disproportionately high number of ethnic minority staff and significantly more women than men were not promoted and/or were made redundant. Rumours are developing within the company that it favours white men when making decisions about promotion, downsizing and changing job practices.

Discussion questions

● What might the company need to do when planning or anticipating future staffing and structural changes?

● What might the consequences be for the company of doing nothing or taking the view that the effect of such changes are 'normal' or 'natural' or don't need to be thought about or anticipated?

 ## Change, motivation and the psychological contract

Underlying most theories of motivation or satisfaction in the workplace is an assumption that key variables are fixed or static. They tend to be non-dynamic models, that is, aspects of the individual, the organisation and the business environment are considered either unimportant or unchanging. In reality the individual, and particularly the relationship he or she enjoys with the organisation, is a dynamic phenomenon. The nature of individual, group and organisational roles and objectives continually change. Change can be a source of frustration, fear and anxiety or a challenge and renewed source of motivation – perhaps even both. Organisational change, and the manner in which it is managed, and, if appropriate, communicated, can have a lasting impact on the motivation of those involved.

When people join an organisation they metaphorically 'sign' a psychological contract. In other words, they enter into an understanding with their employer concerning expected and legitimate behaviours and outputs. This joint agreement usually includes an understanding about the level of commitment expected of employees and of support offered by the employer. In general terms, most individuals would expect equitable treatment, some form of involvement in decision making (especially in a managerial position), a certain level of job security and so forth. Major organisational change can alter these often-taken-for-granted expectations. Employers would expect employees to accept the organisational ideology and its goals, to uphold the image of the company and to show diligence and trustworthiness. At any time different individuals in an organisation might hold different psychological contracts with their employer. Major organisational change might not only violate that contract, but also affect different people in a variety of ways. Similarly, major conflict between individuals and groups and between the organisation and individuals can violate the psychological contract. Such violation can cause bitterness and resentment which might in turn lead to demotivation.

The relentless pressure on organisations to embrace greater flexibility has resulted in the emergence of the flexible organisation. Organisations are adopting flatter structures by delayering and downsizing, they are outsourcing more and employing a smaller core workforce. There is, as a result, a burgeoning peripheral group of employees, some only loosely connected to the organisation. These changes affect individuals within and around the flexible organisation. Roles are becoming broader and more dynamic, individuals are increasingly required to develop multiskill capabilities and job security is waning. These changes have far-reaching consequences for motivation and pose crucial questions for management and employee groups. Ironically, multiskilling, teamwork and change generally demand greater levels of individual motivation on the part of employees, yet all can lead to stress and a feeling of anxiety and insecurity. The motivation equation is most certainly assailed by these developments.

The issue of pay and status frequently emerges within organisations and is particularly relevant during some organisational change processes. Mini-case 4.5 illustrates a thorny problem faced during organisational change. The potential for conflict and demotivation is apparent in this real-life scenario, as is the scope for enhanced motivation – a thin line exists between the two.

Motivation and conflict

The management of conflict in organisations affects the motivation of individuals and groups. Contrary to intuitive understanding, conflict can have positive effects. Research has indicated that conflict can arouse enthusiasm in some individuals, whereas inter-group rivalry may act as a source of cohesion and encourage *esprit de corps* within groups. Schmidt (1974), following empirical research conducted among management executives in the USA, revealed both positive and negative effects of conflict. Many of these 'outcomes' can directly influence job satisfaction and affect motivation and performance in the workplace. He found that conflict can stimulate creative thinking and can inspire people to confront long-standing problems and explore new approaches. It may encourage reflection and help people clarify their views, and heighten their interest in the task at hand. It also tests people's abilities.

Mini-case 4.5: Change and motivation

This mini-case study explores the motivational issues concerning pay and status differentials in the context of the management of change.

In a medium-sized NHS Trust hospital in the UK all cleaning staff, nursing assistants and ward clerks formed a flexible, multiskilled, ward-based team of care assistants. Formal status and pay differentials between employees were reduced and many staff were upgraded and received a basic pay rise as a consequence. The new simplified grade and pay scales or 'spines', which applied to all care assistants, reduced status differentials and simplified the highly complex bonus schemes that had evolved. Some staff were required to change their shift pattern and the total hours they worked within any one week.

At the design stage, managers felt it would improve worker motivation as all would 'feel part of a team'. This would, they believed, particularly apply to the domestics who were often unaffiliated to a ward and consequently were remote from patients and from care assistant colleagues.

Pay issue

One of the major issues discussed at the change project meeting prior to implementation of the project was the proposed pay scales for these new roles. All staff would be classified as either Health Care Assistant 1 (HCA1 – the lower scale) or HCA2 (the higher pay scale) and jobs would be assessed to see into which category they fell (for example, those with supervisory responsibility would be likely to be classified as HCA2 and might be paid higher than HCA1 staff irrespective of whether they were an assistant nurse, ward clerk or domestic). All employees would have protected pay for a year, that is, even if they were placed on a scale and job rate which was below their existing pay, their income would not immediately fall.

Immediately prior to implementation the Director of HRM argued, 'What I'm interested in is whether the underlying principles are right, that is, are all the jobs, nursing [assistant], housekeeping and administration rated equally, allowing for two grades of these personnel?' The Chief Executive, responsible to the Board of Directors for the Trust budget, suggested that he had 'some difficulties with the concept of thinking that these are all valued the same. I intuitively would have put housekeeping at a lower level than administration and nursing. What I'm worried about is that in order to recruit for the administration and nursing we're going to end up with the highest paid domestic workforce in the locality.' The Director of Nursing interjected, 'It's too easy to drop back into "old speak". Why should people, just because they clean the toilet, be any different from those who make beds?'

Discussion question

Should cleaners be paid on the same scale as porters, administrators and nursing assistants? Discuss the motivational implications of these changes, drawing on theories and models presented in this chapter.

Clearly, many of these positive outcomes appear to stimulate thinking and action: they energise or motivate people. However, negative effects of conflict can lead to dissatisfaction, demotivation and reduced performance. Schmidt (1974) found that certain people felt defeated by conflict and, as a result, reduced contact with others and harboured distrust and suspicion. Parties that needed to cooperate in the interests of the organisation tended to pursue self-interest and some executives in the study left their organisation in order to escape conflict. Continued and severe conflict can have a major and sometimes lasting impact on an individual's psychological well-being. Blake and Mouton (1984) suggested that tension, anxiety and resentment result from conflictual situations which threaten individuals' personal goals and beliefs, rendering trusting relationships impossible to maintain. Kohn (1986) suggested that there is a direct link between conflict and resultant motivation. The stress which results from conflict leads to a rigidity in behaviour and thought and a reduction in motivation.

In conclusion, whereas it is thought conflict has its advantages in the workplace, the potential problems, not least to levels of motivation, can be severe. Hence, the careful management and control of conflict falls within the remit of all competent and responsible managers.

Motivation and communication

Communication within organisations, between employees and managers, is a vital ingredient of motivation. Powerful intrinsic rewards require communication to be apparent. For example, employees are likely to be motivated by recognition and constructive feedback from their line manager. It is not enough for employees to be doing a good job, more often than not some recognition of that is important. What is more, communication needs to be two-way. Expectancy theory suggests that people are motivated by attempts to achieve desired outcomes. Employees need to communicate their desired outcomes to their manager. Whereas one employee may be motivated by an end-of-year bonus another may prefer the option to work with a particular team or on a particular project and communicating these needs is essential if they are to be met.

Similarly, mis-communication, sending out inaccurate or misleading information, can cause motivational problems. Managers who promise the earth and do not deliver to employees will not be trusted again, while those who clearly and unambiguously communicate may be trusted and valued for their honesty.

Finally, giving and receiving feedback is a vital ingredient of motivation. Both giving and receiving are useful skills to acquire and skills which many, including many managers, lack. Well-delivered, timely feedback can inspire employees to achieve while poor, negative or even absent feedback can demotivate.

Motivation and diversity

Most of the theories of motivation were devised by Western, usually Anglo-American, men, primarily with little if any focus on issue of diversity in the workplace. They purport to be context-neutral and universally applicable or normative models. As we have seen in Chapter 3, individual differences are strong, not least those stimulated by cultural and gender difference. This said, there is not a well-developed body of research informing motivation in different and more diverse contexts. Considerable work has been conducted in comparative management – the examination of cultural differences and their impacts on organisations (refer to Chapter 10); however, the reader should reflect on the applicability of motivation theories to both genders and in different national and workplace contexts.

Contemporary motivation theories

Some more recent work on motivation has been briefly discussed throughout this chapter. We will now explore further modern research. Critical issues which have occupied researchers more recently have been focused on more complex contexts and jobs, for example, in computing, in learning and in long-term performance. Attention has been paid to how individuals differ and to how we can implement procedures which draw upon and integrate existing theories.

Considerable criticism has been levelled at many of the assumptions implicit in certain motivation theories. Additionally, the practicality of these models as managerial tools is questionable. More recent research in the field has tended to move away from providing all-embracing general solutions to motivation problems. Furthermore, another trend, as indicated in this chapter, is towards a consolidated perspective on the main motivation theories, one that aims to identify and work with the relationships between different theories. Also, emphasis has shifted away from the development of new motivation theories to related areas such as concern with leadership and organisational culture. Research and writing have dwelt on issues of commitment of personnel and of involvement and participation in decision making.

It is recognised that the workplace environment is changing rapidly in many cases and that people themselves reflect changes in their national cultures and subcultures. Maccoby (1988) suggests that there are five social character types, each of which differs in terms of their prime drivers. One type he argues, the self-developer, is more prevalent in the modern age. They are well suited to the demands of modern organisations: they are likely to have higher levels of education and are well imbued with problem solving, information processing and diagnostic abilities. Such people, he argues, are motivated by opportunities for expression, by challenge and development. They require management commitment on responsibilities and rewards and need to be involved in business affairs and have access to information. Clearly, this 'type-environment' fit model rejects the rather simplistic claims of Maslow and others that needs are similar for all individuals and that they are hierarchically accessed.

Progress has been made in the identification of personality dimensions and there is some agreement that there are five basic traits:

- neuroticism;
- extrovertism;
- openness to experience;
- agreeableness;
- conscientiousness.

Of these five, conscientiousness appears to relate most closely to motivation. McCrae and Costa (1990) describe persons high on this dimension as hard-working, achievement-orientated and persevering. Recently, researchers have explored the relationship between personality and different dimensions of job performance. Again, conscientiousness appears to relate most strongly to most job dimension and job performance criteria.

Whereas most traditional motivation theories suggest that individuals largely respond to organisational and other external stimuli, an alternative approach or perspective in the field of psychology suggests that we are not passive receivers and responders (Staw, 1977). Individuals may actively attempt to control factors which influence the rewards they receive. For example, they may employ ingratiation, *the process whereby people manipulate their superiors' opinion of them*, to improve their chances of being awarded desired rewards. This may explain why some employees are more successful in being granted promotion or other rewards.

Work on intrinsic motivation and commitment has shown that individuals who expect to influence or even control performance and reward outcomes for themselves devalue those outcomes if they are imposed or chosen by another. Reactance theory suggests that when freedom and control are threatened individuals are motivated to regain or reassert that freedom or control. Of concern is that if their attempts to regain freedom and control are thwarted, as they so often are in the workplace, individuals who recognise or perceive that they cannot control their rewards experience learned helplessness, a process of giving up and reducing effort. For example, in the competition for promotion that often occurs in organisations, many cannot identify the basis on which others receive promotion. This may lead the 'unsuccessful' to feel disempowered and helpless, a state of mind which may in turn prove demotivating.

Considerable work has been focused on intrinsic rewards and the potential demotivating influences of poorly applied extrinsic rewards. Malone and Lepper (1987) have categorised three types of intrinsic motives:

- need for curiosity, stimulation and arousal;
- need for competence, mastery and challenge;
- need for personal control and self-determination.

New light is shed on the old issue of pay as a source of motivation. Although pay is clearly an extrinsic reward, receiving a bonus, for example, could convey a sense of competence and, hence, satisfy an intrinsic need. Similarly, knowledge of the bonus system and, importantly, personal control over the outcomes that are to be judged, might satisfy the need for self-determination and control.

Intrinsic motivation has also been found not to be a continuous process with employees more likely to pass through motivated phases (that motivation coming from work or contacts they engage with) and less-than-motivated stages (similarly, most employees have to undertake tasks that they would prefer not to and this does not particularly motivate them).

People construct or attribute explanations, often fictitious, for events such as an individual's promotion or the award of a bonus. Heider (1958) and Kelley (1971) have made a major contribution to attribution theory. The four prime explanations given for success are effort, ability, luck and the degree of task difficulty. If an individual attributes his or her success to luck, this person is unlikely to increase motivation to ensure success continues, whereas if the individual believes effort was the root cause then a high level of motivation is likely to continue. Those with a strong internal locus of control tend to believe that events are within their personal control, whereas others attribute external causes to events. The latter may well suggest that receipt of their recent bonus was a matter of luck, the former individuals would suggest that they had earned it by effort and ability. Clearly, this work suggests that individuals differ and that the ability to motivate employees might, in part, depend on their perceived or real locus of control.

 ## Motivation and job design

It is now appropriate to move on from a theoretical and, at times, abstract consideration of how people are motivated to focus upon how knowledge of motivation theories can influence management in the design of jobs. Early concern with job design focused on attempts to improve individual motivation by paying attention to job rotation, job enlargement and job enrichment. Job enlargement involves *increasing the scope of the job, often by increasing the number of tasks to be performed.* Job enrichment is an attempt to build upon Herzberg's two-factor theory by *designing jobs which enrich individuals by giving them opportunity to increase their responsibility and involvement and which allow greater opportunity for advancement, achievement and recognition.*

Existing motivation theory has contributed significantly to job design. For example, expectancy theory predicts that jobs which emphasise the relationship between effort, performance and reward will motivate people, especially those who value an interesting and challenging work experience. Herzberg sought to apply his two-factor theory to the workplace. He argued that in order to enrich jobs, as a mechanism for ensuring satisfaction and enhanced motivation, measures would need to be taken which would enable individuals to benefit from intrinsic rewards and to avoid the potential dissatisfiers. As a consequence he suggested seven vertical loading factors implementation of which may lead to improved motivation. These are shown in Table 4.3 which relates the factors to various intrinsic and extrinsic rewards that might ensue and suggests potential managerial actions which might serve to achieve each loading category.

Table 4.3 Herzberg's vertical loading factors

Vertical loading factors	Potential managerial actions
Increase individual accountability	Enhance sense of responsibility and personal challenge, hence allowing scope for growth and advancement.
Remove controls	Remove sources of dissatisfaction resulting from a controlling style of supervision. Allow greater freedom of action and give scope for personal growth and recognition via trust.
Allocate special assignments	Delegate responsibility and interesting work, hence giving an opportunity for achievement and growth.
Introduce new tasks	Enhance the desirability of the work itself by introducing variety and challenge and, potentially, greater responsibility.
Create natural work units	Allow for enhanced recognition from one's colleagues by forming groups whose members enjoy each other's company and are otherwise compatible.
Grant additional authority	Enhanced responsibility is a form of recognition. It allows for growth and advancement and may reduce the potential dissatisfaction of having to comply with all manner of company procedures and policies.
Provide direct feedback	This provides potential for recognition and scope for coaching to facilitate growth.

The Hackman and Oldham job characteristic model

Hackman and Oldham (1980), perhaps the most significant contributors to work design theory, argued that a well-designed job may enhance employee motivation. Their work drew heavily on the theoretical arguments summarised above, particularly the contributions of Herzberg and some needs theorists, such as McClelland. Motivation increases, they suggested, when individuals achieve three critical psychological states (*see* Figure 4.6):

- experienced meaningfulness;
- experienced responsibility;
- knowledge of results.

There are five job characteristics which should encourage the three psychological states to be achieved and, hence, lead to motivated employees:

- skill variety;
- task identity;
- task significance;

- autonomy;
- feedback from the job.

This theory provides a model to guide job design.

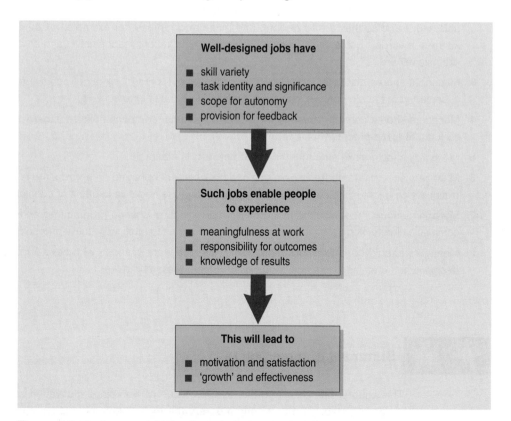

Figure 4.6 Hackman and Oldham's work design model

Source: Based on Hackman and Oldham (1980)

The outcomes from a well-designed job, which considers and incorporates the aspects listed above, include high internal work motivation, growth, general satisfaction and work effectiveness. Hence, the model considers the intrinsic aspects of motivation in addition to job characteristics and individual differences. The model can be used, especially when accompanied by the Hackman and Oldham job diagnostic survey (JDS), to calculate the overall 'motivating potential score' (MPS) for any job.

Managerial implications

Motivation is a complex subject. For managers and aspiring managers with a willingness and desire to learn how to motivate subordinates the plethora of theoretical material can appear confusing. This chapter has attempted to indicate that many of the theories do not in fact significantly contradict one another but, rather, complement each other. Collectively, they shed considerable light on the nature of workplace motivation. In very broad terms, managers need to do the following to motivate others.

1 Managers should identify the needs, drives and ambitions of each individual, the outcomes each employee wants, while recognising that people differ in their personality and needs.

2 Managers should relate these characteristics to the nature of the tasks expected of those individuals and the roles they are to perform and give opportunities, for example, for them to seek both intrinsic rewards, such as achievement, affiliation, recognition, responsibility and advancement, and extrinsic rewards.

3 Managers should clarify for individuals the potential outcomes they might achieve for their efforts, especially if these are positive, desirable, realistic and possible to achieve.

4 Managers should carefully examine their reward systems, company policies, supervision styles and so forth, to avoid potential sources of demotivation.

5 Managers should make sure that the reward system is equitable.

6 Managers should attempt to forge a balance between encouraging an appropriate level and type of rivalry, which might stimulate employees, and avoiding the negative aspects of conflict.

7 Managers should recognise the motivational implications of change programmes and utilise skills of communication to moderate the adverse effects of changes to each individual's psychological contract.

8 Managers should consider motivation theory, and the work of those who have applied this to job design, when creating or changing individual or team tasks and roles.

 Summary of main points

This chapter has examined the complex issue of workplace motivation and drawn upon a range of established and contemporary theory and empirical research. The main points made are:

- motivation theories can be subdivided between process and content theories and between those from the cognitive school and those underpinned by behaviouralist principles;

- expectancy theory is a useful explanatory model of motivation which enables us to consider other process theories, such as equity theory, and content models, such as needs and two-factor theories;

- the management of change, its communication and the involvement of people in the change process, together with the management of conflict, all have potentially profound effects on individual motivation;

- motivation theories underpin and direct efforts to enrich jobs and design tasks and roles to maximise potential motivation and/or avoid demotivation;

- there are a series of implications for management that derive from the work of motivation and job design theorists.

Conclusions

There does not appear to be one universally applicable theory of motivation. However, those presented in this chapter increase our understanding of workplace motivation considerably. Motivation is a complex, dynamic and culture-bound concept and the reader should beware of giving too much credence to simple 'solutions' which might claim to provide *the* answer. If motivation were a simple managerial task then most workplaces would be full of well-motivated employees. The extent to which they are motivated is dependent not merely on the quality of management but on many other personal and environmental factors. Clearly, what motivates people differs between individuals, is related to and influenced by context, and is both culturally dependent and ever changing.

Questions

1 To what extent and under what circumstances might a pay increase serve to motivate people?

2 How can a manager or other employee gain a practical understanding of how to motivate others from studying needs theories?

3 Under what circumstances might organisational change motivate people? Will all people be equally motivated or demotivated by change?

4 How can the work of call-centre employees be designed in an attempt to reduce demotivation?

References

Adams, J. S. (1963) 'Towards an understanding of inequity', *Journal of Abnormal Social Psychology*, 67, pp. 422–36.

Adams, J. S. (1965) 'Inequity in social exchange' in Berkowitz, L. (ed.) *Advances in Experimental Social Psychology, Vol. 2*. New York: Academic Press.

Alderfer, C. P. (1972) *Existence, Relatedness and Growth*. New York: Collier Macmillan.

Blackburn, R. M. and Mann, M. (1979) *The Working Class in the Labour Market*. London: Macmillan.

Blake, R. R. and Mouton, J. S. (1984) *Solving Costly Organizational Conflicts*. San Francisco: Jossey-Bass.

Blum, M. L. (1949) *Industrial Psychology and its Social Foundations*. New York: Harper & Brothers.

Campbell, J. P. and Pritchard, D. (1976) 'Motivation theory in industrial and organizational psychology' in Dunnette, M. D. (ed.) *Handbook of Industrial and Organizational Psychology*. Chicago: Rand McNally, pp. 63–130.

Goodman, P. A. and Friedman, A. (1971) 'An examination of Adams' theory of equity', *Administrative Science Quarterly*, 16.

Hackman, J. R. and Oldham, G. R. (1980) *Work Redesign*. Reading, MA: Addison-Wesley.

Hall, D. T. and Nougaim, K. E. (1968) 'An examination of Maslow's need hierarchy in an organizational setting', *Organizational Behavior and Human Performance*, 3, pp. 12–35.

Heider, F. (1958) *The Psychology of Interpersonal Relations*. New York: Wiley.

Herzberg, F. (1968) 'One more time: How do you motivate employees?', *Harvard Business Review*, 46(1), pp. 53–62.

House, R. J. and Wigdor, L. A. (1967) 'Herzberg's dual-factor theory of job satisfaction and motivation: A review of the evidence and a criticism', *Personnel Psychology*, 20 (Winter), pp. 369–90.

Iaffaldano, M. T. and Muchinsky, P. M. (1985) 'Job satisfaction and job performance: A meta-analysis', *Psychological Bulletin*, 97, pp. 251–73.

Kelley, H. H. (1971) *Attribution in Social Interaction*. Morristown, NJ: General Learning Press.

Kerr, S. (1975) 'On the folly of rewarding A, while hoping for B', *Academy of Management Journal*, 18, pp. 769–83.

Kohn, A. (1986) *No Contest: The Case against Competition*. Boston: Houghton Mifflin.

Lawler, E. E. (1973) *Motivation in Work Organizations*. New York: Brooks-Cole Publishing.

Lawler, E. E. and Suttle, J. L. (1972) 'A causal correlation test of the need hierarchy concept', *Organizational Behavior and Human Performance*, 7, pp. 265–87.

Locke, E. A. (1968) 'Towards a theory of task motivation and incentives', *Organizational Behavior and Human Performance*, 3, pp. 157–89.

Locke, E. A., Shaw, K. N., Saari, L. M. and Lantham, G. P. (1981) 'Goal setting and task performance: 1969–1980', *Psychological Bulletin*, 90, pp. 125–52.

McClelland, D. C. (1961) *The Achieving Society*. New York: Van Nostrand Reinhold.

McClelland, D. C. (1962) 'Business drive and national achievement', *Harvard Business Review*, 40 (July–August), pp. 99–112.

McClelland, D. C. and Boyatzis, R. E. (1984) 'The need for close relationships and the manager's job' in Kolb, D. M., Rubin, I. M. and Macintyre, J. M. (eds) *Organizational Psychology: Readings on Human Behavior in Organizations*. New York: Prentice-Hall.

Maccoby, M. (1988) *Why Work: Motivating and Leading the New Generation*. New York: Simon and Schuster.

McCrae, R. R. and Costa, P. T., Jr (1990) *Personality in Adulthood*. New York: Guilford Press.

Malone, T. W. and Lepper, M. R. (1987) 'Making learning fun: A taxonomy of intrinsic motivations for learning', in Snow, R. E. and Farr, M. J. (eds) *Aptitude, Learning and Instruction: Conative and Affective Process Analyses, Vol. III*. Hillsdale, NJ: Erlbaum, pp. 223–53

Maslow, A. H. (1943) 'A theory of human motivation', *Psychological Review*, 50(4), pp. 370–96.

Pinder, C. (1984) *Work Motivation*. Glenview, IL: Scott, Foresman.

Porter, L. W. and Lawler, E. E. (1968) *Managerial Attitudes and Performance*. Homewood, IL: Irwin.

Schmidt, W. H. (1974) 'A powerful force for (good or bad) change', *Management Review*, December, pp. 4–10.

Schneider, B. (1985) 'Organizational behavior', *Annual Review of Psychology*, 36.

Schweiger, D. M. and Leana, C. R. (1986) 'Participation in decision making', in Locke, E. A. (ed.), *Generalizing from Laboratory to Field Settings*. Lexington, MA: Lexington Books, pp. 147–66.

Staw, B. M. (1977) 'Motivation in organizations: towards synthesis and redirection', in Staw, B. M. and Salancik, G. R. (eds) *New Directions in Organizational Behavior*. Chicago: St Clair Press.

Tolman, E. and Honzik, C. (1930) 'Introduction and removal of reward and maze performance of rats', *University of California Publications in Psychology*, 4, pp. 257–75.

Tyler, T. R. and Bies, R. J. (1990) 'Beyond formal procedures: The interpersonal context of procedural justice', in Carroll, J. S. (ed.), *Applied Social Psychology and Organizational Settings*. Hillsdale, NJ: Lawrence Erlbaum, pp. 77–98.

Vroom, V. H. (1964) *Work and Motivation*. New York: Wiley.

Further reading

Herzberg, F. (1968) 'One more time: How do you motivate employees?' *Harvard Business Review*, 46(1), pp. 53–62.

Huczynski, A. and Buchanan, D. (2007) *Organizational Behavior*. 6th edn, Harlow: Financial Times, Prentice Hall.

Lawler, E. E., III (1971) *Pay and Organizational Effectiveness*. New York: McGraw-Hill.

Maccoby, M. (1988) *Why Work: Motivating and Leading The New Generation*. New York: Simon and Schuster. Outlines the changing nature of the workplace and categorises people into five types. It outlines the characteristics and sources of motivation and demotivation of each.

Maslow, A. H. (1987) *Motivation and Personality*, 3rd edn. New York: Harper & Row.

Moorhead, G. and Griffin, R. W. (1995) *Organizational Behavior*, 4th edn. Boston: Houghton Mifflin, Chapters 4–6.

Mullins, L. J. (2002) *Management and Organisational Behaviour*, 6th Harlow: Financial Times Prentice Hall.

Internet sites

Google or other search engines highlight many sites covering motivation theories such as those illustrated above. No one site has outstanding quality and they do change frequently but few stones are left unturned by the sites under 'motivational theories'. Many university lecturers place their module outlines and sometimes their notes on open access. These often supplement textbook understandings. Other sites can be useful, such as:

www.businessballs.com/motivation This free site has some useful material including links to most of the 'big names' – McClelland, Adair, Herzberg and a lot more. It is well worth a visit.

5

Groups and teams

Hugh Davenport

Learning outcomes

- On completion of this chapter you should be able to:
- understand 'our' many needs to belong to different groups;
- discriminate between groups, psychological groups and teams;
- differentiate between formal and informal groups;
- explain a model for group development and growth;
- understand the dynamics of team roles and norms;
- discuss the dynamics of group performance, effectiveness and cohesiveness;
- differentiate between inter- and intra-group conflict and behaviour;
- appreciate the role technology can play within teams;
- consider the impact of technology on team functioning and communication;
- appreciate what global, cross-cultural, virtual and self-directed teams are;
- appreciate some of the problems inherent with working in groups and teams;
- appreciate communication networks.

Key concepts

- groups and teams
- formal and informal groups
- psychological groups
- team development
- self-directed and self-managed teams
- team roles
- group norms
- team and group effectiveness and cohesion
- conformity and groupthink
- technology, communication and change
- networks and virtual teams
- global and cross-cultural teams.

Most activities that take place in an organisation require some degree of coordination through the operation of group working. Many organisational goals cannot be achieved by members working alone; thus most individuals spend an increasing amount of time working with others in groups. The classical approach to organisation ignored the importance of groups and the social factors at work, but the writings of Elton Mayo and others soon created a cult of the group, and this continues unabated today, albeit in the guise of teams and teamworking. Within this scenario, it is an essential requirement that leaders and organisations should understand the nature of groups and teams, their processes and their behaviour. If managers are to lead and influence the behaviour of a team, team members need to be aware of factors which influence their performance and effectiveness.

Introduction

A popular and important aspect of work is that it is increasingly conducted in groups. Some of the reasons for this increased interest in work groups and teams stems from the rapidly changing conditions facing today's organisations. Organisational restructuring is leading to flatter structures, wider spans of control and a general reduction in layers of management. Following on from this comes the inevitable complementary increase in the empowerment of employees. All of these aspects lead to a greater emphasis on the importance of groups and teamworking. Additionally, the impact of global economic competition, increasing diversity within the workforce and the expanding role played by technology suggest that new ways of working within these teams are required. Within this increasingly volatile scenario Stough *et al.* (2000) have identified that the 'concept of teams and teamwork is increasingly becoming an important key to productivity and employee satisfaction in the contemporary workplace'. Within this heightened team philosophy the successes or failures of teams can be both dramatic and visible, making the need to understand group and team effectiveness a crucial aspect for organisations wanting to thrive in these new conditions. This chapter will investigate the concepts of groups, psychological groups and teams. We will also explore some of the factors which affect their functioning, performance and effectiveness. Mini-case 5.1 explores the characteristics of one such team.

Why gather in groups?

Before identifying and exploring what a group is, it is important to understand why people feel the need to gather in groups and why organisations promote their importance. Having looked into these general areas we will start to focus on the different types of group and the needs those different groups are satisfying. We congregate in social gatherings to satiate our need for it. 'It' is what might be termed a *sense of belonging*. Gathering in groups has always been a characteristic of human behaviour. We are, in Aronson's (2007) words, 'social animals', and often need interaction with others to function effectively as individuals.

However alluring and seductive the above sentiments are, they do not give the whole picture of why groups form and people join them. People do not join groups simply to flock around others, although that may appear to be the case sometimes. Most people belong to a whole variety of groups, both in and out of work, each providing different benefits to its members and satisfying various needs.

Security and protection make up one aspect of why we might want to gather together.

Employees who feel their jobs are under threat from new technology may well join together to reduce their levels of insecurity and fear.

The members of a new product design team may well feel more secure in their decisions because the responsibility for a bad decision is shared with, and spread among, others. A group, without being aware of it, can dissipate the risk.

Mini-case 5.1 Team Ellen

Around the world in 71 days (and a bit)

There can be fewer starker examples of individual heroics and achievements than Ellen MacArthur's staggering circumnavigation of the globe in a record time of 71 days 14 hrs 18 mins 33 secs (to be precise!). It is also a wonderful example of teamwork, often, and quite literally, at a distance, and how the single-handed heroics and brilliance of a team member can sometimes overshadow the performance of the team.

Ellen has herself been at pains to stress the teamworking nature of her feat. For example it took a team of 30 people more than 30,000 hours to build *B&Q* (her boat) over a period of seven months. The whole project was funded to the tune of £4 million by the Kingfisher Group using their DIY company, B&Q, as the main sponsor. But the real teamwork started, ironically, when she was 'all at sea'.

Team Ellen had a very diverse and cross-cultural feel to it:

- Mark Turner (Britain) was the project director. He was often her first point of contact and the 'emotional punchbag'. Be it three a.m. or Christmas Day, he gave Ellen advice or listened to her frustrations. He also decided who Ellen should consult about specific problems.

- Neil Graham (Australia) was the technical director. Having supervised the building project, he was well placed to provide technical solutions for Ellen to carry out at a distance. Daily contact with Ellen would also involve Olivier Allard (France), the expert when it came to the boat's structure, rigging and engineering.

- Charles Darbyshire (Britain) was the technology manager tasked with talking through any communication-type problems, with Rudi Stein (Sweden) being called upon for additional electronics support.

- Lou Newlands (Britain) was the team's media manager. She was responsible for controlling and managing the time-sensitive requests of the media and balancing these against the incessant demands of the record attempt. Kate Steven (Britain) acted as liaison with the sponsors B&Q and Castorama.

- Loik Gallon (France) was the 'other' skipper of *B&Q*, looking after the boat both before and after the challenge. He was also 'in post' to offer sailing advice.

- Ellen's first point of contact for weather was with an American company, and the on-call doctor was an experienced Canadian yachtsman. Juliet Wilson

(Britain) was Ellen's nutritionist and Claudio Stampi (Italy), based at the Chronobiology Institute in Boston, received data on her heart rate and sleeping patterns.

So finally, to rapturous applause, Ellen MacArthur crossed the finish line at 2229 GMT on Monday 7th February to be hailed as the 'greatest sailor in the world'. But maybe it was really all about the 'greatest sailing team'? She said 'It's always been about a team. Thanks to our partners, friends and supporters. Without them we would be nowhere.'

Discussion questions

1 Discuss some of the typical problems which might be encountered when working with such a functionally and culturally diverse team.

2 What would be some of the issues for Ellen when working so remotely from the rest of the team? Which of these issues might more regular teleworkers encounter? How might an organisation, or the teleworker, overcome these?

3 Do you consider Team Ellen to be a proper team? Why or why not?

Regular interactions with a set of people with whom we are familiar can act to fulfil the needs for affiliation and social contact (*see* Chapter 3 for a discussion of needs theories in organisations). At a deeper level, needs for friendship and self-worth are met.

Groups can also give us prestige, recognition and status among our peers.

The phrase 'the whole is greater than the sum of its parts' highlights a seductive property of groups: that they represent synergy. The unachievable becomes possible through group action. As we will see below, informal groups and networks can also provide a mechanism for people to exercise power, an avenue which would not be open to them under the formal structure (*see also* Chapter 8 on power).

Illustration in film

The Great Escape (and *Chicken Run*)

The Great Escape is a story of American and British airmen set in a German prisoner-of-war camp during the Second World War. They form a committee, develop an escape plan and eventually some of them do escape. Teamwork, co-ordination, planning, sabotage, the loose cannon doing his own thing (Steve McQueen) – it's got everything. Consider to what extent team success is due to the individual personalities and role performances of the team members.

Comment on the interpersonal processes within the team, its norms and level of cohesion. Is there greater conflict within the group of escapees or between them and their captors?

If you prefer your films more animated watch the 'same' story unfold in *Chicken Run*.

Groups and teams

What exactly is meant by a group? Consider the following groups:

- 500 ecstatic fans witnessing pop band Circuits performing at a club;
- the newly formed European sales team who have not yet met each other but communicate and interconnect on a daily basis using a range of new technology;
- the comprehensively beaten, but informally run, pub quiz team;
- delayed passengers on the 8.15 train from Euston who together, while sitting in their compartment, brainstorm a letter of complaint and form a commuters' action group;
- the singer Ian McNabb strumming away, in his garden, to a dozen friends;
- the victorious village Sunday morning football team;
- the two dozen residents organising a play and celebration to commemorate the 200th anniversary of the Blisworth Tunnel.

Which of these 'groups' are merely aggregates of people, which of them are something more meaningful, and which of the examples may be categorised as teams?

Groups

There are a number of ways of defining a group. Charles Handy (1993: 150) defines a group as *'any collection of people who perceive themselves to be a group'*. However, this is of limited use when considering effective or ineffective groups in organisational settings and situations. In deciding which of the above groups are something more than merely collections of individuals who just happen to perceive themselves as a group, we are forced to refocus and sharpen our definition.

Arnold *et al.* (2005) expand upon Handy's definition of a group: *'Two or more people who are perceived by themselves or others as a social entity.'*

A more meaningful approach comes from Schein (1988), who frames the group in psychological terms. That is, a group is any number of people:

- who interact with one another;
- who are psychologically aware of one another; and
- who perceive themselves to be a group.

Clearly, this brings into play the ideas that interaction must take place and the importance of awareness.

So the Circuits concert spectators in the list above are not a group, because they do not fulfil all of Schein's criteria. When we use the words 'groups' or 'group relationship' we are, more than likely, referring to the existence of a psychological relationship.

Teams

Social psychology may still talk about groups and group work but organisations are primarily interested in teams and effective teamworking. The focus on teams in organisations represents a move away from a Taylorist view of employees as costs, to a more dynamic approach of viewing people as an investment (*see* Chapter 2). With an increasing concentration on working across functional and geographical divides, and an emphasis on flexibility, empowerment and innovation, the organisations of the twenty-first century will foster collaborative teamworking cultures.

That teamworking is popular cannot be doubted. A survey by the Industrial Society (1995) of 500 HR managers found that 40 per cent worked in organisations with self-managed teams. The average team had around eight people, and the main reasons cited for their use were improved customer service, increased staff motivation and the quality of output. Kreitner *et al.* (2002: 323) quote from a number of newspaper articles about major companies (Siemens, Motorola, Fiat, Ford) which emphasise in different ways their commitment to teams and teamworking. As Kreitner *et al.* say: '*All these huge global companies have staked their future competitiveness on teams and teamwork.*'

According to the Learning and Skills Council (LSC), UK employers value communication skills and teamworking above leadership in the 'soft skills' they look for in a workforce. The National Employers Skills Survey 2005, another recent piece of research from the LSC, also showed the major skills gaps employers are currently facing relate to 'soft skills'. Over half of the employers surveyed cited teamworking and customer handling as gaps in most employees' skill sets.

But what exactly is a team as compared to a 'work group'? Guzzo and Dickson (1996) argue that it is sometimes impossible to distinguish between groups and teams at work and that it is probably a pointless exercise. Martin (2005) states that a team '*implies a small, cohesive group that works effectively as a single unit through being focused on a common task*'. Katzenbach and Smith (1999: 15) in their landmark research present a more comprehensive definition: '*a team is a small number of people with complementary skills who are committed to a common purpose, performance goals, and approach for which they hold themselves mutually accountable*'. Further, they describe a number of groups and teams which distinguish between different levels of collective performance ranging from working groups and pseudo groups to potential teams, real teams and high-performance teams. Their work is useful because it starts to distinguish between real teams and groups of people who may often be called teams but are anything but teams. Table 5.1 extends Schein's definition of a psychological group further to include more specific teamworking elements.

Drawing on Table 5.1 it is possible to consider an effective team as one where:

- there is a clear understanding of the team's objectives;
- there is among the team members the range of skills and know-how needed to deal effectively with the team's tasks;
- a range of team types exists within the team;

Table 5.1 Defining a team

Defining a team
● Definable membership
● Shared communication network
● Shared sense of collective identity and purpose
● Shared goals
● Group consciousness
● Interdependence
● Interaction
● Group structure and roles
● Ability to act in a unitary manner

Source: Based on Huczynski and Buchanan (2007) and Adair (1986).

● team members have respect and trust for each other, both as individuals and for the contribution each makes to the team's performance;

● some form of team rewards and group bonus system exists.

Self-directed and self-managed teams

The notion of self-directed teams has grown out of the work conducted in the Swedish car manufacturing industry (Norstedt and Aguren, 1973; Valery, 1974; Thomas, 1974). One of the best-known experiments was conducted in the engine factory of the Saab–Scania Group at Sodertalje. From earlier experiments, the company decided to redesign the factory layout. The new layout consisted of a conveyor loop which moved the engine blocks to seven assembly groups, each with three members. Each group assembled a complete engine and decided for themselves how their work was to be distributed and scheduled. The whole assembly process was not mechanically driven; each group was simply given 30 minutes to complete each engine and the group decided how that time was spent. Needless to say, productivity increased and labour turnover dropped, product quality improved and absenteeism fell. The assembly workers developed into a more cohesive group who had real ownership of and pride in their output. In time, through 'natural' job rotation, they each developed all, or most, of the skills required to do any part of the engine assembly.

This style of work organisation became known as 'autonomous work groups' and the success of these groups led to the 'high-performance teams approach' used by Digital Equipment (Perry, 1984). This in turn has led to the growing acceptance of self-directed teams. A number of definitions are used to describe self-managed teams. Buchanan (1987: 41) developed one of the earlier descriptions: '*A work group allocated an overall task and given discretion over how the work is to be done. These groups are self-regulating and work without direct supervision.*' They might be viewed as a small group of employees responsible for an *entire* work process or segment. To varying degrees, team members work together to improve their operations or products, plan and control their work and handle day-to-day problems. Added to this they may even manage the recruitment and selection of fellow team members, such as their leader or supervisor. They often become involved in company-wide issues, such as quality and business planning. Salem *et al.* (1994) identified some typical 'benefits', including the following:

- reduced absenteeism;
- increased productivity;
- increased employee satisfaction, morale and cohesiveness;
- multiskilled workforce;
- increased flexibility in work practices;
- decreased need for managers.

Clearly, many of the potential benefits listed above were identified some years previously in the Saab–Scania research of the 1970s involving autonomous work groups. A criticism one could level is that the self-directed and self-managed teams of the 1990s are simply the autonomous work groups of the 1970s under a different name. This criticism may be justified; however, self-directed teams have tended to take responsibility and empowerment a stage further from that enjoyed by the work groups of the 1970s. The types of organisation which promote and develop the use of self-directed teams undoubtedly differ from the more traditional organisation in a variety of ways:

- fewer layers of managers and supervisors;
- reward systems are often skill- or team-based, rather than seniority-based;
- leaders may be elected by the team;
- the leader is more of a coach and facilitator than a director or authority figure;
- information is shared with all employees;
- employees learn all the jobs and tasks required of the team.

Self-directed teams certainly appear to be a blueprint for how the organisation of the future will function: orientated around learning, shared ownership, trust, autonomy and flexibility.

However, as with the development of any new way of working, they are not without their problems. Salem *et al.* (1994) also identified some typical 'pitfalls', including the following:

- the difficulty of rescinding the system once it is established and experienced by the workers;
- varying levels and degrees of resistance by elements in the organisation;
- increasing peer pressure and its consequences.

Balkema and Molleman (1999) discuss a range of barriers to the development of self-organising teams. The first category they identify has to do with the opportunities for self-organisation provided by management. The implementation of self-organising teams affects the 'vertical boundary' between lower-level management and workers at the operational level. The role of the manager needs to become more that of a facilitator and coach. Managers may resist such a new role, supposing that the self-organising team structure will be a threat to their position. This scenario may also be an affront to their already established psychological contract, and may even be tinged with a fear that they cannot facilitate and coach. As noted above, self-organising teams reduce the hierarchy, and managers will realise that this could cost them their jobs or at the very least alter their positions radically. Other barriers identified by Balkema and Molleman pertain to the attitudes of the workers, the skills and learning abilities of the workers involved, and barriers related to the actual need for self-organising teams.

In the current fervour for flatter organisations, teamworking is seen as a panacea for many of the accompanying organisational problems, and self-directed teams (SDTs) are viewed as a potential antidote for the accompanying 'unmanaged' hierarchy.

As Levinson Institute CEO Gerry Kraines explained to *Training* magazine (Gordon, 1994), 'I've yet to hear anyone explain satisfactorily what "team accountability" means. Every time [the Levinson Institute] has checked out a claim of an extremely effective SDT, we've found there's always an accountable manager involved.'

Brower (1995: 13) suggests the term 'empowering teams', which means 'teams that plan, carry out and improve their value-adding work. To do this they develop the ableness of their members so that they become learning teams and engines of development.' What is clear is that to create and support 'empowering teams' or their like will require a thorough transformation of our organisational, managerial and informational beliefs, paradigms and practices. This is a very radical shift for most organisations.

Communities of practice

With the development of knowledge management and organisational learning a number of processes have evolved to help capture, transfer and use this most precious of commodities. Some organisations, including BP Amoco (Greenes, 2002), have developed the notion of communities of practice. These are informal groups of people who are bound together by shared experience and a passion for joint endeavour. They share their learning, experience and knowledge in free-flowing ways that foster and encourage new approaches to problems and transfer this learning from one part of the organisation to another. However, these 'communities' are not necessarily tied up with the traditional structure and boundaries of the organisation. Wenger and Snyder (2000) discuss engineers from different companies who are all engaged in deep-water drilling and thus all encounter a multiplicity of similar problems. Other organisations develop similar networks with their supply-chain partners.

With the uptake of remote working such as teleworking and the dawning of a new age as symbolised by the birth of virtual teams, the necessity for capturing and facilitating this transfer of experience and learning seems even more of a necessity. Communities of practice are likely to work favourably if the interaction required builds upon existing patterns of interaction such as small groups of people who do similar tasks or existing friendships. However, one of the principles is to encourage a diversity of interactions between people, departments and business units that have not had much to do with each other in the past.

So these communities of practice will necessitate a very different type of 'team' and way of working together that hitherto may not have been fully understood within the organisation.

Groups within groups

One can view groups and teams as a series of concentric circles. The outer circle defines all groups and includes psychological groups and teams. The middle circle, in turn, includes all teams. Not all groups are teams, but all teams are psychological groups. In order to be effective, a team must possess all of the criteria for being a psychological group and a group. This is illustrated in Figure 5.1.

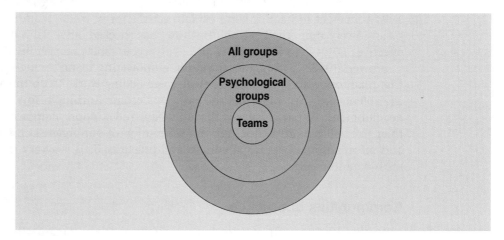

Figure 5.1 Groups within groups

Illustration in film

Daylight

When an explosion blocks New York's Hudson River Tunnel at both ends, ex-Emergency Medical Services Chief Kit Latura (played with typical aplomb by Sylvester Stallone) is the only one with the know-how and experience to save the day. Risking his life, he seeks out and joins a group of survivors in the tunnel. There he finds a feisty writer, an elderly couple, a famous action-man, a quarrelling family, some young hoodlums, a security guard and even a Weimaraner dog. Can he put his own past tragedies behind him (in similar vein to the film *Cliffhanger*) and lead this disparate group to safety?

Daylight, along with a whole range of other action disaster movies, shows a mixed collection of very individual people becoming transformed into a psychological group and even going through one of the various group development models, such as Tuckman's.

In concluding our discussion of groups and teams perhaps all we need say is that teams differ from groups in the extent to which their members are interdependent (there is more interdependence in teams) and that the team as a whole, rather than the individual members, has performance and reward goals. Clearly, the boundaries between the two are blurred, but the important issue is to recognise that there are some general and significant differences between the two. In summary, external circumstances (e.g. a delayed train) can change a small group of people (the passengers) into a fully functioning psychological group (with the objective of producing a letter of complaint) or even a team (the commuters' action group).

Formal and informal groups and teams

Formal groups

Organisations are constantly organising and reorganising their processes and structures. This may involve disbanding various groups and creating others which are formally constructed, usually by middle or senior managers. Formal groups are, therefore, consciously created to accomplish the organisation's collective mission and to achieve specific organisational and departmental objectives. They are primarily concerned with the coordination of work activities and are task-orientated. They are embedded and entrapped in the fabric, hierarchy and structure of the organisation: people are brought together on the basis of defined roles. The nature of the tasks undertaken is a predominant feature of the formal group. Goals are identified and developed by management, and rules, relationships and norms of behaviour are established. They have been consciously created and organised, recruited for and put together by somebody for a reason. Formal groups are an important element of the organisational structure (*see* Chapter 7).

Because the individuals in formal groups share some commonality of objectives, goals and (occasionally) rewards, they are more akin to teams – formal teams. They assist people to:

- accomplish goals much less haphazardly than they would in informal groups;
- coordinate the activities of the functions of the organisation;
- establish logical authority relationships among people and between positions;
- apply the concepts of specialisation and division of labour;
- create more group cohesion as a result of a common set of goals.

If the above list reflects how formal groups assist people to achieve in certain ways, what are the things they are trying to achieve? Charles Handy (1993) identified a number of major organisational purposes for groups and teams. They are to:

- distribute work, having brought together a particular set of skills, talents and responsibilities;
- manage and control work;

- facilitate the problem-solving process by bringing together all of the available capabilities;
- pass on decisions or information to those who need to know;
- gather ideas, information and suggestions;
- test and ratify decisions;
- coordinate and facilitate necessary liaison;
- increase commitment and involvement;
- resolve arguments and disputes between different functions, levels and divisions.

Informal groups

Running alongside and within, cutting across and around these formal groups and teams there exist a number of informal groups, such as:

- the office quiz or bowls team;
- the theatre-going group or the Friday lunchtime people;
- the Monday morning 'let's talk about the weekend' group or the folk who regularly swap the latest music CDs;
- the 'let's moan about the organisation' people.

The list is endless.

We can define an informal group as *a collection of individuals who become a group when members develop certain interdependencies, influence one another's behaviour and contribute to mutual need satisfaction.* Informal groups are based more on personal relationships and agreement of group members than on any defined role relationships. They simply emerge in the organisation, from the informal interaction of the members of the organisation. They may be born out of shared interests, friendship or some other social aspect. What informal groups satisfy, in a way that the formal group may not, is a sense of belonging, the idea that we can be wanted, needed and included for what we are and not because the organisation has put us to work with these other people. These informal groups can also satisfy a range of other needs. They can:

- reduce feelings of insecurity and anxiety and provide each other with social support;
- fulfil affiliation needs for friendship, love and support;
- help to define our sense of identity and maintain our self-esteem;
- pander to our social nature, as 'social animals': they are a means of entertainment, alleviating boredom and fatigue, boosting morale and personal satisfaction;
- provide guidelines on generally acceptable behaviour: they help shape group and organisational norms;
- cater for those often ill-defined tasks which can only be performed through the combined efforts of a number of individuals working together.

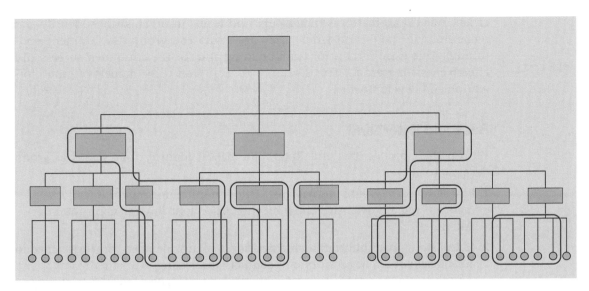

Figure 5.2 Informal groups within the formal structure

As can be seen from the list at the beginning of this section, membership of a group can cut across the boundaries created by the formal structure. Individuals from different parts and levels of the organisation may all belong to the same informal group. Informal groups tend to have a more fluid, flexible and variable membership than formal groups, which tend to be fairly 'permanent'. Figure 5.2 illustrates the way informal groups can exist within the formal structure of an organisation.

 ## Stages of group and team development

With the increasing focus in organisations on groups and teams, there is a growing need to understand how groups form, grow, develop, mature and change. There are a number of models and frameworks which have attempted to encapsulate some, if not all, of the thinking in this area.

These models talk about:

● teams which 'form' and finally 'adjourn'; or

● 'undeveloped' teams which become 'mature'; or

● teams which pass through a variety of 'stages' from 'mutual acceptance and membership' to 'control and organisation'.

Whatever the language of the model, most start with a newly formed, undeveloped group of people who end up being a fully formed, structured and cohesive team. The important point is that, whatever the model, each provides us with a framework, a point of reference, a shared language. The models are a vehicle for aiding discussion and understanding; it does not matter exactly what the stage is called. What does matter is that groups and teams in organisations identify and recognise the stages and where they are along the group development continuum. This is important for team-building and for the continued success and effectiveness of a group. This section now examines three models of group formation and development.

Bass and Ryterband

Within their model Bass and Ryterband (1979) identify four stages in group development.

1 *First stage* – developing mutual trust. Through initial mistrust and fear, group members remain defensive and limit their behaviour through conformity and ritual.

2 *Second stage* – communication and decision making. Members, having learned to accept each other, begin to express conflicts and feelings – in other words, emotions. Norms start to be established and members develop a sense of caring for each other. Open communications develop, along with more constructive problem-solving and decision-making strategies.

3 *Third stage* – motivation and productivity. Members are involved with the work of the group, cooperating with each other instead of competing. They are now more readily motivated by intrinsic rewards, such as a high level of productivity.

4 *Fourth stage* – control and organisation. Work is allocated by agreement and abilities. Members can work independently and the organisation of the group is flexible and can adapt to new challenges.

Woodcock

Woodcock (1979) also views the pattern of team development as having four stages.

1 *Stage 1 – The Undeveloped Team.* This stage is dominated by feelings not being dealt with, or even not being allowed. Although there are unclear objectives at this stage, any established policy prevails. The group is epitomised by a lack of shared understanding about what needs to be done, the leader often having a different view from the led. Personal weaknesses are covered up because the group lacks the skill to support or eliminate them. Mistakes are used as 'evidence' to convict people rather than as opportunities to learn.

2 *Stage 2 – The Experimenting Team.* The team begins to be willing to experiment and thus risky issues are raised. There are higher levels of listening than in the previous stage and members start to raise their more personal issues and feelings. The group, almost inevitably, becomes more inward-looking and may even reject other groups and individuals.

3 *Stage 3 – The Consolidating Team.* More often than not the team decides to adopt a more systematic approach, leading to a more methodical way of working. Rules and procedures are now the agreed operating rules of the team, rather than the edicts from on high, as they were in an earlier stage. The improved relationships

and more exciting methods experienced in Stage 2 are maintained but they are used to build the rules and working procedures which the team will use.

4 *Stage 4 – The Mature Team.* The openness and improved relationships of Stage 2 and the systematic approach of Stage 3 are now used to complete the task of building a really mature team. High levels of flexibility become paramount. Appropriate leadership is established for different situations. There is optimum use of energy and ability. Development increasingly becomes a priority because continued success depends on continued development. Trust, openness, honesty, cooperation and confrontation, and a continual review of results, become part of the way of the team's life – is this team nirvana?

Tuckman

The final model presented (Tuckman, 1965) is probably the one most often quoted, in no small part because of the rhythm of its sequence, which makes it easy to remember: forming, storming, norming, performing and adjourning.

Forming – initially, this stage is involved with the bringing together of a number of people who may be somewhat anxious, wary and unsure. Clearly in this scenario there are few, if any, rules. Ambiguity and confusion reign over the group. Everybody is busy finding out who the other people are. Members are keen to establish their personal identities in the group and make a personal impression, and it is for this reason that considerable anxiety, and even fear, may be generated. Adding to this anxiety is the potential lack of focus and clarity around the purpose of the group and uncertainty about the task ahead and its terms of reference. This anxiety reveals itself in hesitant behaviour, defensiveness and 'scapegoating' aimed at factions outside the group.

Storming – having traversed the slippery slope of 'forming', the group now tackles the choppy waters of 'storming'. This is a period of disagreement, frustration and potential confrontation but every group must go through it. Out of conflict can come good, and the group needs to cling to this sentiment at this time. The potential conflict is there because members now feel more confident to challenge each other, and to express their views more openly and forcefully. There will be some jockeying for positions of power, and frustration at apparent lack of progress. The storming stage is important as it raises the energy (and activity) level of the group and can lead on to significant changes in creativity and innovation. One is reminded of the film *Jerry Maguire*. Embroiled in a heated discussion with a hot-headed football client, sports agent and manager Jerry turns and walks away. The footballer follows him, saying 'Hey, you see that's the difference between us. You think we're fighting and I think we're finally talking!'

Norming – at this stage there is a clear sense of group identity, and guidelines, standards, procedures, roles and structure become formally established. Emotions are now expressed constructively and listened to! In organisational settings, it is at this stage that management should intervene if they are looking to influence the group because it is at this stage that those all-important group norms (the rules for all sorts of behaviour within the group) are developed and established. Intervention is required because it shouldn't be taken for granted that what is put in place by the group will automatically lead to effectiveness in management terms. If the Hawthorne Studies of the 1920s and 1930s (*see* Chapter 2) showed us anything, it was that group norms can certainly influence, and often impose, limits and restrictions on all sorts of key areas like productivity and quality. If dysfunctional groups become fully developed, with an entrenched culture and norms, it is much more difficult to alter, or influence, their members' attitudes and behaviour.

Performing – having progressed through the earlier stages, a team will have created some structure and cohesiveness to work effectively. With these 'mechanics' in place, the team can now concentrate on the achievement of its objectives. It is in this stage that task performance is at its most effective. The group should now be close and supportive, open and trusting, resourceful and effective.

As most teams have a limited life, Tuckman and Jensen (1977) added a further stage to the model, which they referred to as *adjourning*. The group may disband, either because the task and objectives have been achieved to a satisfactory level or because the members have left. However, before disbanding, it is important for the group members to reflect upon their time together – what went well, what didn't go so well and what might they do differently next time and how? Such reflection may be a great source of learning for both the individuals concerned and the organisation.

Illustration in film

The Breakfast Club

The Breakfast Club, directed by John Hughes, is set in the library of an American high school: it's the weekend and five students representing different stereotypes have Saturday detention. There's a prom queen, a nerd, a jock, a misfit and a criminal. These five students have never met each other before, and each is being punished for a different act of organisational misbehaviour. Shut in together in the school library for the day, they are forced to get to know each other. Being from such widely different backgrounds and having such completely different personalities, it's inevitable that some frictions develop. At first they argue and appear to dislike each other. However, as the day progresses they learn that behind the exterior and stereotypes, they are all very similar.

Look out for the 'break points' in the action when the students move from forming, to storming, to norming and finally performing. Try to spot when the leadership of this group moves from one character to another.

Table 5.2 summarises the different models discussed above, and the stages which they propose. All of these models certainly look very straightforward. A group moves from Stage 1 to Stage 2 and onwards to Stage 3 and so on, but is the process as simple and straightforward as this statement implies? Unfortunately, where people are concerned, events do not occur in linear fashion, and teams do not move in straight and predictable lines. In the 'storming' phase groups can generate a general reaction against all prior arrangements and this may well throw the

Table 5.2 Stages in group development

Bass and Ryterband (1979)	Woodcock (1979)	Tuckman (1965)	Glass (1996)
Developing mutual trust	Undeveloped team	Forming	Birth
Communication and decision making	Experimenting team	Storming	Childhood
Motivation and productivity	Consolidating team	Norming	Adolescence
Control and organization	Mature	Performing	Maturity
		Adjourning	

group back into the 'forming' stage. On the surface this may appear a retrograde step but it could lead to far more meaningful and creative solutions and ways forward. In other situations some groups may never develop to the stage of performing, becoming bogged down in an earlier stage. Yet other groups may skip about, backwards and forwards, from one stage to another, sometimes missing out or leaping over stages. Teams composed of people who are accustomed to working in that way may jump straight to the norming stage. In the real, more complex world, the journey of team development is not a precise path. Every team is different and different groups may process information differently and proceed at different speeds through the stages. As a result, an understanding of the general principles involved in these models is more important than a detailed appreciation of any one particular approach. This understanding can help us either to shorten the process or at least to make it a better, more effective one. Moreover, a team whose members understand the dynamics of group formation are less likely to get caught up at one of the intermediate stages.

 ## Roles and routines

Group norms

Groups tend to develop routine ways of behaving and doing things in a very natural and almost unspoken way, a development over time which becomes a shared, 'taken for granted' group psyche. Groups develop habits and rituals, the origins of which they cannot explain. Of course, work groups have some of these rituals and routines spelled out for them and made explicit in the form of procedures, laid down rules and regulations and well-accepted (and documented) working practices. However, as the Hawthorne studies (*see* Chapter 2) demonstrated, work groups can evolve unwritten and more 'informal' rules of behaviour or 'norms'. Norms may act positively or negatively from an organisational point of view. Any violations of the group norms are not conducive to the harmony of the group, and offenders run the risk of punishment, social isolation or expulsion from the group. New members are quickly socialised into the norms and are expected to fit in and comply. Norms can give a group its identity, and can help to differentiate it from others.

Illustration in film

Big

At one level, this 'children's' film, starring Tom Hanks, is simply about the mind of a 13-year-old boy in the body of a 35-year-old man. At another level, it illustrates what is achievable when we approach working from a different perception. Hanks gets a job with a large toy store, F. A. O. Schwarz, and rises quickly up the corporate ladder thanks to his unique childlike insight. When Hanks first joins the toy store, he is placed at a desk in a cubicle in a huge open-plan office. Being a 13-year-old boy, he naively beavers away, processing orders at a fast pace. After a while, the colleague in the next cubicle leans over and tells him to slow down, you're making the rest of us look bad – in other words he has unwittingly broken some of the work norms. He is having so much fun enjoying life away from responsibility, which begs the question why adults get so serious when there is fun to be had in almost any situation. As a result of his free-spirited behaviour, Hanks is promoted way beyond his expectations and experience.

Group roles

Within the framework of norms that groups have developed, there also exists a pattern of roles which members develop and demonstrate in that particular group. The roles that individuals perform in a group have an important effect on its development and cohesiveness. Within a typical group activity, such as a team meeting or a seminar discussion, people will indeed show a consistent preference for certain behaviours and not for others. In helping us to study this group and role behaviour a basic, but useful, exercise is to divide a team's activities, and hence roles, into 'task/content' and 'maintenance/process'. *Task/content activities* are aimed at problem solving and achieving the team's concrete goals, such as developing a new product. *Maintenance/process activities* involve managing how the team works together, its emotional life and the quality of members' interactions. These are focused on areas such as resolving conflict and giving individuals encouragement and support.

In further work on the distinction between task and maintenance, Benne and Sheats (1948) developed a popular system for the classification of member roles. Roles performed in well-functioning groups were classified under three broad headings: group task roles, group building and maintenance roles, and individual roles. Individual roles such as blocking, dominating or avoiding need to be replaced with maintenance, building or task roles before the group can become a truly effective team.

In a similar vein, Ancona and Caldwell (1990) studied the boundary management behaviours of new product teams and found that team members engaged in four varying types of inter-group activity:

● *Ambassador*, who represented the team to others;

● *Coordinator*, who communicated laterally the team's effort on its task with other work units;

- *Scouting*, which was about scanning the team's immediate environment;
- *Guarding*, involved in keeping information and resources within the group.

In keeping with research around team development models, they also found that the team's boundary management activities differed over the period of the product development cycle.

Many other classification systems exist for teasing out and identifying group roles. For example, Obeng (1994) lists only five roles:

- *doers* – who concentrate on the task at hand;
- *knowers* – who provide specialist knowledge;
- *solvers* – who solve problems as they arise;
- *checkers* – who make sure that all is going as well as it can and that the whole team is contributing fully;
- *carers* – who make sure that the team is operating as a cohesive social unit.

Belbin's team roles

Probably the most popular team roles categorisation was developed by Belbin (1996, 2004). He initially identified eight team roles which, upon further development, were expanded to nine. He argues that it is these nine roles that team members need to fulfil if the team is to be effective and successful. Clearly not all teams are composed of nine people, each of whom takes one of the different roles. Usually each person will find it quite natural to fill two or three preferred roles (and it is to be hoped that team members' preferred roles differ from the preferred roles of the other team members). Belbin's team roles are illustrated in Figure 5.3.

Belbin's team roles have proven popular in team development and teambuilding, so popular that he has incorporated them into a computer-scored questionnaire. One of Belbin's key principles is that 'no one's perfect but a team can be'. He preaches the gospel of balance and diversity within teams, stressing that his team roles questionnaire is purely an initial starting point for team composition and subsequent development. Some naive followers of his prescriptions have taken the 'scores' of individuals as the ultimate truth about what that person contributes to a team. This is a misguided practice, particularly when used to recruit and select new people into a team. Belbin's team roles are not to be taken as black or white, yes or no, true or false. The questionnaire itself is not a fully scientifically valid or reliable tool, particularly for measuring stable aspects of personality. However, this should not be read as a criticism of Belbin's work. He would argue that team role scores are a useful guide in forming a profile of a team and a standpoint from which one can start to identify the weaknesses of a team. Further, because the process involves assessing the preferred roles of each team member and encouraging all members to appreciate the characteristics and strengths of the others, his model provides an accessible and shared language to enable this. When using it we are not swamped with data generated from the questionnaire. It is simply a starting point to provide a common understanding from which to pursue team issues further. If Belbin's questionnaire simply raises the awareness levels in a team about their collective strengths and weaknesses, then it has been a success.

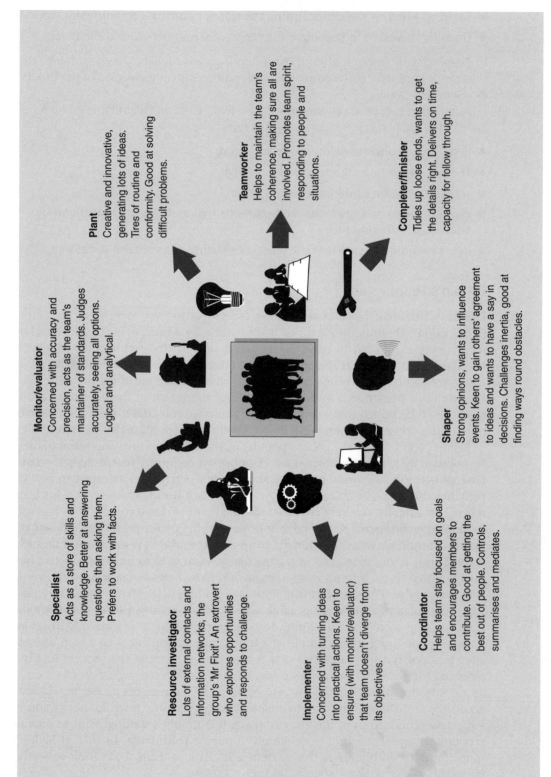

Specialist
Acts as a store of skills and knowledge. Better at answering questions than asking them. Prefers to work with facts.

Resource investigator
Lots of external contacts and information networks, the group's 'Mr Fixit'. An extrovert who explores opportunities and responds to challenge.

Implementer
Concerned with turning ideas into practical actions. Keen to ensure (with monitor/evaluator) that team doesn't diverge from its objectives.

Coordinator
Helps team stay focused on goals and encourages members to contribute. Good at getting the best out of people. Controls, summarises and mediates.

Monitor/evaluator
Concerned with accuracy and precision, acts as the team's maintainer of standards. Judges accurately, seeing all options. Logical and analytical.

Plant
Creative and innovative, generating lots of ideas. Tires of routine and conformity. Good at solving difficult problems.

Teamworker
Helps to maintain the team's coherence, making sure all are involved. Promotes team spirit, responding to people and situations.

Completer/finisher
Tidies up loose ends, wants to get the details right. Delivers on time, capacity for follow through.

Shaper
Strong opinions, wants to influence events. Keen to gain others' agreement to ideas and wants to have a say in decisions. Challenges inertia, good at finding ways round obstacles.

Figure 5.3 Belbin's team roles

In summary, we can say that it is simply not enough for groups or teams who are working towards a common goal to have a ragbag collection of individual skills. The various behaviours (and routines) of the team members must mesh together in order to achieve their group's goals and objectives.

Illustration in film

Oceans Eleven, *Twelve* and *Thirteen*

In heist movies a lot of the fun comes from watching the 'team leader' recruit various specialists and con men for the job. Are they 'in' or 'out'? Will this group of dropouts, misfits and hustlers ever learn to function as a team?

However, what does become clear in the films is that each member of the team has their specific role. One guy knows how to disable the alarm system. Someone else is the getaway driver. Of course, there's also the expert safe cracker!

Roles and responsibilities are explicit.

 ## Building and maintaining effective teams

Some managers may 'play' at human engineering by trying to select exactly the right combination of people, but more often than not they end up in a state of confusion. Effective teams can come about spontaneously, as a result of a particular set of circumstances. The key to success does not always appear to lie in the selection of team members, as many sports teams are composed of talented individuals who work poorly as a team. Likewise, there are many examples of groups of less talented individuals who perform well in a team scenario.

In his classic work *The Human Side of Enterprise*, Douglas McGregor (1960) provides an account of the differences between effective and ineffective groups. According to McGregor the effective group is cohesive, relaxed and friendly. Their discussion is open, hence disagreement is always possible. Effectiveness is a function of group members' orientation and attitude, not simply the behaviour of the leader. McGregor's view of effective groups corresponds to Tuckman's norming and performing stages of group development mentioned earlier. However, the features of ineffective groups are closer to Tuckman's storming stage. A significant difference between these two writers is that McGregor sees some groups as fixed and trapped in their own poor behaviour, whereas Tuckman implies that groups tend to move out of the ineffective stages into more effective behaviour (or at the very least they fluctuate between the two).

Mullins (2002: 477) views the characteristics of an effective work group as being more holistic and humanistic. He sees the underlying feature of these groups as '*a spirit of cooperation in which members work well together as a united team, and with*

Table 5.3 Characteristics of effective work groups

- A belief in shared aims and objectives
- A sense of commitment to the group
- Acceptance of group values and norms
- A feeling of mutual trust and dependency
- Full participation by all members and decision making by consensus
- Free flow of information and communications
- The open expression of feelings and disagreements
- The resolution of conflict by the members themselves
- A lower level of staff turnover, absenteeism, accidents, errors and complaints

Source: Mullins (2002), p. 477.

harmonious and supportive relationships'. According to Mullins, this may be particularly evidenced when members of a group exhibit the characteristics presented in Table 5.3.

A mild criticism of these ideas is that the list in Table 5.3 reflects effective *work teams* rather more than work groups and that this is how it should be – these are teams not groups. Teams operate at the higher order of group dynamics that the list reflects.

Finally, it must be recognised that for a team to be effective it should contain diversity: it should have people with differing outlooks and strengths (Higgs, 1996). To some extent this need for diversity is satisfied (and forced upon us) by the growing inevitability of globalisation and cross-cultural fertilisation. Whereas diversity in terms of occupational or organisational role is an expectation of a team, diversity in terms of nationality, age, ethnicity, personality or even gender is often less readily accepted. It is hard to manage a truly diverse team. Team members invariably have very different values, norms and beliefs about how to behave and even different perceptions of what is going on around them. Kandola (1995) identified that although diverse teams have the potential to be highly effective because of the variety of outlooks they possess, they may often fail to achieve that high potential. Teams need and require integration; this is something that Maznevski (1994) has argued for. This requirement for integration involves a paradox: integration is more difficult to achieve as teams become more diverse (and yet with globalisation, teams will inevitably become more diverse). According to Arnold *et al.* (2005) integration relies on:

- a social reality shared by group members;
- the ability to empathise and see things from others' points of view;
- the motivation to communicate;
- the ability to negotiate and agree norms within the team;
- the ability to identify the true causes of any difficulties which arise;
- self-confidence of all group members.

If one combines Mullins's list with that of Arnold *et al.*, the result is a comprehensive range of characteristics for an effective work team.

Illustration in film

Master and Commander

One of the most effective ways the leader of a team can ensure some 'buy in' from the team members, is to develop and communicate a shared vision for the team – something they can all believe in and relate to.

In *Master and Commander* Captain Aubrey (Russell Crowe) knows what it takes to get the best from his crew. When a cannon-firing exercise – designed to outgun a French warship – takes longer than he likes, Captain Aubrey spurs them on to try harder, shouting out.

Aubrey: Do you want Napoleon to be your King?

Crew: No!

Aubrey: Your language to be French?

Crew: No!

Aubrey: Your children to sing the Marseillaise?

Crew: No!

Aubrey: Then let's try again!

We are left in no doubt about the 'shared vision' of Aubrey and his crew – a free and independent Britain with no interference or influence from France!

Group cohesiveness and performance

Group cohesiveness is related to group effectiveness, and factors which constitute cohesion can be seen to parallel some of the aspects which determine a group's effectiveness. Group cohesion can be thought of as the 'pulling power' of the group, its magnetism, its ability to retain its members. Piper *et al.* (1983: 94) defined it as *'the attractiveness of the group to its members, together with their motivation to remain as part of the group and resist leaving it'*. In a cohesive group, group identity is clear, interpersonal relations are good and people place value upon being a member of the group. Members of such groups experience fewer work-related anxieties and are better adjusted in the organisation than are members of less cohesive groups. They have higher rates of job satisfaction, and lower rates of tension, absenteeism and labour turnover. Cohesive groups develop greater levels of cooperation among their members, and membership in itself can be a very rewarding and enlightening experience. All in all, a cohesive group is likely to be an effective one.

On the question of relatedness, Handy (1993) identified the size of a group as an important moderating factor in its ability to be effective. For best participation and involvement, between five and eight members appears to be the optimum. In work

Table 5.4 Group performance and cohesiveness

Membership development	Work environment	Organisational cohesiveness	Group and maturity
Size of the group	Nature of the task	Management and leadership style	Forming
Compatibility of members	Physical setting		Storming
	Communications	Personnel policies and procedures	Norming
Permanence	Technology	Success	Performing
		External threat	Adjourning

Source: Adapted from Mullins p. 472.

groups, size can be related to cohesiveness and member satisfaction too, with larger work groups tending to have lower morale and more absenteeism. Members start to feel less involved and committed in large groups of over fifteen members: interaction with all members becomes more difficult and the ability to maintain a common goal becomes harder. The incidence of clique formation also increases, thus decreasing overall cohesiveness. Mullins (2002: 472) lists a comprehensive number of factors affecting cohesiveness, as set out in Table 5.4.

What we have said about cohesive groups so far amounts to an impressive list of advantages. They demonstrate greater cooperation, with easier and more flowing communication and an increased resistance to frustration, as well as reduced labour turnover and absenteeism. If a manager aims to develop and lead effective work groups then he or she simply must pay attention to the factors which influence the creation of a group's identity and cohesiveness. However, the tightrope of tension

Illustration in film

Apollo 13

The story is of the ill-fated Apollo 13 moon-shot mission. It was to be the third moon landing, but the ship malfunctioned in deep space. For the better part of a tense week, it seemed that the crew of three might not be coming back.

The key themes of team synergy, creativity, differing roles and technological expertise are explored, along with the very current issues of working with a team of people who are distant (very distant in this case) from the organisation and divorced from the normal work environment.

The NASA team has to constantly invent new solutions to never-before-faced problems – the brainstorming and creativity sessions are there for everyone to see. As an aside, Ed Harris (NASA flight director) has a neat line in viewing the problems from a different angle. In response to a senior official's despondent utterings 'This could be the worst disaster NASA has ever experienced', Harris replies 'With all due respect, sir, I believe this is going to be our finest hour.'

the manager must negotiate in order to develop strong and cohesive groups involves a very tricky balancing act, for very strongly cohesive groups also present problems. They start to look in on themselves too much and can become very defensive and protective of their 'territory' and jealous of, or even aggressive towards, other groups. Life may be difficult for new entrants into the group, thereby restricting the introduction of new practices and suggestions. Linked to this last point, and of great relevance in today's increasingly flexible business environment, is the fact that strongly cohesive groups resist change and the 'invasion' of these new ideas. The status quo is comfortable and satisfying and the cohesive group feels it is invulnerable and strong. This results in a powerful set of forces equipped to resist any proposed changes. It must come as no surprise, either, that these over-cohesive groups are viewed as awkward, overbearing and bombastic by others.

Conformity and groupthink

The 'energy' of very cohesive groups is not just directed at people who fall outside the boundaries of the group. Even in a strongly cohesive group, pressure is placed on members to fall into line and conform to the group norms. The potency of this group pressure to conform was illustrated in a classic laboratory study by Solomon Asch (1951). A group of seven subjects were shown a line and asked to say which of three other lines matched it in length. In fact only one of the subjects was a true volunteer, the other six being stooges. The subjects gave their responses with the real volunteer responding sixth. At the first session, all of the group correctly identified the lines. At the second session, the stooges consistently gave incorrect answers. They would say, within earshot of the true volunteer, that a line clearly shorter than the test line was equal to it. In 32 per cent of cases, the volunteer went along with this opinion despite some initial hesitancy. Asch's study demonstrated the power of a group to elicit conformity of opinion and judgement amongst its members. More importantly, it also revealed how difficult it can be to resist other people's opinions, even when one knows that their opinions are wrong.

Asch's work was anchored in the laboratory, where life, and research findings, are not necessarily the same as one might find in the reality of a business organis-ation. In the light of more recent trends within the business environment towards flatter organisational structures, which empower and entrust individuals to make decisions for themselves, we have to question the validity of Asch's findings. More and more, managers are being encouraged to challenge the status quo and to think more laterally, to be more creative and innovative in a shorter space of time. Organisations are busy developing learning cultures, cultures where everyone has the right to question and where diversity of thinking (not just diversity of people) is positively encouraged and rewarded. Many management consultants, and the tools they use (such as business process re-engineering), are geared towards helping the organisation question and challenge its taken-for-granted assumptions about 'the way we do things around here'. What we can say is that there is always a strong social pressure to conform when amongst our peers but, in the context of a business organisation, this pressure is watered down and moderated for the very reasons listed above.

Table 5.5 Symptoms of groupthink

- Group feels invulnerable; excessive optimism and risk taking pervade the air.
- Warnings that things might be going awry are discounted and rationalised away.
- There is an unquestioned belief in the group's morality.
- Those who oppose the group are ridiculed and stereotyped as stupid, corrupt and weak.
- Pressure is applied to anyone who opposes the prevailing mood of the group.
- An illusion of unanimity develops; silence is taken as consent.
- Members of the group censor themselves if they feel they are deviating from the group norms.
- Self-appointed 'mindguards' are established who protect the group from information and individuals which would disrupt consensus.

Source: Based on Janis (1972).

The work of Janis (1972) developed a theme of Asch's work, that the effective decision-making ability of a group is dramatically and drastically impaired by the presence and pressure of others. Janis's work struck a very practical note of reality because it was extracted and developed from famous cases in world history. There was coined the term 'groupthink', which in Janis's (1972: 9) words is *'a mode of thinking in which people engage when they are deeply involved in a cohesive group, in which strivings for unanimity override motivations to realistically appraise alternative courses of action'*. When making decisions, groups do not have either perfect knowledge or perfect rationality and yet groups suffering from 'groupthink' believe that they possess both of these and a variety of other 'symptoms' highlighted in Table 5.5.

Janis concluded that the historical decisions he looked at were all characterised by a process which involved the group just 'drifting along', which gave rise to the sense of false consensus. Another common factor among the cases was the tendency to curtail discussion and to consider only a very limited range of alternatives. Again we must ask ourselves how applicable these findings about strongly cohesive groups are for today's business organisations. In thinking about this question, one should bear in mind the earlier points noted and the fact that Janis was primarily looking at very significant and important foreign policy decisions.

Illustration in film

12 Angry Men

A classic film of its genre. The jury of the title retires to deliberate, and right away it's eleven votes to one to convict the teenager of the murder of his father. But one dissenter gradually brings the rest around to reconsider their original views. Watch it for the drama or watch it to learn something about groupthink, leadership, group conflict and team dynamics.

Can you 'pin down' exactly what behaviours and strategies Henry Fonda (the sole dissenter at the beginning of the film) employs with his fellow jurors?

Communication and conflict

Teams rely on communication; it's their lifeblood. The global and virtual teams of 'tomorrow' will need it more than ever (Coles, 1998a).

A recent YouGov survey of over 800 employers found that employers look for communication skills (61%), followed by teamworking (58%), self-motivation and initiative (41%) and problem solving (28%).

Typically a communication process involves a sender (or encoder) of a message and a receiver (or decoder) of that message. The sender chooses the words and the medium through which that message is sent and the receiver interprets the message. The sender has an intended message which may well differ from their actual message and the receiver has certain perceptions about what they want to hear, what they think they hear, what they expect to hear and what they actually hear. Thus the receiver creates the meaning of a message in their mind, so interpretation and intention may be poles apart!

There are a number of 'standard' communication networks to be found in organisations.

Centralised networks (typically a chain, a Y-shape or in the form of a wheel) maintain a centralised flow of information or that information is directed through specific members.

Decentralised networks (a circle or all-channel network) involve the communication flow originating at any point and the flow is not directed through certain central group members, akin in action and philosophy to self-directed or self-managed teams.

Centralised networks tend to be governed by members' status within the organisation, whereas decentralised networks are controlled by factors such as proximity or personal preference.

Adding an extra dimension to the complexity of even the simplest communication chain (person-to-person, face-to-face) is the 'noise' factor. This may be genuine noise that is a hindrance, such as distractions or illegible handwriting, inaccurate statistics in a report, poor Internet or e-mail connection or physical distance between sender and receiver.

Many of the problems encountered in a simpler' communication network can be overcome with feedback – checking for understanding, reflecting back what we hear or interpret, summarising the main points as we see them. However, when we look beyond the two-person communication scenario to the linkages and networks among work groups, departmental and organisational members, we are concerned with complex communication networks. Add on to this a layer of telecommunications and a further layer of technology-enabled working and the main types of communication networks illustrated in Figure 5.4 look positively simplistic.

Many management commentators preach individual power and autonomy, self-responsibility, trust, empowerment and the ability to make decisions and act rapidly. This is part of a dominant contemporary philosophy, and if we accept this philosophy, we have to ask the question, 'How relevant are communication networks, when employees are being encouraged to think and act independently?' It

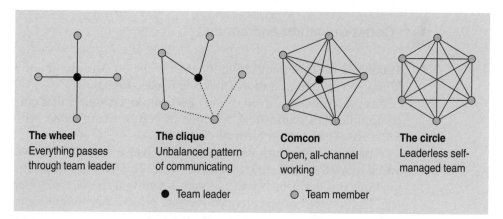

The wheel
Everything passes
through team leader

The clique
Unbalanced pattern
of communicating

Comcon
Open, all-channel
working

The circle
Leaderless self-
managed team

● Team leader   ○ Team member

Figure 5.4 The main communication network patterns in teams

is because we are being empowered to be more autonomous and to take responsibility that we must address this issue.

As long ago as the early 1990s Sproull and Kiesler (1991) compared how small groups make decisions through computer conferences, e-mail and face-to-face discussion. The use of an electronic medium caused participants to talk more frankly and more equally, and to make more suggestions for action. In the face-to-face discussions only a few people dominated. However, they also found that the increased democracy of the electronic media interfered with decision making and raised the levels of conflict. Decisions via email were made more slowly and participants expressed more extreme opinions and vented their anger more openly.

There is no doubt that computer-mediated communication is not only changing the way organisations function but is impacting upon the very building blocks of effective teamwork and communication, namely regular, 'face-to-face' interaction. Clearly non-verbal cues are less important, receivers are empowered as to when and whether they respond, fears of interpersonal contact can be overcome and status differences have a limited impact. Computer-mediated communication is seen as both more open and democratic, but also more subversive (Guirdham, 2002)!

Fulk and Collins-Jarvis (2001) estimate that less than 15% of management meetings are mediated by technology such as videoconferencing, computer conferencing and conference calls. However, mediated meetings will become more common as new ways of working and new organisational forms demand this – just ask the average teleworking manager.

Intra-group behaviour and conflict

Organisations are encouraging higher levels of diversity in teams. Diversity is a gateway to being more effective, and yet the more homogeneous a team is in terms of shared interests, attitudes and backgrounds, the easier it might be for that team to be a cohesive force. Individuals in the team can empathise and relate to each other more readily. Some variety and variation in individual differences, such as personality or skills, may, on the other hand, act as a positive force for cohesion.

However, if these personality differences are particularly accentuated, extreme or acute, personality clashes can occur, and this can be a source of conflict and disruption for the team. Belbin (2004) talks about balance in teams and people complementing each other. More sophisticated recruitment and selection processes may be one way of achieving the right levels of balance in a team, ensuring that a whole range of individual differences in areas such as skills, attitudes, attributes and personality are taken into account. In this way we can predict, and moderate against, potential conflict situations.

Another source of conflict for teams can arise where members of the team are in competition with each other for finite resources. Typically, where a sales team operates in a limited geographical area there may be salespeople in that team competing with each other for revenue, individual incentives and bonuses. Some members of the team will do better than others and in some cases this can trigger the 'stealing' of sales leads and the sabotaging of others. The resulting animosity and conflict can become dysfunctional for the whole team. Clearly, this is an extreme example but the practice of individual incentive payment schemes and the encouragement of intra-team competition do exist. As before, it is all a matter of balance. Some level of competition between members of the same team can be productive in all sorts of ways, but the important point is to know at what level to pitch that competition and how to reward it. Individual incentive schemes in a team, by their very nature, demand a highly accurate process for measuring performance fairly. A growing number of companies are experimenting with schemes based on the output, sales or productivity of a group, section or department (Carrington, 1995; Armstrong, 1996). Incentive schemes based on the discrete performance of a work group attempt to encourage flexibility and cooperation among its members, and to a certain extent provide opportunities for the employees to decide for themselves how to divide up the resulting rewards and incentives. Armstrong (1996) points out that such schemes appear to be more effective when the work groups:

- stand alone as performing units, with clear targets and standards;
- have a meaningful degree of autonomy;
- consist of people whose work is interdependent;
- contain members who are multiskilled, flexible and good team players;
- perform in a directly measurable way.

Although team-based payment schemes can lead to higher levels of motivation, productivity, cooperation and 'teamness' among team members, there can be problems. The team can end up 'carrying' someone, who ultimately reaps the same rewards as the other members but for less effort. However, what we have learned from the Hawthorne studies indicates that it is likely that the other members of the team doing the 'carrying' would address the situation. In this way, it can be argued that team-based schemes encourage the team to take a more proactive role in managing itself. Alternatively, pressure to conform and the requirement for consideration of others can lead to the reduction of effort to the lowest common denominator and the demotivation of high performers. Another disadvantage with these schemes is that they can help to develop an imbalanced, and skewed, pattern of labour movement around the organisation. Individuals will resist transfer out of high-performing teams for fear of a potential drop in individual earnings. Likewise, employees may resist being moved into teams that perform poorly. Probably the most important issue in the development, implementation and success of these schemes is the requirement for there to be a change in the culture of the organisation. There needs to be a move away from an individually orientated work environment, which the scheme itself would facilitate, towards the realisation that the individual's pay will not be totally related to his or her own efforts. Indeed, an individual's pay may well be more closely related to the performance of a colleague than to his or her own. This, in turn, will develop a very real interdependence within teams.

In Sid Joynson's (Joynson and Forrester, 1995: 31) experience the very essence and nature of teamwork can build strong motivation – far stronger than can be given by mere cash incentives: 'In my experience, attempts to motivate through performance-related pay schemes are quite counter-productive and tend to destroy the all-important team ethic.'

Illustration in film

Glengarry Glen Ross

It's a rainy night at the tired firm of John Williamson (one of Kevin Spacey's earliest roles) when Blake arrives to give the loser sales team a pep talk on how to sell right. Blake's angry rantings offend George, upset Dave and annoy Shelley, but none can complain because Blake has proposed a contest. First prize is a Cadillac Eldorado, second prize is a set of steak knives, third prize is the sack! There is no room for losers in this dramatically masculine world; only 'closers' will get the good sales leads.

As well as a fine ensemble piece, adapted from a powerful play, this story demonstrates the destructive notion of individual rather than team rewards and the conflict which this encourages.

Inter-group behaviour and conflict

Groups in organisations are not sealed off from each other; they do not exist and operate within a vacuum. In fact, the situation can be quite the opposite. They can become highly dependent upon each other, and the effectiveness of an organisation often relies upon smooth relationships between its different teams (Ancona, 1987). However, since each group is primarily judged on how well it performs its tasks, there will be tension between the need to focus on its own concerns and the requirement to cooperate with other groups, in order that they might perform effectively. As noted earlier, cohesiveness can be of great benefit to a group but it can also result in tension and conflict between groups. The problem is clear: some degree of conflict or competition between groups is both good and inevitable but the mix of 'friendly' rivalry and competition must be balanced with the need for cooperation. This is where many organisations go wrong when structuring, for instance, their sales teams. They view competition between teams as a way of motivating people and as something that is healthy for the workplace. Teams that consistently perform well might receive large bonuses, or other incentives, at the end of the year. But not everyone can be top; the system may well develop a destructive climate of 'winners' and 'losers'. In extreme cases, this inter-group conflict can operate to the detriment of organisational productivity. However, groups that cooperate can coordinate their activities better, have a fuller exchange of ideas and information, and share both expenses and rewards.

 ## Groups and change

'We have met the enemy and it is us.' (*Walt Kelly*)

The inevitability of change is an accepted truism in today's business environment. However, when undergoing change, groups can present us with some difficult moments of truth; they are not good at handling change!

- Groups will think first about what they must give up.
- They feel awkward and self-conscious.
- Groups have different readiness and acceptance levels for change.
- Some groups will feel very alone.
- Others will worry and fret that they don't have enough resources.
- Groups will revert to their old ways of behaving, particularly if we do not 'constantly' reinforce the change.

The impact of technology

Technology clearly has a considerable influence on the pattern of group operations and behaviour. One of the most striking issues arising from the work of Trist *et al.* (1963) was that the technological changes being implemented in a coal mine under observation had brought about changes in the traditional social groupings of the miners. Technological change created a lack of cooperation between different shifts and a disruption to the integration of small groups (*see* Chapter 2).

The type, level, amount and use of technology available to an organisation can often determine how particular tasks or work packages are carried out. In some circumstances, the technology can strongly influence and change the very essence of a job and the way it is performed. For example, the way the work is organised around the technology may limit the opportunities for social interaction and the extent to which it is possible to identify oneself as a member of a cohesive work group. Consequently, this can have adverse, or positive, effects on attitudes to work and the level of job satisfaction. During the past few decades manufacturing organisations have been striving to eliminate some of the more alienating aspects of mass production by increasing the range and type of tasks and responsibilities allocated to small groups. These attempts include the greater use of group technology approaches, autonomous work groups and self-directed teams, as discussed above.

The downsizing of large-scale centralised organisations into smaller working units can help to develop an environment in which workers may relate more easily to each other.

Global teamworking

With more companies extending their operations across and around the world, the management and leadership of global teams is becoming a new challenge (*see* Chapter 10). That global teams exist cannot be denied. At Hewlett-Packard, the European export administration manager has a team of 35 people in several countries, including 15 in the UK. In the Ford Motor Company, some senior project managers have direct managerial responsibility for 25 people, of whom the most senior might comprise five project managers, based in Europe, South America, Australia, Japan and China.

There are a number of all-consuming and inextricably linked trends which are encouraging this situation. Heading the list is the revolution in technology, particularly telecommunications. E-mail, voicemail, laptops, hand-held organisers, videoconferencing, Internet telephones, interactive pagers – all of these tools make teamwork, mobility and working at a distance a more satisfactory option. The only problem is that technology is changing faster than our attitudes and beliefs about work. Another paradox is that all this wizardry is supposed to help businesses to communicate and manage remote teams. The reality is that few multinationals have started to tackle the challenge. They often have no clear information technology strategy; alternatively, one part of the organisation, due to some technological mismatch, may be unable to 'talk' to another part. Often, few have been trained in the use of new technology and many are unfamiliar with it. Within the same global team the technology can create a two-tier hierarchy of those who can and those who cannot use it.

Illustration in film

Disclosure

Although *Disclosure* is remembered more for the theme of sexual harassment than anything else, as with many Michael Crichton novels there is a parallel theme of technology and its impact on the functioning of global organisations, office 'politics' and 'virtual' teams.

Cross-cultural teamworking

Much of the research into formulating ideas and models around groups and teams – how they form, how they develop, how they thrive and grow – could be accused of being ethnocentric. Many of the ideas have evolved out of a Western mode of thought. The greatest barrier to inter-cultural communication occurs when a person believes that 'only my culture makes sense, espouses the right values, and represents the right and logical way to behave'. If we look at the work of Geert Hofstede (1980), we can identify some key differences between the United States and Japan, for example. The USA is one of the most individualistic cultures, Japan is among the countries where collectivism is strong. Further, the USA is a culture with a low orientation towards authority and can tolerate uncertainty. The Japanese, on the other hand, have a national culture with a strong orientation towards authority and are highly motivated to avoid uncertainty in their work lives. Armed with this information we can hypothesise that Japanese business people would not be at ease taking part in some energetic storming; rather, they would be more willing to (over-)conform when in teams. Whatever we might conclude, it is an inescapable fact that the national cultures of the USA and Japan are very different and therefore people from those cultures will go about the process of forming and working in teams in different ways.

It is vitally important to be aware of the business and cultural protocols of the people with whom you are sharing a global teamworking experience. As an example, imagine the scenario of having a face-to-face meeting of the global design and sales team. The Japanese partners are seated opposite the large windows, looking out, and the most senior of the Japanese visitors is near the door. The seating arrangements may upset your team partners on two counts. First, they will assume that you consider that they are not interested in the meeting, because you have placed them in front of the windows, thus giving them a view to look out on and occupy them. Second, and more traditionally, in Japan, the most senior people are placed furthest from the door, facing it. This dates back to a time in Japan's history of warring samurai factions when the first people to 'get the chop' were the people nearest the door.

Illustration in film

Fantastic Four

When a space voyage goes awry, four people are changed for ever. Reed Richards, the leader of the group, gains the ability to stretch his body and becomes Mr Fantastic. Sue Storm develops the skill to turn invisible and create force fields, calling herself (not surprisingly) the Invisible Woman. Her brother Johnny Storm gains the ability to control fire, including covering his own body with flame. He becomes the Human Torch. Finally, pilot Ben Grimm is turned into a super-strong rock creature calling himself Thing. Together, they use their unique skills and powers to explore the strange aspects of the world and to foil the evil plans of Doctor Doom.

Pretty well much an everyday story of the power of differing skills and diversity within a team! Other 'super-hero' teams and alliances like the X-Men (or Batman, Robin and Batgirl) demonstrate the same principle. Often, individually, they can be seen as 'powerless', but together as a team they are a much mightier force to be reckoned with.

Diversity in teams

As already highlighted, diversity in organisations is a growing need. There is evidence to suggest that businesses with a diverse workforce are more strongly placed to attract and retain quality staff. The same can be said of teams within those organisations. Well-led diverse teams can outperform homogeneous teams by as much as 15 per cent (Watson *et al.*, 1993). Further, companies have identified the benefits that the differing experiences and perspectives of a diverse team can bring to the workplace. It enables them to be more competitive in serving the needs of their customers (a diverse group in themselves), in expanding into new markets and in recruiting talented people from an increasingly mobile workforce.

Of course, diversity is not only limited to the groups of employees that equal opportunities legislation highlights. Functionally diverse teams may consist of individuals with a variety of work, educational and training backgrounds. Europe-wide or even global work teams may further involve cultural, perceptual and even socially developed cognitive differences. Traditional diversity in teams along the lines of functional diversity does ensure that the team will have the adequate mix of skills, knowledge, expertise and experience to guide itself. Also, when people in teams bring different points of view and information to the task in hand, that team may well avoid the dangerous problems of groupthink.

Although diverse teams may well generate higher levels of creativity (Guzzo and Dickson, 1996), be more flexible, adapt to change more readily and have a greater 'global reach', there are team leadership and management problems associated with diverse teams. They may simply be too diverse and 'spread', and can sometimes present all the difficulties of leading people with extremely differing views and opinions about almost anything!

Networks and virtual teams

With the increasing propensity for organisations to downsize and outsource or sub-contract a growing number of tasks and functions, some work teams may have a membership consisting of full-time employees, part-time and temporary (fixed-term) people, two-days-per-week associate partners and outsourced workers (*see* Chapter 7). In *The Age of Unreason* Charles Handy (1989) describes a flexible organisational structure design, which he calls the 'shamrock' organisation. This structure is made up of three distinct groups of people:

- the professional core;
- the contractual fringe;
- the flexible labour force.

Each of these three elements of the workforce has a different kind of commitment to the organisation and a varying set of expectations; each group needs to be managed in a different way. When they are put together in mixed teams, what might you expect some of the outcomes to be? Many organisations are now undertaking joint projects with other organisations, forming strategic partnerships and alliances or creating loosely coupled teams across several organisations, even with their competitors. Learning and developing in groups and teams is starting to cut across the organisation's traditional boundaries. (*See* the works listed in the Further Reading section at the end of the chapter – Hamel *et al.* (1989) or Coles (1998).)

Virtual organisations, workplaces and teams are becoming increasingly commonplace. In a virtual team, the members' primary interaction is through some combination of computer-mediated communications, which allows the members of the team to cross time, space and cultural boundaries (Johnson *et al.*, 2001). If interdependence is the 'glue' which holds more conventional teams together, then communication technologies serve as the bond linking the members of virtual teams. They allow team members to communicate and share data and information despite disparities in location and time zone. In this way, they become the key channel for interaction in virtual teams. (Bell and Kozlowski, 2002)

Virtual teams can be split into:

- Department virtual teams made up of people who all work for the same department but are based in different locations. The team members have common objectives, work under the same day-to-day management and have a detailed understanding of each other's responsibilities and working conditions.

- Company virtual teams which are made up of people who all work for the same company but within different departments and, most likely, locations. They are unlikely to know one another personally but will be used to working within the same corporate culture and have shared working conditions and hours.

- Organisation virtual teams made up of members who do not all work for the same organisation, for example a marketing team that works in partnership with an external agency responsible for carrying out creative work on their behalf. The team members will most likely, have no existing relationship, work under different management and working conditions, have conflicting ideas about what their objectives should be and have no awareness of their colleagues' other responsibilities or big projects.

- Multiple virtual teams made up of a mixture of virtual teams, for example a cross-department team, all based in different locations, that also works with an external supplier based in another country. In addition to the issues highlighted above there will be more complex communication issues that will make it a challenge for members of this team to coordinate their thoughts and ideas collectively.

To summarise, virtual teams are much more likely to involve far more diverse and transient membership across different geographical locations within the organisation; contingent workers from outside the organisation; suppliers and customers; and even resource providers from many different cultures (Sparrow, 2000). Young (1998: 46) makes the distinction between *virtual teams – working together as one across distances simultaneously, with people from the same function* and *cross-functional virtual teams – people working in different functions, business units or across time zones.*

Young stresses that virtual teams free the organisation to run 24 hours a day, helping the organisation to break away from the constraints of traditional working time and staff availability. Cascio (1998) lists a number of advantages of virtual teams, including:

- savings in time and travel expenses and elimination of the lack of access to experts;
- teams can be organised regardless of whether the members are in reasonable proximity to each other;
- allowing organisations to expand their potential labour market, and to hire and retain people regardless of their physical location;
- dynamic team membership enables people to move from one project to another;
- employees can be assigned to multiple, concurrent teams.

Other key benefits associated with encouraging virtual teamworking might include improving the work-life balance of staff, better sharing of information and knowledge across organizations and freedom to allocate projects to the best people regardless of their location. In the case of outsourcing, benefits may include accessing expertise not immediately available within the organization, freeing up staff time to focus on the organisation's core competencies, reduced legal liability and substantial cost savings.

Given these positives, virtual working is a trend that's here to stay. However, many organisations will not experience these benefits despite their best efforts to embrace virtual working, primarily for the simple reason that they will underestimate the many difficulties and challenges that need to be addressed in order for a virtual team to be pulled together in a productive way.

Although significant technological advances have been made in terms of 'telepresence' or 'virtual presence', many virtual teams still find that effective collaborative work is still performed in face-to-face meetings where the issues of trust and ambiguity that surround identity in the virtual world are most easily overcome. The very lack of physical interaction, with its corresponding verbal and non-verbal cues, will be detrimental to the quality of communication. Up to 70 per cent of the meaning of a message is derived from non-verbal cues. The synergies that often accompany face-to-face communication will also be lost. Another disadvantage may well be the increased reliance on technology and telecommunications. Technology will become an all too powerful determinant for the way we communicate and how we organise and manage teams and ultimately organisations. Already technology is moving faster than other organisational activities. Virtual teams add another layer of complexity to any teamwork structure and, though increasingly popular, they are still a relatively under-researched organisational form. They are built around the latest advances in technological communication, so how do team leaders learn not to over-rely on these advances, such as email, newsgroups and interactive groupware? Membership is typically based solely around needed expertise; the teams rarely have any history of interaction, and their performance potential is unknown (Potter *et al.*, 2000). Virtual work teams present a unique set of managerial challenges which organisations are only just starting to tackle (Kiser, 1999; Solomon, 2001). Some people are just not built for remote teamworking (Alexander, 2000), which virtual teams are bound to encourage; how do we manage the people who get left behind by the whole process? To develop and manage virtual teams requires expertise in both team development and virtual team technologies.

It cannot be expected that people who work in different locations, under different management, in different working cultures or in different time zones, with little or no personal contact will automatically find a way to work cohesively and effectively together. Considering that team members will lack established communication channels and a shared line of authority to govern the delivery of their work and it's unsurprising that projects carried out by virtual teams are at particular risk of falling apart, failing to deliver and running over budget.

Teams – are they really that good?

'Hell is other people.' (*Jean-Paul Sartre*)

Hackman's review of teamworking (1990) raises a number of circumstances in which teams do fail. The truth is that they don't always work well. Many management books develop processes in which people from a broad spectrum of backgrounds cheerfully set aside their native prejudices and preferences and march in rhythm, or at least in time, to the heroic leader's drumbeat. But some of these approaches fail to address the fact that people have their own reason for doing things.

Groups could be viewed as the multipliers of underachievement – a small shortfall that one person has on an assembly team is multiplied across the whole team; each weakness adds to the whole weakness. Groups are seldom unanimous, and the striving for unanimity at all costs is unrealistic. Within any group there will be a variety of degrees of commitment and understanding. Disappointments can be magnified by the dynamics. Groups are prone to rumour, supposition and innuendo – negativity can live on when it might have naturally subsided in individuals. Conformity saps diversity, or at least waters it down. The very thing teaming sets out to encourage can be the first thing it eradicates.

Once one delves below the surface one can also find evidence for the frailty and frivolity of working in groups and teams. We have already highlighted some of the 'folly' of groupthink – personality factors can hamper group decision-making. Dominant individuals may exert excessive influence over decisions or solutions even when their solutions are incorrect. Status hierarchy often inhibits the individual with the correct answer from persisting (Maier and Solem, 1952).

Drez (1999) identified a range of reasons for the potential failure of work teams. Amongst these were:

- a lack of (or no) trust;
- weak strategies;
- competitive and authoritarian environment;
- a 'fad' mentality;
- limited experimentation;
- vague assignments;
- poor team skills;
- poor staffing.

This list certainly provides some 'food for thought' for both team-orientated organisations and team leaders.

There is some debate about whether the quality of ideas is superior when individuals work alone or when in real groups. Diehl and Stroebe (1987), in a review of the evidence, suggest that individuals working alone produce a better quality of ideas. Problems of group performance extend also to studies of group decision-making. Research evidence is consistent in suggesting that the quality of group decision-making generally equals but does not exceed the quality of decision-making of the average member.

Meta-analysis (Mullen and Cooper, 1994) of studies examining the relationship between cohesiveness and effectiveness suggested that the direction of effort was from performing to cohesiveness rather than vice versa. Teams which performed well became more cohesive as a result, so organisations need to worry less about creating cohesiveness, for it will come, and more about raising performance. In studies conducted in organisational settings, there's no reliable impact of team-building interventions upon task effectiveness or team performance. Interventions designed to change the interpersonal processes in groups are least likely to effect any change in performance (Tannenbaum *et al.*, 1992).

Some potentially useful teams aren't managed or supported well. Managing a team is a skill, which needs training and development. Further, managing creative and innovative teams is more awkward and difficult, as suggested by the following:

● There may be reaction against the process of forcing people to form and act like a team when a team isn't needed.

● Teamwork can take more time than individual work, particularly at the beginning of a project.

● Often training is required to build a distinct set of team skills.

● Can the work be done better by more than one person?

● Does the work 'naturally' create a common purpose or set of goals for the people in a group?

● Are the members of the group interdependent? Do they have to work hand in glove to get the job done?

There are also the issues around the changing nature of teamworking – virtual teams, teleworking, diversity. Much research now highlights the negative aspects of teamwork – groupthink leading to ineffective solutions, increasing stress = competition between teams, competition over scarce resources. More recently, a number of writers have started to identify a backlash against the excessive use of teams in recent years. Drexler and Forrester (1998: 55) feel that 'the concept of teamwork has been overused and has been employed even in activities which actually require individual efforts and have very little impact on the other group members'. They also discuss issues appertaining to whether particular types of work really require teamwork, and to ask these questions before employing a team-building strategy to anything and everything. Teamwork may not always necessarily be the answer.

These sentiments are echoed by Butcher and Bailey (2000), who report that companies often saw teams as an end rather than a means, setting them up where they were not required. Further, even in situations where their use was justified, their effectiveness was hindered by managers' adherence to strongly held beliefs about how they should operate.

Managerial implications

Collaborative work is often viewed as one of the centrepieces of contemporary management, and team-working is firmly at the middle of that centrepiece. A manager's worth is often weighted against his or her skills as a leader of groups and their ability at evolving, developing and encouraging teamwork. This chapter has covered some of the key aspects of groups and teams and has attempted to raise a number of issues. To consolidate these issues, the following implications are of some importance.

1 Some of the aspects which allow groups to be cohesive are being moderated, and this must be recognised. Physical proximity helps cohesiveness and yet, with new technology and global teams, proximity is no longer vital. In another way, though, the new technology of telecommunications makes us even closer than before.

2 Group norms cannot be completely controlled but they can be influenced. Managers need to learn the art of shaping these norms through clear statements about preferred behaviours, by reinforcing the desired behaviours through their own actions and by linking them to rewards.

3 Leading and managing a team is a balancing act between continuity and diversity, between individual and team incentives, between conformity and individualism, between face-to-face team meetings and distant communications, between different but complementary roles.

4 The power of the informal group to effect change and influence the organisation is often overlooked. Leaders must recognise and use the informal, 'shadow side', of the organisation.

5 The growth in teamworking should lead to a significant and meaningful growth in the incidence of group performance reviews and team incentives. The equitable and fair measurement of a team's productivity or performance will become of paramount importance.

6 In most cases effective teams do not just occur. They need to be consciously built, created and selected for. Roles need to be established and developed, diversity needs to be encouraged, and an open culture of trust sought. The negative aspects of cohesiveness and groupthink should be guarded against.

7 Although many textbooks define formal groups as permanent, many organisations are seeking to implement adaptable structures and develop more flexible and proactive patterns of working. In this sense the permanence of a formal group may be no more than the duration of the project in a matrix structure. Less permanence will be more common.

8 Although making group decisions can be time consuming, trigger conflict and involve inappropriate pressures to conform, the decisions are often more accurate, creative and acceptable. This is because of the innate capacity for groups to demonstrate synergy – 'the whole is greater than the sum of its parts'. But synergy does not just happen, it has to be nurtured and managed.

9 Issues faced by the leaders of global, virtual and self-directed teams include how to manage the anonymous team and what to do about performance management. What is the new social protocol for virtual teams and how do we manage that? Can any of the traditional views of team development still be applied?

10 It is important to understand that teams, and teamworking, may not be the magical panacea for all organisations.

Summary of main points

This chapter has examined the rapidly changing nature of groups and teams. The main points made are:

● humans have an innate 'craving' to be in a variety of groups, and organisational life helps to satisfy this need;

● there are clear differences and similarities between informal and formal groups;

● there are significant distinctions between groups, psychological groups and teams;

● groups occur, grow, develop and are maintained in a number of different but complementary ways;

● there is a fine balance between effective and dysfunctional teams;

● technology is playing an increasingly important role in the life and functioning of teams.

Conclusions

The nature of teams is changing significantly because of changes in organisations and the very nature of the work they do. Organisations are becoming more distributed across traditional geographical boundaries and across industries. What were once competitors are now collaborators, what were once outsiders are now stakeholders, what were once stark boundaries are now fuzzy fences. Organisations have now discovered the value of collaborative work, both inside and outside. There is an increasing emphasis on knowledge management and harvesting the learning from the experiences of people in the organisation.

Globalisation and technology are also having a profound effect on the ways in which organisations structure themselves and their work. Technology has taken on an increasingly significant role in the way we organise, structure and manage teams. It has the potential to change the very nature of groups and teams as we understand them. Although technology can assist groups in overcoming the constraints of space and time, it also demands that groups learn and understand it, so that they may fruitfully appropriate its structures and realise its intended benefits and undoubted shortcomings. How computer-facilitated interaction will affect such critical group and team variables as pressure for uniformity, status and power is as yet largely unknown.

Can all, or any, of the traditional models for group development still be applied? What will become of team roles, group norms and cultural values? How do formal and informal groups fit into virtual organisations and workplaces? The scope for further discussion, exploration and research around this growing area is enormous, for it involves all that you have read up to now about groups and teams.

Questions

1 An argument often put forward in support of teams is that they are 'synergistic' – 'the whole is greater than the sum of their parts'. How true is this? How would you interpret this view?

2 What do you see as the key emerging issues for work teams over the coming decade? How can organisations and teams manage these issues?

3 What processes might the manager of a group of teleworkers introduce to maintain a team spirit and ethos?

4 How might an organisation go about balancing the paradox of having both compatibility and diversity in a team?

5 Think about the different groups and teams you are a member of... at home, in work, at school or college. Try to classify them into groups or teams. What needs does each one satisfy for you? Try to apply a model of group development to each one. What stage of development is each one at?

6 Assess the impact of technology as a key determinant of group behaviour and performance. What action might be taken to help embellish the advantages and reduce the disadvantages?

7 'Belbin's Team Roles Inventory is just a simple little descriptive test which is fun to do but tells you little you didn't already know'. Discuss!

8 Within your own environment, describe which formal and informal groups and teams you are a member of. Is it easy to decide between formal or informal? Is it harder to decide whether they are a group or a team? Are some more difficult to categorise than others? What are the norms for these different groups?

9 There are lots of firms of management consultants, training organisations and human resource providers on the internet. A search under a topic such as 'teamworking' or 'teambuilding' will generate a good range. Search the Internet and investigate what these consultants and organisations are offering in the way of teambuilding experiences and interventions.

- What is the range and what do you think is the effectiveness of the different interventions and offerings?

- What models, theories and frameworks are these different interventions and organisations operating from?

- Is it just about getting the team together for some fun . . . or is it more than that?

References

Adair, J. (1986) *Effective Teambuilding*. Aldershot: Gower.

Alexander, S. (2000) 'Virtual teams going global – communication and culture are issues for distant team members', *InfoWorld*, 22(46), pp. 55–6.

Ancona, D. G. (1987) 'Groups in organizations: Extending laboratory models', in Hendrick, C. (ed.) *Group Processes and Intergroup Relations*. Beverly Hills, CA: Sage.

Ancona, D. and Caldwell, D. (1990) 'Improving the performance of new product teams', *Research Technology Management*, 33(2), pp. 25–9.

Armstrong, M. (1996) 'How group efforts can pay dividends', *People Management*, 25 (January), pp. 22–7.

Arnold, J., Silvester, J., Patterson, F., Robertson, I., Cooper, C. and Burnes, B. (2005) *Work Psychology*, 4th edn. Harlow: Financial Times Prentice Hall.

Aronson, E. (2007) *The Social Animal*, 10th edn. New York and Oxford: Freeman.

Asch, S. E. (1951) 'Effects of group pressure upon the modification and distortion of judgements', in Guetzkow, H. (ed.) *Groups, Leadership and Men*. New York: Carnegie Press.

Balkema, A. and Molleman, E. (1999) 'Barriers to the development of self-organizing teams', *Journal of Managerial Psychology*, 14(2), pp. 134–50.

Bass, B. M. and Ryterband, E. C. (1979) *Organizational Psychology*, 2nd edn. London: Allyn & Bacon.

Belbin, R. M. (1996) *Team Roles at Work*, New edn. Oxford: Butterworth-Heinemann.

Belbin, R. M. (2004) *Management Teams: Why They Succeed or Fail*, 2nd edn. Oxford: Elsevier Butterworth-Heinemann.

Bell, B. S. and Kozlowski, S. W. J. (2002) 'A typology of virtual teams: Implications for effective leadership', *Group and Organization Management*, 27, pp. 14–49.

Benne, K. D. and Sheats, P. (1948) 'Functional roles of group members', *Journal of Social Issues*, 4, pp. 41–9.

Brower, M. J. (1995) 'Empowering teams: What, why and how', *Empowerment in Organisations*, 3(1), pp. 13–25.

Buchanan, D. (1987) 'Job enrichment is dead: Long live high-performance work design', *Personnel Management*, May, pp. 40–3.

Butcher, D. and Bailey, C. (2000) 'Crewed awakenings', *People Management*, August, pp. 35–7.

Carrington, L. (1995) 'Rewards for all', *Personnel Today*, 17 January.

Cascio, W. F. (1998) 'On managing a virtual workplace', *Occupational Psychologist*, August, pp. 5–11.

Coles, M. (1998a) 'Managers tackle worldwide teams', *Sunday Times*, 8 March, p. 24.

Coles, M. (1998b) 'Managers learn value of sharing', *Sunday Times*, 19 July, p. 24.

Diehl, M. and Stroebe, W. (1987) 'Productivity loss in brainstorming groups: Towards the solution of a riddle', *Journal of Personality and Social Psychology*, 53, pp. 497–509.

Drexler, A. B. and Forrester, R. (1998) 'teamwork – not necessarily the answer', *HR Magazine*, January.

Drez, J. (1999) 'Teams and teamwork for the 21st century', **www.siu.edu/departments/cola/psycho/psyc323/chapt13**

Fulk, J. and Collins-Jarvis, L. (2001) 'Wired meetings: Technological mediation of organizational gatherings', in F. M. Jablin and L. L. Putnam (eds) *The New Handbook of Organizational Communication*. Thousand Oaks, CA: Sage, pp. 624–63.

Glass, N. (1996) *Management Masterclass: A Practical Guide to the New Realities of Business*. London: Nicholas Brealey.

Gordon, J. (1994) 'The team troubles that won't go away', *Training*, August.

Greenes, K. (2002) Keynote address. Knowledge Management and Organisational Learning Conference, London.

Guirdham, M. (2002) *Interactive Behaviour at Work*, 3rd edn. Harlow: Financial Times Prentice Hall.

Guzzo, R. A. and Dickson, M. J. (1996) 'Teams in organizations: Recent research on performance and effectiveness', *Annual Review of Psychology*, 47, pp. 307–38.

Hackman, J. R. (1990) *Groups that Work (and Those that Don't). Creating Conditions for Effective Teamwork*. San Francisco: Jossey-Bass.

Handy, C. (1989) *The Age of Unreason*. London: Business Books.

Handy, C. (1993) *Understanding Organizations*. Harmondsworth: Penguin Books.

Higgs, M. (1996) 'Overcoming the problems of cultural differences to establish success for international management teams', *Team Performance Management*, 2(1), pp. 36–43.

Hofstede, G. (1980) *Culture's Consequences: International Differences in Work-related Values*. Beverly Hills, CA: Sage.

Huczynski, A. and Buchanan, D. (2007) *Organizational Behaviour: An Introductory Text*, 6th edn. Harlow: Financial Times Prentice Hall.

Industrial Society (1995) *Self-Managed Teams*. London: The Industrial Society.

Janis, J. L. (1972) *Victims of Groupthink*. Boston: Houghton Mifflin.

Johnson, P., Heimann, V. and O'Neill, K. (2001) 'The "wonderland" of virtual teams', *The Journal of Workplace Learning*, 13(1), pp. 24–30.

Joynson, S. and Forrester, A. (1995) *Sid's Heroes: Uplifting Business Performance and the Human Spirit*. London: BBC Books.

Kandola, R. (1995) 'Managing diversity: New broom or old hat?', in Cooper, C. L. and Robertson, I. T. (eds) *International Review of Industrial and Organizational Psychology*, *Vol. 10*. Chichester: John Wiley, pp. 131–67.

Katzenbach, J. R. and Smith, D. K. (1999) *The Wisdom of Teams: Creating the High-performance Organization*. New York: Harper Business.

Kiser, K. (1999) 'Working on world time', *Training*, 36(3), pp. 28–34.

Kreitner, R., Kinicki, A. and Buelens, M. (2002) *Organizational Behavior*, 2nd Euro. edn. London: McGraw-Hill.

McGregor, D. (1960) *The Human Side of Enterprise*. New York: McGraw-Hill.

Maier, N. R. F. and Solem, A. R. (1952) 'The contribution of a discussion leader to the quality of group thinking: The effective use of minority opinions', *Human Relations*, 5, pp. 277–88.

Martin, J. (2005) *Organizational Behaviour and Management*, 3rd edn. London: Thomson Learning.

Maznevski, M. L. (1994) 'Understanding our differences: Performance in decision-making groups with diverse members', *Human Relations*, 47(5), pp. 531–52.

Mullen, B. and Cooper, C. (1994) 'The relationship between group cohesiveness and performance: An integration', *Psychological Bulletin*, 115, pp. 210–27.

Mullins, L. J. (2002) *Management and Organisational Behaviour*, 6th edn. Harlow: Financial Times Prentice Hall.

Norstedt, J. P. and Aguren, S. (1973) *Saab–Scania Report*. Stockholm: Swedish Employers' Confederation.

Obeng, E. D. A. (1994) *All Change!* London: Pitman Publishing.

Perry, B. (1984) *Enfield: A High-Performance System.* Bedford, MA: Educational Services Development and Publishing.

Piper, W. E., Marrache, M., Lacroix, R., Richardson, A. M. and Jones, B. D. (1983) 'Cohesion as a basic bond in groups', *Human Relations*, 26(2), pp. 93–108.

Potter, R., Cooke, R. and Balthazard, P. (2000). 'Virtual team interaction: Assessment, consequences and management', *Team Performance Management*, 6(7), pp. 131–7.

Salem, M., Lazarus, H. and Cullen, J. (1994) 'Developing self-managing teams: Structure and performance', *Journal of Management Development*, 11(3), pp. 24–32.

Schein, E. H. (1988) *Organizational Psychology*, 3rd edn. Hemel Hempstead: Prentice Hall.

Solomon, C. M. (2001) 'Managing virtual teams', *Workforce*, 80(6), pp. 60–5.

Sparrow, P. (2000) 'Teleworking and the psychological contract', in Daniels, K., Lamond, A. and Standen, P. (eds) *Managing Telework*. London: Thomson Learning.

Sproull, L. and Kiesler, S. (1991) 'Computers, networks and work', *Scientific American*, 265, pp. 116–32.

Stough, S., Eom, S. and Buckenmyer, J. (2000) 'Virtual teaming: A strategy for moving your organization into the new millennium', *Industrial Management and Data Systems*, 100(8), p. 380.

Tannenbaum, S. I., Beard, R. L. and Sales, E. (1992) 'Teambuilding and its influence on team effectiveness', in Kelly, K. (ed.) *Issues, Theory and Research in Industrial/Organisational Psychology*. North-Holland: Amsterdam, pp. 117–53.

Thomas, H. (1974) 'Finding a better way', *Guardian*, 17 January.

Trist, E. L. *et al.* (1963) *Organizational Choice*. London: Tavistock Publications.

Tuckman, B. W. (1965) 'Development sequence in small groups', *Psychological Bulletin*, 63, pp. 384–99.

Tuckman, B. W. and Jensen, M. A. C. (1977) 'Stages of small group development revisited', *Group and Organizational Studies*, 2, pp. 419–27.

Valery, N. (1974) 'Importing the lessons of Swedish workers', *New Scientist*, 62(892), pp. 27–8.

Watson, W. E., Kumar, K. and Michaelson, L. (1993) 'Cultural diversity's impact on interaction process and performance: Comparing homogeneous and diverse task groups', *Academy of Management Journal*, 36(3), 590–602.

Wenger, E. C. and Snyder, W. M. (2000) 'Communities of practice: The organizational frontier', *Harvard Business Review*, January–February, pp. 139–45.

Woodcock, M. (1979) *Team Development Manual*. Aldershot: Gower.

Young, R. (1998) 'The Wide-awake Club', *People Management*, 5 February, pp. 46–9.

Further reading

Adair, J. (1986) *Effective Teambuilding*. Aldershot: Gower.

Belbin, R. M. (1993) *Team Roles at Work*. Oxford: Butterworth-Heinemann.

Coles, M. (1998) 'Managers learn value of sharing', *Sunday Times*, 19 July, p. 24.

Gibson, C. and Cohen, S. (2003) *Virtual Teams that Work: Creating Conditions for Virtual Team Effectiveness*. San Francisco: Jossey-Bass.

Hamel, G., Doz, Y. and Prahalad, C. K. (1989) 'Collaborate with your competitors – and win', *Harvard Business Review*, January/February.

Mullins, L. J. (1999) *Management and Organisational Behaviour*, 5th edn. London: Financial Times Pitman Publishing.

Pringle, D. (1996) 'Is team-working faith misplaced?', *Personnel Today*, 12 March.

Robbins, H. and Finley, M. (1998) *Why Teams Don't Work: What Went Wrong and How to Put it Right*. London: Orion Books.

Senge, P. (1991) *The Fifth Discipline*. London: Random Century.

Wenger, E. C. and Snyder, W. M. (2000) 'Communities of practice: The organizational frontier', *Harvard Business Review*, January–February, pp. 139–45.

West, M. A. (2004) *Effective Teamwork: Practical Lessons from Organizational Research*, 2nd edn. Oxford: Blackwell Publishing.

Internet sites

General

www.emeraldinsight.com A useful general site which can be used to search for journal articles and interviews with management commentators. They also have a 'Journals of the Week' page, featuring free access to two different journals each week.

www.strategy-business.com A site which focuses around its own quarterly journal, with articles, interviews etc.

www.managementfirst.com An up-to-date site with some limited access to selected, and abbreviated, journal articles. Includes 'specialist' functional areas.

www.peoplemanagement.co.uk The site for the Chartered Institute of Personnel and Development (CIPD) and its fortnightly magazine. The current edition is available for perusal. There's always something around groups and teams.

Specific

www.belbin.com A chance to 'make contact' with the man himself, or at least his son!

www.employment-studies.co.uk/press/index.php

http://reviewing.co.uk/toolkit/teams-and-teamwork.htm This is a good site which carries a comprehensive collection and review of teamwork links and sites.

www.teams.org.uk

www.teamwork.demon.co.uk An example of a typical consultancy and its 'teamwork' offerings.

6 Management and leadership

Learning outcomes

On completion of this chapter you should be able to:

- know the difference between leadership and management;
- understand the prime developments in management theory, including the work of Taylor, Fayol and Mintzberg;
- know and understand the main developments in leadership theories encompassed by the trait, behavioural and situational schools;
- appreciate different perspectives on, or approaches to, leadership and management;
- recognise that individuals may operate in limited frames of reference which set limits to their leadership and management capability;
- understand that leadership may be best viewed as a pluralistic concept involving many capabilities which might be shared between a number of leaders;
- understand and analyse the activities of some leaders who have successfully managed change.

Key concepts

- management
- leadership
- traits
- leadership behaviour
- leadership style
- leadership and diversity
- situational theory
- contingency theory
- path–goal theory
- intrapreneurship and entrepreneurship
- leadership frames
- pluralistic leadership
- transactional and transformational leadership
- leadership, conflict, communications and change.

A vital and, some argue, increasingly dominant, aspect of organisation is the role of management and leadership. Research and academic and practitioner interest in management and in leadership has blossomed in recent decades. As interest in and concern about organisational change, globalisation and diversity have grown, the role of leadership has been emphasised. Similarly, the definition of management and management competencies and the concept of managerialism have stimulated considerable debate in political, academic and organisational spheres.

 ## Introduction

An understanding of organisational theory (refer to Chapter 2) is vital to gain an appreciation of the nature and practice of management and leadership. As a consequence, it is appropriate to briefly explore the development of management theory, from the early works of Frederick Taylor to contemporary understandings offered by Henry Mintzberg and others in so much as they reveal the changing nature of management and leadership. The chapter explores the difference between leadership and management before going on to examine the development of leadership theory. This body of knowledge has evolved separately from management theory, although many leadership theories appear as relevant to managers and management as they do to leaders and leadership. In keeping with the overall objectives of this book, this chapter also looks at some contemporary issues and provides two fresh insights into leadership, that is, re-framing and pluralism. It concludes by building on the theme of change, examining both theoretical and case study material, diversity, communication and conflict.

 ## From Taylor to Mintzberg

This section examines four writers who consider the functions performed by management, enabling us to define management and explore how thinking has changed through time.

Frederick Taylor

As discussed in Chapter 2, Taylor's work in the early twentieth century focused on the management of the work task. His emphasis on rationality led to the application of scientific principles to work management in order to establish the most efficient way of working. He argued that efficiency, standardisation and discipline would result from a process of scientific management of work tasks. Taylor suggested that it was a prime managerial function to undertake such analysis.

It is important to locate developments in scientific management in their historical context. In the early twentieth century, management was a little-researched
and very imprecise activity. (Many would argue that little has changed in this
regard!) Taylor's work largely preceded the widespread adoption of mass production techniques. Little systematic research had been conducted and practices
varied considerably. Workers tended to believe that an increase in productivity on
their part would merely result in job losses. Understandably, they took advantage
of poor management controls to slow production. They were able to do so as
workers themselves often designed or organised their own efforts and had little
interest in seeking efficiency.

Many modern organisations still adopt Taylor-like principles in order to maintain
or increase productivity. This is particularly the case when similar or identical outputs are required on a near-continuous process. Whereas Taylor's work was novel in
its time, it is now largely taken for granted. Increasingly, aspects of it have been
rejected in favour of more 'human' or social considerations and the whole approach
has proven less valuable in many modern contexts. Nevertheless, the principles of
division between managerial and worker roles, of standardisation and specialisation, of division of labour and efficiency, remain central in many organisations.

Henri Fayol

Although Henri Fayol did not invent the concept of management, he did distinguish it from other organisational activity and outlined, in some detail, what he
considered to be the prime functions of a manager. His is a normative and prescriptive model: it indicates how managers *should* conduct their activity in order to
achieve efficiency. Some readers may be familiar with Fayol's suggested functions
of management: they are frequently referred to in numerous definitions of management. Fayol suggested that managers have an obligation to:

- *plan and forecast* – prepare a series of actions to enable the organisation to meet
  its objectives in the future;
- *organise* – to fulfil the administrative principles embraced by Fayol;
- *coordinate* – to ensure that resources, actions and outputs are coordinated to
  achieve desired outcomes;
- *command* – to give direction to employees;
- *control* – ensuring that activities are in accordance with the plan, that orders are
  followed and principles of management applied.

He also established 14 principles of management, many of which still profoundly
influence and significantly reflect the way many 'modern' organisations are managed. This could be considered to be seminal work, an important influence on
management theory, and, consequently, is worthy of some consideration here.
Table 6.1 lists these principles and attempts to divide them between those which
primarily relate to organisational structure and those concerning broader management functions (*see also* Chapter 7).

Table 6.1 Fayol: the principles of management

Primarily structural principles	Other principles
Division of work	Discipline
Authority and responsibility	Subordination of individual interest to general interest
Unity of command	Remuneration of personnel
Unity of direction	Equity
Centralisation	Stability of tenure of personnel
Scalar chain	Initiative
Order	*Esprit de corps*

Source: Adapted from Fayol (1949).

Although many of these principles were commonplace in organisations before Fayol's work, it was not until 1949 that they were set out in this systematic manner. Some of the principles have been challenged by modern developments in organisations. For example, the principle of unity of command, where each person has one superior to whom they report, although still the norm, is contravened in many matrix- or project-based organisations. Additionally, the rather rigid principles do not sit well with contemporary developments, such as teamworking, flatter hierarchies, professional control and flexible working.

Peter Drucker

Two more recent writers, Peter Drucker and Henry Mintzberg, have attempted to describe and comment upon what managers *do*. This functional approach has a long tradition in management writing. Whereas Drucker gives a prescriptive analysis of the managerial role, rather in the manner of Taylor and Fayol, Mintzberg seeks empirically to comment upon the reality of managers' roles.

Drucker (1977) identifies three broad tasks:

- satisfying the goals or mission of the organisation;
- enabling the worker to achieve and focus on productivity;
- managing social responsibilities.

In order to fulfil these fundamental roles, Drucker suggests, managers are required to: set objectives; organise; motivate and communicate; measure and develop people. The prime difference between this later work, and that conducted previously, is the consideration of human and interpersonal issues, including recognition of the importance of communications and wider social concerns. It was, largely, the work of the human relations school (*see* Chapter 2 for details) which placed such concerns on the practitioner and academic agendas.

Henry Mintzberg

In 1973 Henry Mintzberg published his influential work on management, following detailed observations of what managers actually did, whereas Fayol and others had presented prescriptive analyses which became 'myths of modern management'. In contrast to what had previously been understood, managers were not found to spend most of their time planning, organising, coordinating, commanding and controlling. Instead, Mintzberg identified ten roles which managers fulfil in the conduct of their jobs: these are categorised into three groups, as shown in Table 6.2. Mintzberg (1973) suggested that managers often attempt, and frequently fail, to sequence their roles logically in the pursuit of their objectives. Figure 6.1 indicates a simple temporal sequence of activity; first, the manager builds relationships with employees and networks internally with other departments. Doing so enables the manager to collect information and to begin to act as spokesperson for the group. As stable relationships develop, they yield quality information (the second stage) which finally leads to the third stage: decision making, objective setting and resource allocation decisions.

Kotter (1982), broadly supporting Mintzberg's findings, found that managers appear to spend very little time in isolation on solitary tasks. They prefer, instead, according to Mintzberg (1973), to work or consult with subordinates (48 per cent of their time), with superiors (7 per cent of their time) and with peers and outsiders (44 per cent). A 'typical' manager's day comprises frequent interruptions for brief conversations, by phone, in person, or increasingly, via e-mail and other electronic

Table 6.2 Mintzberg: managerial roles

Managerial roles	Managerial activities
Interpersonal roles	All managerial behaviours which establish relationships
Figurehead	Performs ceremonial duties – testifies at hearing, opens new offices
Leader	Motivates employees – encourages new employees, recognises achievements, recruits and dismisses
Liaison	Networking – joins professional societies, answers external post
Informational roles	Allowing managers to collect and disseminate information
Monitor	Scans for information – reads sector press
Disseminator	Shares information with employees – holds meetings, writes memos, forwards mail
Spokesperson	Shares information with outsiders – makes speeches, keeps superiors informed
Decisional roles	Managerial behaviours which set, implement and monitor progress towards objectives
Entrepreneur	Seeks to change – looks for new ideas
Disturbance handler	Responds to pressures and crises – acts quickly in crisis, faces problems
Resource allocator	Allocates resources to others – manages the budget, constructs schedules
Negotiator	Reaches agreements – solves work disputes, resolves arguments

Source: Based on Mintzberg (1973).

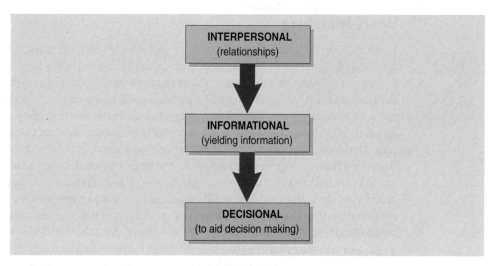

Figure 6.1 Sequence of roles

forms of communication, which serve not only to punctuate activity but also to keep the manager informed. Dailey (1988) suggests that managers should not balk at such interruptions as the resultant impetus given to relationship building and information dissemination proves invaluable in informing decision making.

More recent theorists, for example, Rosabeth Moss Kanter and also Tom Peters and Henry Mintzberg have focused on managers and leaders as critical strategic players in organisations. This has led them to stress the importance of mission and vision and of culture and the leadership of values within a customer-orientated outward-facing business environment. This 'new' approach can be illustrated by the Virgin group of companies and entrepreneur Sir Richard Branson (refer to Mini-case 6.1). Virgin attempts to identify a holistic picture of the conditions necessary for organisational success.

Mini-case 6.1: Virgin

Extracts from the Virgin web site (**www.virgin.com**, January 2008) indicate the importance the organisation places on achieving a group-wide sense of mission, largely focused on customer need and care, in order to provide competitive and commercial value to Virgin.

'We believe in making a difference. In our customers' eyes, Virgin stands for value for money, quality, innovation, fun and a sense of competitive challenge. We deliver a quality service by empowering our employees and we facilitate and monitor customer feedback to continually improve the customer's experience through innovation.'

'All the markets in which Virgin operates tend to have features in common: they are typically markets where the customer has been ripped off or underserved, where there is confusion and/or where the competition is complacent.'

'Contrary to what some people may think, our constantly expanding and eclectic empire is neither random nor reckless. Each successive venture demonstrates our skill in picking the right market and the right opportunity.'

'Once a Virgin company is up and running, several factors contribute to making it a success. The power of the Virgin name; Richard Branson's personal reputation; our unrivalled network of friends, contacts and partners; the Virgin management style; the way talent is empowered to flourish within the group. To some traditionalists, these may not seem hard headed enough. To them, the fact that Virgin has minimal management layers, no bureaucracy, a tiny board and no massive global HQ is an anathema.'

'Our companies are part of a family rather than a hierarchy. They are empowered to run their own affairs, yet other companies help one another, and solutions to problems come from all kinds of sources. In a sense we are a community, with shared ideas, values, interests and goals. The proof of our success is real and tangible.'

 ## Differentiating leadership from management

We are now in a position to define management and leadership and to attempt to differentiate the two. *Managers perform functions in organisations and hold a particular, formal, title and/or fulfil a role.* A typical example is a divisional marketing manager, responsible for the marketing of a product range in a geographical territory, or a personnel manager responsible, for example, for the recruitment and selection of staff for a single site organisation. These managers have a title, a role and a series of functions to perform, including the management of subordinates and of physical and financial resources. They are responsible for the performance and the productivity of their subordinates. Fayol stated that management is often concerned with planning, organising, coordination, commanding and controlling the activities of staff.

Leaders, on the other hand, aim to influence and guide others into pursuing particular objectives or visions of the future and to stimulate them into wanting to follow. Leadership demonstrates the power of one individual over others. Leadership is not necessarily related to hierarchical position, as management tends to be. Informal leaders exist at all levels of an organisation. Leadership is often a dynamic activity concerned with changing attitudes. Leadership is more inspirational and involves more emotional input than management. This latter point is supported by Zaleznik (1977), who suggests that managers adopt a less emotional and more passive attitude than leaders and are more concerned with seeking compromise in conflicting positions and with conserving order than in initiating transformation. Mini-case 6.2 explores the military context where the differentiation between leadership and management may be clearer. It also reflects the critical importance of 'context' in understanding the nature of management and leadership (refer to situational leadership, pp. 171–74).

It is not always the case that individuals are either managers *or* leaders. It is likely, for example, that a manager may show leadership qualities on particular occasions. Indeed, Mintzberg refers to leader roles as one of his ten roles of management. Others, such as Handy (1993), Watson (1983) and Kotter (1990), suggest that leadership is merely part of the broader role of management: it is primarily concerned with interpersonal aspects of the role. Similarly, a leader, focused on

Mini-case 6.2: Military leadership

Field Marshal Slim (1891–1970) suggested, in a speech in Adelaide, Australia, in 1957, that there is no such thing as 'military management' – there is only leadership.

'To begin with, we do not in the Army talk of "management" but of "leadership". This is significant. There is a difference between leaders and management. The leader and the men who follow him represent one of the oldest, most natural and most effective of all human relationships. The manager and those he manages are a later product, with neither so romantic nor so inspiring a history. Leadership is of the spirit, compounded of personality and vision; its practice is an art. Management is of the mind, more a matter of accurate calculation of statistics, of methods, timetables, and routine; its practice is a science. Managers are necessary; leaders are essential. A good system will produce efficient managers but more than that is needed. We must find managers who are not only skilled organisers but inspired and inspiring leaders, destined eventually to fill the highest ranks of control and direction. Such men will gather around them close-knit teams of subordinates like themselves and of technical experts, whose efficiency, enthusiasm and loyalty will be unbeatable. Increasingly this is recognised and the search for leadership is on. . '. The distinction that Slim makes is one reason why management is conducted differently in the military than in civilian environments.

There are two other important and related issues. The first is that unlike civilian organisations there is a very well defined hierarchy in the military and one whereby every serviceman goes through the same progression system and – most importantly – the same training or development courses. So you have a highly trained organisation where everyone has experienced the position of their subordinates and knows exactly what to expect of them in terms of knowledge and capability.

'Mission command' is defined as a style of military command promoting decentralised command, freedom of action and initiative. Subordinates, understanding their commander's intentions, their own missions and the context of those missions, are told what effect they are to achieve and the reason why it needs to be achieved. They then decide within their delegated freedom of action how best to achieve their missions. It is closely related to the concept of empowerment in civilian management. It is worthy of note, however, that although this concept is broadly accepted doctrine amongst NATO nations there are some where their national culture somewhat contradicts the concept.

In the military environment, notwithstanding the degree of information gathering, forward planning and coordination, it is said that 'no plan survives the first contact'. Knowledge of the situation and the capabilities of those around you, personal experience at every level below yours, as well as deep mutual trust and respect will allow the team to act freely for the common purpose.

Source: Brigadier John Hoskinson, 2008

---

attitudinal and organisational change, employing all the political, emotional and symbolic tools of leadership, might also conduct 'normal' managerial responsibilities. Nevertheless, individuals may have a tendency towards either a managerial or a leadership disposition. Many academics have attempted to differentiate leadership from management (for example, refer to Kotter, 1990). Mini-case 6.3 illustrates the activity of Henry V, whom Shakespeare regarded as a leader. Is leadership just about motivating and being inspirational?

Kotter (1990) differentiates between management and leadership at four stages of activity, that is, when creating the agenda, developing the necessary human networks for progressing the agenda, during its execution and when dealing with the

Mini-case 6.3: Henry V from Shakespeare

Probably one of the most stirring leadership speeches in literature, and subsequently on film, is that of Henry V to his army immediately before the battle of Agincourt in 1415. The reader is encouraged to believe that English victory over the French was in large measure due to the leadership of King Henry.

The young king and his army are outnumbered and tired yet he stands among them and addresses his troops:

'We few, we happy few, we band of brothers;
For he today that sheds his blood with me
Shall be my brother; be he ne'er so vile,
This day shall gentle his condition:
And gentlemen in England now abed
Shall think themsleves accurs'd they were not here,
And hold their manhoods cheap while any speaks
That fought with us upon St Crispin's day.'

For many, this is what leadership is about. But, is that what leaders really do and are?

Source: Shakespeare: *King Henry V*, Act IV, scene 3. Also illustrated in two films of the same title, the first starring Laurence Olivier (1944) and the more recent Kenneth Branagh (1989).

outcomes of this activity. Throughout, Kotter suggests that leadership is more concerned with the human, visionary, inspirational, motivational and dynamic aspects of the total management/leadership role whereas management focuses on the tasks identified by Fayol, that is, planning, organising and controlling, together with problem solving and maintaining a degree of predictability and stability.

Another observation you may have made about the debate above, not least embedded in the two mini-cases provided, is that until quite recently the discussion around leadership has been contextualised within the male gender. Shakespeare and Field Marshal Slim can be excused – they write in the context of their time – but the times are changing.

Leadership: schools of thought

There has been considerable interest in leadership for centuries. People have been fascinated with the personality or character of exceptional leaders, whether they brought social good or ill to their followers. It is possible to divide leadership research into three broad schools (*see* Figure 6.2): trait, behavioural and situational approaches.

A concern to discover the personal characteristics, or traits, of good leaders was a particularly salient idea around the middle of the twentieth century. Trait theories can only give a partial and often superficial perspective on the issue of leadership. Later the behavioural theories were themselves criticised, primarily as being non-context specific, a criticism which has led to a focus on the context or situation in which leaders operate. Situational theories deal with the leader in an organisational, or other, context and add richness to the study of leadership.

Trait theories	Behavioural theories	Situational theories
Emphasis on the personal characteristics of leaders	Emphasis on the behaviours of leaders including their style of leadership	Emphasis on the leader in the context or situation in which he or she leads

Figure 6.2 Leadership research: three phases of development

The following section synthesises some of the prime findings of each of these three schools.

Trait theories

Personal traits were, and on occasions still are, thought to have a bearing on an individual's ability to lead. These traits included physical characteristics, such as height, social background, intelligence and a range of personality features. Considerable research attempted, without great success, to establish relationships between many trait variables and leadership success (Stodgill, 1948; Mann, 1959). Many traits are weakly related to leadership. However, Bennis and Nanus (1985) established some relationship between the effectiveness of leadership and the traits of logical thinking, persistence, empowerment and self-control, where logical thinking relates to:

- the ability to translate ideas into simple forms;
- persuasive abilities;
- explaining phenomena in unique ways.

Persistence traits were thought to be:

- considering setbacks as minor mistakes;
- working long hours;
- attempting to succeed against the odds.

Empowerment traits included:

- enthusing people about their goals;
- being enthusiastic and energetic oneself;
- increasing confidence in employees' own abilities.

Self-control traits included:

- working under pressure;
- remaining calm and even-tempered;
- resisting intimidation.

Numerous other academics and researchers have attempted to establish a link between traits and leadership effectiveness, including some meta-analytical work which brings together the findings of dozens of separate research projects (Lord *et al.*, 1986; Kirkpatrick and Locke, 1991). Each produces its own list of leadership qualities; most appear intuitively sound. Unfortunately, there is only limited agreement between all of these studies. For example, a degree of intelligence appears to be necessary to improve leadership effectiveness. The varied interpretations by the researchers, together with the range and complexity of materials with which they are dealing, have ensured that the findings offer little fresh insight. They are, after all, like much research, attempts to relate two or more variables which might be quite unrelated.

Although this work is of some value there are significant problems with trait theories. Some studies are gender, even racially, biased while many more are focused on a rather narrow, albeit at the time often majority, section of the management workforce in North America and the UK – white males. Very few traits appear to correlate strongly with leadership effectiveness. Some assume that leadership ability can be measured simply. In many studies leadership effectiveness, success or ability are assumed to be products of position in the organisation or, alternatively, subjective assessment is used to categorise good or effective leaders. The saying that leaders are born and not made cannot be substantiated; it simply is not supported by research evidence. Additionally, trait theories omit any situational or contextual considerations. Surely, some leaders become effective because the situation is 'right' for them (and vice versa). It may well be that appropriate situations 'make' great leaders. Finally, trait theories can lead to unhelpful stereotyping. They can lead to the assumption that once one has, or has not, the required traits, leadership effectiveness is, somehow, decided. If those traits are physical, or otherwise of a nature which makes it impossible for them to be developed or acquired, the implication is that leaders are born, not made, and that management development or experience becomes meaningless.

Behavioural theories

Rather than focus on the traits or characteristics of the leader, the behavioural approach examines leadership behaviour, particularly that which influences the performance and motivation of subordinates. As a result, emphasis is placed on leadership style.

The Ohio State University studies, in the 1940s and 1950s, examined leadership style, and concluded that there were two fundamental types of leader behaviours: 'initiating structure' and 'consideration'. Initiating structure refers to *behaviour which focuses on the achievement of objectives and includes clear supervision and role clarification, planning of work and a results orientation.* Consideration includes *behaviours which encourage collaboration and focus on supportive networks, group welfare and the maintenance of job satisfaction.*

At the same time as the Ohio studies, researchers at the University of Michigan made similar findings. Leaders and managers exhibited characteristics which were employee centred and/or production-centred. More recently, these broad descriptions have been labelled 'task' and 'people' orientations. As a result of this work, commentators suggested that it was possible to identify the 'one best' style of leadership, that is, a leader who exhibits high initiating structure and high consideration behaviours: a strong orientation to both task and people issues.

 ## Leadership style

Leadership style refers to *the behaviour of leaders towards subordinates, the manner in which tasks and functions of leadership are conducted.* Tannenbaum and Schmidt (1973) suggested a continuum in leadership styles from a so-called boss-centred approach to a subordinate-centred approach. Figure 6.3 illustrates a simple style continuum. The suggestion is that managers' or leaders' style can be 'mapped' along a continuum between the authoritarian and democratic extremes. It is likely, however, that a leader's decisions will always be influenced by the situation in which they find themselves. Hence, even if a leader is able to adjust his or her style according to the particular situations there will be a need to consider a host of contextual factors, such as group effectiveness, the nature of the task environment, pressures of time. Tannenbaum and Schmidt recognised that situational factors were important. They argued that forces in subordinates, for example their level of experience and the style to which they are accustomed, and forces in the leader, including knowledge and preferred style, combine to determine the most appropriate leadership style to adopt. In choosing an appropriate style, managers consider their own value system and leadership inclination, the level of confidence they have in their subordinates and their ability to cope with the uncertainties of the situation. They will evaluate the nature and experience of their subordinates, their readiness to assume responsibility, their knowledge and interest. This refinement to the basic model places their work in the situational school of leadership (*see* pp. 170–73).

A problem with the simple style continuum model is that there is only one dimension. However, other styles, not encompassed in the autocratic–democratic continuum, may be applicable. For example, leaders may consider re-framing a situation, thinking of it differently – in a unique manner or from a different, atypical, perspective (*see* the discussion on pp. 175–77 on re-framing leadership, where reference is made to the work of Fisher and Torbert). This model also implies that leaders make rational decisions based on a wealth of knowledge about the context, themselves and their subordinates – an assumption that is not necessarily proven

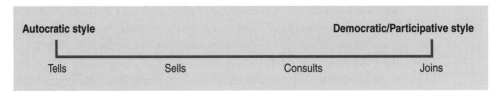

Figure 6.3 Style continuum

Source: After Tannenbaum and Schmidt (1973) and others.

by experience. Nevertheless, the model can prove a useful management development tool and raises the value of self-awareness of one's style of leadership.

Prevailing styles of leadership may vary across different cultures or by gender. Mini-case 6.4 summarises some of the current thinking about female leadership style.

Mini-case 6.4: Female leadership

There is a great deal of anecdotal writing and some research about female leadership style. It is widely argued, for example, that women's leadership style embraces the importance of communication, positive working relationships and teamwork. Other things being equal, women are considered to have better social skills than men and are concerned to keep team members informed. They are thought to put the success of the team before that of themselves and use influencing skills as opposed to authority to achieve their goals. Women may be more tolerant of individual differences and less bound by social traditions. Women may be better at motivating colleagues by their willingness to appreciate others, show their feelings and share their thoughts. Others have suggested that women are less willing to take risks or focus their energies away from the detail towards more strategic considerations.

Discussion Question

Are these beliefs valid? If so, what might be the impact of these understandings on organisational leadership and both women and men?

A simpler version of the work of Tannenbaum and Schmidt suggests that the continuum may involve four distinct styles of leadership, namely:

- *joins* – manager defines the problem, but leaves it open for alternative problem-definitions to arise, and for the scope of the endeavour to expand; then becomes a member of the problem-solving group and hands over decision-making power to the group;
- *consults* – manager both identifies the problem and makes the decision, but only after listening and possibly adopting solutions that have been suggested;
- *sells* – manager decides on the solution to problems and then persuades staff that this decision is most valid;
- *tells* – manager identifies the problems and decides on the solutions, as above, and also expects staff to implement such decisions without questioning.

John Adair

Action-centred leadership, developed by John Adair (1979), prescribes three areas of need which leaders must satisfy, namely:

- task needs;
- individual needs;
- team maintenance needs.

This work builds on that of theorists working in the behavioural tradition and argues that successful leaders need to accommodate both task and people considerations. Figure 6.4 indicates the functions involved in attempting to satisfy each need.

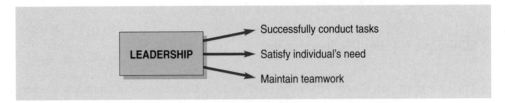

Figure 6.4 Leadership: the fulfilment of three needs
Source: Based on Adair (1979).

As indicated in Figure 6.4, action taken to meet one need may have an impact on another area. A leader who can ensure the successful conduct of tasks while satisfying individual need and maintaining teamwork, is likely to be highly effective. Adair has embraced the two prime dimensions, task and people, and added a third, team maintenance. The latter further emphasises the human and interpersonal nature of leadership and accommodates contemporary recognition of the importance of teamwork for organisational and therefore leadership effectiveness.

Behavioural school: conclusions

From a simple analysis of the material presented above, it is possible to identify four broad leadership styles:

1 Task/structure orientation.

2 People/interpersonal orientation.

3 Directive/autocratic leadership.

4 Participative/democratic leadership.

Styles 1 and 3 are often associated, as are 2 and 4; hence, these four approaches can be further reduced to just two, as is illustrated by the Ohio State University and University of Michigan research and later work by McGregor (1960) and Blake and Mouton (1964). McGregor's now popular contention, his Theory X and Theory Y, was that leaders and managers could be differentiated from one another according to their attitudes and assumptions about human nature. Theory X leaders consider people, notably subordinates, to be lazy, reluctant to assume responsibility and lacking in ambition and so, they require to be controlled, directed and, if necessary, coerced and punished. In Maslow's terms (*see* Chapter 4) they are motivated only by physiological and security needs. Theory Y represents a direct contrast. It assumes that individuals align themselves with organisational goals and, as a consequence, people require little control or direction, seek rewards consistent with their performance, may accept and relish responsibility, possess initiative and creative skills and are potentially motivated by the higher-order needs for affiliation, esteem and self-actualisation.

Blake and Mouton (1964) suggest that a manager's style can be identified and mapped according to the 'people' and 'task', or 'production', orientation. The mapping exercise allows for degrees of people or production orientation, so that it is possible, for example, to have a high people and a high production tendency (a highly desirable state), a high production and a medium people orientation, a low orientation in both dimensions (a rather precarious state) or numerous other combinations.

The work of the behavioural school represents an improvement over the trait approach. Behaviour is observable and can be learned and the focus is on what a leader does, not on what he or she is. Nevertheless, there are problems with this school of thought. It assumes that high consideration, or people orientation, and high initiating structure, or task/production focus, cause high performance. In reality the relationship between the two broad variables may be more complicated. For example, it may be that a task orientation and people concern in subordinates might lead leaders to adopt or maintain that approach as it appears to yield good results. In other words, leadership style might be both a cause and an effect of the followers' style. Also behavioural approaches, rather like trait theories, ignore the context or situation in which leaders and followers find themselves. That context is likely to partly determine the most appropriate style to adopt. For example, an organisation might have a long-engrained norm which necessitates or encourages the adoption of a task orientation. This cultural characteristic may prevent a leader from significantly deviating from that approach. Leadership is context-specific, or at least this is what the situational theories suggest.

Situational theories

When certain aspects of the behavioural and trait approaches are combined with consideration of context, or the situation in which leaders find themselves, a complex but more promising explanation of leadership is apparent. We saw in Chapter 4 that consideration of situational or contingent factors improved our understanding of motivation in the workplace. Similarly, our insight into leadership is enhanced by a consideration of these contingent factors. Once again,

Illustration in film

From *Star Trek: Generations* to *The Incredibles*

The film *Star Trek: Generations* (1994) illustrates how different (male) leaders are required for different situations – of course Captain Kirk was always good in a crisis! The animation film *The Incredibles* (2004), illustrates the stereotypical gender differences and compares the effectiveness of the two – the male action hero versus the flexible (literally) female hero. Of course Mr Incredible was ultimately only successful when he teamed up with the feminine skills of his flexible friend – something about teamwork and embracing difference to achieve success? How might this film relate to organisational reality?

contingency theory adds complexity, but richness, to our understanding of organisational behaviour.

Fiedler's contingency theory

The contingency hypothesis is that *leadership behaviour interacts with the favourableness of a situation to determine effectiveness.* It argues that some situations are more favourable than others and, as a consequence, require different behaviours. This theory requires the assessment of both the leader's style and three broad characteristics of the situation or context:

- *leader–group member relations* – the nature of work group atmosphere and subsequent loyalty, trust and so forth;
- *task structure* – clarity of the group's work and understanding of the group's goals;
- *position power* – a leader's legitimate power to tell others what to do.

Leadership style is said to be relationship-centred, where the leader is motivated to maintain good interpersonal relations, or task-orientated, in which case the leader is motivated to get on with the job. It is ascertained by requiring leaders to indicate their orientation towards their least preferred co-worker (LPC). Those who describe their LPC in 'accepting' terms are relationship-orientated whereas task-orientated leaders believe their LPC has few redeeming qualities. This, Fiedler argues, demonstrates a personality trait referred to as the leader's motivational pattern.

A highly favourable situation would be one where relations were sound and reliable, tasks were clearly structured and goals widely understood and where position power was strong.

A task orientation is considered more suited to highly favourable or highly unfavourable situations. To take an example, if there is an urgent impending requirement, say for the launch of a marketing campaign to meet an advertiser's deadline, the manager may, recognising the nature of the task and relying on position power (*see* Chapter 8), adopt a highly task-orientated approach, giving clear instructions and deadlines and requesting compliance. Alternatively, where a manager enjoys good relations with workers and if the tasks to be performed are clearly structured, that is, not much debate or decision-making ability is required in order to perform them satisfactorily, a task orientation may be best employed to ensure high productivity. The 'simplicity' of the task might not warrant a more participative or people-orientated approach and the good relations that exist could survive the adoption of a task approach. It is argued that this is common in the fast-food industry where little skill is required on the part of kitchen staff overseeing the preparation of burgers and fries!

A relationship orientation is best suited to average situational favourability. Fiedler suggests that an organisation should not focus on attempts to change a leader's personality but should select leaders to match the situation's favourability. Although this approach might be of some value in recognising that both situation and a leader's orientation can determine the appropriate choice of leader, it is of less value as a selection technique or a tool of 'social engineering' within organisations.

House's path–goal theory

Path–goal theory was briefly addressed in Chapter 4 (in the discussion of expectancy theory) and is referred to here as it has implications for leadership. It is a situational and transactional model of leadership, in addition to being a motivation theory. House (1971) suggests that it is a leader's function to clarify pathways for subordinates to achieve their desired rewards. When a subordinate recognises that a desired reward is achievable by adopting a particular course of action, then motivation to achieve that reward should follow. The leader provides the rewards and clarifies the pathways between employee effort and performance and between performance and reward. The leader engages in a transaction giving rewards for performance. This requires leaders to exercise flexibility and to develop abilities to engage in:

- *directive behaviours* – including planning, setting expectations and clarifying instructions;
- *supportive behaviours* – offering friendly consideration;
- *participative behaviours* – involving subordinates in decision making;
- *achievement-orientated behaviours* – setting objectives and expecting them to be achieved.

The leader is required to consider environmental factors and subordinate characteristics and then adopt a flexible approach. The prescriptive model suggests an appropriate style for a variety of combinations of situations, for example:

- Directive leadership best ensures high performance for subordinates who require a high degree of work structuring.
- Achievement-orientated leadership behaviours are best suited to subordinates with a strong achievement drive.
- If tasks are clear and routine dominates, then any leadership behaviour may be redundant.

The situational approach to leadership embraces both style or behavioural issues and context or situation. It is, therefore, more complex but better reflects reality than other, earlier approaches. Nevertheless, not even the models presented above can fully explain the characteristics of effective leadership. They do not adequately embrace the complexities of interpersonal behaviours and relationships nor do they accommodate the rapidity of change which characterises modern organisations. For example, if organisations follow Fiedler's advice and appoint leaders to match the situation, then organisational dynamism might so alter 'the situation' as to make the appointed leader ineffective. Additionally, there remains considerable subjectivity concerning the assessment of an individual leader's style and personality. Someone might appear to have the necessary qualities to match the perceived nature of the situation, yet not be an effective leader (and vice versa).

Although many of the contingency or situational theories take cognisance of many organisational and environmental variables little attention is paid to organisational culture (*see* Chapter 9) or organisational politics (*see* Chapter 8), both of which may have a profound influence over leadership styles and approaches.

Most of the research presented above implies that leadership is an individualistic concept; that is, it considers the role of the leader as an individual. We explore joint or multiple leadership (pluralism) below.

Intrapreneurs and entrepreneurs

It is unusual in organisational behaviour to consider the nature and activity of intrapreneurs and entrepreneurs. Entrepreneurship is the *creation of economic wealth by adding value and involves risking capital, time and energy*. When this activity takes place in an organisation it is referred to as *intrapreneurship*. The intrapreneur often has to succeed in a bureaucratic environment which tends to stifle innovation and dynamism. Both entrepreneurs and intrapreneurs can be considered, in a broad sense, to be leaders. They lead the value-adding capabilities of an organisation, the development of new ideas and ways of solving old problems. They often lead people in accepting novel solutions and new ways of operating. The case below (Mini-case 6.5) illustrates probably the most famous and one of the most successful British entrepreneurs.

Rather like the early trait theorists' attempts to explain leadership as a result of physical or other personal characteristics, much work on entrepreneurship considers entrepreneurs to possess exceptional inherent personal qualities. Peter Drucker (1985) has dispelled this myth and suggested that entrepreneurship is, like many managerial and leadership qualities, something which can be learned, whereas success owes more to hard work than to some romantic notion of sheer entrepreneurial talent. Aldag and Stearns (1987) have attempted to explode some of the conventional wisdom or myths of entrepreneurship (Table 6.3). The study of entrepreneurship is developing rapidly, going well beyond this rather simple search for the entrepreneurial profile.

Mini-case 6.5

Richard Branson and Karen Hanton: 'typical' entrepreneurs?

Sir Richard Branson is a household name. He left school at 17 to start a magazine and did not attend university. Just three years later the Virgin record label was launched. Now the umbrella company has sales of around £6 billion a year. He attempts to exploit weaknesses in existing ways of doing business. Richard Branson appears to enjoy his work and leisure activities and seeks every opportunity to promote his businesses – willing to do almost anything to promote his brand. But this is the public face. Reports suggest that as a manager he invests time in his senior executives, instils them with the need to seek major and ongoing changes and improvements and to always consider customer needs.

Karen Hanton created Toptable.co.uk after starting businesses in property development and the restaurant trade. She has a series of celebrity shareholders and business is growing. Karen argues that she tired of working for others and wanted to stand or fall on her own merits. She thinks of herself as a risk taker. The idea for this business is simple but, at the time when the internet just began to take off, it hadn't been done before.

Table 6.3 Myths of entrepreneurship

Myth	'Reality'
Entrepreneurs are doers, not thinkers	Entrepreneurs do engage in careful planning and forethought
Entrepreneurs are born, not made	Evidence suggests that characteristics are acquired and not inherited (McClelland, 1976)
All you need is money	Commitment and single-mindedness are more vital
All you need is luck	This suggests that entrepreneurial skills are irrelevant

Source: Based on Aldag and Stearns (1987).

Reframing leadership

Not surprisingly, and despite the wealth of research in the field, there is no one accepted, explanatory theory or model of leadership. In more recent times, theorists have explored alternative explanatory frames for leadership. In Chapter 2 we suggested that it is possible and valuable to view organisations as if through different lenses, to analyse them from a variety of different perspectives. Similarly, we can categorise different 'types' of leaders by analysing and evaluating the frames of reference or paradigms into which they are 'locked'.

Leadership frames

Some of the more interesting work in this area has been conducted by Fisher and Torbert (1995). They argue that managers fall into one of six frames which represent stages of managerial development. They are:

- Opportunist
- Diplomat
- Technician
- Achiever
- Strategist
- Magician.

Table 6.4 outlines the characteristics of managers in each frame. People in these frames view many aspects of organisation, the environment, their subordinates, management and leadership, differently from one another. For example, Achievers, it is argued, see leadership as a process of moulding others to their own way of thinking, whereas a Strategist is likely to attempt to encompass a variety of points of view and ways of thinking.

Whereas managers in the first four frames cannot recognise themselves as working in that constructed frame and do not fully recognise that others operate from alternative frames, persons in the fifth frame, the Strategists, show awareness of the ever-present interplay of people operating in different frames. They are, there-

Table 6.4 Managerial style characteristics

Development stage	Frame	Style characteristics
1	*Opportunist*	• short-term focus on concrete things • manipulative, deceptive, hostile, distrustful, flouts power • rejects feedback and externalises blame • dubious ethical standards: stereotypes, punishes on 'eye-for-an-eye' basis
2	*Diplomat*	• conflict avoidance, face saving • conformist, works to standards • belonging, status, gives loyalty to group
3	*Technical*	• problem solving, logic, cause and effect • self-critical, dogmatic, meritocratic • seeks efficiency or perfection
4	*Achiever*	• long-term goals, feels like initiator • welcomes feedback, seeks mutuality • appreciates complexity but blind to subjectivity behind objectivity • guilt if falls short of own standards
5	*Strategist*	• creative conflict resolution • principle, theory, judgement can usefully inform decision making • process- and goal-orientated • aware of paradox, contradiction • relativist, individuality, existential humour • aware of frame or world-view
6	*Magician*	• seeks participation in historical/spiritual transformations, creator of mythical events • reframes situations, blends opposites • action researches, interplay of intuition, thought, action and effect • sees time as symbolic, metaphorical

Source: Adapted from D. Fisher and W. R. Torbert (1995) *Personal and Organizational Transformations: The True Challenge of Continual Quality Improvement.* © McGraw-Hill Companies, Inc. 1995.

fore, concerned with the testing and framing of assumptions encountered in social interplay. It could be argued that when moving from Achiever to Strategist managers might be able and willing to embrace double-loop learning (*see* Chapter 2) and, as Fisher and Torbert suggest, to make more effort to understand subordinates and push the limits of perceived organisational constraints. Fisher and Torbert (1995) suggest that when moving from Achiever to Strategist the leader makes a significant step forward in terms of effectiveness.

As might be expected, research indicates that the proportion of managers in each of the six categories varies. Table 6.5 reports on a sizeable research exercise, involving almost 500 managers in the USA, from first-line supervisors to senior managers and executives. Of course, this and similar work is not without its critics. We can all recognise characteristics of ourselves and others which cut across the

Table 6.5 Distribution of managers by developmental position

Position or frame	%
Opportunist	2
Diplomat	8
Technician	45
Achiever	36
Strategist	9
Magician	0
	100%

Source: D. Fisher and W. R. Torbert (1995)
Personal and Organizational Transformations:
The True Challenge of Continual Quality
Improvement. © McGraw-Hill Companies,
Inc. 1995.

positions identified. Few people appear to correspond clearly to one frame alone, and this could prove to be a major criticism of the whole concept which suggests that people are, albeit not often permanently, 'locked' into just one frame. Additionally, research in this area is notoriously difficult and fraught with problems which question its reliability and validity. There is also an assumption that competence in leadership, especially the leadership of major transformational change, is better performed by Strategists and, if they exist, Magicians. There is no real hard evidence to suggest that this is the case. Nevertheless, thinking about frames of reference, reflecting upon one's experiences and attempting to explore alternative approaches, is of considerable value, particularly in developing managerial and leadership understanding and capability.

 ## Leadership and change

As a theme throughout this book, organisational change is particularly worthy of consideration in any discussion of leadership. After all, one of the key defining elements of good leadership is taking people through successful change. We will begin by exploring an examination of pluralistic leadership of organisational change before exploring transformational leadership and looking at two case studies.

Pluralistic leadership

Traditionally, leadership has been considered an individual or singular activity. That is, one person leads and the rest follow. In reality, leadership and leaders are found in all aspects of our lives. Leadership qualities are exhibited by many people much of the time. Leaders, both formal and informal, are found at all levels of most organisations. Yet, it is usually individual leaders who spring to mind when we think of leadership: rarely do we consider outstanding leadership teams. Bate

(1994) argues that, particularly in the management of change, leadership is best considered as a collective or plural concept. His contention is that it is networks of leadership which prove effective in change, not necessarily individual leaders. He suggests that leadership comprises five main dimensions and each individual leader is unlikely to be able to offer all these qualities. A leadership team, on the other hand, might embrace the plethora of characteristics required to successfully manage transformational change. The five dimensions of leadership, identified by Bate (1994) are shown in Table 6.6.

If each of these five dimensions is placed at the corner of a pentagon, as in Figure 6.5, it may prove possible to 'map' the leadership capacities of any particular organisation. That is, the pentagon can become elastic, with certain dimensions – the organisation's strengths – being illustrated by an extended 'arm' and under-

Table 6.6 The five dimensions of the leadership of organisational change

Dimension	Leadership role
Aesthetic	Leadership of the creation, expression and communication of new ideas
Political	Leadership of political processes involved in gaining acceptance of new ideas in an evolving culture
Ethical	Leadership in the creation and imparting of a framework of moral standards related to these meanings and ideas
Action	Leadership in transmuting agreed cultural meanings into concrete practices
Formative	Leadership in structuring new ideas, meaning and practices into a framework – a new source of legitimacy within the organisation

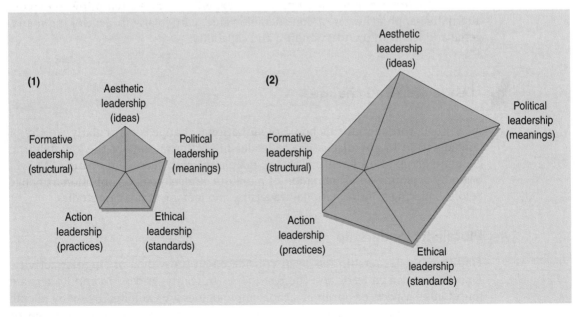

Figure 6.5 The elastic pentagon
Source: Based on Bate (1994).

developed dimensions by a restricted extension. This can prove to be a useful team leadership development activity. The illustration in Figure 6.5 depicts: (1) the elastic pentagon model showing the five dimensions of leadership, and (2) an organisation with strong creative and political leadership skills, but one which is weak on action and the subsequent ability to embed change into its structures.

Organisational change is best accommodated, Bate (1994) argues, by an appropriate blend and balance of leaders who may have differential inputs at various stages in the change process. As a result a network of leaders, with different strengths and at a range of hierarchical levels, will make the change happen.

Transformational leadership

We will briefly look at a useful distinction often made between two categories of leader and examine research which attempts to relate leadership style to types of change. Table 6.7 draws on the work of Bass (1990) and others to illustrate two leadership behaviours, that is, transactional and transformational. It appears that transactional leadership is concerned with managing in relative stability whereas transformational leadership implies dynamism and flux.

The activities of certain so-called transformational leaders, for example Nelson Mandela in the 1990s or Margaret Thatcher in the 1980s, or Richard Branson and Bill Gates from the organisational world, attract considerable media and academic interest. Anecdotal knowledge suggests these leaders possess the trait often referred to as charisma. This trait is difficult to define and virtually impossible to measure, yet, arguably, simpler to observe. The charisma of a transformational leader is thought to inspire and energise followers who, as a result, are more amenable to change, are highly motivated and unquestioning followers. Robbins (1984: 151) suggests that a transformational leader is one who 'inspires followers to transcend their own self-interest for the good of the organisation and who is capable of having a profound and extraordinary effect on his or her followers'.

Transformational leaders engage in major organisational change which involves addressing both political and cultural systems and challenging current norms. They create a vision of a desired future state and mobilise commitment to achieving that goal. The final step, it is argued, is to institutionalise that change, to make it a reality. In order to achieve transformational change leaders require a deep understanding of organisations and the social interaction they embrace. They need to master political dialogue and understand the nature of power, equity, the dynamics of decision making and when to push and when to back off (Morgan, 1989).

Table 6.7 Transformational and transactional leadership

Transactional leadership	Transformational leadership
● Rewards are contingent on performance	● Shows charisma and vision and instils trust, pride and respect
● Focuses on exceptions and deviations from rules	● Inspires, sets high expectations, uses symbols
● Intervenes only when standards are not achieved	● Promotes intelligence and creative problem solving
● Avoids difficult decisions and responsibilities	● Gives personal attention, considers individuals, coaches

Dunphy and Stace's change matrix relates four types of leadership style to four types or scales of change. This model, based primarily on intuitive understandings, suggests that corporate transformation or other major change, when achieved by application of a collaborative or consultative style of leadership, may result in 'charismatic transformation'. Alternatively, transformation may be achieved by adopting a more directive or dictatorial approach. In fact their research, conducted in a range of service-sector organisations, indicated that transformational change was more likely to have occurred as a result of adoption of a directive or coercive style. Nevertheless, Dunphy and Stace (1993) suggest that once change is in process, a more consultative approach is required, particularly at sub-unit level, in order to gain the support of employees. Considerable change management research has commented on the relationship between style and the effectiveness of change initiatives. It is also worthy of consideration that the context of change is a vitally important determining variable in the success, or otherwise, of change management.

Leaders on leadership

Many practising and recently retired leaders from industry, especially those in the public eye, attempt to identify the qualities of good leadership. These often appear in best-selling easy-to-read books. Not all are without merit – a lifetime's successful experience provides a wealth of data on which to reflect. They are not of course 'research' as such, as they don't tend to consciously draw on and extend our theoretical knowledge of leadership. They do, however, often provide scope for reflection. Gary Hoffman, visiting Professor at The University of Northampton and Vice Chairman of Barclays has distilled what he considers to be the nine qualities and roles of a leader (2008 lecture):

- protector of brand and reputation
- creator and champion of ambitions
- inspirer of shared sense of purpose
- champion of customers and colleagues
- creator of commitment and trust
- provider of clear direction
- creator and facilitator of teamworking
- coach/builder of skills
- role model of behaviours.

It is worth reflecting on these roles in the light of the material presented in this chapter. Note, for example, the strong 'people' orientation with reference to 'ambition', 'facilitator', 'trust' and 'coach'. The role of the leader in giving direction figures strongly with reference to 'creator' (three times), 'inspirer', 'purpose' and 'provider of clear direction'. Few roles appear to be directly seeking economic good – there is no mention of business development, for example. Rather, economic value added is clearly to be achieved by setting the 'right' context.

Leadership and change: conclusions

This section primarily comprises two mini-case studies. Mini-case 6.6 explores the leadership of a great man, Nelson Mandela. Was he a 'magician' as well as a transformational leader?

The leadership of change, Mini-case 6.7, considers certain aspects of pluralism in leadership and addresses one of the important themes of this book, that is, the management of change. It acts as a useful prelude to Chapters 8 and 9 on power and politics and organisational culture.

Mini-case 6.6: Nelson Mandela: a 'Magician' and transformational leader

It could be argued that Nelson Mandela, the first black president of South Africa, approximates to the characteristics of Fisher and Torbert's Magician. Not only did he have a tremendous influence over two or three generations of South Africans, he also symbolised an image of great value to many millions of people throughout the world. Incarcerated in jail for decades because of his stringent opposition to apartheid in South Africa, he symbolised hope, justice and courage to most black and many white South Africans. In jail he was penniless, confined, abused, denied fundamental liberties and marginalised, yet with unimaginable courage and magical skill he rose, within just a few years of his release, to lead a nation (black, coloured and white) in seeking greater justice and further hope.

Upon release, he brought a most remarkably diverse nation closer together, gaining overwhelming popular support in free, democratic elections. Diversity, mutual distrust and, often, undisguised hatred were, and, to an extent, still are based on colour, race and tribal difference. Mandela recognised, examined and confronted such differences while simultaneously standing above them. He embraced, literally and metaphorically, leaders of tribes antagonistic to his African National Conference (ANC) and whites who had sought to remove him (and who would probably have murdered him had such an action not been likely to arouse considerable external and internal opposition), overseas leaders who helped to facilitate his freedom and his people whose support he could count upon.

Acute awareness of the human condition, an apparently total lack of personal vice or any desire for vengeance and a fundamental appreciation of the 'real' and the symbolic as one, make Mandela a great leader.

After becoming president, he attended a rugby international in 1995. South Africa were playing and the match was being televised in the country and in most rugby-playing countries. Rugby, as a sport, goes to the heart of the division in South Africa between black and white. It is a game beloved by the white minority and was, and largely still is, the preserve of whites. Mandela's presence at the game represented a symbolic (and real) attempt to integrate the two communities, to bring black acceptance of rugby and its importance to white South Africans to the fore. But Mandela did not just attend the game, he wore a Springbok rugby shirt (not a shirt and tie or his flamboyant tribal dress). Few, if any, black Africans had ever had the privilege of wearing it. What is more he wore a 'Number 6' shirt, that of the captain of the team, Pinaar. He also sang along with the country's new national anthem (as opposed to the old Afrikaans anthem, 'De Stem'). A highly symbolic moment.

This simultaneous challenge and acceptance, being part of many groups of people and different from them and honouring a tradition that had incarcerated him for the prime years of his life, endeared people throughout the world to his magical and inspirational qualities.

Mini-case 6.7

The leadership of change

This mini-case explores the leadership of change in a medium-sized NHS Trust hospital in the Midlands of England. The organisation has been successful in achieving significant and measurable quality improvements, surpassing its broad array of objectives and coping with considerable environmental flux.

Rapidly impending, centrally imposed, change in the NHS created a trigger for action. The internal process of change management conceived of and undertaken by the Chief Executive (CEO) Miah Patel and the senior management team, was based on a cognitive model of change which was not articulated, but served to delimit and guide their leadership activities. That model (see Figure 6.6) is analysed below.

The three processes, shown in the interlocking circles in Figure 6.6, took place in a context which was made receptive to change, in part, through leadership efforts. Leadership held a vision of a desired future

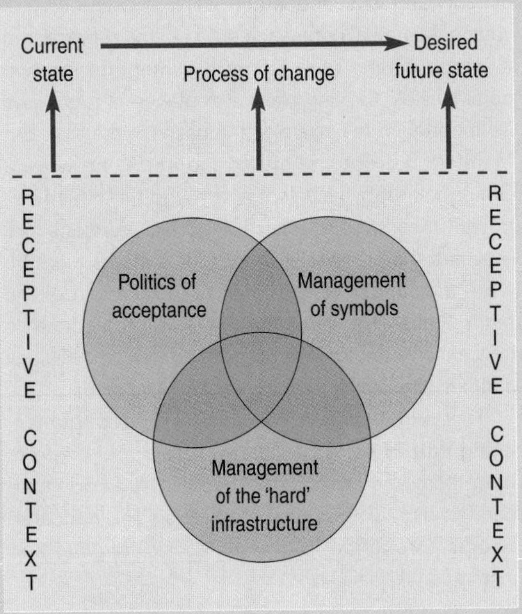

Figure 6.6 A cognitive change model
Source: © Brooks (1996)

state, an ambition or ideal to aim for. This contrasted with the tired and increasingly unsatisfactory current state of affairs and informed the direction, scale and scope of the change. It could be argued that the 'hard' changes, referred to below, together with a genuine attempt to change the culture of the organisation to make it more receptive to innovation, represent the 'content' of the change. The process of change embraced an ongoing time frame, punctuated by symbolic and tangible actions centred around the politics of acceptance and cultural interventions, all led by a leadership team, an example of pluralistic leadership.

A three-pronged approach to change management was employed:

- the conscious and active management of symbols, including 'talking up the crisis', changing dress and behaviour codes, degradation of some dysfunctional rituals and development of new rituals symbolising change;
- a focus on the politics of acceptance; and
- concurrent attention to 'hard' systems and structures.

Although external change provided a trigger for action, the leadership team consciously heightened the existing sense of impending crisis, partly by using 'crisis' language, while instilling confidence in staff that they were competent to cope with the consequences.

The leadership team oversaw the restructuring of the organisation. Business managers were introduced to each clinical directorate, and systems – including new financial procedures – were developed to facilitate the achievement of operational and strategic objectives. These 'hard' changes enabled the organisation to cope with externally imposed change: the rigours of the internal market. However, these changes were not managed in isolation from the political and symbolic leadership processes.

The leadership team paid particular attention to the politics of acceptance, adopting a collaborative, not coercive, style. They engaged in a great deal of discussion at an early stage and involved individuals and groups who held both formal and informal power. Gaining a common understanding of the realities of the environment and subsequent collective action were emphasised. Instilling in others a sense of ownership of both the problem and the solution was viewed as crucial by leadership. Hence, leaders were created and encouraged, at all levels, to champion the change.

It is of value to briefly consider a simple model useful for analysing organisational change. All change can be considered to have four prime parameters, that is, the content, context, process and timing of change:

- content refers to the nature of what is changing, whether it is transitional or incremental or transformational and revolutionary;
- context is the internal and external environment in which the change is occurring. An analyst or change agent would need to consider all manner of internal contextual characteristics, such as the predominant management style, the qualities of leadership, the organisation's structure and systems, and attempt to assess the receptiveness of that context;
- process of change encompasses the series of mechanisms and activities that are employed during the change – how it is undertaken;
- change takes place over a period of time: it is not an event, although certain 'events' often punctuate the change process. The content, contextual variables and processes employed in most significant organisational changes also alter over time.

A knowledge of this model can help us to understand the nature and complexity of organisational change.

 ## Leadership and diversity

Leadership and management have been gendered terms; especially the word 'management' is more closely associated with men than women. As with much organisational research, work on leadership was often conducted by men in the Anglo-American context and aimed largely at the same target audiences. That said, the evidence for sex differences in leadership is mixed yet such differences are apparent. Often the differences in leadership style between men and women are found to be the consequence of different working contexts; these contextual factors moderate what might otherwise be more significant and measurable differences. We remain influenced by the 'traditional' perspective of 'a good leader'; someone who is strong, charismatic and decisive. In fact when a strong female leader, such as Margaret Thatcher, was or is judged, they are often said to possess male characteristics. This raises the question as to whether our picture of 'good' leadership is itself gendered?

Judy Marshall (1993) suggests that female values and male values are not owned by each sex – both sexes have access to them. This enables men and women to be both the same and different. The key is to recognise differences and embrace a breadth of approaches to management and leadership. Many management writers, theorists and practitioners have argued that 'female values', such as interdependence and cooperation, receptivity and acceptance, emotional tone and intuition, are more relevant to the modern workplace than traditional 'male values', such as self-assertion, control, competition and rationality.

A large 'meta-study' by Eagly and Johnson (1990) of management or leadership styles found that although women often adopted more democratic and participative styles compared with men, in general men were no more task-orientated than women while women were no more interpersonally orientated than men. The differences were in fact few.

 ## Leadership and communications

Communications within and external to an organisation goes to the heart of leadership. It is that ability to communicate, to make contact with real people and to interact with them that differentiates leadership from administration or even management. Leaders make speeches, produce written communications, listen and chat to colleagues, observe and respond to needs and otherwise communicate for most of their time in the organisation. Leaders also interact with the external environment, with suppliers, markets, even competitors. What is more, leaders communicate in far more than words. Charisma is a form of communication. All leaders consciously or not, transmit symbolic messages. Mini-case 6.7 shows how a leadership team used symbolic communication as part of a change management strategy.

Communication skills, using all available media and being sensitive to the power of symbols while recognising how people perceive words and actions, are essential skills of the competent leader.

 ## Leadership and conflict

Organisations have many stakeholders, factions which often have different interests in the way the organisations should be managed and led. Conflict is inevitable in organisations and an important leadership role is to manage such conflict. Stakeholder analysis involves the identification of key players and planning how best to accommodate their often divergent needs. Leadership becomes intensely political when attempting to manage such different, often irreconcilable, demands. In a way, leadership earns its legitimacy by succeeding in doing this.

Managerial implications

To an extent, the management implications of the material covered in this chapter are at least implicit but are, nevertheless, emphasised here.

1 Individuals need to develop self-awareness of their behaviour and attitudes while attempting to identify their leadership *and* management credentials.

2 Individuals need to appreciate when leadership qualities, such as developing and disseminating a sense of vision, are appropriate and, alternatively, when managerial skills, such as negotiation and transaction, are required.

3 Managers need to recognise that the early theorists, such as Taylor and Fayol, together with the conditions they reported, remain partially embedded in our collective understanding of management and, hence, remain influential in many respects.

4 Managers should recognise that a wide range of potential managerial or leadership styles exist and that they might seek to develop flexibility and self-awareness to both utilise and value different styles in different circumstances.

5 Managers need to reflect on their own strengths, styles and capabilities and assimilate the responses of others to their activities in an attempt to learn about themselves and to explore self-development opportunities.

6 Individuals need to recognise that the frame in which they operate influences their understanding, attitudes and behaviour; recognition of this fact is a prerequisite for personal development and growth.

7 Similarly, as the frames in which we operate may prevent us from managing change or transformation successfully, knowledge of self and determination to seek development appear to be vital.

8 Managers might consider that leadership can be viewed as a pluralistic concept, in which case organisational change may be considered to be best led by a network of people operating at different levels and possessing different, but complementary, capabilities.

9 Successful management of major change may involve the adoption of transformational leadership capabilities (as opposed to transactional skills and behaviour) and recognition and accommodation of the complex interplay between the symbolic, cultural, political and contextual factors.

 ## Summary of main points

This chapter provides a synthesis of considerable management and leadership theory and other academic work. The main points made are:

- Frederick Taylor and Henri Fayol made a significant contribution to management theory, with the result that their ideas and principles still influence managerial thinking today;

- many eminent academics, such as Peter Drucker and Henry Mintzberg, have attempted to address the questions 'What should managers do?' and 'What do managers do?';

- Mintzberg found that managers tend to spend little time on the basic functions identified by Fayol;
- it is possible, but not always helpful, to differentiate between management and leadership, but less straightforward to label individuals as leaders or managers;
- considerable research has attempted to explore the meaning and nature of leadership and can, broadly, be categorised into three schools of thought: trait theories, behavioural theories and situational theories;
- emphasis is now also placed on other types of leaders in modern organisations, that is, entrepreneurs and intrapreneurs;
- contemporary research on leadership has explored a range of leadership frames of reference, or paradigms, which define the scope of thinking and action available to individual leaders;
- further contemporary writing has suggested that leadership is best viewed as a group or pluralistic phenomenon, as opposed to an individual endeavour.

Conclusions

Despite the extensive research carried out in this field it is still not certain what comprises effective leadership and how we can develop leadership effectiveness. Nevertheless, the material presented in this chapter sheds some light on a number of vital questions. It is important to note the more recent developments in thinking in this regard, while not losing sight of the vital significance that the fundamental principles of management, as outlined by Fayol in the mid-twentieth century, have on modern organisations.

Questions

1   What is a leader? What is a manager? Can a manager be a leader? Is a leader always a manager? Explain your answers to these fundamental questions.
2   Think of someone you know who is considered by you to have leadership skills. What are those skills or attributes? Which of them are personal traits and which are behaviours? Do they have the ability to change their 'style' in different circumstances?
3   What is the value of considering leadership as a pluralistic phenomenon as opposed to an individual orientation?

References

Adair, J. (1979) *Action-centred Leadership*. Aldershot: Gower.

Aldag, R. and Stearns, T. (1987) *Management*. Chicago: Southwestern.

Bass, B. M. (1990) 'From transactional to transformational leadership: learning to share the vision', *Organizational Dynamics*, Winter, pp. 19–31.

Bate, S. P. (1994) *Strategies for Cultural Change*. Oxford: Butterworth-Heinemann.

Bennis, W. and Nanus, B. (1985) *Leaders: The Strategies for Taking Charge*. New York: Harper & Row.

Blake, R. R. and Mouton, J. S. (1964) *The Management Grid*. Houston: Gulf Publishing.

Brooks, I. (1996) 'Leadership of a cultural change process', *Leadership and Organisational Development*, 17(5), pp. 31–7.

Dailey, R. (1988) *Understanding People in Organizations*. St Paul, MN: West.

Drucker, P. (1977) *People and Performance*. London: Heinemann.

Drucker, P. (1985) *The Entrepreneurial Mystiques*, Inc., October, pp. 34–44.

Dunphy, D. and Stace, D. (1993) 'The strategic management of corporate change', *Human Relations*, 46(8), pp. 905–20.

Eagly, A. and Johnson, B. (1990) 'Gender and leadership style: A meta-analysis', *Psychological Bulletin*, 108(2), pp 233–56.

Fayol, H. (1949) *General and Industrial Management*. London: Pitman Publishing.

Fisher, D. and Torbert, W. R. (1995) *Personal and Organizational Transformations*. New York: McGraw-Hill.

Handy, C. (1993) *Understanding Organizations*. London: Penguin.

House, R. (1971) 'A path–goal theory of leader effectiveness', *Administrative Science Quarterly*, 16, pp. 321–39.

Kirkpatrick, S. A. and Locke, E A. (1991) 'Leadership: do traits matter?', *Academy of Management Executive*, May, pp. 48–60.

Kotter, J. (1982) 'What effective general managers really do', *Harvard Business Review*, January–February, pp. 156–62.

Kotter, J. P. (1990) *A Force for Change: How Leadership differs from Management*. New York: Free Press.

Lord, R. G., De Vader, C. L. and Alliger, G. M. (1986) 'A meta-analysis of the relation between personality traits and leadership perceptions: An application of validity generalization procedures', *Journal of Applied Psychology*, 71, pp. 402–10.

McClelland, D. (1976) *The Achieving Society*. New York: Irvington.

McGregor, D. (1960) *The Human Side of Enterprise. New York: McGraw-Hill.*

Mann, R. D. (1959) 'A review of the relationship between personality and performance in small groups', *Psychological Bulletin*, 56(4), pp. 241–70.

Marshall J. (1993) *'Patterns of cultural awareness: Coping strategies for women managers'*, in Long, C. and Kahn, S. (eds) *Women, Work and Coping*, Montreal: McGill-Queens University Press.

Mintzberg, H. (1973) *The Nature of Managerial Work*. New York: Harper & Row.

Morgan, G. (1989) *Creative Organization Theory*. Newbury Park, CA: Sage.

Robbins, S. P. (1984) *Essentials of Organizational Behavior,* 3rd edn. Englewood Cliffs, NJ: Prentice-Hall.

Stodgill, R. M. (1948) 'Personal factors associated with leadership: A study of the literature', *Journal of Psychology*, 25, pp. 35–71.

Tannenbaum, R. and Schmidt, W. H. (1973) 'How to choose a leadership pattern', *Harvard Business Review*, May–June, pp. 162–75.

Watson, C. M. (1983) 'Leadership, management and the seven keys', *Business Horizons*, March–April, pp. 8–13.

Zaleznik, A. (1977) 'Managers and leaders: Are they different?', *Harvard Business Review*, May–June, pp. 67–78.

 Further reading

Adair, J. (1979) *Action-centred Leadership*. Aldershot: Gower.

Bate, S. P. (1994) *Strategies for Cultural Change*. Oxford: Butterworth-Heinemann.

Carli, L. and Eagly, A. (ed.) (2002) *Gender, Hierarchy and Leadership*. Malden, MA: Blackwell.

Fisher, D. and Torbert, W. R. (1995) *Personal and Organizational Transformations*. New York: McGraw-Hill.

Huczynski, A. and Buchanan, D. (2007) *Organizational Behavior*, 6th edn. Harlow: Prentice-Hall.

Moorhead, G. and Griffin, R. W. (1995) *Organizational Behavior*, 4th edn. Boston: Houghton Mifflin, Chapter 12.

Mullins, L. J. (2002) *Management and Organisational Behaviour*, 6th edn. London: Financial Times Pitman Publishing, Chapters 6 and 8.

 Internet sites

There are many sites with information about leadership, some of academic value, and many which discuss particular leaders. Use a search engine to locate sites about your favourite (or your most despised) leaders. You might also look at:

www.ccl.org This non-profit educational institution offers research findings in areas of creative leadership.

www.changingminds.org/disciplines/leadership This is a rich site, well referenced (academically) and provides a useful coverage of leadership.

7

Organisation structure

Stephen Swailes

Learning outcomes

On completion of this chapter you should be able to:

- explain and use the vocabulary of organisational structure;
- compare and contrast the different types of structure commonly found in organisations;
- explain the main factors that influence the structures used by organisations;
- explain how structures affect the people who work in them;
- explain recent developments in structuring;
- appreciate national cultural differences on structuring;
- explain why structures are resistant to change.

Key concepts

- bureaucracy
- hierarchy
- centralisation and decentralisation
- multifunctional, multidivisional and matrix structures
- new organizational forms: network structures, virtual organisations and partnerships
- determinants of structure
- structural inertia
- structural change
- structure–environment fit
- communities of practice.

Organisation structure is one of several key variables influencing how effectively the organization performs in relation to competitors and the attitudes and behaviour of employees. Structural effects on workplace behaviour are of particular interest given the ongoing emphasis placed upon ways of creating and sustaining flexible organisations and the pivotal role that individuals and teams have in achieving corporate objectives. We will see in this chapter how theory and ideas about organisational structure have evolved, and explore current ideas about structuring organisations.

 ## Introduction

Work organisations exist to meet economic and social objectives and the people who work in them wrestle with the task of making them successful. Managers are constantly evaluating market and sector forces and competitor behaviour. As well as this outside focus, managers must keep a close watch on what is happening inside the organisation.

Internal issues and problems may be connected to the way the organisation is structured, and this has a critical influence on the ability of organisations to sustain high levels of individual achievement and performance. The idea that an organisation's structure and processes should *fit* or match its environment has been around for a long time – and firms with good structure/environment fit outperform those without good fit (Habib and Victor, 1991; Ghoshal and Nohria, 1993). Getting the structure 'right' presents problems unique to every organisation because it involves the problems of organising a particular set of employees to 'manage out' inefficiencies to deliver maximum value to the organisation's stakeholders. Structure has a fundamental bearing on how employees behave and on organisational performance. This chapter examines the ways of structuring and highlights some of the factors that influence structural choice and the management issues that arise.

 ## What is structure?

Work organisations rely on ways of controlling the actions of people inside them. Control requires some form of hierarchy, lines of authority and communication to give employees the information and guidance managers feel they need and so they know to whom they are accountable. The various reporting relationships combine to create a hierarchical (scalar) structure. As one ascends the hierarchy, managerial positions become fewer but are associated with higher levels of responsibility. A chief executive figure or dominant entrepreneur sits at the top of the hierarchy with ultimate responsibility for the whole organisation.

Even small organisations group people into different sections or departments. A small clothing manufacturer might organise around functional departments covering design and fashion, purchasing, production, marketing and administration. As organisational size increases, the attraction of organising into divisions and departments becomes stronger for reasons that we will see later.

Thus, a traditional view of organisation structure is that it describes *the way an organisation is configured into work groups and the reporting and authority relationships that connect individuals and groups together.* Structure acts to create separate identities for different work groups and has a big influence on the effectiveness with which individuals and groups communicate. The purpose of structure is to organise and distribute work among the members of an organisation so that their activities are harnessed to meet the organisation's goals and objectives. But we should note at this point that there is a difference between the way an organisation is designed, that is how it looks on paper, and the real operating structures used by employees to make things happen. A more sociological view of structure is that 'its dominant feature is patterned regularity' (Willmott, 1981: 470). In this sense, structures are socially constructed ways of controlling.

 ## Talking about structure

How can we talk about structure? First we need a vocabulary to understand the concepts and variables involved and this is introduced below.

Centralisation and decentralisation

Centralisation is *the extent to which authority for decision making in the organisation is centralised so that it rests with top management.* In heavily centralised organisations tight control is kept over all important decisions. Middle managers may be consulted over decisions affecting them but the balance of decision-making autonomy is held by the centre. Decentralisation, in contrast, is where management gives employees substantial scope to participate in and take decisions at or near the place where the work is performed. Such autonomy, when given, commonly includes freedom to work within a budget, choosing ways of organising tasks, scope to innovate with systems, products and services and to work with suppliers and customers. Centralisation gives overall control to a few people and has the advantage that decisions are more likely to be consistent and jobs at lower levels should be simplified because important decisions are removed. The disadvantages are that it can become a byword for unhelpful bureaucracy that slows the pace of decision making. Front-line employees can feel that they have little opportunity to act on things that are important to them and may feel they are needlessly referring to others decisions they are quite capable of making themselves.

Decentralisation, in theory, provides greater potential for motivating employees and, because decisions are taken nearer the place of work, the organisation can react faster and smarter. However, the concept of decentralisation is far from clear and Hales (1999) cautions that decentralisation alone is unlikely to bring about much change to employee behaviour. Efforts to decentralise need to be backed up with compatible management practices such as appraisal, development and reward if the conditions for new employee behaviour are to be created.

Differentiation

Vertical differentiation is *the extent to which an organisation structure comprises different levels of authority. Horizontal differentiation* is *the extent to which the organisation is divided into specialisms* (Wilson and Rosenfeld, 1990). Thus an organisation with many reporting levels in its hierarchy and which is organised into many different product or service areas would be highly differentiated. An organisation with a small number of employees and which is engaged in a single product area might have three levels of vertical differentiation (directors, middle managers and supervisors) but no horizontal differentiation.

Integration

Integration refers to *the extent to which different levels in the hierarchy are coordinated (vertical integration)* and *the extent to which coordination occurs across functional areas (horizontal integration)* (Wilson and Rosenfeld, 1990). The concepts of differentiation and integration were also used by Lawrence and Lorsch (1967), who saw differentiation as the extent to which an organisation is divided such that different departments focus upon and serve different markets. The more this happens, the more the goals and values and ways of operating different departments vary. Even when high differentiation occurs there is a need to coordinate departmental activities around the common goals of the organisation, and integration refers to the extent to which coordination occurs. Thus we can imagine organisations operating in a complex business environment to be highly differentiated but also highly integrated.

Specialisation

In small organisations where the variety of work is low, employees can move between jobs to build up their versatility and interchangeability. As organisations get bigger and as the nature of the work done diversifies, then it is more likely that employees specialise in the type of work that they do. *Specialisation* is *the extent to which there are different specialist roles in an organisation*: the higher the number of specialist roles the higher the degree of specialisation. Specialisation also refers to *the extent to which employees engaged in similar or closely related tasks are grouped together*. This is called 'routine specialisation' and occurs when jobs are disaggregated such that employees only do one or a few parts of a job but not the whole job. High specialisation has the advantage that employees reach high levels of efficiency, and control is simplified as jobs are tightly defined. Disadvantages include creating a climate of inflexibility, creating workers who do not see the 'big picture', and creating a work climate that depresses job satisfaction as employees simply repeat their experiences.

Formalisation

Formalisation is *the tendency of an organisation to create and impose written policies, rules and procedures that govern the way work is carried out.* This includes job descriptions and staff manuals detailing the procedures for staff to follow in given situations that employees may see as unnecessary.

Span of control

The number of people that can be efficiently coordinated by one person varies with the nature of the work undertaken. *The number of employees that report directly to a manager is called the span of control* and for practical reasons is unlikely to rise above 100 due to problems of control and coordination. The number of subordinates reporting directly to a manager is commonly around 10–20. Above this, some other layer of management or supervision is usually introduced.

Bureaucracy

The term 'bureaucracy' in an organisational context relates to the work of Max Weber (1864–1920). Weber was concerned with understanding the 'rationalisation' of Western society. This is basically about understanding the ways in which the choices that people have over the ways they do things were increasingly constrained by laws, rules and regulations. Bureaucracy is a key part of rationalisation and it embraces several aspects of organisations such as hierarchical structures, responsibilities, rules and procedures, managers having legitimate authority based on their position in the organisation, and employees that are motivated to achieve organisational goals. Weber was concerned that the future held out only prospects for greater rationalisation, and his contribution to organisation theory is expanded in Chapter 2. Looking around British society in general, you may ponder whether Weber's concerns have been realised.

Illustration in film

'Resistance is useless'

Near the start of *The Hitchhiker's Guide to the Galaxy*, a Vogon demolition fleet comes to demolish the Earth to make way for a hyperspace bypass. The Vogon captain positions his ships above the Earth and announces to all mankind that, as all Earthlings should be aware by now, the planet is to be demolished and that it will occur in two minutes. Observing the panic on the planet, the Vogon captain comes over the worldwide public address system and says that there's no point acting surprised about this as the planning charts and demolition orders have been displayed in the Earth's local planning department on Alpha Centauri for 50 Earth years – it's too late to complain now. Moments later Earth is obliterated.

Vogons are one of the most unpleasant races of all – not evil but bad-tempered, bureaucratic, officious and callous. The last surviving Earthman, Arthur Dent, and his companion Ford Prefect, had miraculously been transported onto the captain's spaceship just before his planet was destroyed. With no sympathy for hitchhikers the captain orders them to be thrown out into the vacuum of space. 'You can't throw us into space, we're trying to write a book', cries Ford. 'Resistance is useless', replies the Vogon guard – the first phrase taught to him when he joined the corps and which he repeats in the face of their protests.

The point of this illustration is to show that what seems logical to one part of a bureaucracy may not be logical to someone in another part. What assists one employee may be seen by others as counterproductive. I don't know about you, but I see Vogons everywhere. They have been in all the organisations that I have worked in – usually they end up with good jobs. Often I have left meetings with them thinking 'resistance is useless'.

Catch 22

Another great film that became a powerful exposé of bureaucracy is *Catch-22*, based on the satirical novel of the same name. Indeed, the title of the book has become a byword for illogical bureaucracy. The action takes place on a US bomber group base in World War II and the main character is Captain Yossarian. Realising the madness of war he tries many times to be declared insane in which case he would not have to fly bombing missions and would be sent home. But regulation 22 (the Catch 22 of the title) said that anyone who was concerned for their own safety must possess a rational mind and therefore must be sane. So Yossarian had to keep bombing.

 ## Structural types

Multifunctional (U-form) structures

Large corporations appeared in the USA earlier than in Europe (Hannah, 1976: 2) and were common by the end of the nineteenth century. One of the reasons for their success is thought to come from the structures they used. These commonly involved centralised control and the existence of separate functional departments for purchasing, production, marketing (*see* Figure 7.1). Another aspect of their structure was vertical integration, that is, *the bringing together of operations such as buying materials, production and assembly, distribution and retailing under the control of one enterprise* (Hannah, 1976: 3). Note that this is a different meaning of vertical integration from that given above. Here, vertical integration refers to the extent to which the different stages involved in getting products to customers are owned and controlled by the same organisation, whereas the previous meaning, above, referred to the extent to which an organisation's hierarchical levels are coordinated.

General Motors, the large US car manufacturer, built itself on centralised control over a functionally divisionalised structure and became a benchmark organisation

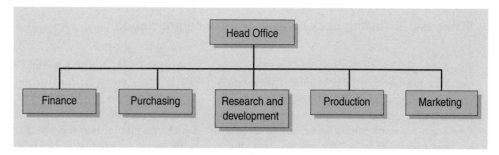

Figure 7.1 Centralised, functionally departmentalised structure in a manufacturing organisation

for other large corporations in the 1940s (Drucker, 1975). The multifunctional form (also called the unitary or U-form) separates and organises according to the various inputs to a firm's business operations. It is viable where products share common production methods and technologies, and it allows employees to become highly specialised in their work. Large US organisations relied upon basically the same structural form for decades, but changes from the 1960s onwards caused them to look at alternative ways of structuring for the following reasons (Drucker, 1975).

- Companies in the developing service sectors needed different structures from those that had suited big manufacturers.
- Firms were using multiple technologies to produce bigger product ranges.
- Multinational operations were growing, and new structures were needed to serve new markets and use new market information.
- New technologies and new markets called for entrepreneurial thinking and faster responses from managers and the growing numbers of knowledge workers.

Drucker did not prescribe what alternative structures should be like but he did make some points that are still relevant today.

1 Structures need to integrate three things: production of the product or service; innovating around future products or services; and management's vision for the future.

2 Structures do not evolve by themselves. They require careful thought and analysis, and should match a carefully articulated vision of what the organisation wants to achieve.

3 Work and jobs should be designed to fit with the aspirations of the people doing them.

4 Hierarchical organisation structure is virtually inescapable. Scalar structures give protection to employees, combined with the freedom to innovate.

Mini-case 7.1 illustrates the relevance of these points today.

Mini-case 7.1: Taking back control: back to centralisation

This case shows how structure can be changed in response to environmental pressures. The company concerned makes feedstuff for cattle, pigs and poultry. It employs around 1500 staff in several locations. Feeds are delivered directly to farms and there are no sales to other sectors. Thus anything that affects livestock levels will be felt directly by the company.

The company ran decentralised businesses with regional managers having substantial power to make their own decisions (high decision autonomy). Adverse conditions affecting farmers resulting from health scares from infected meat, foot and mouth disease and European policy changes forced them to seek cost savings in animal feeds. The company reacted to falling demand and pressure on prices by switching to a centralised, multifunctional form on the grounds that this would hand back tight control over costs to top management.

A consequence of the switch, which involved taking away some of the responsibilities from regional managers, was that staff morale diminished. A classic outcome from multifunctional structures also arose: the sales teams sought a wide range of speciality feeds in order to win business from customers whereas the manufacturing division wanted to reduce the number of product lines and make longer production runs of standard products.

This case emphasises the practical dilemmas that can face top management. On the one hand, they have to react to falling demand for their product. On the other hand, the classic solution of taking control away from people directly involved with the customers can lead to low morale and runs a high risk of quashing the innovative spirit that the company needs to manage its way out of the crisis.

Multidivisional (M-form) structures

Although functional structures were influential in driving economic growth in the early twentieth century, their effectiveness was under question by the 1960s and 1970s. Around this time a more efficient structure, called the multidivisional form, began to replace them (Figure 7.2). In this form, *divisions were created to look after all aspects of the production of a particular product, that is, from purchasing materials through manufacturing and distribution.*

Multidivisional structures are built around an organisation's outputs rather than its inputs since structure centres around the main product/service types, not the inputs, in terms of resources, knowledge and processes needed to create them. They overcome the dangers of weak communication and coordination inherent in multifunctional structures and should allow faster response to market changes. Faster reaction is possible as each division has access to, and control over, the key resources it needs, for example market forecasting and production facilities. The multidivisional form is also referred to as the 'M-form'.

Toyota is made up of separate divisions for Textile Machinery, Compressors, Vehicles, Engines, Materials Handling and Technology Development. The headquarters is divided into a separate Corporate Centre, which deals with strategy and administration of the company, and a Business Support Office, which supports all divisions. The energy company BP, which employs over 100,000 people and which operates in over 100 countries, has four divisions: Exploration and Production; Gas, Power and Renewables; Refining and Marketing; and Petrochemicals. Each of these divisions contains several business units that report to the chief executive.

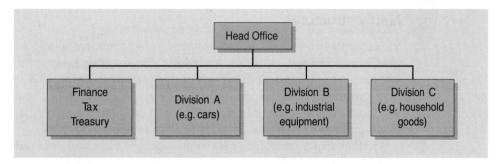

Figure 7.2 Multidivisional structure

Although divisional structures are better aligned to markets, senior management has to ensure that the advantages are not eroded by duplication and diseconomies of scale. When the organisation is structured according to its outputs, extensive communication across functional areas, such as between manufacturing and logistics is essential. A variation of the multidivisional form uses the same structure as in Figure 7.2 but replaces divisions based on product categories with divisions based upon geographic regions in which the company operates. For example, a global vehicles manufacturer could structure on divisions serving North America, Latin America, Europe, Asia–Pacific and the Middle East plus Africa. This type of structure is used by multinational enterprises who feel that the best way of serving geographically diverse markets is to produce and distribute goods locally, allowing managers to meet local product–market preferences arising from cultural differences.

Mini-case 7.2: Restructuring Mobil Oil Australia

Mobil Oil Australia had grown in the 1980s following acquisitions but results had deteriorated. The feeling among managers was that the workforce was well qualified and motivated but that internal processes were inhibiting the ability to compete. Using consultants and work teams a set of major issues was produced:

- Lack of customer focus
- Poor communications with employees about organizational performance
- Functional barriers to integration
- Existing systems were unnecessarily complex
- Excessive reporting but little useful information generated
- Poor strategic planning and product forecasting.

The new organizational design introduced to move the organization forward left behind a functional structure in favour of business units with financial and service objec-

tives. Middle management was also cut back. Cuts were made to expense budgets not only to improve performance but also to symbolise that a 'leaner' culture was being attempted. Restructuring led to refilling of posts, which started at the top and worked down. Jobs were also evaluated such that some employees took redundancy or accepted a lower reward package. Exposure to industrial action was reduced by redesigning jobs held by unionised employees.

Employee behaviour change and the creation of informal networks were seen as a valuable supplement to the new design. The restructuring project cost about two million dollars, excluding redundancy costs, and involved a heavy staff commitment over several months before a new design was reached. While this investment is not big by oil industry standards it does indicate that changes like this are not entered into lightly.

Source: Summarised from Martin and Cheung (2002).

Matrix structures

So far we have seen how organisations can be structured along functional lines to gain benefits of specialisation and along divisional or geographic lines to gain a stronger market focus. A drawback of the divisional structure is the possibility of duplication of effort. For example, if several divisions operate their own purchasing function there may be duplication and possibly a lack of shared information about purchasing that could lead to inefficiencies.

Another structural form open to managers is the matrix (Goold and Campbell, 2003; Wellman, 2007). Its distinguishing feature is that employees have two and sometimes more reporting relationships. One line of authority, often the functional area, manages the formal side of the employment contract such as performance management and salary negotiations. The other lines of authority are used to involve employees in ongoing projects and initiatives that are part of their work (*see* Mini-case 7.3). Matrix-type ways of organising are increasingly used, for instance to coordinate products and brands across countries (Goold and Campbell, 2003).

When there is a real need for staff to spread their time across a range of different activities, matrix structures have something to offer. They can help to push forward

Mini-case 7.3: Matrix structure and IT management

At US motor manufacturer General Motors the information technology (IT) staff had been taken out of the mainstream company to an outside organisation. The outside organisation was running GM's information systems, and leadership of the information technology and systems functions had been dissipated.

A new Chief Information Executive appointed five Chief Information Officers to work with GM's five main geographic divisions, for example North America, Europe and Asia–Pacific. Five Process Information Officers were also appointed to work on technical areas affecting all divisions. These covered supply chain management, product development, production, the customer experience and business services.

Divisional CIOs reported to the Corporate Chief Information Officer as well as to their Divisional Heads. Process Information Officers reported only to the Corporate Chief Information Officer. Over time, the matrix, or 'basket weave' as it became known, helped to cut GM's IT budget by 25 per cent and cut the number of information systems used in half. An advantage of the matrix structure is that the 'creative tension' that arose led to good-quality decisions about priorities and funding.

Given the reported success of the matrix structure for IT at GM, why isn't it used more widely?

The reason is that the matrix suited GM at the time given the structural changes that had occurred previously. It was right for the size of the company and also right to deal with the complexity of the ways that IT was managed. Another reason why more companies do not use a matrix is that not enough top managers are able to control and make positive use of the creative tension that is generated.

Source: Based on Prewitt (2003).

progress on a number of fronts simultaneously and allow staff to reap the benefits of working together in functional areas. The main objections to matrix structures concern their ability to create confusion over the priorities that should be attached to different tasks, loss of accountability and ineffective information management. Since the functional line manager will have position power (*see* Chapter 8) over the project manager(s), and since there are unlikely to be formalised rules and procedures for participation in development projects, there is a danger that unproductive power struggles can evolve. The focus of attention, the project or the customer, can be lost in such struggles as priorities shift towards self-interest and political posturing. However, matrix structures do not have to apply to the whole organisation.

Bartlett and Ghoshal (1990) made the point that the strategies that are followed by leading corporations have outstripped the abilities of organisational structures to support them. They suggested that there is a '*structural-complexity trap*' that paralyses the ability of companies to react quickly to market needs. Hence, they felt that top managers should concentrate less on finding the 'ideal' corporate structure and concentrate more on creating the right attitudes and behaviour in a high-commitment work climate. This is a very important point. One way of enabling it is to get employees thinking of the organisation as a matrix while not actually using a matrix structure. Figure 7.3 shows how a matrix structure might operate in a university business school that groups its staff into four subject groups or 'divisions': marketing, human resource management, strategy and finance. The functional areas of new course development, teaching quality, research and business development cut across the subject groups.

Each division has a Subject Leader who is responsible for day-to-day staff management. The line of authority is through the Subject Leader to the Dean. When lecturers are involved in developing a new course they have obligations to a director of programmes. They may also have a responsibility to colleagues at the same hierarchical level, for example if they are teaching on a course for which a colleague is the course director. Lecturers are also responsible to a director of quality and those who do research have obligations to a director of research. Each person has at least two lines of authority.

The matrix structure shown here replaced a multidivisional form in which about 100 academics were divided into five Schools each one responsible for its own teaching, research and consulting. The old structure had caused inefficiencies in that rivalry between Schools was causing delays in the overall ability to develop and deliver programmes speedily and effectively. Lecturers with very similar teaching interests worked in different schools, inhibiting the exchange of ideas and knowledge.

While they are widely attempted, perhaps the last word on matrix structures comes from St Matthew, who wrote that 'no man can serve two masters'.

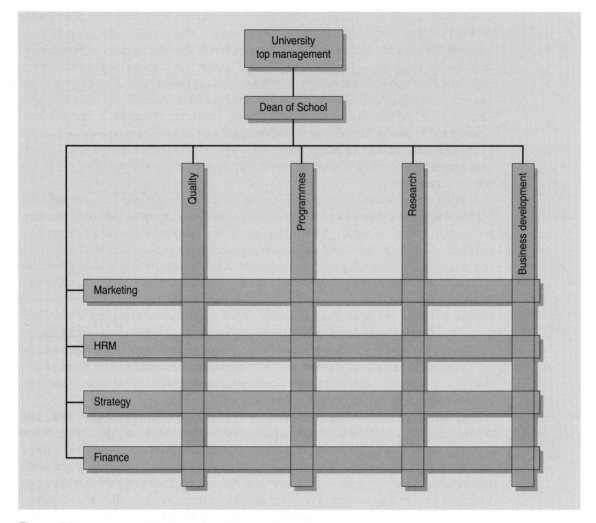

Figure 7.3 A matrix structure in a university business school

Network structures and virtual organisations

What matters most in structuring organisations is not the type of structure used but how well it works. With this in mind, many organisations are now looking to network-based structures to complement multifunctional or multidivisional structures (Sullivan, 1996). Rather than have all, or at least most of, the activities needed to produce a product or service in one organisation, in network structures a small core organisation coordinates, for example, design, production, transportation and marketing across four legally and geographically separate organisations. The central core is rather like a spider tugging on the strands of a web reaching out to the other organisations in the network. These other organisations may be removed or added to give the most flexible arrangement.

Main characteristics of networks

- Decentralisation of authority and responsibility
- Defined by horizontal connections between groups (nodes) of equals rather than vertical connections to superordinates. Links can be voluntary as much as formal
- Tasks are broadly defined and spans of control can be large
- Departmental and geographical boundaries are dismantled
- Many people can assume leadership roles
- Trust, support and shared responsibility are needed between people in different roles
- Informal communication is high and two-way
- Networks need people who are flexible, team-orientated and task-focused and who are good decision makers
- Authority derives from knowledge and skills, not position

Being based on links between teams and individuals, networks create a climate for developing a strong sense of identity with project goals and with other people working towards a common purpose. To achieve this, each team needs to be absolutely clear what it is there for and people can belong to more than one team to help with shared understanding and communication between teams.

Networked structures have many advantages. They maximise the potential and freedom to react quickly to local market needs while retaining large, sometimes global, scale operations. Groups (cells) of people with devolved responsibility can leverage their local skills and knowledge in a positive way. Disagreement and conflict can be tackled in a more constructive, task-orientated climate, in contrast to the often territorial climate present in multidivisional or multifunctional structures.

Virtual organisations

Until the proliferation of information and communciation technology (ICT) there were limits on the nature of organisation structures caused by the problems of coordinating and communicating over large distances. With time and distance much less the barriers they once were, organisations can be created that are geographically distributed but which are held together and enabled by ICT – virtual organisations.

These have been defined as *'almost edgeless, with permeable and continuously changing interfaces between company, supplier and customers. From inside the firm, the view will be no less amorphous with traditional offices, departments and operating divisions constantly reforming according to need'* (Davidow and Malone, 1992). Clases *et al.* (2003) see virtual organisations as a set of economically independent organisations operating together to meet the needs of customers or other stakeholders. The competences and resources of the participant organisations are harnessed in ways that could not be achieved by acting alone. Such an organisational 'structure' is a clear culmination of an information-based and constantly evolving enterprise. Essentially, virtual organisations are like a network of connections into individuals, groups, teams and parts of formal organisations. They are suited to rapid exchanges of information in order to solve problems or locate resources. There is no shared physical location, and the virtual organisation concept is attractive to small organisations that can network with others to access or provide value-adding services.

Virtual organisations can grow naturally out of the historic ties between companies or can be put together by a broker who brings the differing sources of expertise together. To work well, a virtual organisation requires high levels of trust among the partners as they are highly interdependent (Clases *et al.*, 2003). Virtual organisations can be intentionally short-lived and, because of their loose structure, dissolving one or withdrawing from one can occur without protracted and formal legal proceedings.

Ahuja and Carley (1998) explored the structure that arose in the information transmitted in a virtual organisation and found evidence for three dimensions of structure: hierarchical levels; degree of hierarchy, which is the extent to which people reciprocate in information flows; and centralisation. In this sense, the virtual organisation exhibited the characteristics of traditional organisational forms. Their findings are interesting and suggest that even where structure can be reduced it is human nature to recreate it. The key features of the various structural forms discussed above are summarised in Table 7.1.

Table 7.1 Comparison of the main structural forms

Structural form	Key feature	Strong points	Challenges	Comment
Multifunctional	Specialisation along functional lines, e.g. research and development, production	Technical optimisation in functional areas Scale economies in production Career paths in the functional areas Technical competences highly developed High levels of professional development	Achieving meaningful cross-functional communication Responding to market needs Ensuring actions in one area benefit the whole enterprise Struggles when the firm diversifies Getting employees to see the big picture	Viable for smaller organisations but becomes problematic as size increases
Multidivisional	Divisions represent separate business areas	Better focusing of functional areas, e.g. marketing Comparing the performance of different business areas is assisted Clearer view of the causes of problems Development of general management competences	If product-based, certain regions or consumer groups can be overlooked If geographic, is market information shared? Avoiding duplication	On what basis should divisions be created – product, geography or distribution channel?

Table 7.1 Continued

Structural form	Key feature	Strong points	Challenges	Comment
Matrix	Dual reporting relationships	Focuses on responding to market needs Potentially good coordination across functions/divisions Leverages use of employees' competences Expanded roles for employees that develop competences	Confusion among employees One side of the matrix dominating the other (power imbalance) Conflict management Need well-developed management skills to make them work well	Applicable to parts of an organisation
Hybrid	A functional structure but with temporary and permanent teams cutting across the functions	Teams focus on core concerns such as new product development High levels of information sharing	Keeping different process teams focused on mission/strategy	Emphasis is on renewal of structures in response to changes
Networked and virtual organsations	Separate organisations are coordinated by a core Structure is fluid and changes in response to information processing needs	Can be small but with a global reach Fast reactions Customised information shared by large numbers of people High flexibility as component organisations can be changed Potentially the lowest-cost structure	Avoiding goal ambiguity Clarifying lines of authority Getting the best fit between the network structure and its ability to process information Guarding against structure creating itself Lack of organisational identity Retaining and rewarding key people	Seems to be a model for the future

 Partnership working

An example of networking comes from the the UK public sector which uses Local Strategic Partnerships (LSPs) to tackle problems and improve services in areas like regional economic development, crime and housing. In an LSP a range of organisations work together in partnership with local communities. As well as public bodies, business organisations, community and voluntary bodies can be involved. LSPs are voluntary arrangements that vary widely in terms of size, who is in them and what they exist for.

Because of the differing purposes behind LSPs it is important that they are able to decide how to govern themselves. Factors for successful LSPs include the following (Bottrill, 2003; Street *et al.*, 2004):

- All members need a shared understanding of what their respective contributions are.
- Early clarification of what the LSP's aims and objectives are, what it should and should not do, and early setting of realistic targets.
- The power base of LSP members may differ markedly so it is important to clarify where decision-making power lies and how decisions will be implemented. Members with low power need to feel that they are heard and that they make valued contributions.
- Access to ways of resolving major disagreements and conflict.
- Providing personal development to enhance community leadership skills.
- Patience is needed to build trust and confidence. Partners must be aware of how their emotions and behaviour influence the building of trust – being challenging and supportive at the same time does not come easily.
- LSPs should not be overshadowed by bureaucracy, so a light touch with rules is needed while looking out for good practice in other LSPs.
- The LSP should be allowed to decide its optimal organisation structure
- Diverse membership (e.g., police, health services, local authority) may lead to communication becoming bogged down in jargon that becomes incomprehensible to many. Simple language is needed to create shared understanding. Recognising that the diverse organisations in an LSP do things their own way (have different cultures) is also important.

Mini-case 7.4: The Public Finance Initiative

In a change of policy in the 1990s the UK government set out proposals for much more involvement of the private sector in public investment projects such as the building of roads, hospitals and prisons – the Private Finance Initiative (PFI). Big projects involve risk, which is sometimes best handled by private organisations. Where this applies, the logic is that the risks should be transferred to the private sector. If some risk remains that cannot be best handled by private contractors then partial responsibility stays with the public sector.

The PFI has enabled more projects to be undertaken for a given amount of public spending and enables projects to be completed more quickly. The most common form of PFI involves business organisations designing, financing, building and operating a facility based upon specifications drawn up by the public sector. The private sector owns the facility, for example a hospital, and receives payment from the public sector for its use over a contractual period.

PFI projects can be from a few hundred thousand pounds for a school extension to several billion pounds for the Channel Tunnel Rail Link. Most PFI spending is on transportation, health, defence and education. For more details of the PFI and public–private partnerships see Allen (2001) and Ball and King (2006)

New organisational forms

While acknowledging that something is happening in some organisations, Morris *et al.* (2006) urge caution over the extent that post-bureaucratic organisations (such as virtual, shamrock and boundaryless) exist. Despite the downsizing that has occurred the research evidence that there has been large scale structural change that has dramatically altered what people do is anecdotal and may not extend beyond a few 'leading-edge' organisations. They studied Japanese workplaces which are typically very hierarchical and very bureaucratic but achieve flexibility through *keiretsu* (alliances of companies in an industry together with banks) and subcontracting. The effects of traditional human resource practices such as lifetime employment and pay based on seniority which tend towards rigid systems are offset by subcontracting and the use of peripheral, non-core employees.

A study of eight Japanese organisations found that downsizing had occurred in all but one. The pattern was of losing jobs in Japan but of creating them overseas as a result of supply chain decisions. Organisations largely avoided compulsory redundancies of permanent employees and achieved shrinkage through cutbacks in recruitment, by lowering the retirement age and by moving older managers to less well rewarded positions. Six of the eight organisations had delayered their traditionally very hierarchical systems where small differences in status are recognised. Delayering was done to boost faster decision making. The effects were to reduce promotion opportunities and increase the intensity of work especially for middle managers.

Secure employment across a working lifetime remained a priority but the approach was modified. First there were fewer people to offer it to and early retirement was both encouraged and facilitated, for example, by helping older managers to start their own businesses. Greater impact was seen on seniority-based pay. While delayering had reduced promotion opportunities overall, there was more acceptance of faster and bigger promotions and at a younger age for those seen as high-fliers. There were also changes to the bonus system to better reward performance by individuals and groups. In essence, pay practices had become more flexible. The downsides were lower motivation at junior levels due to curtailed promotion opportunities and higher work loads. Also observed was more individualistic behaviour in pursuit of targets at the expense of teamwork.

While changes had taken place in Japan, Morris and colleagues felt that they were not unlike the changes seen elsewhere and certainly not of a magnitude that would categorise them as post-bureaucratic or even as new organisational forms. Despite the changes, 'Japanese practice is deeply embedded . . . and there is as much evidence (if not more) of continuity as there is of change' (p. 1504).

While we can see much more use of networks in the ways that organisations are operating, these findings from Japan should make us reflect on how much change is really happening to the lives of employees.

Mini-case 7.5: Hollywood – an early adopter of new organisational forms?

Lampel and Shamsie (2003) show that new organisational forms are not limited to modern times. Organization structures influence how people behave in organisations and they also impact on how organisations compete. The resource-based view of the firm (Barney, 1991) is based on the idea that some of an organisation's resources are unique and it is these that give strategic advantage. Other resources that are not unique are, by definition, copiable and of reduced usefulness. Organisation structure and the ties that go with it can be a unique asset.

By the 1920s there were eight major film studios around Hollywood, each one with a talent base of producers, directors, writers and actors. Making a movie is about managing a large project from conceptualising the story to release of a film (or 'motion picture' as they were called). Up to and including the 1940s the big studios with hierarchical and vertically integrated structures dominated the industry. Changes in the business environment (such as TV) forced movie studios to restructure. An outcome was a more complex arrangement in which key resources such as financiers, producers and agents split off into separate organisations. This change from having all resources integrated into an organisation to splitting up the resources into a network of organizations is an early example of new organisational forms.

Influences on structure

Having seen the main structural forms, we need to look at some of the main factors that influence the types of structures used. These include organisation strategy, organisation size, the technologies used by organisations, internal power struggles and the nature of the business environment. In other words, structure is thought to be dependent on or influenced by some key variables. This *contingency approach* is discussed in Chapter 2 and is so called because structure is seen to be contingent upon (dependent on) external influences.

Strategy and structure

A classic study of the strategy–structure relationship (Chandler, 1962) stems from work on the strategies and structures of large US companies. Chandler (1962) defined structure as *'the design of organization through which the enterprise is administered'*. One of his main conclusions was that the structure of an organisation follows its strategy; that is, having set out a strategy, an organisation needs to make decisions about roles and responsibilities and about how resources (capital, machinery, expertise) would be distributed in the organisation to assist the implementation of strategy. As an organisation adjusts its strategy, many small and occasionally some large adjustments need to be made to its structure. This line of thinking became widely accepted, but it is important to appreciate the differences between the competitive environments that exist now and those that existed in Chandler's time.

In stable environments the idea that an organisation could rationally determine its strategy and then put in place a structure to achieve it was widely held. In turbulent environments long-term planning is much more problematic and strategy is seen more as something that emerges from the organisation's efforts to stay competitive. While strategy still has a direct effect on structure it also seems likely that structure will influence strategic behaviour.

Olsen *et al.* (2005) studied 200 US firms in terms of degree of centralisation, formalisation and specialisation and their relationship to strategic behaviour. Firms that were highly formalised and centralised (management-dominated) had the lowest orientations towards customers, competitors, innovation and costs. Organisations with moderate scores on the three structural dimensions associated with high to moderate levels of strategic orientation. Organisations with low scores on the three dimensions associated with overall moderate levels of strategic orientation. Structural orientations also varied with organisational performance, suggesting that they do influence the effectiveness of strategic change initiatives.

It is worth noting that data for this study were collected by a questionnaire sent to marketing managers. The questionnaire contained ways of measuring the extent of formalisation, centralisation and specialisation and so each organisation was categorised on the basis of one manager's reported responses to a set of statements in a questionnaire. This comment is not given to diminish the usefulness of the study but to remind readers of the limitations of management research. How reliable an indicator is one person's view of an organisation's position on these complex variables?

Technology and structure

In this context, *technology refers to the processes by which an organisation transforms its inputs into outputs*. It follows that all organisations employ a technology of some sort although the sophistication used may be low. A classic study into the effects of technology on organisations was published by Joan Woodward in 1958 (*see* Chapter 2). She found that when 92 English firms were grouped according to similarities among their production methods and technology (batch, mass production or continuous production) each production system coincided with a particular pattern of organisation. Woodward's main findings were:

1 The number of levels of authority increased with technical complexity from three to six.

2 The span of control of the first-line supervisor was higher in mass production (41–50) than in unit production (21–30), which was higher than in process production (11–20).

3 The ratio of managers and supervisors to employees was higher in process production than in mass production, which was higher than in unit production.

The world has moved on since then but the importance of Woodward's study is that it stimulated a continuing interest in the relationship between technology and organisations (Miller *et al.*, 1991; Perrow, 1967). Aldrich (1972) re-examined the pioneering work of the Aston Group on structure and concluded that technology should be treated as a independent variable, that is, one that 'exerts a causal influence on various aspects of organisation structure' (p. 26).

Information technology

Information and communication technology (ICT) has had a direct effect on structure. Organisations continually react to changes in their markets, and this leads over time to a build-up of new roles and responsibilities. While each new role makes sense, the long-term effect is to add complexity and to slow down decision making. Every so often organisations completely reconfigure their structure in an effort to keep their market alignment. As markets continue to get more complex one might think that structures will reach a limit to their capacity to respond. This, for the moment, is not happening because of the increasing sophistication of ICT, which is proving to be one of the 'levellers' of hierarchy (Day, 1999). ICT, as we have seen, has also led to the configuration of virtual organisations.

ICT increases the quality and quantity of information available to employees. As the amount of information available rises, then managers are able to use it to take more control over processes and operations. Conversely, managers are in a position to push the information closer to the point at which work is carried out and increase the responsibility placed on employees to use it effectively. Since new technologies and the information that goes with them require specialist understanding, then some have been drawn towards teamwork to increase the autonomy of front-line employees. Mukherji (2002) credits ICT with the following impacts on structure.

- Facilitating decentralisation by enabling communication and control from a distance, and assisting matrix and networked structures.
- Increased routinisation of some jobs while at the same time employees have access to much more data.
- Helping to reduce the number of hierarchical levels.
- Creating much closer links with suppliers and customers so that business operations are more integrated.
- Making the boundaries between divisions in an organisation and between organisations fuzzy and less relevant.
- Revolutionising the way small businesses in particular can operate, in particular through the Internet.

The continued development of ICT seems likely to continue to influence structures by further enabling shifts towards networked and virtual forms, at least in competitive and fast-moving markets.

Size and structure

The Aston studies of British firms in the 1960s found that the effect of technology on structure diminished in large organisations and that size (determined by the number of employees) seemed to have a strong effect on structure (Aldrich, 1972; Wilson and Rosenfeld, 1990). As the number of employees grows there is a tendency for staff in different specialisations to be grouped together so that management can achieve the levels of control it seeks and so that employees benefit from sharing knowledge and ideas. As organisations get bigger the problem of managing the various specialist departments increases. One common approach to this problem is to decentralise: to push decision-making authority down the hierarchy to the specialist departments. The appeal of grouping together people with similar tasks, knowledge and expertise, coupled with management's inability to directly manage diverse specialisms, leads to greater formalisation, decentralisation and specialisation.

The studies highlighted some dilemmas with organisation structure. Getting employees involved and participating in their work is a good thing but the hierarchies needed to control activities tend to reduce participation, leading to a waste of potential opportunity. Another dilemma comes from the use of standard work routines rather than personal contribution (standardisation) that could lead to higher levels of job satisfaction and improved work outcomes. The third dilemma concerns specialisation versus common goals since, arguably, groups of specialists may be tempted to work towards their own goals rather than share common goals.

Structures of small firms are much less studied but one exception is of SMEs in the Netherlands (Meijaard *et al.*, 2005). They identified nine structures including:

- 'entrepreneur with submissive team' – here employees working for an authoritarian entrepreneur are mostly independent of each other and have little influence on decisions. Coordination comes from informal teamwork;

- 'co-working boss with open structure' – employees are involved in making decisions at operational but not strategic level and informal teamwork occurs;

- 'singular structure' – employees have some scope for coordinating how they do things, specialisation and formalisation is low-level and there is little organisation into divisions or functional areas.

They also identified the conventional multifunctional, multidivisional and matrix structures. They found that the different structures occurred across the sectors studied and that some structures appeared better suited to one sector than another in terms of organisational performance. Overall, however, there was no evidence to suggest that one way of structuring was better than another.

The business environment

Another classic study concerned organisations and their relationship with the environment (Burns and Stalker, 1961). Their lasting contribution to the structure debate was to propose two ideal types of working organisation – one 'mechanistic' and adapted to stable operating conditions, and one 'organic' and much better adapted to unstable conditions and climates for change.

Burns and Stalker saw mechanistic structures as those in which tasks and problems facing the overall organisation are broken down into specialisms, with each employee fulfilling their task. Tasks are carried out in isolation, and management is responsible for ensuring that tasks are coordinated and meaningful to the organisation. Communication tends to be up and down lines of authority rather than across them. Characterised by structures that look like family trees, interaction flows upwards, is filtered at different levels, and responses are transmitted down the line.

Organic structures are far better suited to unstable operating conditions in which new problems are created which cannot efficiently be solved by mechanistic processes. Organic structures give less attention to describing and defining particular jobs. Demarcation is avoided and people conduct their jobs with knowledge of the organisation's overall purpose and of the contributions made by others. Interaction and communication run across the organisation as much as up and down it.

Burns and Stalker did not describe a structure itself, but rather the characteristics of both slow-moving and reactive organisations. Their findings are still very important for organisation theory. Managers need to continually assess whether the structure existing in their organisation is stimulating the right attitudes and behaviour to bring about change. Table 7.2 illustrates the differences between organic and mechanistic structures.

The Burns and Stalker hypothesis, that the bureaucracy of mechanistic organisations impedes organisational learning and communication, is widely accepted. The organic style has become so sought after that as a general model for the outcomes of a structure it has become 'accepted wisdom' (Bierly and Spender, 1995). An interesting twist to this hypothesis, however, was proposed by Perrow (1984), who analysed high-risk organisations and projects. Perrow argued that technology has advanced more quickly than our ability to manage it. (Global warming and the unfettered use of natural resources testify to this). He pointed to limitations with the organic system argument. In the big picture it does not matter if a single commercial organisation experiments with structure and fails, as others will quickly take its place. But when the risk extends to events such as the loss of military weapons or national secrets, catastrophic pollution incidents or to organisations that absorb massive public spending, then flexible management structures are inappropriate. Managers should reflect on the logic of this argument and consider the operating conditions that put limits on organic structures.

Table 7.2 A comparison of mechanistic and organic systems of management

Organic	Mechanistic
Contributive nature of knowledge and experience to common tasks	Specialised differentiation of tasks
Adjustments and redefinition of tasks through interaction and communication	Changes to roles are slow and procedural
A network structure for control, authority and communication	Hierarchic structure of control, authority and communication
Knowledge located anywhere in the network	Knowledge assumed to reside at the top
Lateral outlooks and communication	Vertical outlooks and communication
Information and advice	Instruction and decisions
Commitment to common tasks	Loyalty to organisation, obedience to supervisors
Value contacts with external centres of expertise	Internal focus

Source: Based on Burns and Stalker (1961).

Summary of influences on structure

So far we have seen four classic influences upon structure: strategy, technology, size and the environment. These factors affect decisions over centralisation and decentralisation, functionalisation and divisionalisation, the amount of specialisation and spans of control. From an organisational behaviour viewpoint, pinpointing the influences on structure and the influences that structure has on individuals and the performance of an organisation is highly complex. There are so many interrelated variables that it requires large and detailed studies of the kind undertaken by Chandler, Woodward, and the Aston group before managers can be confident in their findings. Burns and Stalker show that the effects that different structures can have on a workforce in terms of positive attitudes and behaviour are far more important than the actual structures adopted.

 ## Criticisms of the contingency approach

The Aston group assumed that since all organisations have to develop structures, then patterns and regularities will emerge over time across thousands of organisations. As all organisations are unique then a systematic study of similarities and differences among them should lead to useful organisation theory if the patterns and regularities can be identified. One criticism is that contingency theory does not offer much practical advice to managers who have to organise people and things. It points to some dilemmas for managers to think about, but what else? Another problem is that hundreds of variables influence the attitudes and behaviour of employees. These variables come from aspects of the roles and jobs that people do, from personal factors as well as from aspects of the organisation itself. We are also much more aware now that different national cultures have different approaches to work and organising. These approaches emphasise different variables such as the amount of participation and consultation that employees might expect or how much responsibility for work is individualised or collective. Scandinavian cultures are highly participative whereas the French culture is more authoritarian, for example.

 ## The organisation as a system

Our focus so far has been on the structural forms that are found and what they look like. It is, however, dangerous to place too much emphasis on the tangible aspects because organisation charts only describe grouping and reporting relationships; they do not tell us anything about how the organisation actually functions at the level of the individual or what it feels like to work in a structure. They represent only the way an organisation is designed – not necessarily how it works. They portray the organisation as a closed system, yet it is clear that organisations operate in a network interacting with outside agents as a means of achieving strategic goals.

Mintzberg proposed what became an influential way of seeing structures through six 'basic parts', as shown within the core of Figure 7.4 (Mintzberg, 1989). The largest group is usually an 'operating core', which carries out the daily work and tasks, producing and delivering the product or service. At the top of the organisation is a 'strategic apex' housing the senior management. Connecting the core and the apex is a group of middle managers. A group of technical support staff is needed to assist the core, the middle management and the strategic apex. Mintzberg called this a 'technostructure', and it helps to bring consistency to the way things are done. It includes designers, engineers or information specialists amongst others.

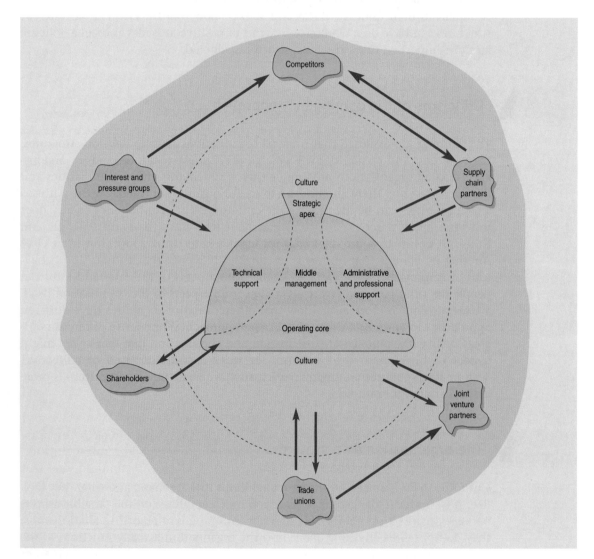

Figure 7.4 External influences on an organisation

Source: Based on MIntzberg (1989).

The fifth group includes administrative support such as financial controllers and human resource managers. The final component of the organisation is its culture (*see* Chapter 9). This is shown in the diagram as bounded by a dotted line, although culture will permeate throughout all staff groups. The dotted line around the whole organisation represents the idea that organisations are not closed to the outside world; instead they are open to it. It is an open system. Variations in the size and strength of the first five parts set organisations apart from each other. The five generic structures that arise from these variations are as follows:

Simple structures – these are found in young organisations but also in well-established ones with an autocratic ethos. The strategic apex dominates the supervision of the work done by the operating core. Numbers of technical and support staff are minimal and there is little in the way of formalised rules and procedures.

Machine bureaucracies – these are found in large organisations in relatively stable settings such as mass production. Standardisation and formalisation are high. The technostructure and support staff dominate activities to try and raise productivity. Machine bureaucracies can be good at delivering consistently to customers but can be weak on creativity and employment relations. The apex can be distant from the core.

Professional bureaucracies – here a large operating core consists of professional employees as might be found in hospitals and universities. The power of the core is strong and it values professional achievement and reputation. Technical and support staffing levels will be low. Decentralisation to professionals carrying out specialist tasks needs to be high.

Divisionalised forms – these are found in very large organisations such as multinationals serving diverse markets. The middle management controls business operations and seeks out new business. Each division with its distinctive structure has its own technical and support staff to help it serve its market.

Adhocracy – these occur in complex, often high technology, environments and in creative industries where fast reactions are needed. The operating core works closely with support staff. Fast-forming teams and matrix structures can be used to see through projects at pace. Decentralisation will be high and there will be a strong professional culture.

Figure 7.4 positions Mintzberg's views relative to other organisations operating in the external environment whose activities influence the structure of the organisation in the centre of the diagram. These other organisations commonly include competitors or, in the not-for-profit sector, organisations with similar goals. The arrows in Figure 7.4 link competitors to supply chain partners, and signify that external organisations may be interconnected. The dotted line around the whole system represents the idea that the organisation's interaction with its operating environment is open, not tightly bounded or closed. The irregular shape of the whole system, and of the external organisations, represents the changing strength and form of the relationships so created. Metaphorically they are rather like single-celled organisms that change shape and divide throughout their lifetime.

In sum, it is useful to see an organisation as existing in a network structure that, with the passage of time, will reconfigure itself as new structural linkages are formed and old ones are dismantled.

 Current issues affecting structuring

Representation of equality groups

Structures have hierarchies and there is plenty of evidence that women are under-represented at the higher managerial levels. Why so? The gender-centred perspective suggests that women's limited representation can be attributed to their particular ways of thinking and to their attitudes and behaviour, which often, but not always, conflict with an ideal type of top manager as aggressive, forceful and decisive. As well as having characteristics that deviate from an ideal type, the way women are socialised towards family obligations can also be considered to clash with the demands of top management roles (Fagenson, 1990).

An alternative view explaining the relative lack of women in top jobs considers that aspects of organisation structure, not sex role socialisation, have an effect. Kanter (1977) proposed two types of job. Advantageous jobs offer opportunity and power and are held by a social majority (men). Disadvantageous jobs offer little power and opportunity and are held by, in numerical terms, a social minority (women). Advantageous jobs stimulate career-boosting behaviour whereas disadvantageous jobs stimulate behaviour that justifies occupying them. Hence, according to Kanter, women's lower commitment and lower power aspirations, among other things, are due to disadvantageous positions not gender.

A third explanation uses a gender–organisation–system approach (Fagenson, 1990), which suggests that it is both gender and structure that influence women's behaviour at work. Additionally it suggests that the organisation's culture also has a big impact. A culture that is rooted in values, history and practices that make distinctions between the roles appropriate for men and women will inevitably affect structures and promotion prospects. Organisations need to look at the representation of women, and other equality groups, in their structures and, where under-representation occurs, think about lawful and non-discriminatory ways of increasing representation.

Ethical business

There seems to have been an increase in recent years of reports of wrongdoing and malpractice in organisations. Enron is one of the most high-profile cases but there are others. Top managers are usually able to accumulate enough money to live out a comfortable lifestyle yet a majority of employees can be put out of work often with their investments in their previous employer worthless. In response to public concerns the US government introduced the Sarbanes-Oxley Act of 2002 to tighten what companies have to do and which made executives more accountable for their actions.

While external frameworks to regulate behaviour are welcome, Stanford (2004) reminds us that internal mechanisms are also needed. But what form should they take? It would be too simple to appoint an executive to oversee ethical practice as it is in the echelons of executives that malpractice is tolerated. Centralised organisations are characterised by a concentration of decision making at the top since that is where authority and autonomy lie. It seems therefore that malpractice is more likely to germinate and grow where centralisation is high. In decentralised structures the opposite is true. There is less opportunity for malpractice due to increased sharing of knowledge and shared accountability for the consequences of decisions.

Organisations should have clear procedures to be followed if and when an employee wants to report things they are concerned about, such as behaviour they perceive to be illegal, unethical or improper. Where employees feel that they cannot access these procedures then one recourse is to 'whistleblowing' – the disclosure of information to people inside the organisation (for example, higher management) or outside (for example, the media) who may be able to intervene.

Communication is a feature of organisational life and communication flows in different structures. Miceli and Near (1992) found that organisational size may influence the likelihood of whistleblowing as individuals in large organisations may see themselves as less able to make a difference than if they worked in a smaller one. Hierarchical, centralised and bureaucratic organisations could be expected to suppress views about speaking out as communication typically is more top to bottom than up and down.

Illustration in film

A Glimpse of Hell

This film is based on the true story of an explosion in a gun turret on the US Navy ship USS *Iowa* in 1989 that killed 47 crewmen. The film shows how the Navy attempted to blame members of the gun crew rather than consider alternative explanations, for example that maintenance of the gunnery equipment might have been neglected. It even tried to insinuate that two sailors were involved in a relationship that had led one of them to deliberately cause the explosion.

At one point, an officer who is concerned about maintenance standards goes to see his father, who was once a senior officer. His father tells him to report his misgivings through the proper chain of command – in this case to his immediate superior.

This film is a good portrayal of how a hierarchical bureaucracy functions when it feels threatened, what it can be like to want to speak out in such a climate, and how the organisation can close ranks to suppress free expression.

King (1999) examined the links between structures and whistleblowing closely and made several propositions:

- Divisional structures will encourage internal whisteblowing as there is decentralised decision making.
- Functional structures encourage external whistleblowing if perceptions of communication channels appear unclear.
- Bureaucratic, top-down organisations will discourage whistleblowing.
- Matrix structures encourage external whistleblowing if clear channels are not available (remember – matrices are vulnerable to creating confusion about lines of authority).

While structure seems likely to have an influence on whistleblowing it seems equally plausible that corporate cultures (norms and values) will have a big effect on the development of moral reasoning among employees and hence on attitudes to reporting perceived wrongdoings. Cultures that tolerate sharp practices will see little reporting regardless of structure. Organisations can encourage ethical behaviour by making commitments to corporate social responsibility objectives, setting out codes of ethics, and establishing committees or groups to oversee organisational progress in that area. There are also implications for the design of human resource management practices. For example, ensuring that performance measurement and reward systems do not encourage unethical practices. This could happen where unrealistic goals are set for people such that employees resort to unethical practices to meet them.

 ## Flexible working

Although people are the most vital resource in an organisation they can be prone to inflexibility and inertia. As a consequence, many organisations have sought more flexible structures and employment conditions. The implications of flexible working and of the flexible firm for organisational behaviour are significant, not least in terms of motivation, teamwork, leadership, structure, communications, culture and change.

Teleworking (using ICT to work at a distance from the employing organisation) may lead an organisation to feel it needs tight controls whereas a looser more organic style may be suited to telecentres. In return for greater freedom from the 'normal' workplace the level of control by a superior increases considerably, and pre-planning work is necessary along with contacts to check progress. Vertical lines of communication are likely, and successful teleworking relies upon a high level of trust (Chapman *et al.*, 1995).

Distancing

Distancing occurs where employees are replaced by subcontractors, and employment contracts are replaced by contracts for service. While commonplace in construction and manufacturing for some time, it is increasingly popular in services and the public sector. It has a significant effect on structure as more and more non-core activities are contracted out. The core–periphery concept (Torrington *et al.*, 2008) applies where a small number of experienced staff work in a stable core whereas others are peripheral and may be employed by satellite organisations and/or as part-time or temporary staff.

Functional and pay flexibility

Functional flexibility involves reducing unhelpful lines of demarcation between jobs in order to encourage effective teamwork and improved productivity. Multiskilling, where workers are trained to undertake a wider variety of jobs, is becoming more commonplace. Pay flexibility involves the harmonisation of terms and conditions across a workforce. Managerial and manual workers, who were often differentiated in terms of hourly pay and salaries, different pension arrangements, sick pay and holidays, are experiencing harmonised reward practices. Pay flexibility also covers the situation where to attract particular skills to different locations employers offer different rates of pay for the same job.

Numbers on flexible working arrangements

By 2002, 18 per cent of the working population of the European Union worked part-time, up from 14 per cent in 1992. Part-time work is more common among working women (33 per cent) than working men (7 per cent). Figures vary from country to country (Corral and Isusi, 2003). Part-time work in the USA is about 13 per cent of the workforce and in Japan is 25 per cent (Buddelmeyer *et al.*, 2005). Research shows that part-time work is associated with fewer training and development opportunities, reduced job security, lower salary and lower protection.

In the UK at the end of 2007, about 7.5 million workers were part-time, of which 76 per cent were women out of a total workforce of about 28 million (*Labour Force Survey*). In addition there are about 1.5 million temporary workers. Research has shown that permanent employees can react negatively to the presence of temporary workers, particularly if they feel their employer would remove their more secure contracts if given the opportunity. Negative reactions can be manifested in lower commitment towards temporary workers and to the organisation (Biggs *et al.*, 2005). Organisations using temporary workers as part of an employment strategy need to work on developing trust between permanent and temporary staff and this starts by explaining to permanent employees the business reasons behind the use of temps (Biggs and Swailes, 2006).

Communities of practice

While structures are created to enable organisations to meet their goals and objectives, there are times when structures can prevent employees from working in the ways that they would like to. Communities of practice come into being to get around these formal obstacles. They are *'groups of people who share a passion for something they know how to do and who interact regularly to learn how to do it better'* (Cross *et al.*, 2006). They share their knowledge and expertise in free-flowing, creative ways that represent new approaches to problem solving and are very good ways of learning (Wenger and Snyder, 2000).

The explosion of knowledge and technology lies behind the proliferation of knowledge workers in organisations. Knowledge is becoming so specialised that knowledge workers want to reach beyond the formal structures and boundaries that organisations constrain them with. They want to collaborate with like-minded people, inside and outside the organisation, and the structural paradox is that classical structuring methods can get in the way (Mini-case 7.6). Paradoxically, the only structure that works is one that members of the community can devise for themselves. Attempts to impose structure run the risk of killing the initiative. If managers try to interfere with communities by controlling their activities then they are likely to dissolve or at best transmute into a formal team or committee. In either case, the spontaneity and creativity of the community is likely to be lost for ever. Table 7.3 summarises communities of practice on their key dimensions.

Mini-case 7.6: Structural barriers and a community of practice

This is a true situation but is anonymous to protect the innocent! Imagine an organisation with 12 departments that are each profit centres. Each has income and expenditure targets and, by and large, the customers of the different departments do not overlap. The budget model in the organisation is such that money follows customers: that is, the money going into one department will not be used to help another department. Suppose that the staff in one department think of an idea for a new service. Usually, the department would develop the service and keep the income from selling it. Suppose though that the new service requires technical help from another department and, if it were ever developed, staff from several departments to deliver it. The problem is that the budget model provides no incentive for staff to help each other develop a new service. Even if a group of employees could do this, the model has no means of rewarding the departments involved for their efforts. Basically, the departmental structure and the overlying budget model are strong barriers to cross-departmental initiatives.

In this same organisation, there are many rules, systems, procedures and committees that exist in the name of protecting service quality. Each department has several sections and the section heads created a community of practice to make sense of all the formal systems that they are supposed to understand. They meet when they feel they need to, have no agenda, and won't meet if any 'outsiders' try to join them. In this informal way, they can help each other with important issues in a non-threatening and supportive environment. Arguably this community does as much to uphold service quality as the formal systems achieve.

Table 7.3 Summary characteristics of communities of practice

Characteristic	Description
Purpose	Adding value, sharing knowledge, building members' capabilities
Membership	Diverse, self-selecting
Size	Can be hundreds
Scope	Narrow or wide, can span several organisations
Structure	Self-organising
Frequency of meetings	Whenever deemed necessary
Ethos	Informal, sharing
Topics covered	Anything defined as useful by the members
Source of cohesion	Members' commitment to the topic
Outputs	Knowledge sharing and new understanding
Organisational support	Funding, interventions to overcome obstacles the community encounters
Typical habitat	Knowledge-driven organisations
Assessment	The stories told by members about performance improvement
Lifespan	For so long as members want it

Source: Based on Wenger and Snyder (2000).

While communities of practice are increasingly used in knowledge-intensive work, Roberts (2006) offers some limitations:

* The context in which a CoP is embedded is central to its success in creating and transferring knowledge.
* In theory, some cultures are more open to them than others, for example, collective cultures should be more conducive.
* Being self-managed their contributions are uncertain (but the same can be said of managed activities)
* They may be less relevant to small organisations given the relative shortage of resources.
* Communities are better suited to decentralised structures.

 Cross-cultural influences upon structure

Multinational companies have some added challenges in relation to domestic organisations arising from the need to cope with different national cultures in terms of the ways they approach structuring. Global and multicultural teams are widely used to coordinate interests and these differ in that their members are dispersed and communicate through ICT. Two particular challenges for 'virtual' teams are the creation of trust among people who do not know each other and who rarely or never meet, and building relationships that will stand up over time, culture and distance (Briscoe and Schuler, 2004).

Chapter 10 explains differences in national cultures in detail. If cultures are seen as systems of values then we can see how values differ – for example, attitudes to risk taking or to the preferred relationships between workers and their bosses. Countries with high power distance between levels would be expected to create more hierarchy and be more centralised, since decision making would be seen as a task for top managers. Cultures that try to minimise uncertainty would create highly formalised structures where rules and regulations are used to govern the routine lives of employees. Such cultures would also value specialisation in terms of the ways that jobs are defined (i.e., narrowly).

Where cultures are more collectivist than individualist, structures should be marked by more group work and group discipline to keep people in check. The ability to cooperate with others and to work as a team member would be more highly valued than in individualist cultures which would be keener to reward individual effort. In cultures that reflect feminine values of support, caring and the quality of relationships, these features would be gathered up by structure. In masculine cultures structures would reflect task achievement rather than relationships.

Hofstede's (1991) cultural mapping suggested that, for instance, Latin countries (for example, South America, Spain, Italy) as well as Japan and South Korea combine both high power distance and strong uncertainty avoidance. Hence, structures in those countries could be expected to be bureaucratic, hierarchical and reliant upon following rules and procedures. In contrast, countries that are tolerant of uncertainty and where power distance is low (Scandinavia, UK, for example) would be more likely to develop flatter structures that are more organic (see Table 7.2) (Schneider and Barsoux, 2003).

Lincoln *et al.* (1986: 361) found clear evidence that Japanese structures differed from US designs and they were less influenced by technology than in the USA. 'Compared with US, Japanese manufacturing organizations have taller hierarchies, less functional specialization, less formal delegation of authority but more de facto participation in decisions at lower levels in the management hierarchy'. These structures were consistent with characteristics of the labour market such as lifetime employment and seniority-based promotion and a general emphasis on groupwork over individualism.

Miles (2006: 305) points out that China, Japan and Korea are 'deeply rooted in Confucian values and ideology'. These stress the importance of sincerity, benevolence, respect for elders and authority and respect for established norms of behaviour (propriety). This leads to structures that are hierarchical and obedient, that emphasise harmony such that priority is given to reaching consensus through discussion not disagreement. Such strong historical forces have to be respected by Western organisations that are setting up operations in these regions.

In sum, it seems clear that national cultures do influence the ways in which work organisations are structured. While adopting a divisional structure overall, a multinational company will need to allow the structure to adapt to local variations in the preferred relationships between people and in the way work gets done. This is necessary to achieve the most productive unit, as imposing structure that works in one culture upon another may not be successful.

Structure and competition: research evidence

The ways in which organisations implement structural change and the causes and effects of these changes are notoriously difficult to research. Much of the research done in the area is small-scale, leading to difficulties in generalising from the findings. One exception is a large European study of the ways in which 450 enterprises were organising in the 1990s (Ruigrok *et al.*, 1999), summarised below. Organisations were defined on three dimensions:

- The structures that link their people and other resources internally and connect them externally to other networks of people and organisations
- The processes that enable production and delivery of products and services. Processes change as new technologies and new knowledge are introduced.
- The boundaries within which they deliver their products and services. Boundaries can be defined in terms of geographic or product or market boundaries.

Structure

The number of management levels between the chief executive and the lowest managers had reduced in 30 per cent of enterprises, and this was consistent across Europe. In contrast, 20 per cent of enterprises had increased the number of management levels. In Northern Europe and German-speaking countries there was a strong trend towards decentralised decision making at both operational and strategic levels. Operational decision-making involves, for example, changing suppliers or production processes. Strategic decision-making involves, for example, long-term planning and major investment decisions. Compared to Hofstede's work on cultures (Chapter 10) there is perhaps a link between greater decentralisation and relatively low uncertainty avoidance (that is, a greater tolerance of uncertainty) and lower power-distance that allows more freedom of thinking down the organisation (Ruigrok *et al.*, 1999: 52).

The study found that functional areas were still very important to European enterprises, suggesting that moves towards more cross-functional structuring were occurring. However, there was more use of project-based organising, requiring less reliance on hierarchy and more reliance on collaborating across internal boundaries, for example between research and development, marketing and production. When strategically important projects are identified, people are relocated from their original functional area to work exclusively for a project team. When the project is completed people return to their functional area or move to another project.

Internal processes

ICT has caused sharp increases in the amount of internal communication, both laterally (across organisations) and vertically. The outcome of this was much more use of internal networks of people that aim to get the best input of skills, knowledge and resources given the increased tendency to decentralise. Another aspect of the ways that organisations are functioning is the use of human resource manage-ment initiatives. Organisations reported growth in the idea of internal labour markets: that is, employees were not seen as being solely confined to a particular functional area where they normally work. There was a rise in the use of planned transfers of people to other parts of organisations, organisation-wide conferences to maximise the capture and use of knowledge, and the use of professional teams to tackle issues and problems. The main thrust of these initiatives is to provide new channels to transfer knowledge throughout organisations.

External boundaries

The research found that organisations were increasingly outsourcing activities that were seen as being peripheral to their main value-adding operations or which, if not peripheral, could be provided more effectively. Research and development is a classic case since it is vital to organisational success in the long term and yet is often very costly, with some organisations spending up to 20–30 per cent of their turnover annually on R&D (Swailes, 2004). Outsourcing all or part of their R&D, perhaps to a network of collaborators, can provide better value to an organisation.

Another alteration to boundaries has come via strategic alliances. A strategic alliance could involve, say, a motor manufacturer, making a commitment to pur-chase from a supplier of components, for example braking systems. The alliance is formed on the basis that supplier and manufacturer work together to find ways of reducing costs and raising quality. The new science of genetics has provided wonder-ful opportunities to create new drugs to treat disease and inherited conditions. The

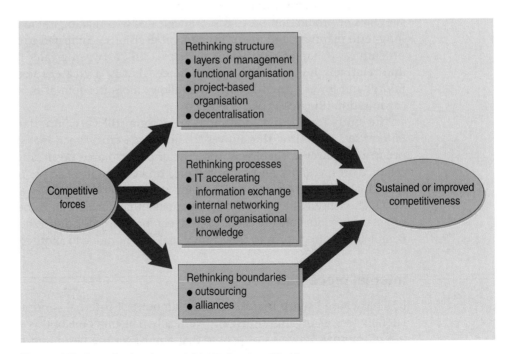

Figure 7.5 Organisational structuring and competitive forces

science is so highly specialised, however, that in practice the larger drugs companies work with smaller research and development companies that have the special know-how. These alliances use joint expertise to find the most economic ways forward. Figure 7.5 summarises the trends in structuring, processes and boundaries.

 Restructuring

Structural inertia

While it is easy to find examples of restructuring it is also true that individual organisations do not change their fundamental structure very often. This tendency is referred to as 'structural inertia' (Colombo and Delmastro, 2002). There are several reasons for this.

- Unless organisations are convinced that a modified structure will lead to a much better performance they will stay as they are.

- Successful organisations are successful, in part, due to a repeatable reliability in what they produce. Repeatability can be attributed to organisation structure which runs standard routines which provide an inbuilt resistance to change.

- For a given structure at a given time, there is a distribution of power and rewards to employees. Structural change calls for a redistribution of these benefits. Inevitably, employees will be concerned to protect their positions and will try to influence the outcomes of redesign and restructuring attempts. As the politics of redistributing benefits is complex and carries high costs, organisations usually resist doing so unless the threat to survival is imminent.

- Since organisations have to invest in new designs and structures, then like other investments, once made the same investment cannot be spent again and represents a sunk cost. A change today also carries an opportunity cost arising from the inability to make a different change tomorrow.

So what makes organisations bite the bullet and go for substantive changes? A performance improvement imperative is one reason. The type of technology used is another, in particular computer-aided manufacturing that allows flexible production systems.

Organisational design and organisation structure

We have noted previously the difference between design and structure. Design is a skeleton on which structure is built. Organisation design charts tell us how the skeleton is supposed to function to support the body of the organisation. Design will stay in place until top managers decide to change it with new divisions, mergers or closures of existing ones and new reporting relationships among them. Structure in contrast can be seen as a much more organic social structure that develops as people interact in the course of their work, making friends and enemies along the way. The real working structure of an organisation can be seen as something that is socially constructed (Bate *et al.*, 2000).

If we accept this view of design and structure we are drawn to an important point. This is that what top managers do in relation to organisational design has, unless there is very close control, at best a loose connection with the social structures that exist and through which things get done. Bate (1995) suggested that when managers focus on design and disregard the social networks that overlay it then there is a danger of 'empty restructuring'. Here, repeated efforts at redesign fail to make changes to the ways managers are managing (management styles), the prevailing subcultures that influence the performance ethic or the processes and systems with which information is used (or not).

Mini-case 7.7 Restructuring health services

The organisational setting was a UK National Health Service Trust with over 3000 employees on three sites. Premises were old and outdated. In common with many NHS organisations a range of professional and occupational groups worked side-by-side to deliver the specialist services needed. The big plan was to relocate to a new purpose-built site.

'Morale had sunk to an all-time low' and relations between the professional groups were 'strained'. Formal structure was built around divisions such as Accident & Emergency and Finance. We can already see that simply redesigning an organisation in this condition would not begin to affect the cultural changes needed.

An action research programme was used, involving researchers working with the Trust employees over two years. The basic model followed was:

1 Diagnosis – of the present state through interviews and participation and through mapping the formal and informal processes that existed.
2 Analysis – to identify issues and problems.
3 Feedback – engaging employees in interpreting the analyses to get ownership of the situation and to create a commitment to change.
4 Action – creating strategies and developing leadership and management capabilities to move forward
5 Evaluation – monitoring progress against agreed success factors and indicators.

This list of five stages is not intended to be linear. Although diagnosis is a starting point the five stages soon became interrelated. For example, the process of giving feedback may clarify part of the analysis and lead to new insights. A key finding was that to move this organisation forward it needed to change in three areas: structure, culture and leadership. To engineer changes in these areas a four stage intervention model was used.

Stage 1 – this stage identified and set out cultural and social issues and made explicit where the organisation was and where it wanted to be – in social terms a move from control to collaboration.

Stage 2 – this involved building bridges between different departments and groups that moved away from an adversarial and untrusting environment to a more constructive one. This stage focused on building the relationships needed to manage change and thus the organisation's capacity to change.

Stage 3 – this sought a more formal set of structures on which change could be built. These structures were not devised and imposed by top managers, but were developed by three project groups.

Stage 4 – here the organisation reflected on what it had done and how it was operating. Stage 4 was not so much an end but a feed into a cycle of identifying issues and new imperatives.

Bate *et al.* (2000) argue that models of change that are top-down and which try to take culture with them are flawed since until there is a consensus around cultural change is reached, structural change will be inefficient.

Source: Bate *et al.* (2000).

Managerial implications

This chapter has dealt with some of the classic material on structure and some of the more recent developments. Against this background we can identify some implications for management.

1 There is not a best way of structuring. To maximise organisational performance, managers must match structure to the demands and challenges of the business environment.

2 Change to organisational design may begin a programme of corporate renewal but, by itself, will not sustain it. To sustain change and renewal, changes to the 'real' structure and to culture are needed.

3 Cultural change requires that managers identify and utilise each employee's distinctive knowledge and capabilities and embed this knowledge in the evolving structure. This is notoriously difficult to achieve.

4 Drives for greater organisational performance create strong temptations for managers to control and closely monitor their workforce. Structures do influence behaviour, however, and control and monitoring mechanisms can depress innovation. Managers must look for ways of balancing these two contrasting requirements.

5 Recognising and making positive use of national cultural differences into structure is important for multinational enterprises.

6 Even the 'best' structure will only take an organisation so far in terms of its ability to compete. Managers need to stimulate positive attitudes and behaviour and link them to the processes used to deliver products or services.

The complexity of the forces affecting structure is shown in Figure 7.6. Pressure to raise performance can show itself in many ways. If performance is unsatisfactory an organisation can become a target for takeover. Improved performance may lead to growth whereas, after a downturn, an organisation may want to cut back some of its activities. An organisation may want to become more flexible and responsive. Particular responses have implications for the skills needed but the mix of skills and activities can influence how these specialisms are best organised. From inside the organisation latent forces emanating from the technologies employed may influence structural choices alongside the more explicit posturing of managers engaged in power struggles. The level of stability in the organisation's operating environment also influences structural parameters.

 ## Summary of main points

The main points are:

- Optimising organisational design and structure is a continual challenge to managers.

- Strategy, size, technology and market conditions all influence structure.

- The main structural forms are multifunctional, multidivisional and matrix structures. Networking is more and more a component of structure as strategies require cooperation.

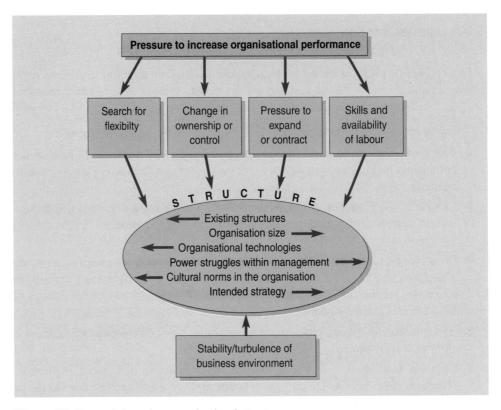

Figure 7.6 Forces influencing organisational structure

● The evidence for any genuinely new organisational forms is limited.

● Current trends are continuing to move away from vertical structures and communications with formal boundaries towards more horizontal communication across fuzzy boundaries. ICT is playing a big role in enabling structural change.

● National cultural differences influence preferences towards structuring.

● Despite rhetoric of flexibility and empowerment organisations still attempt close control.

● Structures influence many things such as culture, learning and communication, which in turn influence vital attitudes like commitment and professionalism.

Conclusions

Structures will change so long as organisations have to be more efficient. Although the determinants and characteristics of different structures are well known, what really matters is the effectiveness of the particular structure used. Big variables like culture and management systems also affect performance, and it is difficult to disentangle their relative influence. Current patterns are towards flatter and more fluid structures with more lateral communication. While organisational design may reflect this, the extent that it is really happening is unclear.

New ways of structuring call for employees to think differently about the way they work and what they are responsible for. They need to think beyond their own interests and to empathise with the interests of other parties, particularly in collaborative and cooperative arrangements. Organisational performance is an expanding concept which extends beyond financial measures to include socially responsible business and ethical behaviour.

Managers should not wait to change structure when performance dips. Prudent managers should keep a watchful eye on structure in relation to strategy and push through changes when action is needed. Failure to align strategy and structure will lead to organisational extinction. It is, of course, the employees who breathe life into new structures, and managers must not lose sight of the personal and professional development that new structures need to make them work.

Questions

1 Why might changes to organisational design have no impact on organisational performance?

2 Evaluate the structure of an organisation in terms of the vocabulary of structure at the start of this chapter.

3 Why might attempts to control communities of practice lead to their quick demise?

4 How can organisation structures affect the levels of innovation and creativity shown by employees?

5 Which of the following statements do you think is the most plausible? Why?

   a Organisation structure influences organisational performance.

   b Organisational performance influences structure.

6 How might different structures influence the likelihood of (un)ethical behaviour by employees?

7 What advice would you give to an organisation that is changing its structure to deliver higher performance?

8 What actions can be taken to increase the representation of equality groups in the higher reaches of organisations?

9 What are the barriers to reducing bureaucracy in organisations?

References

Ahuja, M. K. and Carley, K. M. (1998) 'Network structure in virtual organizations', *Organization Science*, 10(6), pp. 740–57.

Aldrich, H. E. (1972) 'Technology and organizational structure: A reexamination of the findings of the Aston group', *Administrative Science Quarterly*, 17(1), pp. 26–44.

Allen, G. (2001) *The Private Finance Initiative (PFI)*. House of Commons Library Research Paper 01/117, 18 December.

Ball, R. and King, D. (2006) 'The PFI in local government', *Economic Affairs*, 2(1), pp. 36–40.

Barney, J. (1991) 'Firm resources and sustained competitive advantage', *Journal of Management*, 17(1), pp. 99–120.

Bartlett, C. and Ghoshal, S. (1990) 'Matrix management: Not a structure, a frame of mind', *Harvard Business Review*, July–August, pp. 138–45.

Bate, P. (1995) *Strategies for Cultural Change*. Oxford: Butterworth-Heinemann.

Bate, P., Khan, R. and Pye, A. (2000) 'Towards a culturally sensitive approach to organization structuring: Where organization design meets organization development', *Organization Science*, 11(2), pp. 197–211.

Bierly, P. E. and Spender, J.-C. (1995) 'Culture and high reliability organizations: The case of the nuclear submarine', *Journal of Management*, 21(4), pp. 639–56.

Biggs, D. and Swailes, S. (2006) 'Relations, commitment and satisfaction in agency workers and permanent workers', *Employee Relations*, 28(1/2), pp. 130–43.

Biggs, D., Burchell, B. and Milmore, M. (2005) 'The changing world of the temporary worker: The potential HR impact of legislation', *Personnel Review*, 35(2), pp. 191–207.

Bottrill, I. (2003) 'Councillors and partnerships', in *The Councillor's Guide*. London: Improvement and Development Agency.

Briscoe, D. R. and Schuler, R. S. (2004) *International Human Resource Management*, 2nd edn. London: Routledge.

Buddelmeyer, H., Mourre, G. and Ward-Wardmedinger, M. (2005) *Part-time Work in EU Countries: Labour Market Mobility and Exit*, Working Paper Series No. 460, March. Frankfurt am Main: European Central Bank.

Burns, T. and Stalker, G. M. (1961) *The Management of Innovation*. London: Tavistock.

Chandler, A. (1962) *Strategy and Structure*. Cambridge, MA: MIT Press.

Chapman, A. J., Sheehy, N., Heywood, S., Dooley, B. and Collins, S. C. (1995) 'The organizational implications of teleworking', *International Review of Industrial and Organizational Psychology*, 10, pp. 229–48.

Clases, C., Bachmann, R. and Wehner, T. (2003) 'Studying trust in virtual organizations', *International Studies of Management and Organization*, 33(3), pp. 7–27.

Colombo, M. G. and Delmastro, M. (2002) 'The determinants of organizational change and structural intertia: Technological and organizational factors', *Journal of Economics and Management Strategy*, 11(4), pp. 595–635.

Corral, A. and Isusi, I. (2003) *Part-time Work in Europe*. Dublin: European Federation of the Improvement of Living and Working Conditions.

Cross, R., Laseter, T., Parker, A. and Velasquez, G. (2006) 'Using social network analysis to improve communities of practice', *California Management Review*, 49(1), pp. 32–60.

Davidow, W. H. and Malone, M. S. (1992) *The Virtual Corporation: Structuring and Revitalizing the Corporation for the 21st Century*. London: Harper Business.

Day, G. (1999) 'Aligning organizational structure to the market', *Business Strategy Review*, 10(3), pp. 33–46.

Drucker, P. F. (1975) 'New templates for today's organizations', in *Harvard Business Review on Management*. New York: Harper & Row.

Fagenson, E. A. (1990) 'At the heart of women in management research: Theoretical and methodological approaches and their biases', *Journal of Business Ethics*, 9, pp. 267–74.

Ghoshal, S. and Nohria, N. (1993) 'Horses for courses: Organization forms for multinational corporations', *Sloan Management Review*, Winter, pp. 23–35.

Goold, M. and Campbell, A. (2003) 'Structured networks: Toward the well-designed matrix', *Long Range Planning*, 36(5), pp. 417–40.

Habib, M. M. and Victor, B. (1991) 'Strategy, structure and performance of US manufacturing and service MNCs: A comparative analysis', *Strategic Management Journal*, 12(8), pp. 589–606.

Hales, C. (1999) 'Leading horses to water: The impact of decentralization on managerial behaviour', *Journal of Management Studies*, 36(6), pp. 831–57.

Hannah, L. (1976) *Management Strategy and Business Development: An Historical and Comparative Study*. London: Macmillan.

Hofstede, G. (1991) *Cultures and Organizations*. Maidenhead: McGraw-Hill.

Kanter, R. (1977) *Men and Women of the Corporation*. New York: Basic Books.

King, G. (1999) 'The implications of an organization's structure on whistleblowing', *Journal of Business Ethics*, 20, pp. 315–26.

Lampel, J. and Shamsie, J. (2003) 'Capabilities in motion: New organizational forms and the reshaping of the Hollywood movie industry', *Journal of Management Studies*, 40(8), pp. 2189–210.

Lawrence, P. R. and Lorsch, J. W. (1967) *Organization and Environment*. Cambridge, MA: Harvard University Press.

Lincoln, J. R., Hanada, M. and McBride, K. (1986) 'Organizational structures in Japanese and US manufacturing', *Administrative Science Quarterly*, 31, pp. 338–64.

Martin, I. and Cheung, Y. (2002) 'Change management at Mobil Oil Australia', *Business Process Management Journal*, 8(5) pp. 447–62.

Meijaard, J., Brand, M. J. and Mosselman, M. (2005) 'Organizational structure and performance in Dutch small firms', *Small Business Economics*, 25, pp. 83–96.

Miceli, M. P. and Near, J. P. (1992) *Blowing the Whistle: The Organizational and Legal Implications for Companies and Employees*. New York: Lexington Books.

Miles, L. (2006) 'The application of Anglo-American corporate practices in societies influenced by Confucian values', *Business and Society Review*, 111(3), pp. 305–21.

Miller, C. C., Glick, W. H., Wang, Y. and Huber, G. P. (1991) 'Understanding technology structure relationships: Theory development and meta-analytic theory testing', *Academy of Management Journal*, 34(2), pp. 370–99.

Mintzberg, H. (1989) *Mintzberg on Management: Inside our Strange World of Organizations*. New York: Free Press.

Morris, J., Hassard, J. and McCann, L. (2006) 'New organizational forms, human resource management and structural convergence? A study of Japanese organizations', *Organization Studies,* 27, pp. 1485–510.

Mukherji, A. (2002) 'The evolution of information systems: Their impact on organizations and structures', *Management Decision*, 40(5), pp. 497–507.

Olsen, E. M., Slater, S. F. and Hult, T. M. (2005) 'The importance of structure and process to strategy implementation', *Business Horizons*, 48, pp. 47–54.

Perrow, C. (1967) *Organizational Analysis: A Sociological View*. London: Tavistock.

Perrow, C. (1984) *Normal Accidents: Living with High-risk Technologies*. New York: Basic Books.

Prewitt, E. (2003) 'GM matrix reloads', *CEO Magazine*, 1 September.

Roberts, J. (2006) 'Limits to communities of practice', *Journal of Management Studies*, 43(3) pp. 621–39.

Ruigrok, W., Pettigrew, A., Peck, S. and Whittington, R. (1999) 'Corporate restructuring and new forms of organizing: Evidence from Europe', *Management International Review*, 39, Special Issue, pp. 41–64.

Schneider, S. C. and Barsoux, J. L. (2003) *Managing across Cultures*. Harlow: Financial Times Prentice Hall.

Stanford, J. H. (2004) 'Curing the ethical malaise in corporate America: Organizational structure as the antidote', *SAM Advanced Management Journal*, Summer, 69(3), pp. 14–21.

Street, E. *et al.* (2004) *Evaluation of Local Strategic Partnerships: A Briefing Note for LSPs by LSPs*. Office of the Deputy Prime Minister: London.

Sullivan, D. (1996) 'Multinational corporations, organization structure', in Warner, M. (ed.) *International Encyclopedia of Business and Management*. London: Routledge.

Swailes, S. (2004) 'The technological environment', in Brooks, I., Weatherston, J. and Wilkinson, G. (eds) *The International Business Environment*. Harlow: Financial Times Prentice Hall.

Torrington, D., Hall, L. and Taylor, S. (2008) *Human Resource Management*, 7th edn. Harlow: Financial Times Prentice Hall.

Wellman, J. (2007) 'Leadership behavior in matrix environments', *Project Management Journal*, 38(2), pp. 62–74.

Wenger, E. and Snyder, W. (2000) 'Communities of practice: The organizational frontier', *Harvard Business Review*, January–February, pp. 139–45.

Willmott, H. (1981) 'The structuring of organizational structure: A note', *Administrative Science Quarterly*, 26, pp. 470–4.

Wilson, D. C. and Rosenfeld, R. H. (1990) *Managing Organizations: Text, Readings and Cases*. New York: McGraw-Hill.

Woodward, J. (1958) *Management and Technology*. London: HMSO.

Further reading

Huczynski, A. A. and Buchanan, D. A. (2007) *Organizational Behavior*, 6th edn, Harlow: Financial Times Prentice Hall, Chapters 14 and 15.

Kaplan, R. S. and Norton, D. P. (2006) 'How to implement new strategies without disrupting your organization', *Harvard Business Review*, March, pp. 100–9.

Leavitt, H. J. (2003) 'Why hierarchies thrive', *Harvard Business Review*, 81(3), pp. 96–102.

Schneider, S. C. and Barsoux, J. L. (2003) *Managing across Cultures*, 2nd edn, Harlow: Financial Times Prentice Hall, Chapter 4.

Scott, W. R. (2004) 'Reflections on a half-century of organizational sociology', *Annual Review of Sociology*, 30(1), pp. 1–21.

 ## Internet sites

There are some useful web sites to help understand the concept of structure. When searching try looking for 'organizational design' as well as 'organization structure'. Note that the z-form of spelling is the American preference and is far more common than the s-form.

www.organizational.com
www.analytictech.com/mb021/orgtheory.htm
www.analytictech.com/mb021/trendsm/htm
www2.tepper.cmu.edu/bosch/bart.html
www.haygroup.com/ww/Expertise/index.asp?id=504
www.bized.co.uk
www.sociosite_net/topics/organization.php
www.thetimes100.co.uk/company_list.php
www.cwenger.com/theory

8 Organisational power, politics and conflict

Learning outcomes

On completion of this chapter you should be able to:

- understand the unitary, pluralist and radical perspectives and the rational and political models of organisation;
- explain the meaning of, and discuss the links between, organisational power, politics and conflict;
- identify the different sources and bases of power;
- define and understand the concept of powerlessness;
- recognise the power of symbol manipulation;
- understand the influence of power and powerlessness in organisational change;
- understand the effect of power and politics on organisational conflict.

Key concepts

- organisation as a political system
- organisation as a rational system
- unitary, pluralist and radical frames
- power bases
- covert power
- powerlessness
- empowerment
- organisational politics
- interdepartmental conflict
- inter-cultural conflict
- communicating with symbols
- resistance
- negative power.

Power, politics and conflict are often considered as part of the less desirable, more covert, aspects of organisation, yet all are 'real' and endemic to organisations. They fundamentally influence the behaviour of individuals and groups and play important roles in the decision-making and problem-solving activities of organisations. As organisational realities they have stimulated considerable research and debate, which this chapter will explore. We will also relate power and politics to the themes of this book, to conflict, communication and organisational change.

 ## Introduction

There are few aspects of organisational behaviour which, for the inexperienced, appear more mystifying, difficult to appreciate and impossible to manage than power and organisational politics. Managers spend a great deal of their time attempting to avoid or actively managing conflict. They build alliances, compete internally for resources and power or influence and learn that managing their internal 'political' environment is often as vital an ingredient of their success as conducting their business activity. This chapter explores the political perspective, defines and examines power, politics and conflict in an organisational context and discusses the implications of power and politics for change.

The political perspective

It is possible, and potentially fruitful, to view organisations as if they were political systems, that is, from a political perspective. We explored, in Chapter 2, the use of perspectives or frames with which to analyse organisations. From this perspective concepts such as power, politics, conflict and control are viewed as natural common-place aspects of organisational reality with which everyone is involved. Nevertheless, there are alternative frames or perspectives which provide a useful insight. We will begin by briefly exploring a sixfold classification of power relations in organisations. Morgan (1986) identified six types of organisations from this perspective:

- organisations as autocracies – control held by an individual or small group;
- bureaucracies – where rules are written and power relationships clearly specified;
- technocracies – knowledge and expertise rule the system;
- codetermination – opposing parties share a ruling system;
- representative democracy – officers are elected for specific terms by workers;
- direct democracy – everone participates in the right to rule.

Probably the most common form of organisation in the Western world is the bureaucracy although many, perhaps particularly small companies, have auto-cratic tendencies while some, professional organisations, are technocracies.

We now examine two contrasting models of organisation, the rational and the political, together with three frames for analysing conflict, the unitary, pluralist and radical perspectives. If we view organisations as rational bodies, we would consider human behaviour to be based on logic and directed by clear objectives and informed by access to, and assimilation of, perfect information. Nothing is irrational or non-rational, little is random or accidental. For example, communications are open and free and are interpreted similarly by all. The decision process creates and supports clear goals. Decision making is rational: the problem is clearly articulated, alternative solutions are generated, decision parameters which enable choice to be made are known, and alternatives are fully evaluated before the best decision is made. There is an absence of power, politics, conflict and other sources of potential non-rationality or, if present, they do not influence decision making. Decisions always result in optimisation (the best solution is chosen and implemented), organisational members share common values and goals and efficiency is stressed. This is the stuff of dreams!

An alternative view is that organisations are political entities comprising coalitions that have divergent interests and disagree about goals. Communication is not perfect; instead, information is partial and unevenly accessible. What is more, it is open to manipulation and multiple interpretation. Disagreement, tension and conflict are inevitable, with the result that power is required to resolve conflict. Decision making, influenced by differential power, is often non-rational.

It could be considered that in their extremes these two models represent two ends of a continuum and that 'reality' may reside somewhere in between. Organisations that are characterised by complete rationality cannot, in the author's opinion, exist – as human attributes deny this possibility. Similarly, organisations that fully embrace political activity, individual values and differences in goals will prove so dysfunctional as to find survival difficult.

An alternative, although in some ways similar, approach, is to consider organisations from three perspectives or frames: the unitary, the pluralist and the radical frames (see Figure 8.1). Each represents a frame of analysis, a way of examining and interpreting organisational activity and, more specifically, for exploring organisational conflict.

- The *unitary view* suggests that organisations have goals to which all subscribe and that there is a collective understanding of appropriate ways of pursuing those goals. This traditional view was reinforced as a result of the work of the human relations school (*see* Chapter 2). Academics contributing to this view (in the period from the 1930s to the 1960s, although much current management writing implies much the same) argued that conflict and instability in organisations were the result of lack of trust and openness and could be resolved by adoption of a people orientation and by communicating freely. Establishing and embedding shared goals would deny conflict its inspiration.

- The *pluralist view* recognises differences in goals, interests and ambitions and concedes that multiple realities exist. Attempts to forge a coalition of these divergent interests becomes a leadership priority. Conflict is inevitable and endemic. It is a natural phenomenon which cannot be eliminated. As a

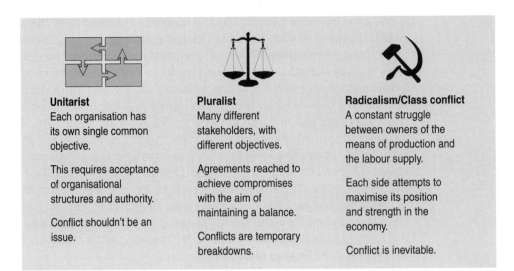

Unitarist
Each organisation has its own single common objective.

This requires acceptance of organisational structures and authority.

Conflict shouldn't be an issue.

Pluralist
Many different stakeholders, with different objectives.

Agreements reached to achieve compromises with the aim of maintaining a balance.

Conflicts are temporary breakdowns.

Radicalism/Class conflict
A constant struggle between owners of the means of production and the labour supply.

Each side attempts to maximise its position and strength in the economy.

Conflict is inevitable.

Figure 8.1 Unitarist, pluralist and radical frames

consequence, conflict cannot be viewed as wholly undesirable, as it would be under the unitary frame, especially as it provides a mechanism for evolutionary change and keeps the organisation responsive to internal and external changes. Within this frame, the manager's role is to manage these divergent interest groups and to achieve compromise and collaboration between stakeholders. There remains an underlying belief that conflict can be resolved and managed.

- The *radical view*, influenced by Marxism, suggests that there are fundamental and powerful social/structural and political divisions in society which make coalition impossible and conflict inevitable. By differentiating ownership of the business from employment in it exploitation and social division are ensured, leading to conflict.

These three frames provide a useful basis for analysing organisational conflict. In some organisations, many employees appear to pursue similar objectives whereas in others considerable and ongoing tension exists between different parties. When an organisation has limited and clear goals, a stable and predictable environment, an empowered staff and a teamworking ethos, conflict may be less apparent than in one where hierarchy and other structural divisions are entrenched, power is fought over, there are multiple and unclear goals and the environment is complex and dynamic.

Morgan (1996: 201) suggests that each frame leads to a different approach to management. He argues, for example, that 'if one believes that one is managing a team, one tends to expect and demand that people rally around common objectives'. Unitary managers cannot sanction conflict and political activity, only legitimate power sources. Pluralist managers, on the other hand, accept the inevitability of conflicts in interest and complex power sources. Their role is to balance this diversity and to work, wherever possible, within the constraints set by organisational goals. Having established these frameworks we will now examine organisational power.

Illustration in film

Antz

In the computer-animated film *Antz,* one worker ant (Z – 4195: voice by Woody Allen) rebels against the mindless devotion to duty and the unquestioned dominance of the elite. He cannot go along with unitarism. His objection shows itself when he dances with a princess in a different style from the multitude of workers on a social occasion and escalates to open questioning of the validity of what they are doing. This behaviour is not acceptable in the ant colony, putting him in direct conflict with leadership. His alternative world-view is not acceptable and an attempt is made to eliminate him.

This celebration of the individual is consistent with American (and increasingly British) culture. Woody Allen's character is a hero whose questioning of the dominant elite saves his fellow ants from destruction.

Organisational power

Robbins (1984: 155) defines power as *'a capacity that A has to influence the behavior of B, so that B does something he or she would not otherwise do'*. The key word here is 'influence', although it is merely a potential that need not be acted upon. If we assume that conflicts of interest exist in organisations, as in any human community, then power, as Morgan (1996) suggests, is the medium through which such conflicts are resolved. In organisations power is thought to derive from numerous sources. The early work of French and Raven (1959) shed light on this and established that it is neither possessed nor used equally by different individuals and groups.

Sources of power

French and Raven (1959) identified five sources of power:

1 *Coercive power* depends on fear and, in 'carrot and stick' terms, it represents the stick, or sanction, and in its extreme it might involve physical abuse. It is unequivocal and the receiver is unlikely to be pleased if this form of power is applied. Compliance may be an immediate response but longer-term commitment is highly unlikely to result.

2 *Reward power* represents the 'carrot', the incentive to behave in a particular manner. It is the power that is derived from an individual's or group's possession and control over organisational resources. People may comply if they consider the resultant benefit to be of value. Hence, in the workplace rewards are often 'used' to exert power over subordinates. In a positive fashion these include the prospect of salary increases, bonuses, certain perks or promises of promotion or, in a negative sense, they can involve the threat of removal of current or expected benefits. It is scarcity of resources which creates potential for them to be used as a power source. In turn, their use may create dependence.

3 *Expert power* refers to influence that is acquired by possessing special skills or knowledge. This may, for example, apply to individuals with superior technical skills and may not necessarily relate to their position in a formal hierarchy. A useful example is that provided by the internal IT technician whose rapid response to 'call-out' is highly cherished. The relative ignorance of the user, often a far more senior employee, provides the technician with an ongoing source of power which can be exercised by altering the speed of response and quality of service given.

4 *Legitimate* or *position power* refers to that derived from holding a formal position in an organisation. In bureaucracies, or in the military services, position power is particularly important, as rank is considered of significance. Weber (1947) referred to a similar concept as 'rational-legal authority'. Its legitimacy derives from social approval, and it provides a mechanism for order and the stabilisation of power relations. The trade union movement has traditionally acted as a counter-force to position power. Power at the top of the hierarchy is countered by collective action among those who individually lack power at the lower end. Morgan (1996: 173) notes that 'to the extent that trade union power is legitimized by the rule of law and the right to unionize, it too represents a type of formal authority'.

5 *Referent power* is derived from one's admiration or respect for an individual. Charisma, meaning 'gift of grace', can inspire followers, thus enabling leaders to exert power over subordinates, a fact recognised by Weber (1947) who referred to this as 'charismatic authority'.

This early work has been further developed. Robbins (1984) distinguishes between the sources of power and the means to exert influence, which he refers to as the 'bases of power'. For example, both position in the hierarchy and an individual's expertise are sources of power, whereas persuasion, knowledge and reward are tools or bases of power. The bureaucrat, holding position power, will have recourse to an array of rules and procedures to enforce or maintain position power. A bully relies on aggressive dominance, the threat of violence or actual physical force. The manager holding reward power will use the principle of exchange in order to exert influence. These are the bases or tools used to exert power. Figure 8.2 illustrates the difference between the sources of power and the tools or mechanisms used to exert that power.

Morgan (1996) noted further sources of power (*see* Figure 8.3). We will briefly examine the sources of power gained from: (a) the control of knowledge and information, (b) the control of boundaries and (c) interpersonal alliances and control of the informal organisation. Each implies some form of control of communication flows.

The ability to control information and knowledge in an organisation is, in part, related to the position held by an individual or group. By choosing to control the timing, destination and 'quality' of information it is possible to define or influence the organisational agenda and create dependencies. For example, British governments of late have employed a number of media and information managers, at very high levels (in the Cabinet), in order to control and influence government news (to put the government 'spin' on things). The 'gatekeeper' role in organisations is a critical source of power manipulation. Information can be screened to

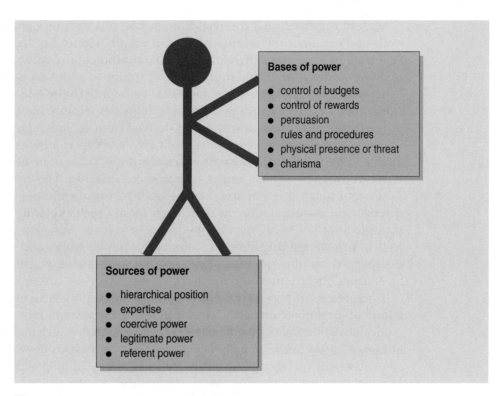

Figure 8.2 The sources and bases of power

ensure that it complies with or supports the accepted world-view and dissenting and potentially dangerous information can be suppressed or altered. Modern technology has increased the potential for information control and centralisation. Systems now enable managers to monitor and review operations, progress and targets from afar. In national politics it is no wonder that major modern political parties pay a great deal of attention to information management. Technology has radically altered the potential for control and manipulation in this regard.

1 Formal authority	8 Control of technology
2 Control of scarce resources	9 Interpersonal alliances, networks and control of 'informal organisation'
3 Use of organisational structure, rules and regulations	
	10 Control of counter organisations
4 Control of decision processes	11 Symbolism and the management of meaning
5 Control of knowledge and information	12 Gender and the management of gender relations
6 Control of boundaries	13 Structural factors that define the stage of action
7 Ability to cope with uncertainty	14 The power one already has

Figure 8.3 Morgan's sources of power
Source: Based on Morgan (1986).

Modern organisational configurations stress collaboration between functions, units and organisations in the creation of wealth. Control of these boundaries, facilitated by extensive networking, control of information and systems or specialised knowledge, can enable individuals or groups to amass considerable power. Whereas it has long been understood that belonging to the 'old school tie' network proved a useful source of power, emphasis has recently turned to the power of the informal organisation and that derived from an individual's wider social network. The skilled organisational politician constructs a network of informal allies and builds mutually supportive relationships. This can be used just as effectively to pacify potential enemies as to woo collaborators. This network, with the skilled politician at its centre, can be used to inform the manager of events throughout the organisation. By more overt means, such as placing of managers in strategic positions in an organisation, a senior manager can gain power by being well informed, gaining access to numerous sub-networks and creating many dependences on him- or herself. Patronage has long existed, probably having been an endemic characteristic of human organisation since the advent of man.

Three aspects of power are worthy of further discussion. First, negative power is a form of illegitimate influence which can be used to disrupt or to resist. This is of particular significance to the management of organisational change. Second, powerlessness, *a state where an individual or group has, or considers themselves to have, no power to influence a situation*, is further debated below. Third, power can be exerted in a highly covert, or invisible, form. These three are discussed, where appropriate, in this chapter.

Illustration in film

Braveheart

In the film *Braveheart* two of the key characters illustrate different sources and bases of power. William Wallace, played by Mel Gibson (a well-known Scot!), used the respect he was shown by fellow Scots as his source of power, referred to as referent power, and considerable expertise in choosing his time and methods of combat. He had little or no formal status with which to lead but charisma formed the basis of his power. Hence, he was able, in the film, to command almost magical respect, leading tens of thousands into battle against the 'auld enemy'.

On the other hand, the King of England (Edward II) enjoyed considerable resources and coercive and legitimate power. He used his ownership of land and his right as king to bestow title on any individual to buy off the Scottish nobles and to buy in sizeable armies. Most people respect and admire individuals who possess expertise and charisma. We choose to follow them. Those who rule by law, coercion and resource power do not tend to stimulate such fervour in their followers. Hence, it made a great movie – the triumph of good over evil.

Covert power

Power can be transparent, even tangible, or invisible and covert. For example, many managers are thought to control information, to accelerate or slow down its dissemination. Many staff members, especially in traditional organisations, do not have access to certain information. When access is denied, power is being exerted. Similarly, by exercising control of budgets, managers can exert influence in an 'invisible' manner, with few, if any, colleagues recognising the 'political' decisions that are being taken. Covert power can be used to control decision agendas. Power influences what actually appears on the agenda of a group. Conversely, power can be exerted openly, for example by giving a clear verbal or written order or instruction to a subordinate, or symbolised openly, such as when the Chief Executive parks his or her expensive new car in a named, allocated parking slot.

Dalton (1959) found that cliques were an important part of power relations in organisations. Cliques often form across departmental and organisational lines to pursue the self-interest of individuals. The cliques more often than not do not follow established organisational heirarchical or horizontal structures.

Covert power can be used negatively or to resist. For example, the Hawthorne experiments (referred to in Chapter 2) recognised that workers can determine the pace at which production occurs; they can increase or slow the rate of work while still giving the impression of being busy. This represents the exercise of power, covertly but by 'agreement'. Often, as we shall see, there is a form of individual and/or collective resistance to attempts to force the pace of organisational change. Subordinates do not often openly refuse to comply but instead pay lip-service to new ideas, sometimes going along with them without being convinced, or concerned, about their merit and, at most, temporarily change their overt behaviour. This represents the exercise of covert power.

As a result of this work, it is possible to analyse departmental power sources in any organisation and attempt to assess the relative power each department might yield. Alternatively this model can be used as a management tool for departmental managers to increase their power by attempting to build or acquire these power sources.

Powerlessness

Powerlessness, *a real or perceived state of having little or no power*, is an organisational reality for many. A feeling that one has little control over organisational decisions, particularly those that affect one's work life, is commonplace. It may be considered to be a relative concept: if A has less power than B then A may well feel powerless. Ironically, employees, irrespective of their rank or role, express feelings of powerlessness from time to time. Even senior managers, who recognise that their organisation is more powerful than any individual within it, or who believe that the environment in which they operate is determined for them, express concern over their perceived lack of power to influence matters.

What distinguishes management from other professions in this regard is dependence. Dependence is a potential trap. Managers direct activities and give orders: these need to be obeyed for power to be exercised. If subordinates do not obey they are withholding compliance and utilising their power to resist and to reinforce mutual dependence. As a result, the credibility of managers is under constant threat. Managers cannot control everything: they do not possess all the information and skills they require to manage successfully and they have many interested parties, or multiple stakeholders, to satisfy. It is not surprising, therefore, that reference has been made to 'the paradox of power' (Calabria, 1982), where the powerful are powerless.

There are, of course, many employees who do not possess the sources of power referred to by French and Raven (1959) or Morgan (1996). Additionally, others feel that they are not supported in what they are trying to do and are isolated and criticised. These employees may be considered to be genuinely powerless. Clearly, the salience of an individual's feeling of powerlessness is, in part, a product of the strength of that person's need to be empowered. 'Perceived' powerlessness is, therefore, a function of:

- the strength of an individual's desire or need to hold power; and
- the perceived power of players within the individual's working environment *vis-à-vis* their own power, that is, perceived relative power.

'Real' powerlessness is a function of:

- the relative strength of an individual's sources and bases of power.

Powerlessness can operate at the collective or group level. Some groups of employees, for instance women, first-line supervisors, some ethnic minorities and disabled people, often consider themselves to be relatively powerless. A collective expression of powerlessness can manifest itself in a variety of ways, not least in trade union activity, pressure group lobbying (e.g., for equal opportunity legislation), collective frustration and low morale and even partial exclusion from the workplace.

Powerlessness in the workplace serves little purpose. Individuals often retrench and become frustrated and disenchanted. They may lose confidence and, curiously, shun responsibility. They may create real or artificial boundaries between themselves and others. Concerned with 'turf' issues and resistant to change which they perceive will further erode their limited power, they can detract from an organisation's attempt to become dynamic and flexible. The solution, many argue, is to empower staff.

Empowerment

In Chapters 2 and 7 we noted that vertical hierarchy and centralisation of power were and, to a large extent, still are the norm in organisations. There is, however, a move towards the development and acceptance of flatter hierarchies and greater devolved power. This manifests itself in the development of self-managed teams (*see* Chapter 5), organic structures, reduced layers of hierarchy, and devolved budgetary control and decision making. *Empowerment occurs where authority to make decisions and to resolve organisational problems is delegated to subordinates.* It is believed that giving power to those doing the work of the organisation should improve flexibility, speed of decision making and the motivation of staff.

Conger and Kanungo's (1988) research indicates that an individual's need for *self-efficacy, a desire to produce results or outcomes*, is better satisfied as a result of empowerment. They argue that motivation is boosted as a result of improvements in the individual's effectiveness and the individual's ability to choose how to complete the task using his or her creative skills (*see* the discussion of intrinsic rewards and needs theories in Chapter 4). The reward resulting from personal control and real or perceived effectiveness in turn improves motivation. A virtuous circle of involvement, effectiveness and motivation is apparent.

Tannenbaum and Cooke (1979) argue that empowerment actually increases the total amount of power, presumably power to do good, in an organisation. The implicit suggestion is that power is not a zero-sum game, but that it grows through empowerment. The cake gets bigger! Senior managers gain power because of the resultant increases in morale, flexibility and productivity whereas subordinates gain the power and authority to make decisions and to act autonomously. There is a degree of intuitive logic to this assumption. However, as many managers will note, increased autonomy, expertise and authority at lower levels can and do make some middle and senior managers redundant, metaphorically and literally: positive for the organisation, potentially disastrous for the individual. For this and other reasons, such as a lack of trust or faith in subordinates' ability, some managers are reluctant to empower their employees.

Daft (1992) outlined the management of the empowerment process (*see* Figure 8.4). In his model, the first stage involves the diagnosis of organisational impediments to empowerment. These might include excessive rules, inflexible systems

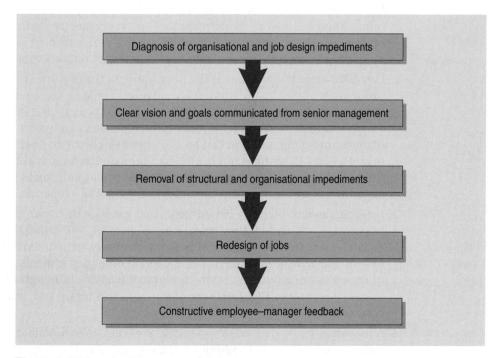

Figure 8.4 Managing the empowerment process

or procedures, too narrowly defined tasks and reward structures that ignore innovation. A clear vision and rationale for change needs to be communicated from senior managers. The stifling aspects of job design and organisational structure need to be changed. Empowering job design features will need to be considered and implemented, where rules and procedures need to be reviewed, relaxed and often removed. Additionally, structured change, for example to reduce levels of hierarchy and improve communication, may need to be implemented. Both during the process of change and when staff are empowered, regular constructive feedback between managers and employees is essential. Since empowerment is often viewed as a necessary prerequisite for organisational flexibility, innovation and change, it appears likely that measures to devolve authority further in organisations will continue.

Inter-departmental power

The sources and uses of power at the level of the group or organisational department are of value in the study of organisational behaviour. They shed light on organisational activity, structural configuration and power issues, not at the level of the individual but horizontally between departments or functions within organisations. Saunders (1990) and others suggest that power at departmental level derives from five potential sources (*see* Figure 8.5). It is possible that these power sources may overlap. They are as follows:

1 *Dependency* – when Department A depends on Department B for information or other cooperation in order to conduct its own tasks and to be effective, Department B has a source of power *vis-à-vis* Department A. For example, if the information technology department in a university largely controls the IT budget, all other departments are reliant upon this department and, rather like a monopoly, it has little incentive to provide a highly responsive service.

2 *Centrality* – this is a measure of the importance of the department's work to the prime goals of the organisation. Alternatively it could be considered as a measure of how dispensable the department is to the organisation. For example, the provision of food and refreshments to employees of a typical service or manufacturing organisation can be, and increasingly is, provided by outside organisations. Catering is not central to a car manufacturer, with the result that the power a catering department holds in that situation is small. Few departments are significantly dependent on this service function.

3 *Financial resources* – clearly departments that generate their own financial resources, particularly if they provide excess income, will (other things being equal) benefit from this source of power. Conversely, departments which earn a low income may be dependent (*see* above) on other departments. Centralisation of resources can reduce inter-departmental differences, although this clearly makes the centre or HQ the source of power in this regard and, as a consequence, disempowers all departments.

4 *Non-sustainability* – this relates to the issue of centrality. Sustainability is a measure of how easy it would be for the department's function to be performed by others. For example, in the motor manufacturing example given above,

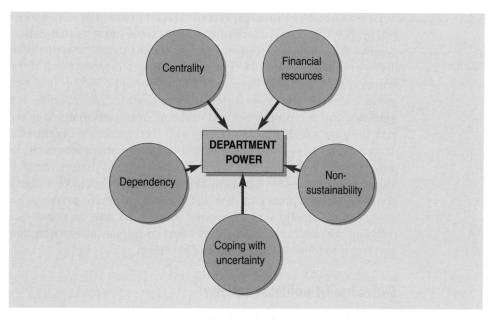

Figure 8.5 Horizontal, inter-departmental power sources

whereas the production department of a car manufacturer would not wish to assume catering responsibilities it is straightforward for it to contract out such services, as a highly competitive contract catering market exists in most modern economies. It is less easy, although not impossible, to contemplate a motor manufacturer dispensing with its production capability. A company with a brand name of repute could, conceivably, contract out its production and instead focus on design and brand marketing.

5 *Coping with uncertainty* – departments that have the ability to reduce the uncertainty for others will gain power. For example, the uncertainty created by technological developments can earn the technology or IT department a valuable source of power. It can, if it wishes, cushion other departments from the realities and uncertainties of technological advance.

 ## Organisational politics

Conflict, power and politics are closely related organisational realities. Conflict, for example, can arise as a consequence of power differentials and political activity and, in turn, can necessitate the use of power and political skills to help resolve or manage actual or potential conflicts. Hence, *politics can be considered to be a 'process of bargaining and negotiation that is used to overcome conflicts and differences of opinion'* (Daft, 1992: 403). An alternative definition of politics incorporates *the more sinister and self-serving activity that is not sanctioned by the organisation and which can increase the potential for conflict and friction.*

Political activity in organisations results from the conversion of power into action. It is the consequence of the diversity of interests that exists in most human communities and, more directly, from attempts to use power to affect organisational decision making or from activities which are self-serving and not organisationally sanctioned. It cannot be assumed that the amount of power held by an individual or group is directly related to their ability to exert influence. Political activity acts as a mediator and is omnipresent and endemic in organisations. It is both the lubricant and the glue which simultaneously frees and binds the organisational machine: it can and does have both positive and negative consequences. In its least desirable guise, politics is considered as a covert, shadowy and dysfunctional aspect of organisation; yet, conversely, political skills are of considerable value if used to forge change, gain acceptance of new and more appropriate courses of action, or to promote job satisfaction and improve morale. In any case, political activity is an ongoing organisational reality, a product of human interaction, fuelled by scarcity, and legitimised by the acceptance of pluralism.

Domains of political activity

Daft (1992) refers to four domains or areas in which politics appears endemic:

- structural change;
- inter-departmental coordination;
- resource allocation;
- management succession.

These domains of power are commonplace and often essential areas of organisational activity, and frequently give rise to intense political activity. The four domains are illustrated in Figure 8.6.

Structural changes reallocate legitimate or position power. During such changes managers will negotiate, bargain and engage in all manner of political activity to preserve or enhance their power position. As a result, power and political skills are required to manage such change. Inter-departmental coordination, Daft (1992) argues, lacks rules and precedents. The resultant conflicts over issues of territory

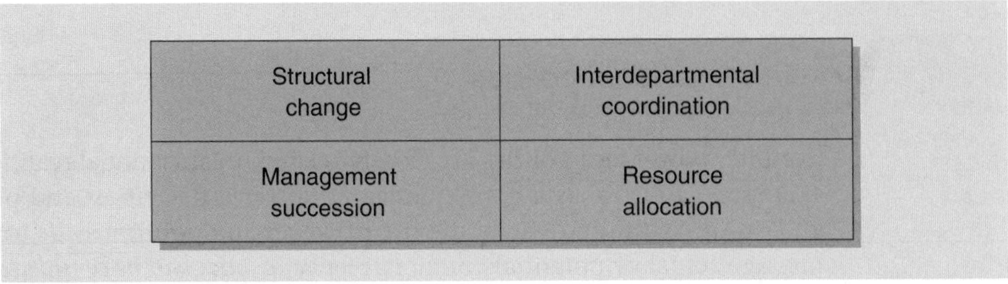

Structural change	Interdepartmental coordination
Management succession	Resource allocation

Figure 8.6 Domains of political activity

and responsibility require political activities to be resolved. Often, at the level of the individual, succession is a contentious issue. Promotion criteria are often opaque and open to interpretation and misinterpretation. Networks, formal and otherwise, alliances and enmities all play a part in creating tension and conflict between parties. Finally, resource-allocation decisions enhance or reduce power bases and the ability of individuals or groups to wield resource power. Budgeting is an intensely political activity, itself requiring sound political skills to manage in order to avoid or suppress dysfunctional conflict.

Political activity is certainly not confined to business or public-sector organis-ations. Politics in sport is rife and often subject to public scrutiny (*see* Mini-case 8.1). No human activity is entirely devoid of political activity if we assume that the pluralistic frame, outlined above, approximates reality. The situation presented in Mini-case 8.1 illustrates that point.

Mini-case 8.1

Politics and sport

It is often suggested that there is no room for politics in sport. However, the two are frequently linked at a variety of levels. At a macro or international level, the political activities of governments frequently influ-ence sporting activity, or inactivity, in their country. For example, in South Africa during the 1970s and 1980s the extreme activities of the apartheid regime ensured that world condemnation of their policies meant that economic, political and social sanctions were enforced. Most sporting links between South Africa and the rest of the world were severed: a bitter blow to the sport-enthusiastic South Africans. Hence, the Springbok rugby team, the South African cricketers and many individual sportsmen and -women could not compete at international level. In broad terms the sanctions were successful in bring-ing pressure to bear on the regime in power. There have also been occasions when national govern-ments have withdrawn or restricted the activities of their own teams in protest against political decisions of others. There is an ongoing debate about whether the England cricket team should play in Zimbabwe, as they did in the winter of 2004, due to the human rights situation in that country.

However, it is not just at this level that politics impinges on sport. All sports teams, sporting associations and individual clubs are, like other organisations, political entities. A football team or the Rider Cup golf teams, for example, have all the ingredients for political activity. Competition is rife, many individuals and groups have collective and individual representatives, they are in the public domain and the customers often feel passionate about their performance. Football abounds with clichés which symbolise control or the subversion of individualism: they are 'political' clichés. Hence, we are frequently reminded that 'no player is bigger than the team', representing an attempt by manage-ment to control staff by bringing collective pressures to bear. Players are 'only as good as their last match' – again a political interchange between management and players. Players frequently 'do not fit in with the style of play', often a euphemism for backroom conflict that has occurred. Managerial and boardroom rows figure in the folklore of many teams. Furthermore, there is constant conflict between football at club and national level. Who holds the power and from what sources does it derive in this case?

Organisational conflict

Conflict is apparent when at least one party perceives that it exists and where an interest or concern of that party is about to be or has been compromised or frustrated. Conflict occurs between individuals, groups and departments: it is, therefore, both an intra- and an inter-group reality. Conflict is common between individuals in the same department or group, between employees at different levels of the organisation, between those with different roles and responsibilities or between otherwise close colleagues. Similarly, conflict can and does occur between workers, often represented by trade unions, and managers, between designers and production managers, between accountants and marketers and so forth. Some conflicts are stimulated by deep-seated fundamental differences, which might be ingrained in the broader society or the context in which the organisation operates. At the other extreme, some conflicts are ephemeral, of immediate concern and often easily and quickly resolved.

Conflict is inevitable (a view consistent with the pluralist perception of organisation). It is a result of interaction in the organisation between individuals and groups: interaction is an organisational necessity (it would not be an 'organisation' without it). The causes of conflict are many and varied (*see* Figure 8.7). They include the following:

1 Differences in status, often created by legitimate or hierarchical power differentials, create barriers to communications, foster feelings of inequity and cause consequent friction which can lead to ambiguity and confusion over responsibilities.

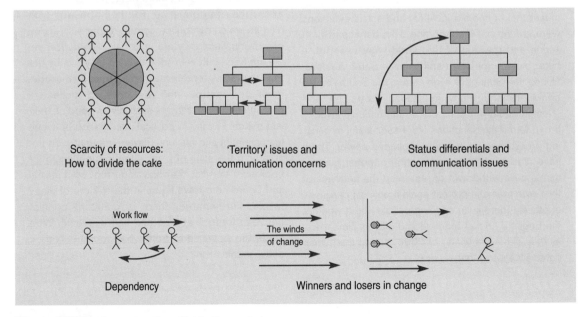

Scarcity of resources:
How to divide the cake

'Territory' issues and
communication concerns

Status differentials and
communication issues

Work flow

Dependency

The winds
of change

Winners and losers in change

Figure 8.7 Some causes of conflict in the workplace

2 Scarcity of resources, such as promotion prospects, bonus payments and departmental budgets, creates competition which often escalates into conflict.

3 Complex organisational structures or configurations frequently make one group, or individual, dependent on another: in this case conflict may occur between the parties, if only as a result of different priorities.

4 Quite often the objectives and tasks of individuals and groups can directly conflict with one another in the same organisation: a zero-sum game might apply where A's gain is B's loss.

5 Differences of opinion and of influence create friction and win–lose situations.

6 Cultural differences were discussed above: conflicts occur between cultures or subcultures within organisations. Such conflicts in the NHS have been referred to as 'tribalism'.

7 Dynamism in the environment, and consequent organisational responses, can create friction between individuals and groups. Change disrupts existing patterns of resource allocation and stable structural relationships. It often creates scope for 'winners' and 'losers': opportunities for growth and development for some and loss of scope, esteem and power for others.

Conflict and diversity

Conflict in the workplace can result from a failure of individuals or groups to recognise diversity; from ignoring cultural difference or preference, for example. An assumption that cultural difference is unimportant and that one's own cultural beliefs, understanding and attitudes prevail is often unintentional but nevertheless potentially highly damaging. This can take many forms in organisations. Some people deny that there are significant differences between themselves and fellow employees based on gender, age, religous belief or race, for example. They make assumptions about situations which derive from the way they view that situation and trivialise or ignore differences in the way others read situations. They may minimise any differences and characterise them as trivial side issues. Mini-case 8.2 identifies an interesting conflict scenario.

Mini-case 8.2: Conflict and diversity

A long-serving employee, who has recently become a 'born again Christian', comes into work wearing a large crucifix around their next. In the staff room during refreshment breaks they start to distribute religious material to other employees inviting them to 'find salvation'. A few weeks later another employee approaches her line-manger and complains that they have been 'harassed' by this employee and accused of being a 'sinner' and a 'heathen' (this other employee is living with a partner, but they are not married, and the partner is a Hindu).

Discussion Questions

● How should the organisation respond to this situation? Discuss various options and possibilities in the context of the individual employees and supervisory/managerial staff.

● What may be the consequences (positive and negative) of not doing anything?

Source of further information: ACAS Guide on Religion or Belief and the Workplace Equalities Act 2006.

Sterotyping is another discriminatory action which can and does lead to conflict in the workplace. Stereotyping represents an oversimplification of another group's characteristics. It can take many forms and include the often unintentional light-hearted jibe – 'Oh, men, they always take the simple way out' or 'Women simply are not so good with numbers'. It is often received with due disdain, leading to dis-connection or disengagement from the source and potential conflict.

Sociologists have explored industrial conflict and its many forms. For example, Reed (1989) distinguishes between collective and individual conflict, the former exemplified by actions such as strikes, working to rule and restrictive practices. A number of people act collectively and live out a rational plan in pursuit of a given objective. Individual conflict, on the other hand, is more random, varied and, often, short lived. Taylor and Walton (1971) note that acts of sabotage are a barometer for underlying conflict in an organisation. They represent attempts by employees to assert control over their work situation and reflect an underlying sense of powerlessness. Theft by employees can be motivated by similar causes.

In each of these cases the positive use of power and political skills can help to reduce conflict, to make it manageable and reduce the potentially dysfunctional out-come of friction. However, the existence of power differentials and/or the negative or overt use of power can stimulate further conflict. Clearly, an ambiguity exists. Power is both a cause of, and a mechanism to help resolve, conflict in the workplace.

Management of conflict

Whereas organisational theory has developed to accept that conflict is inevitable, management theory and practitioner concerns demand that conflict be managed and resolved in the workplace. We discussed above the unitary, pluralist and radi-cal frames of organisation. Each of these frames, or rather managerial acceptance of each, would lead to a different approach being adopted for the management of conflict. Managers who believe that the unitary organisation is a desirable and realisable state will view conflict as marginal, the outcome of ineffective manage-ment or, more likely, as being caused by rogue elements. They will seek to eradicate it. Managers who recognise that organisations are complex pluralist enti-ties may seek to understand the nature and causes of conflict, appreciate the divergence of interest and seek compromise or collaboration: they aim to manage conflict. Pluralists accept that conflict is inevitable and therefore view their role as being to coordinate and balance the conflicting demands and interests: this is the basis of stakeholder analysis and strategic management.

An alternative but related approach, *the interactionist perspective, suggests that managers intentionally encourage conflict and its resolution as a catalyst for change.* A group that is harmonious can become static and accepting, blinkered to environ-mental dynamism and changing priorities and unresponsive to the need for change. A degree of intra- and inter-group conflict can, it is argued, enable groups and individuals to maintain a self-critical and creative edge. This perspective on conflict management has been acknowledged since the 1960s, not least by Pfeffer

(1981). Hence, management might use conflict to seek radical change, to alter existing power structures and entrenched attitudes. A change agent might openly challenge, and/or seek covert support for a challenge to, accepted behavioural norms or power structures, or might seek to create conflict between groups who represent the new way forward and those that embrace the status quo. Similarly, creating a manageable level of inter-group conflict might create greater intra-group cohesion, a desire to pull together to compete with other, hostile groups. This might lead to improvement in effectiveness. Successful sports teams use the competitiveness they feel towards their opponents as a mechanism to bind them together as a team.

Clearly, a balance needs to be struck between the creation and the control of conflict. Whereas it is probably not possible to suggest what is an appropriate level of conflict, it has been argued that both too much and too little are dysfunctional. Performance, particularly of a group, is maximised when conflict is neither too high nor too low: this is illustrated in Figure 8.8. When conflict is very low, apathy and stagnation may breed. The individual, group, department or organisation may be unresponsive to change and may lack creativity. Work life becomes just too predictable and it becomes difficult to inspire staff to think and act differently and to take the organisation forward. Conversely, too much conflict is disruptive, is time consuming to deal with and leads to a lack of cooperation and collaboration in pursuit of organisational goals. The middle ground might provide for sufficient conflict to promote self-criticism and innovative attitudes and behaviours.

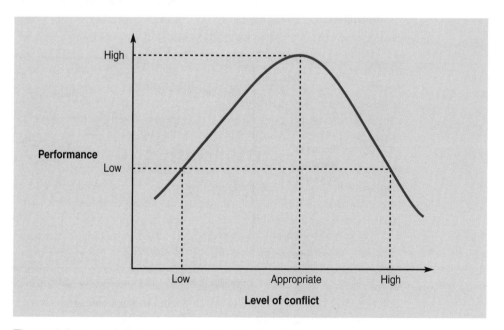

Figure 8.8 Functional and dysfunctional levels of conflict

Conflict-handling model

Thomas (1976) has produced a normative or prescriptive model for managing conflict resolution. It is based on two conflict-management dimensions, themselves reflecting different styles of management. The two dimensions, the degree of assertiveness in pursuit of one's interests and the level of cooperativeness in attempting to satisfy others' concerns, are places along two continua and are illustrated in Figure 8.9. Five conflict-handling strategies emerge which are of relevance and interest to the individual and the manager.

The five conflict-handling styles are:

1 *Avoidance* – one or more parties in conflict may seek to avoid, to suppress or to ignore the conflict. They may take recourse in bureaucratic procedures or otherwise stall the conflict. This approach may not lead to conflict resolution and if the root causes are endemic and/or likely to become apparent again, avoidance will achieve little or will make matters worse.

2 *Accommodation* – this involves one party putting the other's interests first and suppressing their own concerns in order to preserve some form of stability and to suppress the conflict. Again, if the causes of conflict are endemic or lasting, accommodation may never resolve these root issues. The accommodating party may underperform as a consequence.

3 *Compromise* – often seen as the optimum solution: the word 'compromise' in the English language is viewed as positive and constructive. Each party gives something up and a midpoint is often accepted after negotiation and debate. However, in compromise, both parties lose something: there may be a better alternative.

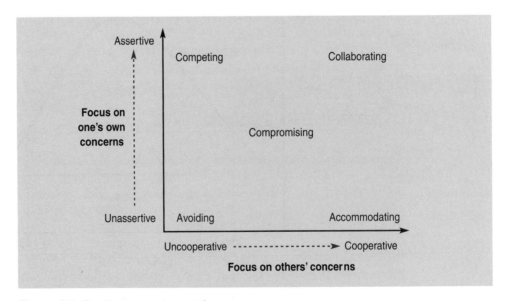

Figure 8.9 Conflict-management style

Source: Adapted from Thomas (1976).

4 *Competition* – this is a state where both or all parties do not cooperate, instead they seek to maximise their own interests and goals. It creates winners and losers. The resultant power plays, dysfunctional behaviours and uncooperative activities might prove damaging to the organisation as well as to at least one of the parties. Even the 'winner' may be damaged in the process.

5 *Collaboration* – from both the individual party's and the organisational point of view this is likely to be the optimum solution. Differences are confronted and jointly resolved, novel solutions are sought and added value ensues: a win–win outcome is achieved.

Thomas (1977) has identified the situational or contextual factors which inform the use of each style of conflict management. The main contingent factors, that is, those which influence the choice of style, include:

- the time available to resolve the conflict;
- the level of importance of the issue(s) stimulating the conflict;
- the preferred style(s) of the participants in the conflict;
- whether one style (or more) is unacceptable in the particular circumstances, for example, where compromise proves vitally dysfunctional for the organisation;
- where issues of commitment, motivation, precedent and lack of information are important.

Implicit in this model is the likelihood that individuals and groups choose a particular style after consideration of the contextual variables. Whereas organisational experience can undoubtedly enable individuals to 'read' a conflict situation better and to respond appropriately, many individuals do have a preferred style. For example, some people, both in the workplace and in their home and social lives, thrive on competition and even conflict. This model has inspired the development of tests for personality type which assess an individual's 'natural' degrees of assertiveness and cooperativeness. Such tests attempt to identify a preferred style or styles of conflict handling.

 Power and communications

Although power and communication are inextricably linked we will briefly examine the use of symbols as sources of power. *A symbol, tangible or otherwise, carries meaning which stands for something other than itself.* Not suprisingly, that meaning can reinforce existing power bases and positions and can be used to exert power. More obvious organisational symbols include company logos or mottoes, the buildings and works of art that adorn organisations, the use of space in buildings, the type of furnishings and so forth. Less tangible symbols include the tremendous power of language – including the use of imagery and metaphor. All of these, consciously or otherwise, carry meaning, they say something about the organisation. For example, hierarchy is, in many organisations, reinforced by symbols. Senior managers often have large offices, are supported by secretaries, have superior quality furnishings and a larger company car than those of their subordinates.

Manipulation of symbols is an expression of power: successful manipulation can create new or reinforce existing power positions and shape the organisational environment in favour of the powerful. It can create meaning – which is a vital ingredient, if not the essential essence, of leadership. Leaders assist in defining situations and in forging new meanings for employees. They use symbols in the process. Chapter 9 explores, in some detail, the use of symbolism in organisations.

 ## Power and organisational change

Change is central to the study of power and politics. Change can threaten existing power structures, while it requires astute political awareness and activity to manage. We will briefly explore one particular aspect of change management which has a particular relevance to the study of power; more specifically, to perceived powerlessness and to negative power: that is, resistance to organisational change.

Resistance to change

Much has been written about resistance to change. It is viewed as an inevitable aspect of the change process, one which counterbalances the pressures or forces encouraging change. Resistance itself can take many forms, from overt, often aggressive, behaviour to covert sophisticated non-compliance. Bedeian (1980) identified four causes of resistance to change:

● parochial self-interest;

● misunderstanding and lack of trust in management;

● contradictory assessments of the implications of change;

● a low tolerance for change.

Organisational change alters the status quo and frequently entails a loss of power for some individuals and groups and a gain for others. Shifting power sources and bases create friction and conflict between real or perceived winners and losers. Organisational change frequently reduces a group's access to resources; structural change can lead to diminishing legitimate or position power, whereas reorganisation can disrupt previously useful relationships and networks. It is hardly surprising that people who perceive or know that their power source(s) may be eroded by change are likely to resist or, alternatively, seek to participate in the process with the intention of altering the nature and consequences of change.

When people exercise power, either individually or collectively, to resist change they are said to be exploiting 'negative power'. The use of the word 'negative' may imply that such resistance is always dysfunctional. That may not always be the case. Successful resistance could be highly desirable and functional for departments or groups. Resistance to a change which is ill-informed may prove beneficial to the organisation.

Managerial implications

A number of managerial implications become apparent when one has a basic knowledge and under-standing of power, politics and conflict in organisations. Many of these suggest tactics for building or securing power and could be used to abuse power as well as to use power to pursue organisational objectives. Managers may benefit from the following:

1 Recognising the political aspect of their work and making attempts to hone their political skills in order to be more effective. It is unlikely that organisations are rational or adopt a unitary frame; rather, they are political, pluralist, human groupings. Therefore, it is important to recognise the sources of power and the causes and domains of conflict and political activity.

2 Enhancing their legitimacy through developing expertise in important areas. This often applies to particular skills, for example in IT or process technology, which are in short supply at the level at which managers operate.

3 An awareness of sources and flows of information is important. A Machiavellian extension to this point is the ability to restrict others' access to information and to select favourable information for others' consumption (see the Mini-case 10.2 in Chapter 10 on practice in Russia). For example, decisions can be influenced by the items that are put by agendas and even by the sequence in which they are placed (Pfeffer, 1981).

4 Building coalitions which might involve communicating freely, warmly and frequently with individ-uals and groups in the organisation whose support enhances power. Merrell (1979) suggested that effective managers huddle in small groups to resolve issues, thus stressing the power of the informal, social network. The aim should be to build positive relationships involving interpersonal liking, trust and respect. This may involve reaching out to dissenters and old enemies.

5 An expansion of their networks. Related to coalition building is the need to build similar relation-ships outside, for example among suppliers and customers, as well as internally.

6 Recognising that successful and effective empowerment creates a win–win situation but that this may necessitate managing fundamental organisational change.

7 A recognition and understanding of other employees' feelings of powerlessness and their conse-quent behaviours and attitudes.

8 A recognition that the successful management of change involves the use of sophisticated political skills and an emphasis on balancing, coordinating and managing the many and varied interest groups that hold power.

9 An awareness of the power of symbols and, in particular, of the unintended symbolic significance of words and deeds.

10 Avoiding making their power open and explicit. There is a general dislike of the open demonstra-tion or abuse of power as most people recognise that self-serving behaviour damages the organisation and its employees. Instead, managers should make their goals and aspirations explicit and leave power implicit. People know who holds power; Kanter (1979) argues that explicit claims to power are only made by the powerless.

Summary of main points

This chapter has explored power, politics and conflict within organisations. The main points made are:

- the chapter has offered a definition of the key terms power, politics, powerlessness, empowerment and conflict;
- there are many sources of power in organisations and mechanisms of power execution: similarly, there are many causes and domains of conflict;
- power, politics and conflict are closely related;
- organisations can be viewed as unitary entities, pursuing common goals, or pluralist, embracing different interests and goals;
- conflict can be viewed as endemic and normal (even desirable), or as exceptional and entirely dysfunctional;
- the use of power and sophisticated political skills is essential in the management of change;
- power can be used to resist change and manipulate its nature and outcomes, just as power is used to manipulate the understanding and interpretation of organisational and environmental events.

Conclusions

This chapter has stressed the intensely human nature of power, political activity and conflict in organisations. Despite the covert nature of much of this activity it is a very 'real' and important aspect of all organisations. The exercise of power, engagement in political activity and involvement in conflict can inspire all manner of human responses, from extreme satisfaction and the resultant dynamism, joy and energy to dire frustration, low morale and withdrawal. Power is an organisational reality and knowledge of its causes, forms and consequences is invaluable both to those who seek to analyse, interpret and understand organisations and to those who wish to work and thrive in the workplace.

Questions

1 In an organisation with which you are familiar identify the sources and bases of power of each of the main players.

2 In your university or other higher education institution what are the sources of power for (a) students, (b) academic lecturing staff and (c) the head of the department or school or faculty in which you are studying?

3 Surely empowering people is straightforward and can only bring benefits to all concerned? Is this the case?

4 Identify one dispute or conflict you have experienced recently which was resolved. What styles of conflict management did the parties, including yourself, employ?

References

Bedeian, A. G. (1980) *Organizations: Theory and Analysis*. Hinsdale, IL: Dryden Press.

Calabria, D. C. (1982) 'CEOs and the paradox of power', *Business Horizons*, Jan.–Feb., pp. 29–31.

Conger, J. A. and Kanungo, R. N. (1988) 'The empower process: Integrating theory and practice', *Academy of Management Review*, 13, pp. 471–82.

Daft, R. L. (1992) *Organization Theory and Design*, 4th edn. St Paul, MN: West.

Dalton, M. (1959) *Men who Manage*. New York: John Wiley

French Jr, J. R. P. and Raven, B. (1959) 'The bases of social power', in Cartwright, D. (ed.) *Studies in Social Power*. Ann Arbor, MI: University of Michigan, Institute of Social Research, pp. 150–67.

Kanter, R. M. (1979) 'Power failure in management circuits', *Harvard Business Review*, July–Aug., pp. 65–75.

Merrell, V. D. (1979) *Huddling: The Informal Way to Management Success*. New York: Amacon.

Morgan, G. (1986) *Images of Organization*. Newbury Park, CA: Sage.

Morgan, G. (1996) *Images of Organization*, 2nd edn. Newbury Park, CA: Sage.

Pfeffer, J. (1981) *Power in Organizations*. Marshfield, MA: Pitman Publishing.

Reed, M. (1989) *The Sociology of Management*. Hemel Hempstead: Harvester Wheatsheaf.

Robbins, S. P. (1984) *Essentials of Organizational Behavior*, 3rd edn. Englewood Cliffs, NJ: Prentice-Hall.

Saunders, C. S. (1990) 'The strategic contingencies theory of power: Multiple perspectives', *Journal of Management Studies*, 27, pp. 1–18.

Tannenbaum, A. S. and Cooke, R. S. (1979) 'Organizational control: A review of studies employing the control graph method', in Lamners, C. J. and Hickson, D. J. (eds) *Organizations Alike and Unlike*. Boston: Routledge and Kegan Paul, pp. 183–210.

Taylor, L. and Walton, P. (1971) 'Industrial sabotage: Motives and meanings', in Cohen, S. (ed.) *Images of Deviance*. Harmondsworth: Penguin Books.

Thomas, K. (1976) 'Conflict and conflict management', in Dunnette, M. D. (ed.) *Handbook of Industrial and Organizational Psychology*. Chicago: Rand McNally.

Thomas, K. W. (1977) 'Towards multidimensional values in teaching: The example of conflict behaviours', *Academy of Management Review, July, pp. 484–90.*

Weber, M. (1947) *The Theory of Social and Economic Organization. New York: Oxford University Press.*

Further reading

The references below represent a variety of texts and writings on power in organisations. Additionally, reference can be made to the sources referred to in this chapter.

Huczynski, A. and Buchanan, D. (2006) *Organizational Behavior,* 6th edn. Harlow: Financial Times. Prentice Hall.

Morgan, G. (1996) *Images of Organization*, 2nd edn. Newbury Park, CA: Sage, Chapter 6.

Mullins, L. J. (2007) *Management and Organisational Behaviour*, 8th edn. Harlow: Financial Times Prentice Hall.

Pfeffer, J. (1981) *Power in Organizations*. Marshfield, MA: Pitman Publishing.

 **Internet sites**

A search engine will help locate sites on power, organisational conflict and organisational politics. You might try this:

www.socresonline.org.uk This offers a series of sociological research papers and articles of interest and value on the subject of power and related issues

www.internationalalert.org/pdf/publA/ResPK-section5.pdf This is an annotated bibliography on conflict resolution

You can also often open full-text articles from emeraldinsight.com, a major publisher of management and business academic journals.

9 Organisational culture

Learning outcomes

On completion of this chapter you should be able to:

- define organisational culture;
- explore the cultural perspective in some depth by identifying the various schools of thought and consequent approaches to the study of organisational culture;
- discuss the ways in which cultural knowledge is learned and stored;
- examine the role played by organisational culture in influencing organisational strategy, performance, diversity and change.

Key concepts

- organisational culture
- national culture
- subculture and cultural diversity
- rituals, symbols and stories
- organisation *is* a culture – organisation *has* a culture
- cognitive knowledge
- culture and organisational performance
- cultural change
- culture clash and conflict
- cultural communication.

Organisational culture is frequently cited as being responsible for all manner of organisational ills and, on occasion, credited with creating positive qualities. It is essential, therefore, that we explore this concept more thoroughly to enable us to understand behaviour of organisations and to diagnose and interpret organisational problems and activities. In short, an intimate knowledge and awareness of culture should improve our ability to analyse organisational behaviour in order to manage and to lead.

 ## Introduction

This chapter explores the theoretical underpinning and complexity of the cultural metaphor. It opens with a discussion of the concept of organisational culture within a broader societal context. The nature and influence of national culture, business sector and group norms and individual personalities are considered. It is recognised that culture is a metaphor and a 'way of seeing and analysing' organisations and, as such, is one of many potential 'perspectives' or frames used for organisational analysis. We also explore the vastly different approaches taken in the literature to the study of culture, the consequences of which influence our understanding of the concept, of its relationship with organisational performance and its impact on management and organisational change. A precise definition of culture is avoided, as will become clear, for such definitions often serve to reduce or constrict our understanding of this complex notion. Rather, we will explore a myriad of definitions and discuss a variety of key issues which have an impact on our understanding of organisational culture, thus preserving the value and insight into organisational life that this concept provides.

The current fascination with organisational culture began in the 1970s and early 1980s with the work of Peters and Waterman (1982), Deal and Kennedy (1982) and Kanter (1983). However, academics had drawn attention to the notion of culture operating at the organisational or unit level much earlier. For example, in the 1960s Blake and Mouton (1969) suggested a link between organisational characteristics that we might now refer to as cultural and organisational performance. In 1952 Jacques referred to the culture of a factory as 'its customary and traditional way of thinking and of doing things which is shared . . . and which new members must learn' (Jacques, 1952: 251). He argued that culture comprised behaviours, attitudes, customs, values, beliefs and 'the less conscious conventions and taboos' (ibid.). Nevertheless, despite the emphasis given to this concept for over 50 years, there remains considerable debate and contention surrounding the nature of, and the value of studying, organisational culture.

Organisational culture in context

Culture is a shared phenomenon and in the case of organisational culture that sharing takes place at the level of the organisation. Individuals in a culture differ and this is, in part at least, a product of personality differences. Culture can make one group of people behave, think, and even look, different from another. These different groups may have different beliefs, different values, and different interpretations of things around them.

Illustration in film

The Last of the Mohicans

The film of the classic book *The Last of the The Mohicans* (1992), set in the late eighteenth century in North America, illustrates the virtues and tragedy when different cultures collide. The French, the British, native North Americans and the colonists enjoy very different ways of being. The film depicts the perspectives of each group and the massive cultural divides between them. Daniel Day-Lewis plays Hawkeye, white adopted son of an Indian; he rescues Cora Munro, daughter of a senior British officer, played by Madeline Stowe. In their escape they come across a British settlement where everyone has been murdered by hostile native Americans. Cora thinks Hawkeye callous and uncaring for not stopping to bury the bodies. Hawkeye, recognising both the strength of the attraction between them and the cultural difference they experience, suggests that it is best if neither tries to understand the thinking of the other.

It is also possible to have a culture which comprises two or more subcultures. For example, in the National Health Service (NHS) in the UK, as in most healthcare sectors throughout the world, a series of subcultural groups work alongside one another. Doctors, nurses, professions allied to medicine (PAMs), ancillary workers and managers, each have their own cultural identity. Each group has its own values, beliefs, assumptions and norms which guide its activities, each has its own rituals and ceremonies, its own stories to tell about organisational life and its own interpretive systems which influence its understanding of organisational symbols. These groups are differentiated by qualifications and, often, by gender. These subcultural groups frequently conflict with one another: NHS staff often refer to the inherent 'tribalism' of their service. Mini-case 9.1 illustrates a series of rituals, which are an important aspect of culture, shared by many ward-based nurses in an acute-sector NHS Hospital Trust in the UK.

Mini-case 9.1

Rituals in nursing

Organisational routines are an effective coping mechanism for people. They anchor and reassure employees in the workplace and are shared by processes of socialisation and interaction. Routines help give order to our working lives. Some of the routines assume ritualistic significance, which helps both to preserve them and to raise their significance in the organisation. Rituals can become enduring aspects of the culture or the professional culture. Practical justification of the behaviour becomes irrelevant. Thus a ritual is a *prescribed activity, often rigidly observed in a solemn or ceremonial fashion, which has symbolic significance*. Rituals are part of an organisation's culture and help to reinforce the prevailing paradigm. The interpretation of ritualistic behaviour gives us an insight into the culture of an organisation.

Rituals

The morning drugs and drinks round: often as early as 6 a.m., patients are woken, administered drugs and given a drink of tea. The ritual serves to enhance the power of the night nurses and to avoid conflict between them and their day-shift colleagues. Often additional sleep would serve to speed patient recovery.

Multiple patient records: all medical professionals and professions allied to medicine keep separate patient records, with the result that some patients – in-patients in particular – are often asked to give personal information as much as five or six times. This ritual serves to enhance or maintain the power and social identity of each professional group (e.g. nurses, doctors, physiotherapists).

Daily changing of the dressing on patients' wounds: although daily changing of dressings is now less common, many nurses still consider it part of their duty of care to replace bandages daily, or even more frequently, in spite of the cost and often adverse affects of this on the healing process. This ritual serves to maintain the social identity of, and the requirement for, nurses.

The cultural knowledge of individuals is not identical. Individual difference, perhaps arising from different home, educational and microsocial contexts, leads to intra-cultural variation. Hence within any culture, or even subcultural group, differences exist. Most cultures are tolerant of such differences, in fact it may provide a mechanism for cultural change or dynamism. For example, national subcultures, based on criteria such as socioeconomic class, ethnic or religious background or occupation, stimulate both debate and conflict, which can provide an opportunity for learning and change.

Although culture is created and sustained in social contexts, such as in an organisation, it is dynamic and constantly evolving. At the organisational level culture is learned by recruits through the process of socialisation, including training and managerial interventions, whereas educational systems, the media, history, political processes and the like, help shape national culture. In a business sector, such as retailing or iron working, Grinyer and Spender (1979) have shown how organisations tend to adopt similar strategic responses when faced with pressures for change. These behaviours are learned by the processes of business-sector interaction, such as through labour movements in the sector, the trade press and formal managerial or worker associations. Hence a 'recipe', which sets limits for action, is broadly agreed by organisations in a business sector. This recipe is a 'taken for granted' set of beliefs and assumptions which is held, relatively uniformly, throughout organisations within a business sector. The recipe, rather like culture at the organisational level, assists managers to make sense of their world.

Hence, values, beliefs, assumptions, norms and ways of interpreting meaning can be shared on numerous levels, from small subcultures which might thrive in parts

Subculture

The shared characteristics of a group, potentially of virtually any size, that composes a subset of a larger organisational or professional culture. For example, permanent ward-based night nurses in NHS hospitals are a subculture of the wider group of nurses of the hospital or unit culture where they work and of the broad organisational culture of the NHS.

Professional culture

The shared characteristics of members of a profession or trade. For example, we could refer to doctors or engineers as having common, cultural ways of doing and thinking. These groups have experienced similar education and training and 'sign up' to professional norms and obligations. Often, they experience divided loyalties between organisation and profession.

Organisational or corporate culture

This is, primarily, the focus of this chapter – culture at the level of the organisation or corporate body. Most organisations have a unique culture, even if this has numerous subcultures and/or professional cultures within it. The relative 'influence' of culture at this level will depend, to an extent, on the strength of corporate identity and influence on its constituent units.

National culture

Possibly the most transparent manifestation of culture lies at this level. For example, there are many significant cultural differences between the British, the French and the Germans. In addition of course, many ethnic groups, who share strong cultures, cross existing national or political boundaries. Chapter 10 explores this in more detail.

Supra-national culture

Characteristics which peoples from many countries or states share in common (across national boundaries). At a very broad level one might refer to Western and to Chinese cultures: the former broadly based on Christianity and including peoples from most of Europe, North America and Australasia and the latter based on Confucianism.

Figure 9.1 Culture at ascending levels

of larger organisations, through organisational culture, corporate culture, business-sector recipes, to regional, national and supranational cultures (*see* Figure 9.1). It is at least intuitively sound to suggest that influence is exerted between these various levels. For example, the patterning of national values, assumptions and beliefs appears to have some influence over organisational activity in countries. Hence the work of researchers at the national level on culture, such as Hofstede, Laurent, Adler and Trompenaars (referred to in Chapter 10), is important for the understanding of culture at micro levels.

 ## Organisational culture: definition and debate

There is considerable debate concerning the nature of organisational culture, which has far-reaching consequences for management and all manner of organisational activity including change, corporate strategy and financial and other measures of performance. It is, therefore, vital that we explore the different definitions and implications of the concept of culture in order to enhance our understanding of organisations themselves.

One source of divergence of opinion as to the meaning and value of organisational culture derives from the different subject fields which study the concept. Much work in the 1980s, for example, derived from business and management schools. The aims and main contentions of this writing differed significantly from that which adopted a more anthropological or sociological perspective. Many definitions of culture are incompatible with one another along a number of dimensions. For example, if we define culture in an objective manner as an organisational variable then the understanding that culture can and should be actively managed is implicit. If we view culture as interpretative, intangible and indistinguishable from the organisation itself, we tend to accept that it is a much deeper concept which can only be understood in subjective terms. In the latter case, the management and intentional change of culture is viewed as a more haphazard and doubtful experience.

In the early 1980s the cultural metaphor received considerable attention from academics and managers hoping to discover the answer to many difficult managerial questions. Far from providing *the* answer, the plethora of research and writing about organisational culture stimulated an active, often contentious, debate. One of the early influential works suggested that strong cultures had a positive effect on organisational performance (Deal and Kennedy, 1982). Strong cultures were thought to exist in organisations which exhibited a close fit between themselves and their environment, possessed a rich and complex system of shared values, a well-specified and routine set of behavioural rituals and an articulate cultural network. Deal and Kennedy (1982), inspired by the strength and cohesiveness of Japanese organisational and national culture, urged a return to the ideas of America's early business leaders in achieving strong cultures. Such cultures, it was argued, provided a system of informal rules which gave guidance to employees and which motivated people by making them feel better about what they did. Hence the research suggested a panacea, a prescription to cure the observed organisational ills in the USA. Their work, like much management research and writing, is primarily aimed at the American manager and academic. Its ethnocentrism is often apparent. This work, together with that of Peters and Waterman (1982), in their best-selling book *In Search of Excellence*, proved extremely influential in both determining the managerial and furthering the academic agendas of the 1980s.

Another popular concept of culture was provided by Schein (1985) (*see* Figure 9.2) who suggested that culture is found at three levels, that is:

- at the core lie people's assumptions and beliefs which influence our 'commonsense' view of the organisational world. These include assumptions about the nature of the business environment, about human nature in general and about relationships in the workplace. These fundamental and taken-for-granted assumptions and beliefs inform
- cultural values which lie at the intermediate level and
- at the surface, culture manifests itself, Schein (1985) argued, in behaviours and cultural artefacts, such as building design features and technology.

Although in many ways appealing, this model provides a rather static view of a dynamic concept. It also underplays the role of symbolic activity in organisations and the role that symbols and stories, for example, play in creating and communicating cultural meaning for people in the workplace. However, it does suggest that what many writers refer to as culture, with such definitions as 'the way we do things around here', might merely be an overt, tangible, surface-level artefact of that culture.

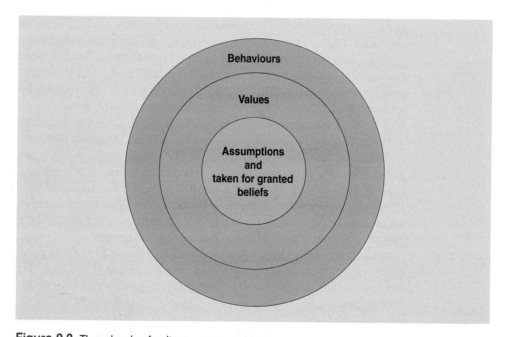

Figure 9.2 Three levels of culture

The 'structural' view of culture relies more upon how roles are structured in an organisation. An example of this is the work of Charles Handy (1989), adapted from Harrison (1972), on culture. This work identified four 'types' of culture based on structural design features. The link between organisational structure, design and culture is clear. Handy (1989) suggests that power cultures are found in small entrepreneurial firms, role cultures in larger bureaucratic organisations, task cultures dominate in matrix-type organisations, where power lies at the intersection of roles, and person cultures are common where the individual is the key element. He identifies the factors which influence the type of culture found in an organisation, some of which, such as organisational size, locus of power, types and levels of technology and characteristics of the business environment, will already be familiar to you.

Power cultures, Handy argues, are found in small, entrepreneurial organisations. In these, as illustrated in Figure 9.3, power lies at the centre of a web. The organisation depends on informal communications and people who adopt the attitudes and norms of the central power source (often the owner/senior executive) will be valued and trusted. Power relations are clear. *Role cultures* have high levels of bureaucracy and coordination is provided by a small, elite, senior management. An organisation characterised by role culture is departmentalised, often into clear functions and areas of specialisation. Employees have clear roles clarified by job descriptions. Work is rationally allocated and organisational life is impersonal. The organisation is suited to stable environments where efficiency is stressed and required. Role cultures provide security for employees. The *task culture* adopts a project focus and is represented in Figure 9.3 by a net where power lies at the intersections. A task culture is common in matrix organisations (*see* Chapter 7) where a team culture exists alongside autonomy. As a consequence these organisations are more flexible than those characterised by a role culture and they can react to changing markets. Finally, in the *person culture*, the individual is paramount. These cultures are common to professional organisations, such as firms of accountants or solicitors. There is limited formal control and communication links are informal.

It is, however, important to place this analysis in a broader context. For example, it derives from a school of thought that links structural factors closely with organisational culture. In fact it does not fully differentiate between structure and culture: it does not recognise them as separate perspectives or frames with which to view organisations (as is illustrated in Chapter 2). It implies that major structural change will lead to cultural change and suggests that the management of culture, like any other organisational variable, is quite possible and likely to yield positive results. It is also a deterministic model, that is, it suggests that a particular type of culture will result from a particular, given set of structural criteria. All of these assumptions are challenged by other writers and theorists in this field, who argue that Handy's work takes a rather superficial, even trite, view of this complex, all-embracing and symbolic concept which is culture.

A similar model, developed by Miles and Snow (1978), suggests that there are different types of organisations *vis-à-vis* their strategic outlook. The culture, structure and other design features and human qualities of organisations conspire to enable managers in organisations to 'see' their world in a restricted way. For example, Miles and Snow (1978) suggest that there are conservative organisations which adopt low-risk strategies and well-tried solutions. These 'defenders' contrast with the more innovative 'prospector'-type organisations. Although this model is of value, its limitations are apparent. It is a simple categorisation of a complex human organisational phenomenon that takes little or no account of the potential uniqueness of culture. However, it does link culture with organisational strategy.

Power culture

Frequently found in small entrepreneurial organisations, power culture relies on central power, informal communication and trust. A unity of purpose negates the need for bureaucracy. The competence, flexibility and dynamism of the central power force, often the owner, are essential. Increased size might 'break' the tight web-like relationships, in which case the organisation might establish a satellite or replicate itself elsewhere. Power cultures place considerable demands on staff.

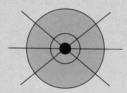

Role culture

In contrast to the smaller power culture, this cultural type is characterised by high levels of bureaucracy and formality. A small group of senior managers control the coordination between specialists and functional areas, as the diagram below illustrates. Rules, procedures and job descriptions are the norm. Work is thought to be rationally allocated to staff. Suited to stable environments, role cultures find change difficult to cope with. They provide security and predictability for staff.

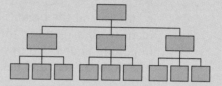

Task culture

Task cultures are often found in matrix organisations where power resides at the intersection of responsibilities. Employees tend to hold joint or multiple responsibilities and work relatively autonomously. Influence is based on expertise as opposed to rank. The need for authority is reduced by the existence of both individual control and teamwork. Operational decisions can be made quickly, making the organisation flexible. These organisations find specialisation, or achieving economies of scale, difficult.

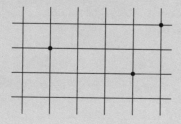

Person culture

The individual is the key feature in this culture, which only exists if individuals come together because they see some mutual benefits ensuing. Teams of professionals, or even 'hippie' communities, illustrate this culture type. There is no formal control and no single or overriding objective: individual objectives predominate in the constraints that 'organisation' involves. Influence is shared and based on expertise and mutual respect. Individuals tend to share common interests. There is little, or no, formal structure, as shown below.

Figure 9.3 Handy's cultural types

Source: Based on Handy (1989) and Harrison (1972).

In contrast, the interpretative view of culture embraces the complexity and subjectivity of culture while rejecting any simple causal relationships between culture and organisational structure. It may be too simplistic to view culture from either of the two perspectives identified here, as both interpretive–symbolic and structural aspects work in tandem in organisations. Johnson and Scholes (1994), in attempting to illustrate the complexities of strategic management in a cultural context, suggest that the organisational paradigm, or 'way of seeing', is embraced in a cultural web (*see* Figure 9.4). The cultural web comprises 'hard' structural and systems characteristics of organisations, together with 'soft' symbolic features and thus attempts to embrace both the broad schools of thought outlined above.

The cultural web is a useful model for examining the complex interrelationships between various cultural features and cultural contexts. Implicit also is that, in order to make significant changes to the organisational paradigm, some or all of the 'hard' and 'soft' supporting mechanisms need attention. The web also brings to the reader's attention the potential significance of ritual, of organisational stories and of symbols in both creating and sustaining organisational culture. The routines and rituals represent the taken-for-granted but symbolically significant aspects of organisational life. Some rituals are dysfunctional in as much as they contradict or countermand the organisation's objectives. Yet rituals help to give the culture its identity; they reinforce the 'way things are done around here' and indicate what is important and valued by employees. Organisational stories serve to 'locate' the culture in the history and development of the organisation. They also demonstrate the

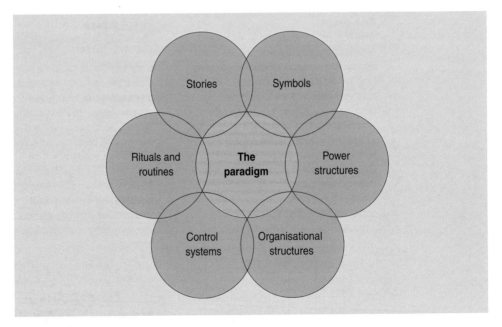

Figure 9.4 The cultural web
Source: Johnson and Scholes (2002).

nature of the culture and the limits of cultural behaviour. Hence they both delineate and reinforce culture. All aspects of organisation and of behaviour by employees and managers can carry symbolic significance. Similarly the systems, tangible artefacts, organisational structure and consequent organigrams (organisational structure diagrams) all convey important information about the organisation. These symbols are interpreted by organisational members. Language itself, notably that of more senior and powerful personnel, carries particular symbolic significance. It helps people to understand what is required and expected, what the norms and values of the organisation are and how to comply with them (as well as the consequences of non-compliance). Some argue that symbols and their interpretation lie at the heart of the concept of culture and this indicates a possible avenue for those who desire to manipulate or change the culture.

This debate continues later in this chapter, in the context of organisational change and performance. First, we briefly explore the mechanisms by which organisational and other levels of cultural knowledge may be learned, shared and stored.

Diversity and organisational culture

It can be argued that diversity and culture are incompatible ideas. How can you have diversity – different behaviours, values, norms, beliefs – in one organisational culture? After all, culture focuses on those things that are similar between people in the organisation: the values, beliefs and norms that bind them together. It is indeed a conundrum, probably best explained by accepting that all cultures contain diverse elements, perhaps subcultures, and most are tolerant of a degree of internal difference. But, can cultures be 'male-dominated' or assume female characteristics, for example?

When work organisations and management were first formed, often hundreds of years ago, the workforce was dominated by males and men held power in organisations, almost without exception. This was the norm. As a consequence, it can be argued that organisations today still reflect a male managerial culture. Similarly, most organisations in the United Kingdom and Ireland, or the USA and Australia, were dominated both numerically and in power terms by Anglo-Saxon people, such that organisational cultures may still reflect these historically derived characteristics. As we have seen, cultures are quite resistant to change – values, norms and beliefs have legs! Bennis (1993) argues that most organisations retain a macho, control-and-command mentality as a consequence of their male dominance initially even where such dominance is not necessarily apparent today.

We increasingly become aware of concepts such as institutionalised racism or sexism. This suggests that racism and sexism are embedded in the organisational culture, not necessarily manifesting themselves as overt discrimination but via more subtle behaviours and attitudes often not fully understood or wilfully displayed by organisational members. If this is indeed the case then removing discrimination from the workplace becomes a task of changing cultures (and national cultures also – refer to Chapter 10).

Organisational culture and change

As suggested above, the structural and interpretative views of culture would lead us to adopt very different approaches to the management of major organisational change. Since the early 1980s organisational culture has become increasingly considered as both an obstacle to change and a vital ingredient of organisational success or failure.

Kanter (1983) argued that there are, broadly, just two types of culture: segmentalist and integrative. She outlined the characteristic features of each (*see* Figure 9.5 for an illustration of some of these characteristics) and suggested that some organisations which possess all or many of the integrative features will embrace organisational change and will thrive in a dynamic environment. Segmentalist cultures, on the other hand, are, at best, slow to react and struggle when required to change. She outlines the characteristics of each; in many cases the two categories represent polar opposites.

The management of cultural change, which many argue is essential to ensure continuous organisational dynamism, is the subject of considerable debate. Many researchers have suggested models of cultural change. For example, Dobson (1988) identified a four-step approach: (a) change recruitment, promotion and redun-

Segmentalist culture

- Views organisational problems narrowly
- Locates problems and hence responsibilities narrowly within department's or individual's remit
- Has segmented structure, divided into departments, and functions often work against one another
- Shuns experimentation
- Avoids confronting problems and conflicts
- Has weak coordinating mechanisms
- Emphasises precedent, policies, procedures and systems
- Inward-looking

Integrative culture

- Sees problems as related
- Views problems and responsibilities as shared and connected
- Has matrix or team/project-based structure
- Innovates and test assumptions: invites experimentation
- Invites confrontation and eventually transcends differences
- Creates mechanisms of coordination for sharing information and ideas
- Looks for novel solutions
- Is outward-looking

Figure 9.5 Segmentalist and integrative cultures
Source: Based on Kanter (1983).

dancy policies in order to influence the composition of the workforce, which involves an active HRM role in identifying both employees who display the beliefs and values the organisation wishes to promote and those who do not; (b) reorganise or restructure the organisation to ensure that those employees and managers who display desired qualities are given positions of power; (c) effectively communicate the new values; (d) change systems in order to reinforce the new beliefs and values. Such models imply that cultural change can be achieved by a combination of personnel, structural and systems changes. However, the political power required to both initiate and implement such changes led Dobson (1988) to suggest that change is 'top-down' and imposed.

A somewhat broader, yet similarly prescriptive, model of cultural change is suggested by Cummings and Huse (1989). They argue that cultural change may result if the following prerequisites are in place: a clear strategic vision; top management commitment; symbolic leadership; supporting organisational changes and changing organisational membership. In their work, which is similar to but broader than Dobson's work, Cummings and Huse (1989) locate such change in a strategic framework. They also accept the need for symbolic intervention, such as 'visioning', and the use of symbolic behaviours and language.

These models are based on empirical research, although both can be criticised as they tend to underestimate the difficulty involved in changing culture. They have been widely criticised as being too simplistic and putting forward recommendations which are too general to be of use to individual organisations (for example, Gordon, 1985; Hassard and Sharifi, 1989). Mini-case 9.2, explores the management of organisational cultural change.

Mini-case 9.2: A model of change

The management of organisational cultural change

This mini-case explores a cultural change process in a medium-sized NHS Hospital Trust in the Midlands of England. The organisation was successful in achieving significant and measurable quality improvements, exceeding its broad array of objectives and coping with considerable environmental flux in the mid-1990s. It was widely considered that aspects of the organisation's culture had changed.

Successful leadership of cultural change required the leaders to think culturally, to be guided by a mental map which indicated where they were coming from and what the intended destination was actually like. They employed cultural tools to negotiate this journey. Additionally, they could not ignore the politics of change nor the hard systems and structural changes that were needed to reinforce and symbolise major change. They used the real or perceived crisis caused by the imminence of a change of status (to quasi-independence or Trust status) as a trigger for change. This crisis increased the receptiveness of employees and of the context in general.

Of particular interest were the cultural, symbolic 'tools' which were employed. Whereas many managers ignore or trivialise the concept of culture and, at best, only think about culture, the CEO in this case thought culturally: that is, he considered the situation in cultural terms. He made every effort to utilise the power of symbols. He showed awareness that his actions carried overt face-values, influence and symbolic significance. This awareness enabled him to calculate the effects of his language, dress, style and actions in symbolic and, therefore, cultural terms.

▶

His insistence on wearing jeans and T-shirts and playing loud pop music at management away-days was a symbolic attempt to reduce barriers and to signal change. The suggestion was that experimentation and change were exciting. He graphically symbolised innovation and enthusiasm by his style of facilitating meetings: darting from flip chart to flip chart, encouraging brainstorming and ideas, publicly embracing employees' concerns and views. Additionally, he frequently gave small gifts to 'islands of progress', sub-units in the hospital which had exceeded targets. This symbolised the rewarding of desired behaviours and attitudes.

Rituals

New rituals were created which symbolised change. Hence, reclassification of hospital porters, cleaners, domestic staff and caterers as ward assistants signalled a new and enhanced social identity for this group which helped to overcome some of the old demarcation issues. Away-days became a ritual of 'sense-making', attempts to listen and explain and to help people through the ensuing changes.

Stories

Organisational stories symbolise what is important in an organisation and help to shape its culture. The stories of how this CEO held meetings, refusing to sit down, inviting criticism and challenge to existing ways of doing things and engaging in open and frank discussion, signalled that experimentation was welcomed.

Values

Collectively held values underpin organisational culture. It is not surprising that attention to the organisational value system became a top priority for the management team. From the early stages, planned workshops and impromptu discussions with senior and middle managers and clinical consultants worked on developing the organisational mission – perhaps the prime symbolic expression of any organisation. The workshops sought to build gradually a value statement which reflected both individuals' personal values and the fundamental purpose of the hospital. The resulting statement is simple and holds few surprises – but, far more importantly, it is 'owned' by many.

Other researchers, while accepting that cultural change occurs, take a more considered view of the ease and pace with which such change takes place. Schein (1985) argued that it is essential to understand how the existing culture is sustained before it can be changed. An analysis of the values, assumptions and beliefs which underlie organisational activities reveals culture, he suggested, as an adaptive learning process. Schein's (1985) approach places emphasis on the way organisations communicate their culture and how assumptions are translated into values. Burnes (1996: 117) suggests, 'seek to understand the mechanisms used to propagate culture and how new values and behaviours are learned'. Clearly, once these mechanisms are revealed, such knowledge forms the basis of a strategy of cultural change. However, Schein (1985) was critical of the idea that cultural change can be achieved by a top-down, management-led approach. Others have suggested that the time frame for cultural change is from 6 to 15 years (Uttal, 1983), though some writing, by the less well-informed and empirically weak, naively suggests the time frame can be as little as one year.

Pettigrew (1990) recognises the difficulty of managing culture. He identifies seven reasons why culture is difficult to change, an explanation which cuts across some of the definitional divides addressed here. The seven issues are:

1 Levels – culture exists at a series of levels, from beliefs and assumptions to cultural artefacts (*see* Schein, 1985).

2 *Pervasiveness* – not only is culture deep, it is broad and embraces all organisational activity.

3 *Implicitness* – much of culture is taken for granted. Therefore, it is difficult to change things which are implicitly part of people's thinking and behaviour.

4 *Imprinting* – culture has deep historical roots.

5 *Political* – culture has connections with the power distribution in an organisation, as certain power groups have a vested interest in the prevailing beliefs and cultural behaviours remaining as they are.

6 *Plurality* – organisations often have plural or more than one culture, that is, a set of subcultures and different group norms and behaviours.

7 *Interdependence* – culture is closely connected with the politics of the organisation, with its structure, systems, people and priorities.

Pettigrew (1990) recognises the role of power and politics in organisations and the interconnectivity of all organisational phenomena and processes. He therefore takes a broad view of culture and cultural change. His paper draws on empirical research in Jaguar Cars and ICI and suggests a list of 13 prescriptions for management to follow to improve the chances of successful change occurring.

Cultural change programmes are often managed by one or more senior managers working with the Human Resource Management (HRM) or Human Resource Development (HRD) department. However, the part played by HRM and training and development in the reproduction and change of organisational culture extends well beyond recruitment, selection, redundancy management and other 'organisational membership' measures. Many management development and training activities are concerned, implicitly or explicitly, with reinforcing or changing culture. For example, if a company wishes to instil a collective value of better customer care, then this is often facilitated through training and development programmes. It is also often built into performance appraisal and reward systems. Hence a coherent and consistent series of direct HRM interventions aims to reshape an aspect of organisational culture. It is quite possible to add to these training interventions and systems changes an element of symbolism. For example, if people who displayed ideal customer orientations were made into heroes and if a ceremony were held to acknowledge and reward such examples, then that ritual might transmit new or evolving meaning to organisational members.

Brooks and Bate (1994), when commenting on the limitations of many traditional top-down methods of change, suggest that successful cultural change requires:

● an awareness of the present culture;

● an awareness of the desired future culture;

● 'management' of the politics of acceptance; and

● a trigger for change.

Thus an essential rule for any cultural change should be: 'know your own culture, then change it' if necessary. Similarly, the holding of ideals or ambitions, a vision or model of the desired future state, would appear essential to facilitate purposeful change. It is important to recognise that politics and culture enjoy a complex relationship. It all depends on how we view organisations. Certainly, for any new paradigm to take hold in an organisation, it needs legitimisation. Hence, as culture is collectively 'owned', it seems reasonable that some attention needs to be paid to collective, political acceptance of the need for dynamism and of the direction of intended change. Finally, it is often considered that successful cultural change is facilitated by a real or perceived crisis, 'a state of affairs that acts as a trigger or catalyst for second-order change' (Brooks and Bate, 1994: 189).

Wilson (1992: 78) argues that 'following an interpretive view of culture leads us to a very different analytical and methodological perspective on how sense may be made of organizational change'. What becomes important is not the notion of an amenable and malleable culture but the cognitive and interpretative processes by which individuals in the workplace make sense of the change and, as a consequence, either support it, facilitating it for others, or seek to destroy or resist it. Thus the interpretation of symbols, such as language, lies at the heart of this view. Although culture may appear more obscure and less readily analysable from this perspective it need not necessarily be so. Symbols abound in organisations and the importance given to them is significant. Recognition that the way in which change and other management initiatives are interpreted is seen as vital from this perspective. Hence 'reality' becomes a social construction, that is, what is real is influenced by the complex cognitive processes of individuals and the myriad of social interactions between people in the workplace. A collectively held, socially derived interpretation of events then becomes a cultural belief. For example, Isabella (1990) views organisational transition itself as subject to change from an interpretive perspective. Hence, during a change process people will view that change and the 'realities' of the change process and its outcome differently at different stages of the process (*see* Figure 9.6).

It is argued that this interpretation of the change process, especially if it is a collective or cultural interpretation, will influence the eventual acceptance, or otherwise, of the change and the future success of the organisation. In order to answer the question 'What will the change mean for me?', people make sense of information and piece it together within a rich context of past and present organisational events. In this view of culture, managers are not powerless to change culture but need to pay attention to the symbolic consequences of their actions, while aiming to foster desired values. However, they can never control culture – as many management writers suggest is possible.

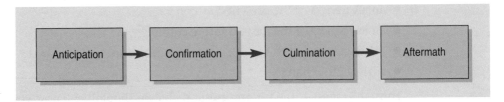

Figure 9.6 Evolving interpretations of a change process
Source: After Isabella (1990).

If we consider organisations themselves as if they are cultures, as Wilson (1992) and Isabella (1990), above, have done, then this fundamentally influences our understanding of management action and of business strategy. For example, if managers as strategists are part of the culture then both the process of strategy making and the resultant strategies will be profoundly influenced by the subjective processes found in that culture. Partly as a consequence of this, some academics argue that culture neither can nor should be consciously changed. Meek (1982: 469) commented that 'culture as a whole cannot be manipulated, turned on or off . . . culture should be regarded as something an organization "is", not something it "has": it is not an independent variable nor can it be created, discovered or destroyed by the whims of management'.

Finally, the ethics of management's attempts to control culture are worthy of consideration. It has been argued (for example, by Van Maanen and Kunda, 1989) that managerial interest in organisational culture is motivated by a desire to control what employees think, feel, do and say. Any such attempts to intervene and change culture may be viewed as little short of cognitive control. If culture is a collective concept then the 'right' to manipulate it to one group's advantage may be ethically questionable.

Organisational learning and change

Organisational learning is a much-debated contemporary issue of particular significance in the study of culture and of change. It was briefly discussed in Chapter 2. The question 'can organisations learn?' invites often heated and contentious debate. Clearly, individuals in organisations can and do learn, yet we have evidence that organisations as a whole (as well as individuals in them) continue to repeat activities which sometimes lead to dysfunction and lack of success. It appears to many that organisations fail to adapt to dynamic markets, neither do they learn, except slowly, to cope with a dynamic environment. Argyris (1964) and later Argyris and Schön (1978) argued that the important distinction in this debate lies between an organisation's ability to engage in single-loop or double-loop learning. They conclude that most organisations are locked into mere single-loop learning. Single-loop learning occurs where an organisation learns to conduct tasks, as if by rote, or to manage itself in a particular, predictable way. Double-loop learning involves greater questioning of both the organisation's objectives and its methods of achieving them in a continuous and progressive fashion. In double-loop learning an organisation will not automatically attempt to solve a problem or conduct a task in the same way as it has in the past but will possess the ability to reflect on previous experiences, to learn from them and to innovate and experiment with alternatives.

Single-loop learning is likely to be common in segmentalist (Kanter, 1983) organisations, whereas double-loop learning requires individuals and groups to be willing to discuss sensitive issues openly and to confront differences of view and seek ways of clarifying vague and ambiguous ideas and data. They must attempt to engage in collective reflection and problem resolution.

Culture, conflict and communications

We have seen how symbols can act as cultural communicators when consciously or otherwise employed by leaders (*see* Chapter 6) and as powerful tools in management (*see* Chapter 8) so we will not repeat that material here. However, we will explore the conflict that exists between cultures.

Conflict between subcultures

Rather like the conflicts that exist between departments in any organisation, friction is commonplace between different organisational subcultures. In order to maintain collective understanding and unity it is necessary for subcultures to devise initial socialisation processes and ongoing mechanisms which induct and continually forge individuals into the group. Collective behaviours, norms and values are essential qualities of a subculture. Collectiveness better ensures a basis for power. Disparate individuals, whether in the workplace or in wider society, lack power. Collectively, as in a culture or subculture, they 'speak with one voice', develop a distinctive social identity and, potentially, tap into the sources of power needed to enhance their socioeconomic status.

Illustration in film

Dead Poets Society

The film *Dead Poets Society* (1989), starring Robin Williams, illustrates how a newcomer to an organisation, in this case a school, holds beliefs and engages in behaviours which are alien to the culture. He tries to unleash students' creativity and their individuality. The resultant behaviour of students and teacher (John Keating, played by Robin Williams) is unacceptable to the staid administration and Keating is fired. Watching the film, you might look for some of the physical artefacts, the values, norms and behaviours experienced in the school and assess how those encouraged by Keating clashed with the prevailing culture.

Mini-case 9.3 illustrates the power conflicts that exist between subcultures in the health service. Subcultures in organisations, such as doctors or nurses or managers in a typical hospital, engage in ritual activities in order to enhance their cultural identity and preserve their standing. This is also true of many professional groups, such as accountants, solicitors and teachers. Each has exacting examinations and educational requirements which must be met before individuals are allowed to 'join' and each has a formal or implicit code of practice. Many subcultural groups seek the same, or similar, sources of power as identified above. Hence, in the National Health Service in the UK there is a constant, ongoing, struggle for power between managers and medical personnel. Managers draw on considerable position or legitimate power and, notably, usually have control over resource allocation (reward power). The expertise of medical personnel is their prime source of power.

Other subcultural groups preserve their power by creating scarcity and restricted access to their expertise. The Chartered Institute of Accountants, for example, is reported to alter the pass mark in its entry examinations in order to protect against an oversupply of accountants in the marketplace. The resultant scarcity increases accountants' power to negotiate favourable terms for their services.

Mini-case 9.3: Subcultures and power imbalances in the National Health Service

There are few organisations where differences between definable groups are more strongly evidenced than in the National Health Service (NHS) in the UK, Europe's largest employing organisation. Despite the claims that medical personnel work as a care team to ensure quality patient care, numerous subcultures exist and strive for power. A complex 'pecking order' ensures that each group struggles to maintain or enhance its power base.

In a typical hospital ward, for example, there are cleaners or domestics, ward clerks, assistant nurses, staff nurses, sisters, junior doctors, registrars and consultants. Additionally, patients on that ward are often visited by physiotherapists and radiologists, to name just two of the many professions allied to medicine (PAMs), and rely on pharmacists and numerous specialists to ensure recovery and quality treatment. Each of these groups represents a subculture in the broader hospital culture or medical community. Power differentials exist and are often obvious. These differentials are based on many of the sources of power, such as access to resources, expertise, legitimate power, access to information and to networks and coalition building. Even in one group, such as qualified staff nurses or doctors, micro level subcultures exist. For example, permanent night nurses do not enjoy the same recognition (of their skills and expertise) as their day colleagues and, hence, are relatively powerless. When attempts are made to introduce annualised contracts and internal day–night rotation on wards, night nurses are relatively powerless to stop this trend.

Of additional interest is the complexity of power interdependencies in NHS hospitals and the role and power position of managers and managerialism. Managerialism has been promoted by government-inspired reforms of the 1980s and 1990s.

Management has enhanced its power *vis-à-vis* most other groups, with the result that managerial pay, particularly at senior levels, has increased more rapidly than that of, for example, nurses (a relatively powerless group) and their influence has increased significantly. Nurses have attempted to address this position by union or association action (e.g. by Unison and/or the Royal College of Nursing) although a shortage of nurses in 1998 and beyond may increase the power of this group as their expertise becomes in short supply. Many subcultures gain power by making others dependent on them. In modern hospitals, managers control most of the resources: this better ensures that the dependencies which occur are controlled by management.

Rituals, medical jargon and precedent are all used to hold on to power and to reinforce existing social divisions. Only certain grades of personnel or those holding particular qualifications are allowed to conduct certain tasks. Demarcation between groups, even when there is little or no rational reason for it, is strong and pervasive. Attempts to remove differences are fraught with difficulties. For example, a recent attempt at a Midlands hospital to issue identical uniforms and to unify pay levels for ward-based domestics, ward clerks and unqualified assistant nurses was greeted with considerable opposition, particularly from ward clerks, who consider the clerical responsibilities they hold to be greater than the domestic responsibilities of cleaners. The uniform symbolised that change and although the staff chose the actual uniform it was almost universally disliked (except by many of the ex-domestics who were net gainers in the change).

Discussion question

How do doctors and consultants preserve their power?

Managerial implications

Knowledge and increasing awareness of organisational culture have significantly influenced managerial thinking and practices in recent decades. Yet, as we have seen above, there remains no clear understanding and/or agreement over the meaning or value of this concept. That said, managers should be open to the following ideas.

1   Be aware that most people view organisations from one or a limited number of perspectives and that what we see is strongly influenced by that 'lens'.

2   Reflect on their perspective(s) and embrace or experiment with others which may shed new light on old organisational problems and may lead to the generation of novel solutions.

3   Understand that culture is shared and pervasive, and influences every aspect of organisational life, including strategy, structure, employee relationships, communications, interpretation of the business environment and so forth.

4   Be sensitive to the multiple influences on culture, such as the role of gender, ethnicity and other factors in shaping organizational norms and behaviours.

5   Be sensitive to an organisation's culture as an essential prerequisite for successful management of change.

6   Be aware that culture changes and may be changed, but it is likely that 'cultural tools' will need to be employed to achieve success.

7   Understand that everything one does, wears or says carries symbolic significance and sends meaning to employees: understanding how they might interpret that meaning could prove valuable.

8   Accept that many organisational routines become ritualised and carry symbolic significance: they are often dysfunctional and do little in themselves to achieve organisational objectives but serve to bind groups together.

 ## Summary of main points

This chapter has been critical of the often simple and trite way in which culture is discussed and has sought to delve more deeply into this complex concept. The main points are:

● culture is an intensely 'human' and shared phenomenon which exists in a rich international, national and organisational context;

● identifiable subcultures thrive in many, especially large and diverse, organisations;

● there is considerable contention concerning the nature of organisational culture, with many suggesting, or implying, that it is an organisational variable, like structure, and others arguing that organisations *are* cultures;

● there are many typologies of culture, which are attempts to identify a small number of cultural types into which all organisations can be classified;

● although apparently paradoxical, culture is both enduring and ever-changing;

- cultural change processes are the subject of considerable organisational and managerial research and practical concern but all agree that culture is difficult to change;
- culture is related to organisational performance, change and organisational learning;
- conflict between cultures occurs within organisations.

Conclusions

Organisational culture is a complex field of study stimulating definitional and methodological debate and contention. It can be seen that the concept has been linked to organisational performance, to management behaviour and to organisational change, structure and strategy. Consequently, whatever views carry most salience with the reader, the concept of organisational culture must be recognised as of vital importance to the understanding of organisation and all activities and processes operating within and in connection with organisation.

Questions

1 What is a ritual? Describe one in the organisation where you are studying.

2 Discuss some features of any culture, at any level, with which you are familiar. How do strangers cope with that culture?

3 Can you change culture easily? What 'tools' would you use to try to change culture? Should you attempt this in the first place? After all, the culture is not yours to change.

References

Argyris, C. (1964) *Integrating the Individual and the Organization.* New York: Wiley.

Argyris, C. and Schön, D. A. (1978) *Organizational Learning: A Theory of Action Perspective.* Reading, MA: Addison-Wesley.

Bennis, W. G. (1993) *Beyond Bureaucracy.* San Francisco: Jossey-Bass.

Blake, R. R. and Mouton, J. S. (1969) *Building a Dynamic Corporation through Grid Organization Development.* Reading, MA: Addison-Wesley.

Brooks, I. and Bate, S. P. (1994) 'The problems of effecting change within the British Civil Service: A cultural perspective', *British Journal of Management*, 5, pp. 177–90.

Burnes, B. (1996) *Managing Change: A Strategic Approach to Organisational Dynamics.* London: Financial Times Pitman Publishing.

Cummings, T. G. and Huse, E. F. (1989) *Organizational Development and Change.* St Paul, MN: West.

Deal, T. and Kennedy, A. (1982) *Corporate Cultures: The Rites and Rituals of Corporate Life*. Reading, MA: Addison-Wesley.

Dobson, P. (1988) 'Changing culture', *Employment Gazette*, December, pp. 647–50.

Gordon, G. (1985) 'The relationship of corporate culture to industry sector and corporate performance', in Kilmann, R., Saxton, M. and Serpa, R. (eds) *Gaining Control of the Corporate Culture*. San Francisco: Jossey-Bass.

Grinyer, P. H. and Spender, J. C. (1979) 'Recipes, crises and adaptation in mature businesses', *International Studies of Management and Organization*, 9(3), pp. 113–23.

Handy, C. (1989) *Understanding Organizations*. Harmondsworth: Penguin.

Harrison, R. (1972) 'Understanding your organization's character', *Harvard Business Review*, 50, May–June, pp. 119–28.

Hassard, J. and Sharifi, S. (1989) 'Corporate culture and strategic change', *Journal of General Management*, 15(2), pp. 4–19.

Isabella, L. A. (1990) 'Evolving interpretations as a change unfolds: How managers construe key organizational events', *Academy of Management Journal*, 33(1), pp. 7–41.

Jacques, E. (1952) *The Changing Culture of a Factory*. New York: Dryden Press.

Johnson, G. and Scholes, K. (1994) *Exploring Corporate Strategy*. Hemel Hempstead: Prentice-Hall.

Johnson, G. and Scholes, K. (2002) *Exploring Corporate Culture: Text and Cases*, 6th edn. Harlow: Financial Times Prentice Hall.

Kanter, R. M. (1983) *The Change Masters*. New York: Simon & Schuster.

Meek, V. L. (1982) 'Organizational culture: origins and weaknesses', *Organization Studies*, 4(4), pp. 453–73.

Miles, R. E. and Snow, C. C. (1978) *Organizational Strategy, Structure and Process*. New York: McGraw-Hill.

Peters, T. J. and Waterman, R. H. (1982) *In Search of Excellence*. New York: Harper & Row.

Pettigrew, A. M. (1990) 'Is corporate culture manageable?' in Wilson, D. C. and Rosenfeld, R. H. (eds) *Managing Organizations*. New York: McGraw-Hill, pp. 266–72.

Schein, E. H. (1985) *Organizational Culture and Leadership: A Dynamic View*. San Francisco: Jossey-Bass.

Uttal, B. (1983) 'The corporate culture vultures', *Fortune*, 17 October, pp. 66–72.

Van Maanen, J. and Kunda, G. (1989) 'Real feelings: Emotion expression and organizational culture' in Staw, B. and Cummings, L. (eds) *Research in Organizational Behavior*, 11, pp. 43–103.

Wilson, D. C. (1992) *A Strategy of Change: Concepts and Controversies in the Management of Change*. London and New York: Routledge.

Further reading

Books and papers on organisational culture exist which directly confront and contradict one another. Having read this chapter you should be more able to appreciate the value of most works on culture. Any of the references above may be of value but those listed here represent a cross-section.

Kanter, R. M. (1983) *The Change Masters*. New York: Simon & Schuster.

Morgan, G. (1997) *Images of Organization*, 2nd edn. Newbury Park, CA: Sage, Chapter 5.

Schein, E. H. (1985) *Organizational Culture and Leadership: A Dynamic View*. San Francisco: Jossey-Bass.

Smircich, L. (1983) 'Concepts of culture and organizational analysis', *Administrative Science Quarterly*, 28, pp. 339–58.

Internet sites

There are very many web sites accessible via search engines with useful information on orgnisational culture. One of the best is:

www.new-paradigm.co.uk/Culture.htm This site brings together considerable material and includes numerous links to relevant materials. It has extensive links to cultural theory, to culture and equity (diversity), case studies and a lot more.

10

The impact of national culture on organisational behaviour

Jon Stephens

Learning outcomes

On completion of this chapter you should be able to:

- understand the concept of national culture and some of the factors that influence cultural differences;
- appreciate different ways of classifying culture, especially the work of Laurent, Hall, Hofstede and Trompenaars;
- have an appreciation of the difference between culture shock and culture shift;
- evaluate the ways in which national culture can influence individual and organisational behaviour, including motivation, leadership and management styles and practices;
- comprehend the difference between convergence and divergence in management styles and how this is linked to globalisation;
- consider the crucial role of communication in overcoming cross-cultural problems in organisations;
- understand how cultural differences might lead to conflict or may hinder changes, with particular reference to international mergers and alliances and also flexible working trends;
- appreciate some core cultural competencies and the importance of cultural intelligence for international organisations.

Key concepts

- national culture
- determinism
- high-context and low-context cultures
- power distance, uncertainty avoidance, individualism/collectivism, masculinity/ femininity, Confucian dynamics
- ethnocentrism
- cultural differentiation and profiling
- shock

- culture shift
- perceptual gaps
- management styles
- cultural stereotyping
- convergence/divergence.

With the increased move towards internationalisation and globalisation of business activities, the impact of national cultures on organisations is becoming of increasing importance. Differences in national cultures may have a bearing on how organisations deal with each other and also on behaviour within organisations which comprise a mix of nationalities. This chapter therefore explores the concept of national culture and then seeks to examine areas of organisational behaviour where cultural differences may be significant.

Introduction

The environment in which most organisations exist is increasingly dynamic and turbulent. Rapid change affects the workings of the organisation and organisational behaviour. One of the factors that is creating change in the environment is internationalisation and globalisation. The world is becoming a much smaller place as a result of changes in transport and technology. For instance, it is now feasible to commute from London to Paris, Lille and Brussels by means of high-speed rail links (Eurostar), with further routes throughout mainland Europe being opened up as the high-speed train network grows. Air travel is growing at about 7 per cent a year, with increased deregulation creating cheaper prices so that business people and tourists can more easily travel between continents. Information technology has also shrunk the world in that communication across borders has never been easier, with e-mail, the Internet and, increasingly, teleconferencing providing swift links between people in organisations in different countries.

At the same time more and more companies are seeking an international presence as a means of diversifying their markets, helped by the development of trade blocs. In the European Union (EU), for example, the single market programme sought to remove a range of barriers that had previously inhibited trading and business across borders. Despite the Asian crisis of 1997, that region has continued to attract massive investment from other countries, with China overtaking the United States as having the highest level of foreign direct investment (FDI). With opening up of the Chinese market and the rapid changes that are taking place in Eastern Europe, and with the EU growing to 27 members, there has been a surge of international mergers, alliances and joint ventures as companies seek to achieve competitive advantage through internationalisation.

These developments mean that an increasing number of organisations are operating in several countries, and thus managers in the organisation's host country are having to deal with nationals from other countries. From a European perspective it is not merely European companies investing and developing overseas; it is also organisations from other countries which have invested in Europe. Again there is a likelihood of increased contact with managers in other countries, even if the organisation operates predominantly in one country. These developments have placed the issue of national culture much higher on the organisational agenda. There is clear evidence that an increasing number of organisations are having to deal with cultural issues and that the success or otherwise of their efforts may have a significant impact on the organisation's overall effectiveness. However, before an organisation can deal with issues arising from national cultural differences, it must first be able to identify what these differences are likely to be and also consider specific issues of significance. Identifying and discussing these is the prime objective of this chapter.

National culture

One of the biggest problems we face when looking at national culture is to find an acceptable definition. Kroeber and Kluckhohn (1985) found over 160 definitions of culture in their research. This may be because culture can be viewed from an anthropological or sociological perspective as opposed to a purely organisational one, although the latter is the area on which this chapter focuses. Two useful examples of definitions of culture are as follows. Mead (1951) suggests that culture '*is a body of learned behaviour, a collection of beliefs, habits and traditions, shared by a group of people and successively learned by people who enter society*'. Hofstede (1984) defines culture as '*the collective programming of the mind, which distinguishes the members of one human group from another . . . culture, in this sense, includes systems of values*'. A more thorough definition and discussion of culture, predominantly at the level of the organisation (as opposed to the nation), is given in Chapter 9.

The most deep-rooted element of culture is the set of values and fundamental, taken-for-granted assumptions held by a group of people. Such values and assumptions about all manner of phenomena, including those about what is 'right' and what is 'wrong' and what is 'good' and what is 'bad', manifest themselves in people's attitudes and behaviours, as was identified in Chapter 3. Often surface behaviour is driven by a much deeper value, assumption or belief which is itself a product of cultural conditioning. As will be shown, cultural differences can be substantial and may lead people to view 'similar' phenomena in quite different ways. For example, people in a particular country may cherish their personal right to freedom of speech, whereas another culture may feel that such a right should be subordinate to what is in the best interests of society as a whole.

The discussion above implies that culture comprises some commonly held values among a group of people which have been determined by the environment in which they grew up and which, to some extent, will influence their behaviour both inside and outside the organisation. Because of Hofstede's work on classifying cultures there is a tendency to look at this in purely national terms, although there may be substantial subcultures within a society: for example, the Catalans see themselves as having a different culture from that of the rest of Spain, although there are points of similarity. A country may have several strong subcultures which may not always correspond with national stereotypes, and businesses sometimes need to be aware of this. Culture is shared; however, that is not to say that everyone in a particular culture thinks and acts in the same way (as Chapter 3 makes clear). Individual differences are significant. When describing cultures we look for 'typical' values, beliefs and attitudes and 'norms' of behaviour. Subcultures can also exist, based on other than geographical criteria. In some countries subcultural differences may follow social class, gender, age, ethnic origin, religion or occupational group, for example.

Figure 10.1 illustrates the origins of commonly held values. As can be seen, these are all factors that may influence how our values develop within the society in which we grow up and work. Perhaps one of the most critical factors is that of language. Returning to the example of Catalonia, we may note that the Catalans have a different language from Spanish (Castilian), and this serves to bond the people of the region together and to reinforce their culture. Sometimes the introduction of new languages, for example those which are compulsory in schools, may have an impact on culture. An example here is the marked shift towards Mandarin Chinese in Hong Kong before Hong Kong was returned to China in 1997. People believed that with Hong Kong's integration into the People's Republic of China, there would be increased opportunities for those speaking Mandarin Chinese, as opposed to the type of Chinese spoken in Hong Kong (Cantonese). It remains to be seen how this switch in use of language will influence the evolution of culture. Sometimes, changes to language which are influenced by other cultures can be fiercely resisted, as we have seen in France, where the Académie Française has been trying to prevent the introduction of 'pop-culture' words which were mainly English.

Religion may also have a significant bearing on culture. The effect may be especially pronounced in countries where the religious and political systems are closely interlinked, such as in Iran or Israel, but it will also be significant in determining the types of values developed. For example, Confucianism has certainly influenced the collectivist views and long-term perspective held throughout Asia. Perhaps the Protestant work ethic has influenced the degree of individualism that

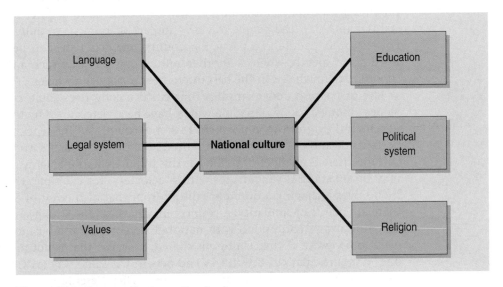

Figure 10.1 Factors affecting national culture

is encountered in many Anglo-Saxon countries, and Catholic countries are often linked with high power distance and uncertainty avoidance (see the discussion below of Hofstede's analysis).

Numerous factors help to determine the way we look at things in the world, how we see ourselves and how we see others. Murdoch (1945) identified many specific factors in which there may be cultural differences. These include:

- courtship;
- dream interpretation;
- food taboos;
- use of gestures;
- greetings between friends and business contacts;
- joking;
- meal-time behaviour;
- use of personal names;
- religious rituals.

Although these areas are of great interest to the anthropologist, they may also be significant when one is negotiating across cultures.

 Perspectives on culture

Kluckhohn and Strodtbeck

Some of the earliest work on analysing culture was carried out by Kluckhohn and Strodtbeck (1961), who essentially approached culture from an anthropological perspective. It was based on studies in rural communities in the south-east of the USA, although it was applied in a much wider cultural context. Kluckhohn and Strodtbeck were able to classify values into six basic orientations to the world, from which a cultural profile would emerge. The six orientations of value were:

- the nature of individuals;
- the person's relationship to their environment;
- the person's relationship to other people;
- the nature of the person's activity;
- the time dimension of the person's activity;
- the space dimension of the person's activity.

These orientations were then further subdivided as shown in Table 10.1.

Nancy Adler

Nancy Adler (1997) looked at these dimensions from an American perspective and suggested that Americans see individuals as a mixture of good and evil who are also capable of changing and improving themselves: hence, the demand for books and

Table 10.1 Kluckhohn and Strodtbeck's value orientation dimensions

Perception of	Possible dimensions		
Individuals	Good	Good and evil	Evil
Relationship to environment	Dominant	Harmony	Subjugation
Relationship with others	Individualistic	Extended groups	Hierarchical groups
Nature of activity	Doing	Controlling	Being
Relationship to time	Future-looking	Present-looking	Past-looking
Relationship to space	Private	Mixed	Public

Source: Adapted from Kluckhohn and Strodtbeck (1961) and Adler (1997).

programmes which propose to make people better managers or put them more in touch with their inner self. In terms of their relationship to the environment, Adler suggests that Americans see themselves as dominant over nature and their environment rather than feeling a need to live in harmony with their environment, as people with a more Confucian-type perspective would do. When it comes to relationships with other people, the American culture can clearly be seen to be individualistic as opposed to depending more on groups. There is still the belief that anyone can rise to the top with the right combination of skills and drive, sometimes called the 'log cabin to president' philosophy. They believe that your birthright should be no barrier to your development in society. People who achieve are seen as the 'champions' of the country, whether it is Bill Gates with Microsoft or Michael Jordan on the basketball court. Adler suggests that the individual will be expected to make decisions and perform independently whereas, in the more group-orientated or collectivist cultures, there is greater dependence on the group, whether it is the extended family (as in Chinese family businesses) or the company (such as in the giant groups of interlinked companies in Japan called *keiretsu*).

When we consider the nature of people's activity we can see clearly that the Americans are 'doers' or action-orientated: if there is a problem you go and sort it out yourself. This may have a significant impact on management style and activity in the organisation in that individuals will be expected to engage in problem-solving activity by themselves rather than rely on others for a solution. A television series in the UK called *The Tourist Trap* exposed people of different nationalities to similar experiences in order to evaluate their reactions. One 'event' involved intentionally leaving the breakfast in a deserted kitchen to see how the groups would react. The American group soon found the kitchen and organised the breakfast themselves without any complaint, whereas the Japanese group remained politely waiting in the main room. It took them a long time to go and find the kitchen and even then they were reluctant to take over from the staff who were temporarily absent.

When looking at the time dimension of their activities, Adler found the Americans to be future-orientated in that they believed you should look at issues and assess the potential future benefits that could be produced, although they tended to look at these benefits very much in the short term rather than in the long term. Past-orientated cultures are more likely to be found in Europe and Asia.

This might partly be a result of a greater sense of history or a belief that actions should fit in with beliefs and traditions. It is also noticeable that many Asian companies adopt a longer-term perspective, and this may explain Japanese companies' preference for long-term market growth rather than short-term profits.

The final dimension of Kluckhohn and Strodtbeck's work refers to how individuals address the space dimension of their activities. This is often reflected in office layouts. In some cultures there may be separate offices, and access to people may be restricted or guarded by a 'gatekeeper' or secretary. Other cultures have a more open approach and may value the openness of managers in the organisation. Whereas, Adler suggests, Americans prefer considerable private space, there is considerable evidence from Japanese companies that they are happy with smaller offices. This can be seen in the Japanese company Sony, which has a plant in Bridgend, Wales, where it is company policy that managers should spend some time of the day with or near the workers and also mix in their company canteen.

The Kluckhohn–Strodtbeck model is a useful introduction to cultural analysis and many aspects of it were developed by other writers, especially Trompenaars (1993). It must be remembered, though, that it was based on anthropology rather than organisation studies and that the research was not carried out in a wide range of countries.

Illustration in film

Borat

This 2006 film evolved from a character created by Sacha Baron Cohen and covered the exploits of a hapless 'Kazakh' reporter on his journeys through the United States. Cohen creates humour in the film by seeking to create cultural misunderstandings, in many cases to the later embarrassment of people in it. In fact the film's subtitle, *Cultural Learnings of America for Make Benefit Glorious Nation of Kazakhstan*, hints at Cohen's understanding of different cultural factors to create situations of misunderstanding, especially as the United States has a very ethnocentric-type culture. We have seen from Kluckhohn and Strodtbeck how Americans prefer considerable private space, and in one of the early scenes 'Borat' seeks to kiss other men on the cheek as a form of greeting which creates some humorous and sometimes quite violent responses. The scene with the 'humour coach' also plays on cultural misunderstandings. Needless to say the film didn't go down well in Kazakhstan!

Edward T. Hall

Edward T. Hall (1976) approached the issue of culture from an anthropological perspective but has created some useful frameworks for cultural analysis. His main approach was to look at how people communicated between different cultures, and he picked up on three areas where differences in communication and relationship can occur.

The most significant distinction he made was between what he called *high-context cultures* and *low-context cultures*. He suggests that in some cultures it is the context of the communication or negotiation which is as significant as the actual content. For example, in Asian or Arab cultures (which are seen as high-context cultures) there will be much more in the way of non-verbal communication. Silences may be significant and what *isn't* said may be just as significant as what is directly communicated. Tayeb (2003) talks of how Japanese often communicate with a minimum of words, called *haragei* or belly language. In terms of negotiations the objective in high-context cultures may be to build a relationship (see section on China later in this chapter) rather than reach a specific conclusion, and ultimate agreements will be built around trust rather than a written contract. It is easy to see how this contrasts with low-context cultures such as the United States, where 'what you say is what you mean' and where negotiations will be expected to reach a conclusion with a signed legal agreement. It also suggests possible areas of confusion or conflict when looking at mergers and joint ventures between high-context and low-context countries.

This may be further exacerbated by two other dimensions identified by Hall, namely how personal space and time might vary between different countries. It seems that there is a difference in terms of how comfortable people are in proximity to other people, a concept which Hall calls *proxemics*. For example, in the UK and Germany people like a certain physical distance between each other, so the handshake is used frequently in business and also in social life. In other countries people are used to being much closer, so that in Egypt, for example, it would be expected that someone would speak very closely to your face and there would be more touching. This is obviously significant in business meetings, and includes the style of greeting at business events and social events linked to the business, and again is an area where confusion can occur. The final area identified by Hall is how time is perceived in different cultures, a point picked up on later by Trompenaars. Hall called these perceptions of time *monochronic time* and *polychronic time*. Monochronic time tends to be linked with low-context cultures and tends to see time as compartmentalised and something that must be planned and adhered to. Thus if a meeting is scheduled for 2.15 p.m. then everyone is expected to be there with a set time schedule to finish the meeting and arrive at a conclusion. High-context cultures tend to a stronger polychronic time dimension in that here the focus is on building social relationships and completing transactions, but not around any rigid time schedule – thus the understanding and use of time can be more 'flexible'. This may mean that appointments may start late or be missed altogether. The issue of how time is managed is seen to be critical for the success of joint ventures and alliances, and this factor can be very significant when there is a high-context/low-context mix.

André Laurent

Laurent (1983) developed our understanding of national culture further, and his research built on that of Kluckhohn and Strodtbeck. It was manager-focused and was based on about 60 questions to assess managers' work values. Its geographical spread was much greater as it included nine West European countries and the USA, and it was also expanded by Laurent *et al.* (1989) to include Japan, Indonesia and the People's Republic of China (PRC). Laurent was essentially seeking to prove that commonly held beliefs by managers in a country were a result of national cultural factors and, thus, he argued that care should be taken when assuming a universality of management and organisational theories. Such theories, particularly the prescriptive ones, might suggest an approach that would work in one country but prove less effective in another (*see* below and also Chapter 3 on contingency theory).

Mead (1998) and Adler (1997) have identified some key aspects of Laurent's analysis, and focus specifically on the issues of:

- managers' attitudes towards hierarchy;
- the willingness to bypass lines of hierarchy in the organisation;
- managers' relationships with subordinates;
- the importance of managers in society.

These four themes were reflected in the following statements:

- 'The main reason for a hierarchical structure is so that everybody knows who has authority over whom' (Statement 1).
- 'In order to have efficient work relationships it is often necessary to bypass the hierarchical line' (Statement 2).
- 'It is important for managers to have at hand precise answers to most of the questions that their subordinates may raise about their work' (Statement 3).
- 'Through their professional activity, managers play an important role in society' (Statement 4).

The responses to these statements can be seen in Table 10.2.

This evidence clearly supports Laurent's hypothesis that much of management behaviour is culturally determined or influenced. This is especially clear in relation to attitudes to authority in the organisation. Evidence of the Confucian principle of respect for and obedience to elders and superiors is shown by people's preference for clearly defined hierarchical structure and their unwillingness to bypass this structure. We also see the more individualistic American culture, with less respect for hierarchy and the belief that individuals should be willing to undertake their own actions, even if it means bypassing the established hierarchy.

What is more interesting from Laurent's analysis is the massive diversity which he found in Europe. Indeed if you contrast, say, Sweden and the Netherlands with Spain and Italy you see marked differences in practically every area. Thus, although we might predict that the Confucian-influenced Asian countries would expect superiors (managers) to have precise answers for questions (not least because of the fear of losing face), we see very similar responses in Spain and Italy, so in some respects the values of their managers are closer to those found in Indonesia than to those in Sweden. This finding has implications for situations when managers in Europe come together through acquisitions, joint ventures or strategic alliances. Ronen and Shenkar (1985) have identified nine clusters of countries which, they argue, have similar cultural characteristics. It is interesting to note that member

Table 10.2 Laurent's analysis of managers' roles

Country	Statement 1 % agreeing (1989)	Statement 2 % disagreeing (1989)	Statement 3 % agreeing (1989)	Statement 4 % agreeing (1983)
Spain	–	74	77	–
Denmark	–	37	23	32
UK	34	35	27	40
Netherlands	31	44	17	45
Germany	26	45	46	46
Sweden	30	26	10	54
Switzerland	–	41	38	65
Italy	42	56	66	74
France	43	43	53	76
Belgium	–	42	44	–
USA	17	18	52	
Japan	50	–	78	–
Indonesia	83	51	73	–
PRC	70	59	74	–

Source: Based on Laurent (1983), Laurent *et al.* (1989).

countries of the European Union fall into five separate cultural groups. For example, the United Kingdom and Ireland are in their 'Anglo' cluster (together with Australia, the USA, Canada and New Zealand), the Scandinavian countries of Sweden, Denmark and Finland are considered 'Nordic', France, Belgium, Italy and the Iberian countries are 'Latin-European', Greece is 'Near-Eastern' and Germany and Austria are 'Germanic'. It is not surprising that there are differences in perception and in substance between EU members' national governments.

Geert Hofstede

In many ways Geert Hofstede is seen as the major writer on cross-cultural analysis because the model he developed (Hofstede, 1980, 1984, 1991) has survived the test of time, is relatively easy to use and is comprehensive. Hofstede was influenced by Laurent's work but decided to take his analysis further by defining some clear themes for analysis. He extended Laurent's original Western Europe/USA spectrum to a more global one. His data for this were provided by gaining access to the American computer company IBM. Through this he was able to investigate the attitudes of 116,000 employees in 50 countries, clearly a more extensive analysis than that of Laurent. Table 10.3 illustrates his findings.

Four cultural dimensions, discussed below, emerged from his extensive data. They are referred to as:

- power distance;
- individualism/collectivism;
- uncertainty avoidance;
- masculinity/feminity.

Table 10.3 Hofstede's cultural criteria

Country	Abbreviation	Individualism		Power distance		Uncertainty avoidance		Masculinity	
		Index (IDV)	Rank	Index (PDI)	Rank	Index (UAI)	Rank	Index (MAS)	Rank
Argentina	ARG	46	28–29	49	18–19	86	36–41	56	30–31
Australia	AUL	90	49	36	13	51	17	61	35
Austria	AUT	55	33	11	1	70	26–27	79	49
Belgium	BEL	75	43	65	33	94	45–46	54	29
Brazil	BRA	38	25	69	39	76	29–30	49	25
Canada	CAN	80	46–47	39	15	48	12–13	52	28
Chile	CHL	23	15	63	29–30	86	36–41	28	8
Colombia	COL	13	5	67	36	80	31	64	39–40
Costa Rica	COS	15	8	35	10–12	86	36–41	21	5–6
Denmark	DEN	74	42	18	3	23	3	16	4
Ecuador	EQA	8	2	78	43–44	67	24	63	37–38
Finland	FIN	63	34	33	8	59	20–21	26	7
France	FRA	71	40–41	68	37–38	86	36–41	43	17–18
Germany (FR)	GER	67	36	35	10–12	65	23	66	41–42
Great Britain	GBR	89	48	35	10–12	35	6–7	66	41–42
Greece	GRE	35	22	60	26–27	112	50	57	32–33
Guatemala	GUA	6	1	95	48–49	101	48	37	11
Hong Kong	HOK	25	16	68	37–38	29	4–5	57	32–33
Indonesia	IDO	14	6–7	78	43–44	48	12–13	46	22
India	IND	48	30	77	42	40	9	56	30–31
Iran	IRA	41	27	58	24–25	59	20–21	43	17–18
Ireland	IRE	70	39	28	5	35	6–7	68	43–44
Israel	ISR	54	32	13	2	81	32	47	23
Italy	ITA	76	44	50	20	75	28	70	46–47
Jamaica	JAM	39	26	45	17	13	2	68	43–44
Japan	JPN	46	28–29	54	21	92	44	95	50
Korea (S)	KOR	18	11	60	26–27	85	34–35	39	13
Malaysia	MAL	26	17	104	50	36	8	50	26–27
Mexico	MEX	30	20	81	45–46	82	33	69	45
Netherlands	NET	80	46–47	38	14	53	18	14	3
Norway	NOR	69	38	31	6–7	50	16	8	2
New Zealand	NZL	79	45	22	4	49	14–15	58	34
Pakistan	PAK	14	6–7	55	22	70	26–27	50	26–27
Panama	PAN	11	3	95	48–49	86	36–41	44	19
Peru	PER	16	9	64	31–32	87	42	42	15–16
Philippines	PHI	32	21	94	47	44	10	64	39–40
Portugal	POR	27	18–19	63	29–30	104	49	31	9
South Africa	SAF	65	35	49	18–19	49	14–15	63	37–38
Salvador	SAL	19	12	66	34–35	94	45–46	40	14
Singapore	SIN	20	13–14	74	40	8	1	48	24
Spain	SPA	51	31	57	23	86	36–41	42	15–16
Sweden	SWE	71	40–41	31	6–7	29	4–5	5	1
Switzerland	SWI	68	37	34	9	58	19	70	46–47
Taiwan	TAI	17	10	58	24–25	69	25	45	20–21
Thailand	THA	20	13–14	64	31–32	64	22	34	10
Turkey	TUR	37	24	66	34–35	85	34–35	45	20–21
Uruguay	URU	36	23	61	28	100	47	38	12
USA	USA	91	50	40	16	46	11	62	36
Venezuela	VEN	12	4	81	45–46	76	29–30	73	48
Yugoslavia	YUG	27	18–19	76	41	88	43	21	5–6
Regions:									
East Africa (1)	EAF	27	(18–19)	64	(31–32)	52	(17–18)	41	(14–15)
West Africa (2)	WAF	20	(13–14)	77	(42)	54	(18–19)	46	(22)
Arab Ctrs (3)	ARA	38	(25)	80	(44–45)	68	(24–25)	53	(28–29)

Source: Hofstede (2001).

Power distance

Power distance represents *the social distance between people of different rank or position*. For example, in a country with a high power distance score (e.g. Malaysia) subordinates would be unwilling to question superiors, and would look to them for direction. Thus they may well accept an unequal distribution of power and autocratic leadership styles. Low power distance suggests less dependence between superiors and subordinates. A leader may have to earn respect in a low power-distance country. This is one of the most significant of Hofstede's dimensions and can clearly be seen to concur with Laurent's earlier work. In Table 10.3, the higher the index number for power distance (PDI), the greater will be the gap between managers and subordinates. A low PDI figure suggests that there is a much smaller gap.

Individualism

Individualism reflects *the extent to which an individual relies on a group (a collectivist approach) or takes individual initiative in making decisions, solving problems and engaging in productive activity*. We have already noted that the American culture has a tendency to be very individualistic, whereas Asian cultures tend to be much more collective. In some cultures relationships in key groups (whether at work or within the family) may be highly significant. The Chinese have a concept, *guanxi*, which means connection or relationship, and much time is spent in cultivating relationships both within and outside the family, and in building up networks. Thus, rather than rely on themselves individually, they can use these relationships and expect them to be used in return. This collectivism is found in many Asian countries although there have been some changes in Asian countries more exposed to Western influences.

In Table 10.3, the higher index numbers (IDV) for individualism suggest cultures where there is more individualism. Not surprisingly, the USA tops the list, with the UK and other 'Anglo' countries scoring high. This dimension may be significant for managers who are developing an appropriate managerial style when they are operating overseas: they may encounter problems if they try to get their subordinates to act more independently rather than in groups. In Korea, for example, people would not be happy if required to act independently and to justify their independent action; they would fear the loss of face they would suffer if there was any criticism from a superior. Social interaction in China or Korea is carried out with the express purpose of not allowing people to lose face, and a Western manager needs to be aware of this.

Uncertainty avoidance

Uncertainty avoidance essentially reflects *people's attitudes to ambiguity* in a society or country. Hofstede found that in some cultures there was unhappiness or uncertainty with ambiguous situations and that people wanted more direction and were less comfortable with change, especially when it was not explained to them. People who are not comfortable with uncertain or ambiguous situations may develop anxiety or stress and, thus, work less effectively in an organisation where there is little direction and considerable uncertainty. They may be happier with written rules to cover every situation (as they might find in a bureaucratic organisation) and with job security.

From Table 10.3 we can identify a country which has a high level of uncertainty avoidance, such as Greece. The description above would apply to Greek people. From the table we can also see that there are a number of countries with low uncertainty avoidance, such as Sweden. Their low score suggests that people in these countries are more willing to take risks and are much less resistant to change than those in high-uncertainty-avoidance countries. The managerial implications are obvious. If we imagine a Swedish company with a subsidiary in Greece, where it is seeking to introduce new methods, or perhaps a change in corporate culture, we can see that the process will have to be handled carefully. The risk of resistance and conflict if changes are pushed too quickly, in a culture which is resistant to change and ambiguous situations, is very real.

Masculinity

Masculinity is one of the more complex variables introduced by Hofstede. It reflects *values which are widely considered to be more 'masculine', such as assertiveness, competitiveness and results orientation*, whereas 'feminine' values can be seen to be cooperative and to show greater awareness of feelings and equal opportunities. This value also relates to the degree of discrimination against (usually) women in the organisation.

From Table 10.3 it is not surprising to find that Japan has the highest masculinity (MAS) score and Norway one of the lowest, although you will find considerable variance among Western European countries, which confirms Laurent's findings that it can be misleading to talk of a 'European' culture.

Hofstede's findings indicate four areas of potential difference between cultures, but it is now commonly accepted that a fifth variable exists. This resulted from the Chinese Values Survey carried out by the Chinese Culture Connection Group (1987), which sought to evaluate the effectiveness of Hofstede's cultural dimensions in a specific Asian context where there would be a significant influence of Confucianism. Their evaluation was further tested by Bond and Hofstede (1988), who showed that three of the four dimensions identified by Hofstede were present, the missing one being uncertainty avoidance. What did emerge from the study by the Chinese Culture Connection Group (1987) was the evidence of a fifth dimension which seemed particularly applicable to Asian cultures and which indicated that most Asian countries had a long-term perspective about work and the organisation. In the study this was labelled 'Confucian dynamics' but Hofstede called it 'long-term orientation' (LTO). This orientation may be useful for explaining the different behaviour of, say, Japanese organisations and Western organisations. The Japanese may be much more influenced by long-term market share than immediate short-term factors, such as dividends. It may also explain why Asian companies are keen to build long-term relationships with Western companies rather than attempt takeovers or other short-term activities.

A further development which stems from Hofstede's work is the idea that one can place countries in clusters where cultural similarities may be highlighted, drawing on Hofstede's cultural dimensions. If we apply data from Table 10.3 and focus specifically on the cultural dimensions of power distance and uncertainty avoidance, we could identify some possible clusters built around these dimensions, and an application of this can be seen in Figure 10.2. In this figure PD represents power distance and UA represents uncertainty avoidance. We can identify one group with low power distance and low uncertainty avoidance and another group with high power distance and high uncertainty avoidance.

From Figure 10.2 we can see that some countries, even on the same continent, are close on these two dimensions (Italy and Spain) and others are far apart (Italy and Denmark). It would suggest that managers in Spain and Italy would be comfortable with having large power distances from their subordinates and would also both be unhappy with ambiguity or uncertainty, and thus might suggest that both might be happier with a more autocratic management style. One can contrast this with the possible complications that might arise in this respect in an Italian–Danish collaboration.

There have been some criticisms of Hofstede's model. One of the most obvious is that although his study included a substantial number of countries, there were none from Eastern Europe and Russia, and many Asian countries were ignored. The explanation is, of course, that the survey was explicitly based on IBM, and in 1980 and 1984 IBM did not have a significant presence in these countries. This

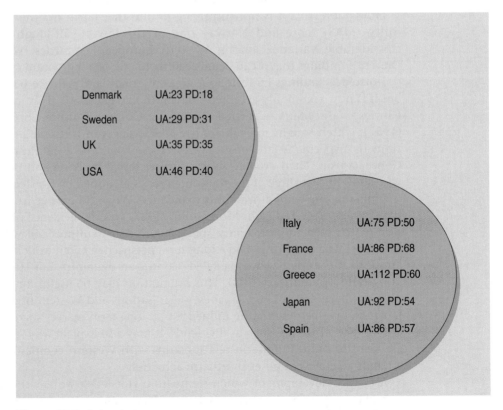

Denmark	UA:23 PD:18
Sweden	UA:29 PD:31
UK	UA:35 PD:35
USA	UA:46 PD:40

Italy	UA:75 PD:50
France	UA:86 PD:68
Greece	UA:112 PD:60
Japan	UA:92 PD:54
Spain	UA:86 PD:57

Figure 10.2 Cultural clusters

omission has to some extent been corrected by the Chinese Values Survey and more recent work applying the work of Hofstede to Eastern Europe. However, this leads to a second criticism in that the results were based on an organisation with a very strong corporate culture which may have distorted the findings. Despite this, most subsequent research has upheld the validity of his analysis, and it remains the most popular model which is used worldwide to evaluate cultural differences between countries and assess their implication for organisational behaviour.

Fons Trompenaars

Fons Trompenaars' (1993) work draws on that of Kluckhohn and Strodtbeck and also that of Hofstede, but seeks to extend the analysis. Whereas Hofstede sought to explain differences in cultures, Trompenaars, coming from a consultancy background, was more concerned with practical problems and solutions for managers dealing with a cross-cultural environment. Trompenaars' questionnaire survey directed to 15,000 respondents provided data enabling him to identify seven dimensions of culture, namely:

- universalism *v* particularism;
- collectivism *v* individualism;
- affective *v* neutral cultures;
- specific *v* diffuse relationships;
- achieving *v* ascribing status;
- time as sequence *v* time as synchronisation;
- inner-directed *v* outer-directed.

One of these dimensions, collectivism *v* individualism, is familiar to us from Hofstede's work but the others require further explanation.

Universalism v particularism

The *universalist* approach suggests *a culture that is driven by rules and prefers a rational and logical approach in the belief that there are universal rules which should be respected.* A *particularist* culture is based more on people relationships (e.g. *guanxi*) and may encourage more flexibility in the interpretation of rules. High universalist countries include Canada, the USA and the UK, and particularist countries include China and Thailand. This may explain the confusion often experienced by Western managers when negotiating in Asia, especially if they are under the misapprehension that Western rules of business behaviour will apply in the East, particularly in terms of contractual negotiations.

Affective v neutral cultures

This dimension relates *the extent of emotional behaviour found in a culture.* In affective cultures, such as Italy, emotions are revealed more openly in the organisation than they are in neutral cultures, such as Japan and Germany, where such openness would be frowned upon and where people might find emotions difficult to handle. The implications for international teamworking may be significant if some members exhibit emotional behaviour in the way they communicate and others prefer 'the stiff upper lip' approach. The use of emotion may distort the meaning of communications, whereby an individual who displays inhibition may be hiding his or her true feelings or viewpoints and thus may contribute less effectively to the group.

Specific v diffuse relationships

In a *specific* culture, Trompenaars argues that *managers separate their work relationships from other relationships*: that is, the manager–subordinate relationship may be observed at work but at the squash club people are on first-name terms and treat each other as equals. This contrasts with behaviour in a *diffuse* culture, where the relationship at work influences all relationships outside work: so a person who is a subordinate at work would be very cautious about approaching his or her superior outside work in a relatively open manner without some prompt from the manager concerned. Diffusion is very strong in cultures where there is high respect for seniority and can be clearly linked to Hofstede's power distance factor.

Achieving v ascribing status

In an *achieving* culture *status is considered to be achievement-based*, whereas in other cultures status is ascribed to an individual because of factors like age or gender. Thus high-ascribing cultures are to be found in Hong Kong, Argentina and Egypt whereas achievement cultures are found in the USA and Scandinavia.

Time as sequence v time as synchronisation

Time as sequence suggests *a rational, linear approach to issues* ('one step at a time'), whereas *time as synchronisation* suggests that *time is seen as circular* with the possibility of parallel activities, such as might be found in Japan. Trompenaars suggests that this relates to Bond and Hofstede's (1988) dimension of 'long-term orientation' (or 'Confucian dynamics') and that it may be very significant for organisational behaviour. In cultures where time is seen as sequential there may be a tendency towards short-term relationships, and timing may be seen as very important. There is potential for conflict with people in cultures where the concept of time is more elastic and where long-term relationships carry more weight.

Inner-directed v outer-directed

The dimension of inner or outer direction contrasts countries like the USA and Switzerland, where there is *a belief that the individual should seek to control the natural and human environment*, with nations like China, where man aims to be in harmony with nature: this belief is central to both Confucianism and Buddhism. It is this belief which may explain why, in countries like Japan, organisations are seen holistically as operating in harmony with their surroundings and with the people within the organisation, and could further explain why direct conflict or confrontation is often resisted.

Trompenaars has developed his work with Charles Hampden-Turner (1993, 1997), and they have extended their field of analysis, especially in Asia. They replaced the affective/neutral dimension with an equality/hierarchy one which corresponds more clearly to Hofstede's findings. In many ways they have confirmed and developed the work of Kluckhohn and Strodtbeck, Laurent and Hofstede. The work of analysing culture still goes on (*see* Gatley *et al., 1996*), but a common thread that emerges from all of these studies is that organisations operating in a multinational context need to be aware of the cultural differences they are likely to encounter if they are to avoid potential problems. They also suggest that there is no unalterable formula for reconciling cultural differences but that every case should be seen on its own merits. However, the awareness of the likely cultural problems to be encountered could, ultimately, give an organisation competitive advantage over its rivals.

Culture shock and culture shift

Imagine the following scenario. You have just moved to start a new job in an exciting new country with a totally different culture from that of your own. The initial reaction to this may well be one of excitement as you read the guide books and start to learn a few words of the language. The first few days of your new job may be exciting as you begin to absorb some of the new sights and sounds: what Torbiorn (1982) calls 'the honeymoon'. Then, with mounting horror, you begin to realise that your command of the language is seriously inadequate. Furthermore, you are finding that relationships with people in your organisation and socially are not going smoothly. You appear to have offended someone without realising it. From a feeling of euphoria you rapidly descend to feeling that you are in an increasingly hostile environment, in which you feel alienated and lost. This experience is referred to as *culture shock*: that is, *the startling experiences and difficulties first encountered when entering an alien culture*. This is increasingly being recognised as a serious issue for companies which send managers overseas. The manager may end up disillusioned and may even leave the company as a result of this bad experience. If this happens, it represents a major loss for both the individual and the organisation.

The ability of the individual to overcome these problems to some extent depends on his or her own personality, but there is an increasing recognition that managers overseas need increased support from the organisation. It is also interesting to note that many of the early problems faced by Eurodisney near Paris were cultural in origin and were partly the result of American management coming into contact with French culture.

Another factor of which organisations should be aware is reverse culture shock, which occurs when a manager who has been overseas for some years, and has adapted well to his or her new culture, is faced with returning to the home country, perhaps because of some organisational restructuring. Imagine a British manager who has been in Malaysia for the last twenty years returning to the UK of 2008, having been used to the UK of 1988. Such a move can cause culture shock and may require support for the manager from the organisation. Awareness of the possibility of reverse culture shock might also explain why the long-term posting of managers overseas is becoming less commonplace: there is a trend towards their being replaced by locally employed managers.

Culture shift is *cultural change or, more specifically, the extent to which a culture can change and the speed at which such changes occur.* There are many factors that might induce cultural shift in a country. Changing economic conditions, high levels of investment by overseas multinationals and social, political and religious upheaval can all affect culture and, in turn, be further influenced by the evolving culture. Mead (1998) highlights the case of the *shinjinrui* in Japan. Traditional Japanese workers were exceptionally loyal to their company and leader and would regard the company's interests as paramount. *Shinjinrui* means 'new human beings' and reflects the influence of a number of predominantly younger workers who are less loyal to the company and who would not, for example, automatically work overtime. In Hofstede's terms, this reflects a move towards more individualism and, therefore, represents some degree of cultural shift, although Mead cautions against overstating the nature of this change, as the extent of the shift is at present quite small.

Another interesting case is that of Hong Kong, where the population is over 90 per cent ethnic Chinese and yet there has been significant investment by overseas multinationals, especially American companies. Table 10.4 illustrates Hofstede's and Trompenaars' rankings applied to Hong Kong, China and the United States (in order to see how close the Hong Kong culture is to the Chinese one) in areas where there may have been an element of cultural shift.

It appears that Hong Kong remains close to China in terms of power distance, individualism, achievement, universalism and affectivity, as their common cultural origins might suggest. On the other hand Hong Kong is closer to the United States in terms of uncertainty avoidance, masculinity, internal control and specificity, which suggests there has been a degree of culture shift as a result of Western influence. Hong Kong remains an essentially Chinese culture but one with a much more individualistic, risk-taking and non-deterministic nature than that of mainland China.

Illustration in film

French Kiss; Fools Rush In; The Tourist Trap

The issue of culture shock has been the basis of many films and is usually approached from the humorous dimension of misunderstandings between people of different cultures. A typical example would be *French Kiss* with Meg Ryan and Kevin Kline, in which much of the film revolves around misunderstandings between the two main characters (French and American). The writer's favourite film in this context is *Fools Rush In* with Matthew Perry and Salma Hayek, in which the cultural mix is between an American man and a Mexican woman; it is both well observed and very funny, especially the meeting of the two sets of parents and their complete cultural misunderstanding. Refer also to the television series *The Tourist Trap*, mentioned earlier in the chapter, which deliberately sought to identify cultural differences between four national groups.

Table 10.4 Cultural comparison of the USA, China and Hong Kong

	Mainland China	Hong Kong	United States
Hofstede (1980)			
Power distance	20	15	38
Uncertainty avoidance	1	49	43
Individualism	23	37	1
Masculinity	54	18	15
Trompenaars (1993)			
Achievement	32	20	2
Universalism	39	38	7
Internal control	19	8	7
Specificity	34	16	17
Affectivity	41	38	20

Source: Adapted from Hofstede (1980) and Trompenaars (1993).

Organisational behaviour and national culture

This section briefly explores the interaction of culture with many of the prime areas of interest in organisational behaviour (OB) which have been covered in this text. It examines the culturally specific nature of many of the theories in OB and criticises their essential ethnocentrism.

Convergence or divergence?

The assumption of cultural convergence dominated business, organisational and management studies up to and including the 1960s. The convergence hypothesis argues that *management is a universal phenomenon and that 'good practice', which usually emanated from the USA or Europe, could and should be applied throughout the world.* Theodore Levitt (1983) argued that national cultures were converging, with the result that culture was becoming an unimportant variable for business to consider. However, in recent decades, and especially since the 1980s as we have seen, considerable attention has been paid to cultural differences between nations. There is a growing acceptance that 'good' managerial practices may be those which best fit and are in keeping with a particular culture. Differences between cultures have been increasingly recognised, with the result that the divergence hypothesis is now given considerable credence. Supranational organisations like the European Union, which were founded on the convergence belief, have had to recognise significant national differences.

Culture and individual behaviour

One of the most challenging issues in OB is the extent to which national culture influences individual behaviour and, as a result of this, whether behaviour needs to be modified when faced with a different culture. National cultures influence most aspects of individual behaviour including the cognitive framework through which we view people of other countries. People who have been predominantly influenced by their own culture, and who have had little or no exposure to cultures of other countries, may tend towards a more ethnocentric or parochial view, whereby all contacts with other cultures are seen through the eyes of the individual's own culture and are judged accordingly. This can lead to a very narrow view of the world, in which other cultures may be considered negatively. This may influence behaviour and lead to a perceptual bias on the part of the individual.

In practice there may be very different cognitive styles in different cultures. For example, a study by Abramson *et al.* (1993) showed clear differences between Canadian and Japanese cognitive styles: the Canadians looked for quick decisions and had little interest in building relationships whereas the Japanese favoured relationship building and did not like being rushed into making a decision. The problems of negotiating in this context are clear. This finding can be related back to Hofstede's work, where the individualism index for Canada is much higher than that for Japan (*see* Table 10.3). The Japanese approach to decision making is described by Min Chen (2004), who suggests that they use the processes of *nemawashi* and *ringi seido* for decision making. *Nemawashi* literally refers to dealing with the roots of trees but reflects *the process of informally sounding out employees' ideas about a proposed policy or action, often under the cloak of anonymity. Ringi Seido* is more formalised, in that *a proposal originating in one part of the organisation is circulated around the organisation for others to make comments; the final decision on the proposal will be taken by senior managers after they have viewed all the feedback.* The purpose of both methods is to eliminate dissension when the proposal is carried out. It reflects the more communal approach that is found in Japanese culture, reflected in the practice of Quality Circles.

With the development of multinational activity involving more cross-cultural contact, there is a need for individuals to develop a more 'global' mindset, where issues are considered from a wider perspective than from a traditional ethnocentric position. The challenge in international companies is to move managers from an ethnocentric to a global mindset.

There are many problems inherent in measuring determinants of individual behaviour, such as personality, across cultures. The effectiveness of personality testing may be diminished in cultures where there is no familiarity with such tests (Lonner, 1990). Jackson (1993) and Cronbach (1990) further support the argument that the value of intelligence tests and personality profiles may be limited, according to the cultural context in which they are applied: they can be discriminatory if not designed for that culture.

Table 10.5 Mutual perceptions of British and Italian managers

British of the Italians	Italians of the British
• excessively flexible	• obsessed with rules/procedures
• entrepreneurial	• inflexible
• creative	• good planners
• people-orientated	• formal
• emotional	• avoid confrontation
• undisciplined	• disciplined
• not very time-conscious	• hide emotions
• unable to meet deadlines	

Source: Based on Hoecklin (1995).

Another area where culture could influence individual behaviour is in the field of perception. Adler (1997) shows that there is likely to be a high level of selective perception between different cultures and countries, especially if the individual has an ethnocentric view. Selective perception can, in turn, lead to perceptual stereotyping, *the tendency to group or pigeon hole people according to a single or limited number of apparently dominant characteristics*. All too often the dominant characteristic is nationality. This has the potential to affect relations between managers of different nationalities and cultures when they have to work together. Hoecklin (1995) describes a situation where a group of British and Italian managers were brought together for a joint project in a chemical company. Their mutual perceptions of each other are illustrated in Table 10.5.

In the situation described by Hoecklin, one can see that there is the potential for misunderstanding, confusion and even resentment if the respective managers carry their mutual perceptions into their dealings with one another. However, Hoecklin explains that the company took time to explore these perceptual differences with the combined group in order to establish a clear way of working together. Ultimately their project was successful. This case highlights the critical role of communication when dealing with perceptual bias and stereotyping. It is only through communicating effectively with people from other cultures that these cultural stereotypes can be managed. Mini-case 10.1 illustrates the need to consider communication in inter-cultural activities.

Culture and motivation

There has been considerable debate as to the validity in a cross-cultural context of some of the motivation theories described in Chapter 4. Adler (1997: 166) argues that 'American motivation theories, although too often assumed to reflect universal values, have failed to provide consistently useful explanations for behavior outside the United States'.

Mini-case 10.1: Verbal and non-verbal communication in Malaysia

Malaysia is a very pluralistic society, with over half the population being Muslim Malays, over a quarter Chinese and with substantial minorities of Indians and other groups. There are distinctive subcultures within the Malaysian culture. It is a collectivist society where social harmony is very important and influences individual behaviour as well as relations in the community and in organisations. Therefore, the organisational approach is very much towards collective decision making and consensus.

The right form of communication is crucial for the visitor to Malaysia. One of the first issues is how to address people. In Hofstede's survey (see Table 10.3) Malaysia ranked highest on power distance, so it is important to assess the rank or status of an individual and adjust one's approach. Professional or honorific titles are important to individuals, so these must be respected.

King (1998) identifies some situations which a Westerner from a highly individualistic culture might encounter. People in individualistic cultures are quite comfortable engaging in open debate about an issue (possibly a proposed business contract) and might stress their side of an argument forcibly. This tendency towards openness in discussion may not be greeted with universal acclaim in Malaysia, where social harmony is important and where compromise is preferred to confrontation. The Malaysian will go to great lengths in order to save an individual from 'losing face'. A low-key approach which spares the feelings of others would be productive for the Westerner.

In terms of non-verbal communication, the smile can mean many things in Malaysia. A smile and a nod may suggest that the person respects your opinion but does not necessarily mean that the person agrees with it. A smile can also signify embarrassment or even annoyance, especially when a person is being put in a situation where there is the possibility of losing face. Silences are also perfectly acceptable in Malaysia as they are seen as a sign of politeness in that an individual is reflecting on a comment made before answering. Westerners may find problems with this.

It is important for people from one culture to respect another culture in which they find themselves. They should certainly not take the ethnocentric view – expecting the foreigners to respond as people would in their own home country.

Hofstede (1980), in his analysis of different cultures, identified the culture of the United States as being one of high individualism, high masculinity and low power distance and having a low need to avoid uncertainty. A more collectivist culture, such as is found in China, would have a very different profile, which makes some of the assumptions around which motivational theories were built less relevant. For example, Maslow's (1943) model of motivational needs has been questioned by many writers such as Onedo (1991) who, when studying motivation in Papua New Guinea, found that security needs were ranked as more important than autonomy needs. Similar inconsistencies were found in countries having a high need for uncertainty avoidance, such as Japan and Greece. Nevis (1983), in his study of the People's Republic of China, found that security needs (linked to loyalty to the nation) were the overriding motivational need and that self-actualisation, which is the highest level of need in Maslow's model, was considered of little significance. As might be expected, the need to belong (to family and/or community) was found to be a more powerful driving force, often more important than seeking to meet basic physiological needs. This reflects the more collectivist view held in China at that time, although it has been pointed out that China has changed considerably since the Cultural Revolution, when the study was carried out, and that there may have been some culture shift in China in the 1990s which could lead to more individualism.

Herzberg's (1968) model of motivation has an equally uncomfortable evaluation when exposed to cross-cultural studies. Hines (1973) tested the model in New Zealand and found that some of the concerns that acted as hygiene factors in Herzberg's analysis, such as supervision, were seen as motivators in the sample studied. Adler (1997) suggests that the motivator/hygiene model seems to vary according to the culture in which it is tested and so the universality of the model must be in doubt.

McClelland's needs theory (considering the relative needs for achievement, power and affiliation) (McClelland and Burnham, 1976) does fare a little better in a cross-cultural context, although Hofstede (1984) suggests that the concept of achievement is a Western one. The model seems to be especially applicable in countries having low uncertainty avoidance and high masculinity, although the actual need to achieve may be lower in some cultures than others, especially in less individualistic ones.

Vroom's (1964) expectancy theory assumes that individuals are rational decision makers who will choose between alternatives on the basis of which course of action is likely to give them most advantage. The theory seems to work best in cultures where there is an emphasis on 'internal attribution', where the individual feels he or she has the ability to influence the environment. This appears to be most applicable in cultures which exhibit Trompenaars' concept of 'inner direction' and in cultures with high individualism. However, it is likely to be much less effective in collectivist cultures where individuals have an external locus of control and where maintaining harmony between the individual and the organisation is of paramount concern.

 ## Culture and leadership

The issue of leadership and leadership styles is important to international managers when they are operating in a different country. Increasingly, prospective international managers are encouraged to undertake courses of study which seek to improve their cultural awareness. One of the most important factors will be that of power distance. The French manager is used to significant power distance when dealing with employees, and so more autocratic styles of leadership are tolerated in a French cultural context (Barsoux and Lawrence, 1990). There are very clear lines of hierarchy between the leader and subordinates, and it is unlikely that these will be circumvented. Contrast this with the American manager, who is probably used to low power distance, has easier accessibility to subordinates, and probably deals with people at all levels of the hierarchy on first-name terms. Clearly the more democratic leadership style adopted by American managers may cause confusion if applied in a French context, where people are used to more formality and authoritarian leadership styles. Effective leaders in an international context need to adapt to the constraints and expectations of the particular culture in which they are operating, otherwise there is always the danger of conflict through misinterpretation. The early years of Eurodisney in Paris were hampered by such conflicts between an American management and an essentially French workforce, and it was only when a French chief executive officer was appointed that matters improved.

 ## Culture and structure

With the increase in internationalisation that has been taking place from the latter part of the twentieth century, the issue of organisational structure is becoming increasingly important when companies seek to develop by expanding overseas. Some of the most significant work in this regard has been undertaken by Hofstede (1984, 1991), who has looked at bureaucracy from a cultural perspective. Given the nature of bureaucracy, the two elements of Hofstede's model which appear most relevant are power distance and uncertainty avoidance. Hofstede has built his models of bureaucracy around these, as can be seen in Figure 10.3.

The most traditional model of bureaucracy is referred to as 'full bureaucracy', which has its roots in Hofstede's dimensions of high power distance and high uncertainty avoidance. An organisation characterised by this model is dominated by rules and regulations (which remove uncertainty) and has a strong hierarchical system with clear power distances between individuals at different levels. It is characterised by vertical top-down communication, conveyed by formal means. An alternative model is 'marketplace bureaucracy', which relates to cultures with low power distance and low uncertainty avoidance. There is greater flexibility in this model than there is in the full bureaucracy, with more willingness to bypass hierarchy and fewer rules. An organisation characterised by this sort of bureaucracy would have little difficulty moving towards a more flexible type of organisation, such as a matrix or flexible firm (*see* Chapter 7). The two hybrid models are 'per-

	Uncertainty avoidance (UA)	
	Low	High
Low **Power distance (PD)** **High**	Low UA, low PD **Marketplace bureaucracy** *e.g. UK, Scandinavia*	High UA, low PD **Workflow bureaucracy** *e.g. Israel, Germany*
	Low UA, high PD **Personal bureaucracy** *e.g. Hong Kong, India*	High UA, high PD **Full bureaucracy** *e.g. Belgium, France*

Figure 10.3 Hofstede's bureaucratic types
Source: Based on Mead (1998), adapted from Hofstede (1984).

sonal bureaucracy', characterised by high power distance but low uncertainty avoidance (which Hofstede links to the Chinese family model), and 'workflow bureaucracy', which is suited to cultures with high uncertainty avoidance and lower power distance. The latter may resemble a professional organisation in which there are experts who are readily accessible, but which is still driven by tight rules and procedures.

One of the criticisms of bureaucratic models of organisational structure is that they are slow to react to changes in their environment because of rigidity in their communications and the inflexibility of their rules and regulations. Recent shifts have been towards organisational structures that can respond more quickly to their changing environment, such as matrix structures or the modern flexible organisations with their core and periphery workers (*see* Chapter 7). From a cultural perspective, it would appear that the types of cultures most likely to adapt to these changes are those with a low power distance and low uncertainty avoidance. These newer structures are likely to operate more easily in the USA, the UK and Scandinavian countries, for example.

Change in Eastern Europe

Each of the Eastern European countries has a distinctive economic and social history. Before the Second World War (pre-1939), Hungary maintained close ties with Germany, and Romania had close ties with France. Russia, however, had been far more isolated since the revolution of 1917. After the war (post-1945), Russian influence extended across Eastern Europe, forming a massive economic trading bloc. Industry was dominated by large, state-controlled conglomerates that produced a vast range of industrial and consumer goods to targets set by the state and which were inefficient by Western standards. There were substantial imports and exports between bloc countries, and competition, as we know it, was largely absent. Private enterprise was allowed but only took place on a very small scale and was closely regulated.

After around forty years of existence, the Soviet bloc began to disintegrate in the late 1980s. This was a mostly peaceful transformation, and what is interesting about it to organisation theorists is the truly revolutionary nature of the forces for change that had an effect in such a short time. In the new order, organisations, many of which were in monopoly situations before, were faced with sudden falls in revenues as guaranteed markets and government subsidies were dismantled. Managers of the large conglomerates were left to their own devices as state control was rolled back. A further high-impact change was that these organisations had to start competing in capitalist markets which operated according to different 'rules' and values. Organisations that were relatively inefficient, by capitalist standards, had to cope with a profit-driven focus.

Due to the recent nature of events in Eastern Europe it is too early to be firm about issues of organisation structure. We can, however, note some issues that were typical of those facing these conglomerates and which would have implications for design of structure. The following points are taken from Pearce and Branyiczki (1993):

1 Because of the dominance of state control, employees and managers looked upwards for instructions and guidance.

2 Faced with such mould-breaking changes it was the people working in them not the organisations themselves that were faced with attitudinal and behavioural change. New roles in areas like marketing or financial management had to be learned.

3 Existing roles like procurement and manufacturing had to be upgraded to approach the sophistication of Western levels.

4 Employees had to cope with unlearning attitudes and behaviours that had sustained them in a state-controlled conglomerate but which would not help a smaller private organisation operating in free markets.

5 New attitudes and behaviours had to be implanted, for example greater openness to feedback and willingness to contribute to change, from other managers in the organisation and from the marketplace.

6 Organisations needed to implement new control and reporting structures, and people unused to managerial positions had to face up to tough decision-making responsibilities.

The implications of these general observations for structure differ between countries. The differences arise as there are wide divergences of approach to management in Eastern Europe. For example, on Hofstede's individual–collective dimension of culture, managers from Poland, Hungary and Slovenia would tend towards individualism whereas managers from the Czech Republic would be relatively more collectivist. A study of Czech and British managers revealed some differences in their views of themselves and others (Pavlica and Thorpe, 1998). British managers tended to emphasise the need for continual development of work skills, and saw the manager as a communicator among a diverse set of people. In contrast, Czech managers did not put much value on staff development and de-emphasised the needs of others at work. They saw subordinates as incompetent or lazy and held the view that the manager is a dominant male (*see* Table 10.6).

The rough but informative contrast presented in Table 10.6 suggests that different culture-driven managerial 'types' may well invoke different organisation structures, given their contrasting beliefs and assumptions about the people working in those structures. It also serves to remind us that, although structure can impede the

Table 10.6 Contrasting attitudes of British and Czech managers

British managers	Czech managers
• See employees as part of a flexible labour force who need communication and interaction	• See employees as incompetent or lazy
• Stress personal and interpersonal skills	• Stress individual personal qualities
• See manager as social communicator	• See manager as dominant and superior male
• Have concern about staff development	• Underestimate the needs of others, neglect staff development

Source: Based on Pavlica and Thorpe (1998).

progress and performance of an organisation, a good structure will be unable to overcome unhelpful attitudes endemic in an entire, or part of a, workforce.

One of the interesting aspects is in relation to attitudes towards hierarchy, which characterised the old system. Whilst new organisational structures developed in the 1990s, a high degree of hierarchy remained. Edwards and Lawrence (2000) have described how in many Eastern European countries traditional hierarchies (with high power distance) have been re-established, and Michailova (1996) also noted that system change didn't change attitudes towards hierarchy in Bulgaria. On the other hand it will be interesting to see how the Eastern European countries that joined the EU in 2004 will change in the face of much more exposure to Western European influences and whether it will result in an element of culture shift.

Change in China

One of the biggest changes in the world as it moves into the twenty-first century has been the emergence of China. Since 1979, when China began its reform programme, it has encouraged a shift towards private enterprise and also increasingly had an 'open door' policy towards foreign direct investment in the country, usually through joint ventures. This has resulted in consistently high levels of economic growth in the country (it was barely affected by the 1997 Asian crisis) and China becoming the world's number one location for overseas investment as many companies have sought to take advantage of its burgeoning market and also its potential for efficient manufacturing allied with lower labour costs. In addition many Chinese companies are beginning to look to markets outside China. This in turn has seen more and more Western companies forming alliances or joint ventures with Chinese companies and even acquiring some of them, meaning that there has had to be a steep learning curve for many Western managers when dealing with their Chinese counterparts.

One of the key differences is that many Western managers come from low-context cultures and they are coming into contact with a Chinese culture that is certainly a high-context one. Whereas the Western cultures often have relatively low levels of power distance and uncertainty avoidance they are coming into a culture which is still influenced by Confucianism with its high level of respect for older people and where there will usually be a high power distance between the employer and employee. In a high-context culture there will be a high level of personal interaction designed to build up trust between managers, and this will be seen as a gradual process until the level of trust is strong enough for the business relationship to develop – and this interaction will involve both verbal and non-verbal communication.

A critical aspect of business in China is the development of *guanxi*. Chen (2004) describes it as 'connection' or 'relationship', and it is central to Chinese culture. Within any organisation, individuals will be seeking to develop their relationship or *guanxi* with people at all levels, especially where it might be advantageous for them. This relationship suggests the continual exchange of favours which binds them together. This places network-building at the heart of Chinese organisations, and this will extend to their relationships with overseas companies. In fact the Chinese have a word *zouhoumen,* which means 'walking through the back door': it suggests that you get things done through your *guanxi* network of relationships rather than, perhaps, direct negotiation.

A second critical factor which interlinks with *guanxi* is the issue of 'face'. It relates again to the Confucian philosophy which underpins much of Chinese and Asian behaviour and is also significant in Arab countries and South America. Face is linked with preserving harmony by preserving one's self-respect and the self-respect of others, and thus it becomes essential in social and business interaction that nobody is forced to lose face. Chen mentions two types of Chinese face: *lian* and *mianzi. Lian* is linked with personal interactions – for example for a student to criticise a teacher or professor in a lecture would be seen as a profound loss of face for both concerned, which is why there is little open dissent in Chinese society. *Mianzi* is something that can be achieved and which is linked to a rise in status. The link with *guanxi* is that if you do not follow the rules of *guanxi,* through mutual reciprocity, then it can lead to a loss of face; this has been developed by Huang (1989).

 ## Change, conflict and communication

We have already seen in this chapter how the changes brought on by internationalisation and globalisation have led to greater emphasis being given to national cultural issues. The danger with such changes is that if cultural factors are not addressed, there will be the potential for conflict. If one looks back at the case of the Italian and British managers, referred to earlier in the chapter, one can see that there was the potential for conflict in the project they were undertaking if the cultural issues had not been addressed. Some of the potential pitfalls of dealing with Russia (see Mini-case 10.2) reflect some of the problems of communication and negotiation which are developed further in this section.

The significance of communication in a cross-cultural context

The underlying themes of this book are change, conflict and communications. All of these relate to the field of cross-cultural behaviour and management and can be seen as central to the success of companies that are seeking to internationalise by entering into an alliance or joint venture with an organisation from another country, or even if they are just communicating in a business or social context. We have already seen how communication may be very direct in low-context cultures and yet more restrained in high-context cultures. The nature of the communication may also be determined by the extent of the power distance between the individuals, and this in turn will be significant in terms of how other people are addressed (i.e. in high-power-distance cultures people may insist on being addressed by their titles and would be upset to be addressed by their first name). The significance of non-verbal communication will be enhanced in high-context cultures. Gestures may be very important and how hand, head and eye movements are used may be very significant – for example in Asia it is rude to point the soles of your feet at people. Negotiators from low-context countries have to learn to understand key features of non-verbal communication when dealing with high-context cultures. Elfenbein (2006) has done some work on interpreting facial expressions in terms of seeking to interpret the emotions being portrayed by facial expressions; for example a negotiator from a high-context culture such as China is unlikely to directly contradict a negotiator from a low-context culture, even if they strongly disagree with what is being said. The reasons for this will be an unwillingness to make anyone lose face and to destroy the harmony by direct confrontation, so there is a need to try and interpret facial expressions – such as a furrowing of the brows – which might indicate dissatisfaction and unhappiness.

An additional factor to handle with communication is the language chosen for the communication. In a cross-cultural context companies often choose a company language and this inevitably means that the person speaking in their first language might have an advantage over people speaking in a second language in which they are not fluent. Feeley (2003) shows how the second language user may not contribute because of uncertainty over their linguistic skills or because of fear of losing face if they are not strong enough in the language: this in turn can distort the power–authority relationship and lead to possible resentment. The answer lies in better language training or more use of translators, although even this might not train the manager enough for the interpretation of non-verbal language found in high-context cultures. Ultimately, effective cross-cultural communication will become an important competency for international managers when working globally.

An interesting example of confusion between high-context and low-context communication was in the *Celebrity Big Brother* show in 2007 when there was a media frenzy about the racist bullying of Shilpa Shetty, a well-known Bollywood actress, by three other participants, led by one Jade Goody. It led to a record 30,000 complaints to OFTEL, the then Chancellor, Gordon Brown, having to apologise whilst visiting India, street protests in India and the sponsor of the programme pulling out. Whilst there were unpleasant overtones, the root cause was probably inter-cultural communication misunderstandings. Shetty, coming from a high-context culture, had a communication style that sought to avoid making people lose face, her tone was generally soft, people weren't criticised in front of others and expletives would not be used with other people about. Goody, by contrast, coming from a low-context culture with a very direct communication style, was quite happy to use expletives in front of others, spoke in an aggressive manner and and called Shetty a 'liar' in front of others. From Shetty's perspective Goody had made her lose face and as a result Goody lost face in her eyes whereas from Goody's perspective, she saw Shetty as not answering directly and thus hiding things from her and not being genuine. Although this was an extreme case it does show how communication problems can lead to conflict situations in international organisations. For the record Goody was removed from the show and Shetty won it.

Illustration in film

Lost in Translation

This film was shot entirely on location in Japan and stars Bill Murray as Bob, an American film star, in Tokyo to shoot a commercial, and Scarlett Johansson as Charlotte, a young wife tagging along with her workaholic photographer husband. They both sense and experience elements of culture shock being in Tokyo, and some of the best scenes are Bob's attempts to communicate when being directed for his advert – a classic case of problems in cross-cultural communication. Much of the film is about how they gradually escape the isolation of their luxury hotel and go and meet some Japanese and experience parts of Japanese life, besides the relationship that they build between each other – it is a beautifully understated film which is as amusing as it is charming.

Conflict and national culture: the importance of cross-cultural negotiations

With the internationalisation of business there has been an increase in international negotiations between organisations, and this is another area where cross-cultural factors may have to be considered if some conflict is not to occur which could lead to the failure of negotiations.

There are several phases to the negotiation process: the first phase will involve the building of a relationship between the negotiators; the second phase will be the exchanging of information and stating of negotiating positions; the third part will be the discussion and persuasion phase; and finally there will be the final agreement with any concessions agreed between the two parties. It is clear that culture can impact on all these phases. For example, relationship building will be extremely important in high-context cultures such as China and Japan; this will also include informal meetings such as meals together, and thus may require several meetings for the relationship-building (the Chinese *guanxi*) to be strong enough to proceed with the key details of the negotiation. In contrast the negotiator from a Western culture will be looking for an early closure of the negotiations, and this contrast can lead to confusion and potential conflict.

In the actual negotiations themselves the question of presentation of positions may differ, in that in Eastern cultures it is seen as rude to interrupt at any stage whereas this may be seen as normal in the West as a means of clarification. We have also seen that silences are quite acceptable in the East, which might be confusing to Western negotiators. In the persuasion stage, issues like the use of threats or the use of promises can be significant; again, the ability to 'read' the non-verbal communication signs of negotiators may be significant, and the issue of 'face' has to be considered when dealing with certain countries. Finally, in the agreement phase there may be differences in terms of how the negotiation is decided: in the West it would usually be by a complicated legal document whereas in the East contracts and agreements are very short because they are built on a position of trust and therefore long contracts are not seen as important.

Mead (1998) also suggests that the timing of the negotiation and the composition of the negotiators may be significant. He suggests that you may have to consider the best time of the day to negotiate (certainly not in lunch periods for southern European cultures) or even times to avoid for religious reasons (e.g. Ramadan). The composition of the negotiating team may have to be considered when dealing with a different culture in terms of deciding the rank of people involved, their age and their gender. For example, when dealing with the Japanese, they would tend to negotiate in groups and have higher respect for older males of significant rank in the organisation. There might be problems sending younger female managers with limited status to act as negotiators in this context (see Case Study 3 'It's been a bad week at the office').

Change and national culture: the case of flexible working

The shift to flatter working structures and the increased need for the ability to react quickly to the business environment have led to a significant increase in flexible working patterns so that organisations can expand or contract more quickly in response to sudden changes in their business environment.

The traditional form of adjustment has been the use of shift work, where extra shifts of workers are added or cut in response to demand but the organisation still has significant control over the workers. Increasingly we are seeing a move towards more part-time work, with flexible hours and a shift to contract working (e.g. the use of external call centres to outsource operational functions) and teleworking. These tend to be more flexible but they pose more of a challenge for the organisation as to some extent the organisation is networking as well as controlling. Some recent studies (*see* Raghuram *et al.*, 2001) have explored whether national cultures affect the approach of companies towards flexible working and thus how they handle changes in this area.

Mini-case 10.2: Doing business in Russia

A study conducted by Barnes *et al.* (1997) questioned executives from a number of Western firms who had undertaken strategic alliances with Russian partners. Many of these had experienced culture clashes which in some cases had led to the alliances or joint ventures breaking down where incompatible cultures had caused conflict, despite the great potential offered to expand into new markets or to exploit abundant raw materials at low cost. Some of the key cultural problems that arose from the survey were an emphasis on hierarchy, the importance of national pride, *blat* (see below), the

value of mutual protection and the lack of organisational loyalty.

The emphasis on hierarchy was a leftover from the previous economic and political structures which reinforced the relatively high level of power distance in Russia. There was a need to please people in authority positions. Given the emphasis on hierarchy, knowledge and information were seen as levers of power. Withholding of information was a source of power in the organisation, a situation which contrasted with Western practice, where people are more used to sharing information throughout the organisation. This lack of openness was a means of avoiding conflict with superiors but meant that negotiations and discussions were difficult.

The importance of national pride should not be underestimated in Russia. Jones (1998) points out that there is a cultural inheritance in Russia that regards foreign investment and alliances with suspicion and often hostility. Western organisations have to be careful to avoid offending Russian pride, and certainly will not progress far if they imply superiority in one matter or another.

Blat is the process of giving favours to others based on private, often family, links. It is a mixture of nepotism and *guanxi* which is found in China. Many business agreements or activities will only succeed because of *blat*. Although networking also occurs in the West, most business dealings are based on a more open procedure, so the process of *blat* causes confusion and misunderstanding for Western businessmen or -women when dealing with Russians.

The value of mutual protection reflects the perceived need to protect each other and reinforces the need for trust to be developed. Trust is developed through personal contacts over a longer time

span than may be usual in the West. This reflects the more collective society in Russia, as compared with the individualism of the West. There is a preference for working with groups and connections rather than alone. The mutual protection afforded may relate to business or personal activities but can also be linked to corruption and crime.

The lack of organisational loyalty is difficult for some Western or Asian managers to comprehend. It stems from the old output planning system, in which there were few rewards for commitment and effort. Workers did not see themselves as part of the organisation and certainly did not trust their managers, and these attitudes have persisted.

It can be seen that some of the solutions to cultural problems with Russian strategic alliances or joint ventures lie in the areas of building good personal relations, learning to work with the hierarchical system, avoiding an ethnocentric perspective on Russia and developing organisational loyalty. These may not solve all the business problems, but may help avoid cultural conflict.

Source: Based on Barnes *et al.* (1997).

Making use of the Hofstede framework they applied it to a number of countries to examine their approach to flexible working and found a correlation between those countries with high uncertainty avoidance and high power distance, where there was a tendency to use the shift-work alternative. In countries where there was both high individualism and low power distance there appeared to be a greater willingness to explore more flexible approaches such as teleworking, and this was most noticeable in the Scandinavian countries. This suggests that cultural dimensions will have an impact on the choice of flexible working, and that to bring in too many of the more flexible approaches in countries with high uncertainty avoidance, high power distance and low individualism might lead to confusion and even conflict.

Developing cultural competencies

Given the increasing internationalisation of organisations and the growth of multicultural workforces within our own countries there is an increasing need to develop cross-cultural competencies within the organization, especially at managerial level. International managers are now more likely to have several short stays in a variety of countries, rather than the traditional expatriate manager who spends many years in one location, so the pressure is on to find managers who can adapt quickly when working in other countries and cultures. Schneider and Barsoux (2003) suggest some of the key cultural competencies are likely to be:

- the ability to build relationships and trust (especially with high-context cultures);
- some linguistic ability (a minimal level often sufficient as it shows respect);
- having the ability to cope with uncertainty;
- having some cultural empathy (through understanding of different cultures);
- having a strong sense of self (including the ability to be self-critical);
- having a good sense of humour (good as a stress reliever and important for building relationships);
- having the ability to respond to different cultures simultaneously.

Some of these factors will be inherent personality traits and may be a product of family background and early international experiences. However, some of them can be developed through professional training and education such as learning about non-verbal communications as described earlier. In Chapter 3 we looked at the growth of emotional intelligence (EI) as becoming an increasingly significant trait looked for in potential employees, and there is a similar concept of developing **cultural intelligence** (Earley and Mosakowski, 2004). It is essentially developing attitudes and skills that affect mental approaches and coping mechanisms in different cultures, having knowledge of different cultures, having a strong locus of control and self-efficacy and the ability to develop a range of physical adaptations (such as use of body language and adjusting proxemics).

Brewster *et al.* (2007) suggest that cultural intelligence (CQ) has similarities to emotional intelligence (EI) but just occurs over several cultures, rather than one, even though that could be challenged if one accepts that dealing with a multicultural workforce within one's own country is increasingly common. The discussion as to what makes for effective CQ within the organisation continues (see Triandis (2006) and Hampden-Turner and Trompenaars (2006)).

Managerial implications

Many implications for managers involved in working overseas or in other cross-cultural contact have been identified throughout this chapter. The prime implications include the following.

1 An awareness of cultural characteristics can help prepare a manager for visits overseas or for working in international management teams. This may reduce cultural shock and improve interpersonal relations with those with whom they deal.

2 Managers should be aware of cultural stereotyping and the effect this may have on relations with overseas partners, customers or suppliers.

3 Managers should be aware of effective verbal and non-verbal communication when working in different cultures.

4 Managers should consider obtaining appropriate training in cross-cultural management prior to commencement of an overseas posting or engaging in cross-national negotiation.

5 Caution should be exercised when attempting to apply organisational behaviour theories which originate in one culture (most often Anglo-American) to individuals, groups or organisations in other cultures.

6 Certain management structures, such as bureaucracy, may work better in some cultures than in others, so international managers should take culture into account when planning structural changes to the organisation.

7 International managers should develop communication and negotiation skills when dealing with other nationalities and pay particular attention to non-verbal communication in high-context cultures.

 Summary of main points

The main points made in this chapter are:

- national cultures may influence all manner of management activity and leadership styles in different countries;

- a number of key dimensions of culture have been identified by researchers in the field which serve to identify significant and measurable differences between national cultures;

- when first encountering a new culture, foreigners may experience a form of 'shock';

- cultures are always evolving, a process referred to as 'culture shift';

- national culture impacts on perceptual stereotyping;

- many theories covered in this book and in OB generally are ethnocentric and are often less applicable to non-Western cultures than they are to those from which they derive;

- the need for effective communication when seeking to collaborate with people in different cultures.

 **Conclusions**

This chapter illustrates that there is a danger in looking at organisations from a purely national, or ethnocentric, perspective. This is because organisational behaviours that are thought to be exhibited in one culture may not be commonplace in another. Prescriptions for 'how to manage' developed in the USA or in the UK or Europe will not be universally applicable. With the trend towards internationalisation and globalisation seeming ever stronger, these issues will become increasingly important for managers and workers in organisations who will have growing contact with people from other cultures and countries.

Questions

1 Identify some of the cultural differences you encountered when you last went abroad. Did these differences fit your previous perceptual stereotype of the country and did you encounter any culture shock?

2 Choose three countries and identify the commonly held perceptual stereotypes about these countries. Is there any evidence of culture shift in these countries?

3 Given the perceptions of British and Italian managers identified by Hoecklin (see Table 10.5), what problems might have ensued if the two groups had not sought to identify cultural differences at the beginning of the project? Do the countries differ significantly according to Hofstede's criteria?

4 'With new technology and globalisation pushing to ever-increasing convergence of management styles, national culture will cease to be of importance.' Discuss.

5 You are leading a team from a British company which is about to start a joint venture project with teams from China and Germany. Do you feel that your team would benefit from any cross-cultural training, and what issues might you focus on? (Make use of Hofstede's data to identify some potential areas of confusion and advise your team on possible areas of behavioural modification.)

6 Critically evaluate the extent to which national culture can influence the potential effectiveness of trans-national mergers.

References

Abramson, N., Lane, H., Nagai, H. A. and Takagi, H. (1993) 'Comparison of Canadian and Japanese cognitive styles: Implications for management interaction', *Journal of International Business Studies*, 3, pp. 575–87.

Adler, N. (1997) *International Dimensions of Organizational Behavior*, 3rd edn. Cincinnati, OH: South-Western College Publishing.

Barnes, J., Crook, M., Koyabaeva, T. and Stafford, E. (1997) 'Why our Russian alliances fail', *Long-Range Planning*, 30(4), pp. 540–9.

Barsoux, J.-L. and Lawrence, P. (1990) *Management in France*. London: Cassell.

Bond, M. and Hofstede, G. (1988) 'Confucius and economic growth: New trends in culture's consequences', *Organisational Dynamics*, 16(4), pp. 4–21.

Brewster, C., Sparrow, P. and Vernon, G. (2007) *International Human Resource Management*, 2nd edn. London: Chartered Institute of Personnel and Development.

Chen, M. (2004) *Asian Management Systems*, 2nd edn. London: Thomson Learning.

Chinese Culture Connection Group (1987) 'Chinese values and the search for culture-free dimensions of culture', *Journal of Cross-Cultural Psychology*, 18(2), pp. 143–64.

Cronbach, L. (1990) *Essentials of Psychological Testing*. New York: Harper Collins.

Earley, P. and Mosakowski, E. (2004) 'Cultural intelligence', *Harvard Business Review*, October, pp. 139–46.

Edwards, V. and Lawrence, P. (2000) *Management in Eastern Europe*. Basingstoke: Palgrave.

Elfenbein, H. (2006) 'Learning in emotion judgments: Training and the cross-cultural understanding of facial expressions', *Journal of Nonverbal Behavior*, 30(1), pp. 21–36.

Feeley, A. (2003) 'Communication across language boundaries', in *International Management*, Tayeb, M. (ed.) Harlow: Financial Times Prentice Hall, pp. 206–37.

Gatley, S., Lessem, R. and Altman, Y. (1996) *Comparative Management: A Transcultural Odyssey*. Maidenhead: McGraw-Hill.

Hall, E. T. (1976) *Beyond Culture*. New York: Doubleday.

Hampden-Turner, C. and Trompenaars, F. (1993) *The Seven Cultures of Capitalism: Value Systems for Creating Wealth in the United States, Britain, Japan, Germany, France, Sweden and the Netherlands*. New York: Doubleday.

Hampden-Turner, C. and Trompenaars, F. (1997) *Masking the Infinite Game: How East Asian Values Are Transforming Business Practices*. Oxford: Capstone.

Hampden-Turner, C. and Trompenaars, F (2006) 'Cultural intelligence: Is such a capacity credible?', *Group and Organization Management*, 31(1), pp. 56–63.

Herzberg, F. (1968) 'One more time: How do you motivate employees?', *Harvard Business Review*, 46, pp. 53–62.

Hines, G. (1973) 'Cross-cultural differences in two-factor theory', *Journal of Applied Psychology*, 58(5), pp. 375–7.

Hoecklin, L. (1995) *Managing Cultural Differences: Strategies for Competitive Advantage*. Wokingham: Addison-Wesley.

Hofstede, G. (1980) *Culture's Consequences: International Differences in Work-related Values*. Beverly Hills, CA: Sage.

Hofstede, G. (1984) *Culture's Consequences: International Differences in Work-related Values*, abridged edn. Beverly Hills, CA: Sage.

Hofstede, G. (1991) *Cultures and Organizations: Software of the Mind*. Maidenhead: McGraw-Hill.

Hofstede, G. (2001) *Culture's Consequences: Comparing Values, Behaviors, Institutions and Organizations Across Nations*, 2nd edn. Thousands Oaks, CA: Sage Publications.

Huang, Guo-gang (1989) 'On the modernization of Chinese family business', in Jiang Yi-Wei and Min Jian-Shu, *Ancient Management Practices*. Beijing: Economic Management Press, pp. 121–34.

Jackson, T. (1993) *Organizational Behaviour in International Management*. Oxford: Butterworth-Heinemann.

Jones, A. (1998) 'Assessing the obstacles to FDI in Russia', Paper presented at CREEB Conference.

King, V. (1998) *A Simple Guide to Malaysia*. Folkestone: Global Books.

Kluckhohn, F. and Strodtbeck, F. (1961) *Variations in Value Orientations*. New York: Peterson.

Kroeber, A. and Kluckhohn, C. (1985) *Culture: A Critical Review of Concepts and Definitions*. New York: Random House.

Laurent, A. (1983) 'The cultural diversity of Western conceptions of management', *International Studies of Management and Organization*, 13, pp. 75–96.

Laurent, A., Adler, N. and Campbell, N. C. (1989) 'In search of appropriate methodology: From outside the People's Republic of China looking in', *Journal of International Business Studies*, Spring, pp. 61–74.

Levitt, T. (1983) 'The globalization of markets', *Harvard Business Review*, May–June.

Lonner, W. (1990) 'An overview of cross-cultural testing and assessment' in Brislin, R. (ed.) *Applied Cross-Cultural Psychology*. Newbury Park, CA: Sage.

McClelland, D. C. and Burnham, D. H. (1976) 'Power is the great motivation', *Harvard Business Review*, 4, March–April, pp. 99–112.

Maslow, A. H. (1943) 'A theory of human motivation', *Psychological Review*, 50(4), pp. 370–96.

Mead, M. (ed.) (1951) *Cultural Patterns and Technical Change*. Paris: UNESCO.

Mead, R. (1998) *International Management*, 2nd edn. Oxford: Blackwell Business.

Michailova, S. (1996) 'Approaching the macro–micro interface in transitional societies: Evidence from Bulgaria', *Journal for East European Management Studies*, 1(1), pp. 43–70.

Murdoch, G. P. (1945) 'The common denominator of cultures', in Linton, R. (ed.) *The Science of Man in the World Crisis*. New York: Columbia University Press, pp. 123–42.

Nevis, E. (1983) 'Cultural assumptions and productivity: The United States and China', *Sloan Management Review*, Spring, pp. 17–29.

Onedo, A. (1991) 'The motivation and need satisfaction of Papua New Guinea managers', *Asia-Pacific Journal of Management*, 8, pp. 121–9.

Pavlica, K. and Thorpe, R. (1998) 'Managers' perceptions of the identity: A comparative study between the Czech Republic and Britain', *British Journal of Management*, 9(2), pp. 133–49.

Pearce, J. L. and Branyiczki, I. (1993) 'Revolutionizing bureaucracies: Managing change in Hungarian state-owned bureaucracies', *Journal of Organizational Change Management*, 2, pp. 53–64.

Raghuram, S., London, M. and Larsen H. (2001) 'Flexible employment practices in Europe: Country versus culture' *International Journal of Human Resource Management*', 12(5), pp. 738–53.

Ronen, S. and Shenkar, O. (1985) 'Clustering countries on attitudinal dimensions: A review and synthesis', *Academy of Management Review*, July, pp. 445–54.

Schneider, S. and Barsoux, J.-L. (2003) *Managing across Cultures*, 2nd edn, Harlow: Financial Times Prentice Hall.

Tayeb, M. (ed.) (2003) *International Management: Theories and Practices*. Harlow: Financial Times Prentice Hall.

Torbiorn, I. (1982) *Living Abroad: Personal Adjustment and Personnel Policy in an Overseas Setting*. New York: Wiley.

Triandis, H (2006) 'Cultural intelligence in organizations', *Group and Organisation Management*, 31(1), pp. 20–6.

Trompenaars, F. (1993) *Riding the Waves of Culture*. London: Nicholas Brealey.

Vroom, V. H. (1964) *Work and Motivation*. New York: Wiley.

 ## Further reading

Adler, N. (1997) *International Dimensions of Organizational Behavior*, 3rd edn. Cincinnati, OH: South-Western College.

Chatterjee, S. and Nankervis, A. (2007) *Asian Management in Transition*. Basingstoke: Palgrave Macmillan.

Gatley, S., Lessem, R. and Altem, Y. (1996) *Comparative Management: A Transcultural Odyssey*. Maidenhead: McGraw-Hill.

Jackson, T. (ed.) (1995) *Cross-Cultural Management*. Oxford: Butterworth-Heinemann.

Mead, R. (1998) *International Management*, 2nd edn. Oxford: Blackwell Business.

Schneider, S. and Barsoux, J.-L. (2003) *Managing across Cultures,* 2nd edn. Harlow: Financial Times Prentice Hall.

Tayeb, M. (2003) *International Management: Theories and Practices*. Harlow: Financial Times Prentice Hall.

Warner, M. and Joynt, P. (2002) *Managing across Cultures: Issues and Perspectives,* 2nd edn. London: Thomson Learning.

 ## Internet sites

www.executiveplanet.com This is a highly recommended site to find out behavioural and cultural issues relating to a wide range of countries.

www.cyborlink.com For information on international business etiquette and manners.

www.itapintl.com Typical example of a company offering cross-cultural consultancy services.

www.international-business-center.com Has useful links, e.g. Hofstede analysis.

Case studies

This final section of the book contains three case studies, each of which draws upon and reinforces many of the principles, concepts and understandings covered in this book. The reader is invited to analyse critically the scenarios portrayed in an attempt to 'get beneath the surface' of human behaviour in organisations.

The grid below illustrates the fit between each case and each chapter. Whereas each case can illustrate many aspects of organisational behaviour it might, equally, be used to focus on one area, such as motivation or teamwork.

Chapter:	2: Organisational theory	3: Individual	4: Motivation	5: Groups and teams	6: Leadership	7: Structure	8: Power and politics	9: Organisational culture	10: National culture
Case 1 ● Motivated teams: an inter-cultural case	**	*	***	***	**	**	*	**	***
Case 2 ● Organisational change: multiskilling in the healthcare sector	**	**	**	***	**	**	***	***	
Case 3 ● 'It's been a bad week at the office . . .'	***	*			*	*	**	*	***

Key

*   some relevace

**   significant relevance

***   major relevance/focus

Case 1

Motivated teams: an inter-cultural case

This case explores how a simple yet sound recognition of the value of people in the workplace takes shape on the ground. The context is a Swedish-owned heavy truck assembly plant which is located in France. The case outlines the novel processes of work organisation employed in this complex multicultural setting. Although both are European countries, Sweden and France are, in key cultural terms, polar opposites, and this case represents an example of a successful inter-cultural business activity.

The case looks at the nature of, and differences between, Swedish and French national cultures in an attempt to account for the success of the plant and the skill of its managers in overcoming potential cultural pitfalls and discusses the contributions made by each culture to the success story. It is based on a series of semi-structured interviews with senior management from both France and Sweden and observation of activities on the ground.

 Scania, Angers (SAN)

The plant is owned by Scania, a Swedish multinational organisation primarily concerned with the manufacture and marketing of trucks and buses. Trucks for the French, Italian and Iberian markets are assembled in Angers in a converted combine harvester plant covering 50,000 square metres. Since it opened in 1992, output has increased significantly and production plans suggest that a continued increase is possible for some time to come. The plant produced 7 trucks a day in January 1994, increasing to 30 trucks a day in 1995. In 1998 it produced around 40 trucks a day, 45 in 2001, 50 in 2005, and this can now be almost doubled by the introduction of a second shift.

There are just four levels of hierarchy in the plant including the managing director and seven senior managers. All but one of the senior managers are Swedish, serving fourteen French cluster managers and their teams.

Management philosophy and the cluster team

A teamwork approach filters through all aspects of organisational life. Involvement in teamwork is not an option. Thorough socialisation and continuous training and coaching is the norm. One of the few French senior managers, Geraldine Proux, spells out, in a style characteristic of her culture, SAN's philosophy (*see* Figure C1.1). Teamwork is central to this

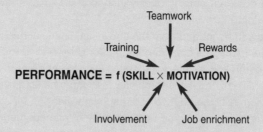

Figure C1.1 Teamwork and the performance equation at Scania, Angers

function as a prime mechanism for the development of skills and as an important source of personal motivation.

Teamwork and employee involvement in plant-wide work processes and in the broader aspects of company activity are regarded by management as a vital motivational tool and, therefore, as a performance-enhancing investment. Training is viewed similarly.

The work cluster

The basic form of work organisation focuses on the cluster team. Clusters are described by the managing director as '*a technical unit of production made up of workers who assemble components forming a semi-finished or manufactured product*'. They are a team which is responsible for a discrete element of production. For example, one cluster is responsible for assembling the cab, others for construction of the engines and the brake systems; another manages delivery of the trucks.

The focus in the plant is the cluster organisation. All managers are clear in their determination to insist that all activities have to be justified in terms of their value added to the cluster operation. The cluster manager has overall responsibility for the team of between 20 and 25 employees. No further formal hierarchy exists in each cluster although each comprises people with differing skill levels and experience. In general terms each cluster member is multiskilled (French = *polyvalent*) and enjoys a long period of initial training and induction, partly in the cluster, before becoming fully operative. This multiskilling allows greater flexibility and frequent job rotation possibilities in a teamwork setting. With a supervisory or managerial ratio of about 1 : 20, clearly cluster teams are largely self-directed.

Although the precise responsibilities of each team vary depending on the array of tasks they are expected to perform, they are all responsible for:

- budget (including salary negotiations);
- materials handling;
- quality inspection;
- recruitment;
- components subassembly and line assembly;
- daily preventative maintenance;
- cleaning up.

SAN does not employ quality inspectors. Clusters are charged with the goal of achieving continual improvement.

As can be judged from the above list, financial decisions are largely decentralised, giving cluster managers considerable personal responsibility. Costs, the financial manager argues, 'are controlled at the point where they are generated'. Hence the senior finance manager, rather like his quality and human resources colleagues, actively serves the clusters in helping them fulfil their duties and responsibilities.

It is seen as a prime responsibility of management to develop employee motivation by giving the necessary leadership and support to teams. Hence cluster managers will establish the team targets, in conjunction with group members. Teams then enjoy a degree of flexibility in how they achieve these targets.

All new employees undergo a lengthy period of training which has two prime objectives. First, workers learn the skills required to operate effectively in one of the clusters. Second, they are educated in the way of working, the operational philosophies, team ethos and management styles.

Have cluster teams proven successful?

Productivity in the plant has exceeded targets established in Sweden. Quality levels have shown continuous improvements since the plant opened in 1992 and are already comparable to those in Sweden and Holland. Output has increased significantly and is set to continue to rise. Absenteeism is very low by any standards, at about 2–2.5 per cent. This compares favourably with the French norm for manufacturing and assembly plants of 5 per cent. Safety standards are continually measured and all targets have been met or surpassed. The working environment appears relaxed and relatively stress-free. Staff at all levels appear to be well motivated.

Teamwork at all levels and in all relationships

Teamwork is a central tenet of the management philosophy and culture of SAN. Teams operate at all levels, in all departments, at all functions and between each level, department and function. Hence there are small, often temporary, teams in each cluster, such as a small subassembly group. The cluster itself is managed and operates as a team. Workers feel a sense of belonging to the whole cluster and, as quality standards suggest, take a pride in their cluster's output. In this participative environment teams contribute to defining and developing action plans at one level and are actively encouraged to show an interest and become involved in company-wide activities and concerns.

The management at SAN has attempted to identify the requirements for successful corporate teamwork. This is viewed in the context of the customer–supplier or the inter-group relationship. The responsibilities of each are made clear during initial, and often subsequent, training and are also continually reinforced by management and peer group feedback. The receiver or customer is required to:

- define their needs clearly;
- justify those needs in respect to the objectives of SAN;
- ensure that meeting the request will contribute added value;
- give feedback to the sender or supplier.

The sender or supplier is expected to:

● know, and if necessary help define, the customer's requirements;

● manage priorities in the interests of overall SAN objectives;

● seek consensus in the exchange of information;

● keep their clients informed of progress;

● supply a service which meets reliability, quality, time limit and cost standards.

Customer–supplier relationships are encouraged at the interface between cluster teams. Hence the boundary is characterised by cooperation and the adoption of a supportive attitude. This helps to ensure a seamless handover of each cluster's finished product.

All managerial personnel in SAN employ a consultancy-style approach with those colleagues who avail themselves of their service. In fact SAN management argues that the customer–supplier relationship extends to all contact of an interpersonal, interdepartmental and external nature and that customer satisfaction is the prime objective.

Individualism and trust

No one is required to clock in or out of the plant and no formal check is kept of people's timekeeping. Obviously expectations are set and these are, with very few exceptions, met. Yet this individual responsibility is monitored, more often than not, by peers within a team framework.

Each cluster member has an annual review with the cluster manager. This serves two major purposes: to negotiate salary on the basis of experience and skills level and to ascertain training and development needs. During the interview managers establish the record of the worker over the past year from both a quantitative and a qualitative perspective. Objectives for the forthcoming year are also set during the review. The assessors are given training to assure fairness, consistency and objectivity in this process. This method of pay negotiation rejects uniformity and aims to ensure that merit awards are based on each individual's results. Collective bargaining does not exist. Hence the cluster manager has a considerably wider brief than the more traditional supervisor in an assembly plant.

The performance interview is also viewed as a management tool to help forge a strong, company-orientated, organisational culture. Marie Robidou (HRM Director) argues, 'The interview . . . represents a concern for fairness in that everyone who takes part must be aware of any difference between the company's system of values and their own.' It is clear that certain attitudes are required of all employees. As a senior manager suggests, 'No one must be able to say "that is not my concern, I am not responsible for that".'

Consequences of cultural differences and similarities

Scania is a Swedish company and the managing director and the majority of its senior management team are Swedish and exclusively male. Almost the entire workforce, including junior managers and cluster managers in the plant at Angers, are French. Table C1.1 shows the rankings of Sweden and France on Hofstede's (1980) four indices (see Chapter 10).

Table C1.1   Swedish and French rankings on Hofstede's cultural indices

Cultural variable	France*	Sweden*
Power distance index (1st = large hierarchial power distance)	15	47
Uncertainty index (1st = strong containment of uncertainty by creating order)	10	49
Masculinity–femininity index (1st = highly masculine culture)	35	53
Individualism index (1st = individualism is culturally strong and collectivism is weak)	10=	10=

* Ranking, out of 53 countries.
Source: Hofstede (2001).

On three of the four indices in Table C1.1 there is a significant difference in score and ranking between French and Swedish cultures. Ironically on the fourth, the individualism index, the two countries are identical. It is this index, individualism–collectivism, which is most successful in predicting the possibility of successful teamwork. The index implies that teamwork, or collective concern and endeavour, does not come easily to either culture. It may account for the degree of individualism still apparent in this teamwork context and, hence, the compromises that exist. For example, salary negotiations, performance payments and training needs analyses are all conducted at the level of the individual. The rankings of other countries on the individualism index include: USA 1st, UK 3rd, Germany 15th, Japan 22nd.

The two most significant differences between the countries are on the power distance and uncertainty avoidance indices. On these two important criteria Sweden and France represent extremes in a European context (*see* Figure C1.2). French culture supports the maintenance of large power distances between different groups, both in the workplace and in society in general. Swedish culture seeks to minimise such differences and embraces a

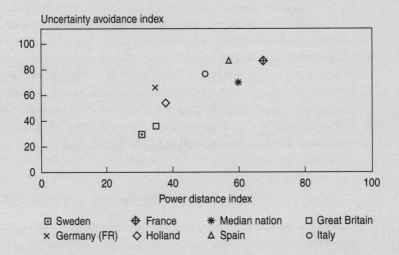

Figure C1.2   France and Sweden: cultural comparisons on power distance and uncertainty avoidance
Source: Data from Hofstede (2001).

strong commitment to egalitarianism. Just a handful of countries in Hofstede's sample score lower on the power distance index than Sweden. The Swedish belief in people is legendary. A number of historical, social and economic factors conspire to encourage this enviable trait. Associated with the egalitarian norm is the norm of accessibility: Swedish managers tend to be highly approachable and open. In fact it is argued that in Sweden managers have to have a good reason for not seeing an employee!

The difference between the two cultures is significant in relation to their desire to avoid uncertainty and associated anxiety. The French have a firm desire to avoid uncertainty, which usually means that rules and bureaucratic procedures dominate. This contrasts sharply with the more laid-back Swedish character. The Swedish are very tolerant of uncertainty in the workplace and are less concerned to organise, regiment or tie down everything and everyone.

The work environment in France is likely to be characterised by authoritarian, top-down management styles, hierarchies and formal procedures. Theory and logic are stressed. By contrast the Swedish are likely to be more informal and easy-going. Lateral communications and networks are more important, as is consensus building.

Evidence abounds in SAN that managers not only think about culture, but also think culturally, both at the level of the organisation and on a national level. This is evidenced not least by the choice of the word 'cluster', which was chosen intentionally as a culturally neutral term in France. The Swedish management team are acutely aware of the potential tensions that exist and the natural tendencies of many employees to revert to traditional attitudes and behaviours.

Some problems, possibly of cultural origin, do occur. These problems highlight some issues with which managers in inter-cultural settings have to cope. They stress the need for continuous cultural vigilance. Managers take steps to prevent any mass retreat of people to their cultural homeland. The Swedes at this plant are experienced international managers; thinking culturally is second nature to them.

Conclusion

This case has outlined the prime features of a management philosophy being acted out in a cross-cultural setting. Managers at Angers are not complacent; they are fully aware of the continued efforts needed on everyone's part to ensure that the cluster philosophy takes root and grows. They are also aware that teamwork does not come naturally to culture-bound individuals from either France or Sweden. However, their unswerving belief in people transcends all differences and difficulties and promises continued success for this and other plants adopting similar principles.

The management style and methods of work organisation outlined in this case represent a significant compromise with French cultural norms. They have been required to make more sacrifices than their Swedish masters. One may suggest that the Swedish are guilty of cultural imperialism; however, their actions have created a paradoxical scenario, that of imposed empowerment. They have required French workers and management to conform, by and large, to their culture-laden management philosophy. It appears that they have been vindicated by success.

Reference

Hofstede, G. (2001) *Culture's Consequences: Comparing Values, Behaviors, Institutions and Organizations Across Nations, 2nd edn. Thousand Oaks*, CA: Sage Publications.

Questions

These questions should help to relate this case study to the materials presented in the book. This case study covers considerable OB territory and these are but a few potential questions of value.

Motivation and groupwork

1 With reference to Chapter 4 of this book, which covers motivation, attempt to explain why employees at Scania, Angers, are or appear to be well motivated.

2 Why might a group-based work process achieve greater productivity and lower staff turnover than more traditional production-line operations?

Organisation and leadership theory

3 How do the management philosophy and practices at SAN differ from those suggested by Henri Fayol (*see* Chapter 2)? How is control achieved in this plant?

4 How would you describe the prevailing leadership style employed in the plant? How have situational variables influenced that style?

National culture

5 What 'contribution' does each culture make to the apparent success of this plant; that is, what are both the Swedish and French qualities which contribute to this success? Do you consider this to be a case of cultural imperialism?

6 A few problems have been encountered at SAN which may, in part at least, be cultural in origin. For each of the problems identified below, attempt to suggest a plausible cultural explanation.

a *Problem*: the French, who make up the vast majority of the workforce, are not natural team players. Perhaps the real problem is that neither are the Swedish!

b *Problem*: cluster managers oppose a reduction in their 'territory' as new clusters are added.

c *Problem*: rapid expansion has led to a reduction in socialisation training: a few workers have experienced problems fitting in.

d *Problem*: (i) there is some confusion among employees over hierarchical grade and pay and status differentials; e.g. two specialist engineers are unwilling to work alongside as 'equals' with the half-dozen technicians; and (ii) workers in clusters are not hierarchically graded and have no official title. Many want to be given a title with an associated grade like their colleagues in other French firms.

e *Problem*: some French managers tend to put a great deal of effort into paperwork which is of marginal value. As one Swedish manager put it, 'they produce lots of stuff which is done very well but serves little purpose [whereas] we do practical things but don't necessarily do it well'.

Organisational change: multiskilling in the healthcare sector

Introduction

This case study looks at an attempt to introduce multiskilled, ward-based teams of support workers in a medium-sized NHS Trust hospital in the UK. Although only directly involving about 250 people in an organisation employing over 2800 staff, the change represented part of a wider, strategic transformation in the NHS with its focus on human resource issues. The driving force is an attempt to realise continual improvement in quality and value for money.

This case is relevant to those studying organisational behaviour, human resources management (HRM) and organisational change: analysis is reinforced by an understanding of motivation, group and teamwork, organisational theory, power and politics, leadership, change management, organisational structure and culture and various HRM issues.

The microcontext: a medium-sized NHS Trust hospital

The case is set in a NHS Trust which provides a full range of acute and midwifery services to a population of about a quarter of a million people. The Trust's income is around £70 million a year and it employs over 2800 personnel (about 1650 full-time equivalents). Of its employees, 62 per cent work part-time; over 80 per cent of all personnel are female. Forty-three per cent of staff have over five years' tenure. The staff turnover rate is rather low compared with that of many urban hospitals and is declining. Absenteeism, for sickness, currently stands at 3.6 per cent which compares favourably with many hospitals and other public- and private-sector organisations. Absenteeism among ancillary staff, those largely affected by this change, is about double the hospital average.

The Site Services Directorate was responsible for the implementation of generic, or multiskilled, working. This directorate broadly comprised two major areas of responsibility, one of which is Hotel Services, in which domestic and portering staff are located, managed by a Deputy Director of Site Services, Alf Turner. Hotel Services and, more specifically, its Director, Michelle Stacy, 'owned' the change and defined and refined it during residential management team meetings and subsequent attempts at implementation.

Change content: the generic worker concept

This section outlines the nature of, and rationale for, the attempted introduction of the generic worker concept. It was one of seven key changes outlined in the Trust's business plan, 2000–01, which included significant reductions in waiting times, compliance with government initiatives and the introduction of major new information systems. The relevant objective states: 'To introduce teams of generic hotel service assistants at ward level so as to improve flexibility and responsiveness to patient needs by combining the role of porters, domestics and catering staff.' The change aimed to devolve all portering and domestic staff to ward level. They would be multiskilled and consequently able to undertake a full range of domestic and portering roles, including cleaning, transporting patients, moving equipment and serving food.

The change involved all porters and domestic staff. In total these roles account for 151 whole-time equivalent (WTE) staff, of which porters account for 44 WTE and domestics (cleaners and 'ward hostesses') 107 WTE. As many domestics work part-time the total headcount involved in this change was approximately 250 people. Some of the porters are assigned to specific departments or directorates, such as X-ray, but most are 'located' in a central pool and respond to demand for their services. There are three porter-managers. The domestics are divided into teams under a supervisor and are designated an area of the hospital to clean and in which to conduct other duties, such as serving food and assisting nursing ancillary staff. They can, on occasion, respond to domestic emergencies and alter their normal routines. All these staff are employed in the Site Services Directorate, and report to managers in that unit, a fact which often creates frustration elsewhere in the Trust. This is particularly so in the case of ward managers, who have little control over the activities of the domestics.

The management philosophy underpinning the generic worker concept is a familiar one. A multiskilled, flexible workforce is thought to facilitate operational planning and enhance both the efficiency and effectiveness of service provision. The assumption is that employees benefit from the resultant job enrichment and cooperative teamwork; cost savings are there for the making via enhanced efficiency, and patient care is improved.

The scope and scale of change

It was proposed that all domestic and portering staff were to be based at ward level rather than, as at present, in a central 'pool'. Most would require additional training to undertake food serving, cleaning and portering roles. Staff would then undertake a wider array of tasks and be required to embrace flexibility and teamwork. All existing formal status and pay differentials between members of Hotel Services, with the exception of management, would be removed. As a consequence of generic working, many staff were to be upgraded and all would receive a basic pay rise representing 2 per cent for porters and 8 per cent for domestic staff. Performance pay was to be based upon attendance. Overtime and weekend working would be carefully monitored in an attempt to reduce costs. Some staff would be required to change their shift pattern and the total hours they work in any one week. The change directly involved about 250 people and included taking on an extra 35,000 hours' work a year previously allocated to nursing assistants.

Talk on the ground

It was thought that the successful implementation of generic working would bring many potential benefits from a managerial perspective. Almost without exception, managers stressed its positive features. The Finance Director, Dalbir Khangura, argued that successful implementation would help to 'provide good value for money' and 'make cost savings'. It would ensure, for the time being at least, competitiveness with external commercial players. The single grade and pay spine, which would apply to all 250 generic workers, would reduce status differentials and simplify the highly complex bonus schemes that had evolved. From an operational point of view it would bring enormous benefits of flexibility and would simplify work scheduling. Managers argued that it would serve to 'even out' the workload for porters and improve efficiency by avoiding 'waiting for action time' and 'wasted journeys' and other 'duplication of effort'. Therefore, not inconsiderable cost savings could be realised. It would formalise control, especially over porters who are 'difficult to track down'. It might, for example, stop porters using their 'pull' over nursing staff. The HRM Director, Philippa Davies, felt it would improve worker motivation as porters would 'feel part of a team' and 'be included if chocolates were given out or nights out were planned'. They would 'take a pride in their work' and be 'recognised at ward level'. One manager responsible for its implementation suggested that generic working is 'going to make it very clear what I am providing and to whom', so facilitating the provision of an up-to-date service-level agreement and competitive tendering.

Terry Abra, the manager responsible for establishing the pilot scheme which ran on one large ward, argued that 'The domestics think it's a great idea', 'Women will go for it to see the men cleaning' and 'They really enjoy the varied workload'. Others attempted to explain why staff were positive about change with comments like, 'Now they don't know what other duties they're going to be doing and they really enjoy that so their job satisfaction has gone up'. However, managers were far less effusive when asked to identify likely reasons for, or sources of, resistance to the implementation of generic working. Issues focused on likely demarcation concerns at the interface between Hotel Services and other groups such as nurses and, within Hotel Services, between porters, cleaners and domestic staff.

Friction

Mr Abra, concerned over the issue of 'ownership' of tasks, commented that 'Basically if anything needs moving we move it, if it needs feeding we feed it, if it needs cleaning we clean it and that's what generic working is about'. Needless to say, tensions arose at the interface between Hotel Services and nursing. The manager responsible for establishing the pilot scheme which ran on one large ward, commented, 'We looked at taking over the service of dispensing food to patients'. Hotel Services believed their staff to be better trained to carry out food dispensing duties. Some ancillary nurses were reported to have 'felt very threatened' and responded with, 'Oh well, that's your job now, I'm not doing it'. Part of the change process involved the reallocation of duties, such as food dispensing to

Implementation: structure and process

patients, from nursing to domestic staff. This amounted to 37,500 hours' work a year and a movement of resources from clinical directorates to the Site Services Directorate.

Personal involvement in the change process was heightened for those managers at the interface between domestic staff and supervisors, as success in introducing generic working would have eased many of the tensions involved in operating the current system. Scheduling tasks would be simplified as would pay and bonus schemes. A number of managers and staff expressed a strong desire to reduce the level of uncertainty they faced under the current system. One porter commented at the commencement of the project, 'At present the porters are understaffed and suffering from low morale with a poor sickness record. The portering service can best be described as "fire-fighting" – there is no service-level agreement in place against which to measure performance.'

One of the major contentious issues which arose during the pilot scheme was that of work rotas. A Directorate General Manager (DGM), Lucy Brooks, from a clinical directorate, commented: 'The goalposts have been endlessly moving . . . it changes with the wind. One minute they were going to be doing XYZ and then the next minute it was ABC.' Another argued, 'They were told that all the rotas would be displayed [and] there would be no names attached – they would apply for which rota they wanted. When they saw the rotas they reckoned that they were all fixed for specific people.' Another manager, 'close' to the change, argued, 'The rotas are so difficult to follow [that] when they went up on the board it was "Where's my job? I haven't got a job", so if they vote no it's because we've changed hours and changed rotas.'

Implementation: structure and process

A small management team comprising the Director of Site Services, her deputy and the managers of domestic and portering staff fine-tuned, 'customised' and planned the implementation of this initiative. The manager specifically responsible for the day-to-day implementation of the concept, the head of the domestic staff, Terry Abra, was a junior/middle manager, at the fourth tier of management. She played a relatively minor role in the decision to introduce the initiative in the hospital or in its inclusion in the Trust's business plan. A subordinate of hers, a first-line supervisory manager responsible for portering staff, Gaurav Dhama, managed the daily 'portering' operations in a pilot scheme on the Ivan Goode Ward. The small management team were enthusiastic and dedicated. They articulated the benefits of the scheme with conviction.

A pilot scheme ran for a year, during which time issues were raised and discussed, changes were made and plans were altered. The pilot involved about 12 domestic and portering staff. The original aim was to appoint a team leader who would allocate duties as they arose. This was thought to have created unnecessary sources of uncertainty and a system of management allocation of tasks on a more permanent basis was soon adopted in the pilot. Those managing the change did not gather the whole workforce together to discuss the changes. Such a process, they felt, would prove difficult. Instead they believed that if it could be made to work well on the pilot scheme then the good news would spread and people would come on board. Thus they relied quite heavily on the undoubted power of the informal communication process as opposed to numerous team briefings. They also utilised the staff noticeboard to display rotas and other important developments.

Teething problems

Many of the porters, almost exclusively male, quite openly expressed their unwillingness to undertake cleaning duties, which some thought were 'women's work'. This gender issue raised its head in many consultations between porters and managers and was a frequent topic of conversation between porters. One manager commented, 'Porters believe the girls are going to be running off doing portering duties all the time and they are going to spend all their time cleaning . . . and they've got these views from the union.' Other 'demarcation' issues were also brought to the fore during the pilot scheme. A group of domestics, known as 'ward hostesses', enjoyed a somewhat privileged position among their colleagues whose work focused almost exclusively on cleaning, involving little or no contact with patients or clinical personnel. The subgroups comprising the generic worker role were often referred to as 'tribes' by managers from across the hospital. One Hotel Services manager said, 'We arranged awareness sessions with nursing staff but no one turned up to them.' One manager, expressing a certain powerlessness, summarised the nature of the problems: 'It is about boundaries between groups. We have nurses, PAMs [professionals allied to medicine], physios, doctors – all these groups, and making them work in teams is impossible.'

Terry Abra suggested domestic staff believe that this is simply 'a cost improvement exercise'. The trade union (UNISON) convener, Pete Frost, openly and persistently recorded his disapproval of the extent of the proposed changes. It strongly opposed generic working from the outset and advised all its members not to facilitate its implementation. Such a change would fundamentally alter the terms and conditions of employees and would necessitate contractual changes and facilitate local determination of pay and conditions. This would contravene national union policy and UNISON's clear position regarding local bargaining. Employees had not yet accepted the principle, let alone the practice, of local determination of pay and conditions.

In a series of meetings between managers in Hotel Services and UNISON representatives debate was often hostile and, allegedly, personal. Few minutes were kept of meetings and little signed and agreed documentation exists. A senior manager suggested that, 'If you're going to negotiate with the unions you get your shopping basket and work out what it's going to cost you' and 'There were few minutes [which] were not jointly signed and nobody had worked out the costs beforehand and [as a consequence] they were always arguing about things which one side thought was agreed three meetings ago.'

Tension before the ballot

The pilot scheme ended with a union ballot aimed at ascertaining the staff's position vis-à-vis acceptance or otherwise of generic working. On the eve of the vote, managers in Hotel Services felt it would be a close-run affair. They were unsure of staff collective opinion and nervous about the outcome. A number of managers argued that the union vote was couched in terms that were tantamount to a vote of confidence in the union itself. One suggested that, 'In a way they were being asked to vote "do you support your union?": management one side, union the other'. Emotional investment in the change process was not inconsiderable, as Terry Abra's comment suggests: 'I'll be very sorry if they do throw it out . . . I'll be quite upset from their point of view. It'll be easier to manage and the main reason we are here is for the patients.'

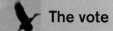 ## The vote

Union members in Hotel Services were eligible to vote in the UNISON-organised ballot on the single issue of generic working. Twelve staff voted in favour of change, 150 against, the rest abstained. The scale of rejection left little doubt concerning the level of resistance to the change initiative. In the face of this clear rejection the planned change as proposed by management will not now be implemented in the foreseeable future. This result does not indicate, however, that the change scenario was a failure; judgement of that nature would depend on one's perspective.

It is appropriate to conclude this case with the HRM Director's thought-provoking comment: 'Inside the hospital is a little cottage with roses hanging over the door, where everything is just as it has always been, and it's all quite happy. Nothing is touching that. Nothing is touching the real heart of what is going on.'

Questions

Motivation

1 How might the motivation of staff have been affected during the change process? Use any theoretical frameworks presented in Chapter 4 to support your answer.

Team/group work

2 What are the merits and drawbacks of the kind of multiskilled teams which this change would have helped to encourage?

Organisational structure

3 What does this case tell us about contemporary management thinking regarding organisational structures and individual roles?

Change, culture and politics

4 What sources of power, or power bases, are threatened by this change?

5 How important is the context of change to the implementation process? How did the context in this case influence the final outcome of the change process?

6 What was the scale of this change for those staff involved in the process, that is, those who were expected to become generic workers?

7 Why was this change initiative, which held so much promise and generated such enthusiasm from management, so emphatically rejected by staff? Drawing on the work of Morgan (1986, 1996) as noted in Chapter 2, together with materials presented elsewhere, attempt to give (a) a managerial, (b) a cultural and (c) a political explanation for the 'failure' of this initiative.

Case 3

'It's been a bad week at the office ...'

Ellen Harris put the phone in her office down slowly with her mind racing. She had just telephoned her partner Martin to ask if he could pick up their seven-year-old daughter Claire from school as the school had rung Ellen five minutes earlier to say Claire was feeling under the weather and should go home. Martin had claimed that he was in the middle of important business and unable to pick up Claire, yet Ellen had her doubts as he had been acting defensively ever since she had got the promotion. In addition she had a further meeting in an hour with Mr Hayashi and his team about the proposed strategic alliance between their companies and she sensed that things had not gone well in the meeting they had had yesterday. As she started working her way through friends who could pick up Claire she found herself muttering under her breath, 'it's been a bad week at the office ...' and started thinking back to the events of the week.

As she reflected, she thought that in many ways she felt positive in her work. The company she was working for, Glazers Lawn Solutions, was back on track after having had a rocky couple of years under the old management team. The company, based in Cobblerton, specialised in producing motorised lawn-mowers which were quite expensive but of good quality and which were used for customers requiring large expanses of grass to be controlled. The company was medium-sized with 140 employees but had gone into decay through a lack of new ideas and investment from the family firm that originally controlled it. Six months ago it had been bought out by a new investor who had put new funds into development and had also completely restructured the company to make it flatter and more flexible than previously. The new owner, Mike Lynch, had also decided that the future lay in internationalising the company and had set up talks with Fujimori Mowers from Osaka in Japan, which specialised in smaller mowers, with a view to developing a strategic alliance between the companies, built around distribution of each other's products and joint marketing and development projects. A large team from Fujimori Mowers had arrived this week for crucial talks, on which the future of the alliance probably depended.

Ellen had benefited from the restructuring and reorganisation which Mike Lynch had carried out in the company. She had joined the company four years earlier as a Marketing Assistant with special responsibilities for linking product development with promotion in the marketplace. She had a degree in Marketing and business experience (although not in mowers) and settled in well with her colleagues and mixed well with them, helped by her sense of humour and approachability. At this stage Martin had been quite happy for her to take the job as it added to their joint income, although Ellen had to ask for some flexibility from the firm in order to pick up Claire from school, whenever one of her friends was unable to do this. The Marketing Director, Bob Gannon, seemed a bit remote but his deputy, Bill Murray, was friendly towards her and helped 'to show her the ropes' whilst she settled into her job, as he had been with the company for several years and was now in his mid-fifties. Ellen had been happy in her job although she was frustrated about the lack of Marketing strategy in the company and had written a couple of reports about this which seem to have lain, undisturbed, on Bob Gannon's desk.

The arrival of Mike Lynch had changed everything with his desire to turn the company around and move it forwards. He had spent a couple of months evaluating things in the company and then brought forward dramatic changes by delayering the company, improving communications and developing teamworking as a means of developing innovation within the company. He was keen to share information around the organisation and change the culture to a much more proactive one. Unfortunately this had led to casualties with some redeployment of jobs and some jobs disappearing altogether. One of the first casualties had been Bob Gannon who quickly left to join another company. Everyone had assumed that Bill would take over the Marketing role but Mike Lynch had asked Ellen to apply as well, having finally read some of her reports about Marketing Strategy and having been impressed by them. This had been quite a shock for Ellen but an even greater shock when she had actually been appointed Marketing Director by Mike Lynch. He had said that although she was only 36 she had shown the drive and strategic awareness that he felt was needed if the company was to change its culture and move forward.

Ellen had been in the job for four months now and although she had found herself very busy, she had also found it challenging and with her income now substantially higher than her husband's, she felt it would help the family and maybe they could move to a bigger house in the future. She had spent much of her time in developing a new strategic marketing plan and in restructuring the Marketing Department in order to split responsibilities and devolve decision-making to people. She had also tried to increase the number of team meetings in the group as well. Whilst she had enjoyed the challenge of the new work in terms of devising the new strategy and meeting key clients, she had increasingly felt that all was not well in the Marketing Department and some events this week had made her think increasingly about this problem.

One of these was the attitude of Bill Murray who was now effectively Ellen's deputy. Although Bill was always polite to her she felt that he wasn't too happy about being overlooked for the promotion and that a distance was growing between them. Even worse was the fact that she had asked Bill to map out the marketing implications of the proposed joint venture and the report he had done for her was, frankly, lacking in depth and limited in scope. It had been a complex challenge for Bill but he had assured her that he could handle it. One of the younger members of the Marketing Department, Pavel Sokota, had been keen to be involved in the Japanese project and Ellen was thinking of asking him to upgrade the report that Bill had done before submitting it, with her recommendations, to Mike. The problem was that Bill thought he coped well with the report and that it was fine as it stood.

Another issue that had troubled her was that of her relationship with the other members of the marketing group. She had always got on well with them and sometimes enjoyed a drink with them after work when they would wind down and discuss the events of the day. Now that she was Marketing Director she had thought it would be good to get together again after work on occasions, despite the problems of arranging child cover for Claire when Martin was unavailable for this. She had thought that by having some informal drinks together they could bond more effectively and build a positive culture within the group. The first proposed meeting had been two days ago when she had suggested that they pop to a local wine bar for a few drinks immediately after work. To her disappointment some people, including Bill, had not turned up and those that had turned up seemed to be a little cautious of her and seemed to hold back a little. She hoped that they would relax with a couple of glasses of wine as they had done in previous days but the only person who seemed to be relaxing and enjoying the wine was her friend Linda who worked for another department inside the company. Overall Ellen had found the experience disconcerting.

Then there was the issue of yesterday's meeting with Mr Hayashi and the rest of his team from Fujimori Mowers. She had attended the meeting with Bill Murray and Pavel Sokota with the objective of working out the marketing implications of the proposed alliance between the two companies. Mr Hayashi had arrived with three other male colleagues, although they were clearly younger than he was and deferential towards him.

On meeting, all the Japanese managers shook hands and Mr Hayashi presented his business card, followed by the others. As the senior representative of the company, Ellen had taken Mr Hayashi's card and immediately put it in her top pocket as she was used to doing in the UK. There had seemed to be a sort of pause in the Japanese managers and Mr Hayashi's eyebrows had furrowed. They had then sat down round the table and Ellen had started to lead the discussion about the proposed marketing arrangements for the alliance. To her increasing annoyance, Mr Hayashi kept responding mainly to Bill Murray, who had seemed quite pleased by this and had sought to lead the discussions himself. Ellen had felt increasingly angry at the fact that there was little direct discussion towards her and even that the Japanese seemed to be avoiding eye-contact altogether. Bill had made a point to which Mr Hayashi was responding when Ellen had interrupted and challenged a point made by Mr Hayashi which she felt was an irrelevant one. Again there had been a long silence with the Japanese managers and she could see that they had furrowed their brows again and were all looking down at the table.

To his credit Pavel had intervened with a positive comment on a technical matter which had got discussions going again and they began to cover some ground. Ellen had sought to lead the discussion again and had received polite answers from the Japanese managers although she still sensed that something was wrong. At the end of the meeting she had suggested that they sign an agreement to cover the main points discussed but the Japanese managers had suggested that further meetings were required before any agreement could be reached and that they were still considering whether to proceed with the alliance at all. Mike Lynch had heard that the meeting hadn't gone that well and had asked to sit in on the meeting she was going to have with the Japanese in one hour.

Ellen felt tired but realised that she had to concentrate and formulate some plan of action. The immediate thing was to arrange for someone to pick up Claire, there was the meeting with Mr Hayashi and his team in one hour and there were some issues in her department that needed sorting out soon. So what to do?

Questions

1 What factors are driving the attitudes of members of the Marketing Department? Is there any evidence of cognitive bias or cognitive dissonance?

2 How far can the problems encountered with Mr Hayashi be linked to national cultural differences?

3 Formulate Ellen's plan of action and identify possible solutions for her.

Index